CIMA Official *Learning System*

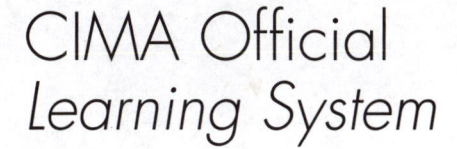

Operational Level

E1 – Enterprise Operations

Bob Perry

ELSEVIER

AMSTERDAM   BOSTON   HEIDELBERG   LONDON   NEW YORK   OXFORD
PARIS   SAN DIEGO   SAN FRANCISCO   SINGAPORE   SYDNEY   TOKYO

CIMA Publishing is an imprint of Elsevier
Linacre House, Jordan Hill, Oxford OX2 8DP, UK
30 Corporate Drive, Suite 400, Burlington, MA 01803, USA

Copyright © 2009 Elsevier Ltd. All rights reserved

No part of this publication may be reproduced, stored in a retrieval system
or transmitted in any form or by any means electronic, mechanical, photocopying,
recording or otherwise without the prior written permission of the publisher

Permissions may be sought directly from Elsevier's Science & Technology Rights
Department in Oxford, UK: phone (+44) (0) 1865 843830; fax (+44) (0) 1865 853333;
e-mail: permissions@elsevier.com. Alternatively you can visit the Science and Technology
Books website at www.elsevierdirect.com/rights for further information

Notice
No responsibility is assumed by the publisher for any injury and/or damage to persons
or property as a matter of products liability, negligence or otherwise, or from any use
or operation of any methods, products, instructions or ideas contained in the material
herein.

British Library Cataloguing in Publication Data
A catalogue record for this book is available from the British Library

Library of Congress Cataloguing in Publication Data
A catalogue record for this book is available from the Library of Congress

978-1-85617-790-0

For information on all CIMA publications
visit our website at www.elsevierdirect.com

Typeset by Macmillan Publishing Solutions
(www.macmillansolutions.com)

Printed and bound in Italy

09 10 11   11 10 9 8 7 6 5 4 3 2 1

**Working together to grow
libraries in developing countries**
www.elsevier.com | www.bookaid.org | www.sabre.org

ELSEVIER   BOOK AID International   Sabre Foundation

Contents

The CIMA *Learning System*   ix
Acknowledgements   ix
How to use your CIMA Learning System   ix
Guide to the icons used within this text   x
Study technique   x
Paper E1 – Enterprise Operations   xiii

1 The Global Business Environment   1
    Learning Outcomes   3
1.1   Introduction   3
1.2   Free trade and economic nationalism/protectionism   4
    1.2.1   International trade   4
    1.2.2   Liberalisation – free trade   4
    1.2.3   Economic nationalism   5
1.3   Comparative and competitive advantage   6
    1.3.1   Comparative advantage   6
    1.3.2   Competitive advantage – Porter's Diamond   7
1.4   Outsourcing and offshoring   9
    1.4.1   The growth of outsourcing   9
    1.4.2   Advantages of outsourcing   10
    1.4.3   Drawbacks of outsourcing   10
    1.4.4   Offshoring   10
1.5   Emerging market multinationals   11
    1.5.1   Globalisation   11
    1.5.2   How transition economies change   13
    1.5.3   Emerging market multinationals and international influence   13
1.6   National account balances and monetary policy   15
    1.6.1   Fiscal policy   15
    1.6.2   International trade   16
    1.6.3   Monetary policy   17
    1.6.4   Impact on business and markets   19
1.7   Cross-cultural management   19
    1.7.1   Managing across cultures   19
    1.7.2   Hofstede   20
    1.7.3   Other models   21

1.8	Stakeholders: society and government		24
	1.8.1	Stakeholders	24
	1.8.2	The role of society	24
	1.8.3	The role of government	25
1.9	Corporate social responsibility		25
	1.9.1	General principles of CSR	25
	1.9.2	The scope of international variation: developed and developing economies	26
1.10	Corporate governance		27
	1.10.1	Why corporate governance?	27
	1.10.2	Stakeholders and government	27
	1.10.3	General principles (The Combined Code)	28
	1.10.4	The benefits of corporate governance	29
1.11	The impact of regulation on the firm		29
	1.11.1	The legal environment	29
	1.11.2	The impact of regulation	30
1.12	Corporate political activity		30
	1.12.1	Business and politics	30
	1.12.2	Developed markets	31
	1.12.3	Developing markets	32
1.13	Country and political risk		32
	1.13.1	Country and political risk	32
	1.13.2	Political risk analysis	32
1.14	Summary		34
	References and further reading		34
	Revision Questions		35
	Solutions to Revision Questions		37

2 Information Systems 39

	Learning Outcomes		41
2.1	Information and information systems		41
	2.1.1	The role of information systems in organisations	43
2.2	Organisational dependence on information systems		46
	2.2.1	Emerging IS trends in organisations	47
	2.2.2	IT – enabled transformation	52
	2.2.3	Teams: dispersed and virtual	53
2.3	Information technology, contexts and change		54
2.4	Challenges in IS implementation		55
	2.4.1	Evaluating information systems	56
	2.4.2	Privacy and security	57
	2.4.3	Changeover approaches	59
	2.4.4	Managing systems implementation	59
2.5	Organising and managing IS activities within a corporate framework		63
	2.5.1	IS outsourcing	64
	2.5.2	Aligning information systems with business strategy	65

2.6	Summary		66
	References and further reading		66
	Revision Questions		69
	Solutions to Revision Questions		73

3 Operations Management — 81

Learning Outcomes — 83
3.1 Shifting perspectives — 85
    3.1.1 Procurement and operations — 85
    3.1.2 Strategic issues — 86
3.2 Operations and organisational competitiveness — 88
    3.2.1 Operations strategy and the organisation — 88
    3.2.2 The supply chain — 91
3.3 Operations and service organisations — 91
3.4 Sustainability in operations management — 92
3.5 Quality management thinking — 93
    3.5.1 Methods of quality measurement — 96
    3.5.2 Approaches to quality management — 97
3.6 Process design — 101
    3.6.1 Process maps — 102
    3.6.2 Systems used in operations management — 104
3.7 Lean management — 107
    3.7.1 Managing inventory — 108
    3.7.2 Managing operational capacity — 109
    3.7.3 Practices of continuous improvement — 111
3.8 Planning quality programmes — 113
    3.8.1 Implementing TQM — 114
3.9 Supplier relationships — 115
    3.9.1 Supply chain management — 116
    3.9.2 The lean supply chain — 118
3.10 Summary — 118
    References and further reading — 118
    Revision Questions — 121
    Solutions to Revision Questions — 125

4 Marketing — 131

Learning Outcomes — 133
4.1 The marketing concept — 133
    4.1.1 Differing business philosophies — 134
4.2 The marketing environment — 136
4.3 Marketing in a not-for-profit context — 137
    4.3.1 Marketing for Charities — 138
    4.3.2 Marketing for non-governmental organisations — 138
    4.3.3 Marketing for the public sector — 138
4.4 The social context of marketing behaviour — 139
    4.4.1 Social marketing — 139
    4.4.2 Corporate social responsibility in a marketing context — 140
4.5 Consumer behaviour — 142

		4.5.1	Factors affecting buying decisions	142
		4.5.2	The buying process	143
		4.5.3	Buyer behaviour	144
		4.5.4	Theories of consumer behaviour	144
	4.6	Market research, segmentation, targeting and positioning		145
		4.6.1	Market research	145
		4.6.2	Market segmentation	147
		4.6.3	Targeting and positioning	149
	4.7	The marketing mix		150
		4.7.1	The product mix	151
		4.7.2	Place	152
		4.7.3	Promotional tools and promotional mix	152
		4.7.4	Price	157
		4.7.5	Extending the marketing mix	158
	4.8	Marketing contexts		159
		4.8.1	Consumer marketing	159
		4.8.2	Business-to-business marketing	160
		4.8.3	Services marketing	161
		4.8 4	Direct marketing and distribution channels	162
		4.8.5	Interactive marketing	163
		4.8.6	e-marketing, e-business and e-commerce	164
		4.8.7	Internal marketing	164
	4.9	The market planning process		166
		4.9.1	Strategic marketing	166
		4.9.2	Product development and the product life cycle	169
		4.9.3	Investing in products	170
		4.9.4	Pricing strategies	172
	4.10	Branding		174
		4.10.1	Brand equity	174
		4.10.2	Experiential marketing	174
	4.11	Summary		175
		References and further reading		175
		Revision Questions		177
		Solutions to Revision Questions		181

5 Managing Human Capital — 189

		Learning Outcomes		191
	5.1	Human resource management and organisational success		191
		5.1.1	Human resource management, motivation and opportunity	194
		5.1.2	The psychological contract and retention	197
		5.1.3	Employees and the corporate dimension	198
	5.2	Ethical behaviour		199
	5.3	Developing the human resource		202
		5.3.1	Recruitment	203
		5.3.2	Selection	204
		5.3.3	Induction	209

	5.3.4	Appraisals	210
	5.3.5	Development and training	213
	5.3.6	Career planning	218
	5.3.7	Employment practices	220
5.4	Motivation and incentives		222
	5.4.1	Designing reward systems	223
5.5	Improving the opportunities for employees contribution		228
5.6	Line managers and human resource practices		230
5.7	HR planning		232
5.8	Summary		235
	References and further reading		235
	Revision Questions		237
	Solutions to Revision Questions		241

6 Preparing for the Examination — 251

Revision technique — 253
    Planning — 253
    Getting down to work — 254
    Tips for the final revision phase — 254
Format of the examination — 255
    Section A: compulsory objective test questions — 255
    Section B: compulsory short answer questions — 256
    Section C: a choice of questions — 256
Examination-standard revision questions and solutions — 256
A style revision questions — 259
Solutions to A style revision questions — 265
B style revision questions — 271
Solutions to B style revision questions — 275
C style revision questions — 287
Solutions to C style revision questions — 295

Exam Q & As — 317

Index — 319

The CIMA Learning System

Acknowledgements

Every effort has been made to contact the holders of copyright material, but if any here have been inadvertently overlooked the publishers will be pleased to make the necessary arrangements at the first opportunity.

How to use your CIMA Learning System

This *Enterprise Operations Learning System* has been devised as a resource for students attempting to pass their CIMA exams, and provides:

- a detailed explanation of all syllabus areas,
- extensive 'practical' materials, including readings from relevant journals,
- generous question practice, together with full solutions,
- an exam preparation section, complete with exam standard questions and solutions.

This Learning System has been designed with the needs of home-study and distance-learning candidates in mind. Such students require full coverage of the syllabus topics, and also the facility to undertake extensive question practice. However, the Learning System is also ideal for fully taught courses.

The main body of the text is divided into a number of chapters, each of which is organised on the following pattern:

- *Detailed learning outcomes* expected after your studies of the chapter are complete. You should assimilate these before beginning detailed work on the chapter, so that you can appreciate where your studies are leading.
- *Step-by-step topic coverage.* This is the heart of each chapter, containing detailed explanatory text supported where appropriate by worked examples and exercises. You should work carefully through this section, ensuring that you understand the material being explained and can tackle the examples and exercises successfully. Remember that in many cases knowledge is cumulative: if you fail to digest earlier material thoroughly, you may struggle to understand later chapters.
- *Readings and activities.* Most chapters are illustrated by more practical elements, such as relevant journal articles or other readings, together with comments and questions designed to stimulate discussion.

- *Question practice.* The test of how well you have learned the material is your ability to tackle exam-standard questions. Make a serious attempt at producing your own answers, but at this stage do not be too concerned about attempting the questions in exam conditions. In particular, it is more important to absorb the material thoroughly by completing a full solution than to observe the time limits that would apply in the actual exam.
- *Solutions.* Avoid the temptation merely to 'audit' the solutions provided. It is an illusion to think that this provides the same benefits as you would gain from a serious attempt of your own. However, if you are struggling to get started on a question you should read the introductory guidance provided at the beginning of the solution, and then make your own attempt before referring back to the full solution.

Having worked through the chapters you are ready to begin your final preparations for the examination. The final section of the CIMA *Learning System* provides you with the guidance you need. It includes the following features:

- A brief guide to revision technique.
- A note on the format of the examination. You should know what to expect when you tackle the real exam, and in particular the number of questions to attempt, which questions are compulsory and which optional, and so on.
- Guidance on how to tackle the examination itself.
- A table mapping revision questions to the syllabus learning outcomes allowing you to quickly identify questions by subject area.
- Revision questions. These are of exam standard and should be tackled in exam conditions, especially as regards the time allocation.
- Solutions to the revision questions. As before, these indicate the length and the quality of solution that would be expected of a well-prepared candidate.

If you work conscientiously through this CIMA *Learning System* according to the guidelines above you will be giving yourself an excellent chance of exam success. Good luck with your studies!

Guide to the icons used within this text

Key term or definition

Equation to learn

Exam tip to topic likely to appear in the exam

Exercise

Question

Solution

Comment or Note

Study technique

Passing exams is partly a matter of intellectual ability, but however accomplished you are in that respect you can improve your chances significantly by the use of appropriate study and revision techniques. In this section we briefly outline some tips for effective study during the earlier stages of your approach to the exam. Later in the text we mention some techniques that you will find useful at the revision stage.

Planning

To begin with, formal planning is essential to get the best return from the time you spend studying. Estimate how much time in total you are going to need for each subject that you face. Remember that you need to allow time for revision as well as for initial study of the material. The amount of notional study time for any subject is the minimum estimated time that students will need to achieve the specified learning outcomes set out earlier in this chapter. This time includes all appropriate learning activities, for example, face-to-face tuition, private study, directed home study, learning in the workplace, revision time, etc. You may find it helpful to read *Better exam results* by Sam Malone, CIMA Publishing, ISBN: 075066357X. This book will provide you with proven study techniques. Chapter by chapter it covers the building blocks of successful learning and examination techniques.

The notional study time for *Enterprise Operations* is 200 hours. Note that the standard amount of notional learning hours attributed to one full-time academic year of approximately 30 weeks is 1,200 hours.

By way of example, the notional study time might be made up as follows:

	Hours
Face-to-face study: up to	60
Personal study: up to	100
'Other' study – e.g. learning at the workplace, revision, etc.: up to	40
	200

Note that all study and learning-time recommendations should be used only as a guideline and are intended as minimum amounts. The amount of time recommended for face-to-face tuition, personal study and/or additional learning will vary according to the type of course undertaken, prior learning of the student, and the pace at which different students learn.

Now split your total time requirement over the weeks between now and the examination. This will give you an idea of how much time you need to devote to study each week. Remember to allow for holidays or other periods during which you will not be able to study (e.g. because of seasonal workloads).

With your study material before you, decide which chapters you are going to study in each week, and which weeks you will devote to revision and final question practice.

Prepare a written schedule summarising the above – and stick to it!

The amount of space allocated to a topic in the study material is not always a very good guide as to how long it will take you.

It is essential to know your syllabus. As your course progresses you will become more familiar with how long it takes to cover topics in sufficient depth. Your timetable may need to be adapted to allocate enough time for the whole syllabus.

Tips for effective studying

1. Aim to find a quiet and undisturbed location for your study, and plan as far as possible to use the same period of time each day. Getting into a routine helps to avoid wasting

time. Make sure that you have all the materials you need before you begin so as to minimise interruptions.
2. Store all your materials in one place, so that you do not waste time searching for items around the house. If you have to pack everything away after each study period, keep them in a box, or even a suitcase, which will not be disturbed until the next time.
3. Limit distractions. To make the most effective use of your study periods you should be able to apply total concentration, so turn off the TV, set your phones to message mode, and put up your 'do not disturb' sign.
4. Your timetable will tell you which topic to study. However, before diving in and becoming engrossed in the finer points, make sure you have an overall picture of all the areas that need to be covered by the end of that session. After an hour, allow yourself a short break and move away from your books. With experience, you will learn to assess the pace you need to work at. You should also allow enough time to read relevant articles from newspapers and journals, which will supplement your knowledge and demonstrate a wider perspective.
5. Work carefully through a chapter, making notes as you go. When you have covered a suitable amount of material, vary the pattern by attempting a practice question. Preparing an answer plan is a good habit to get into, while you are both studying and revising, and also in the examination room. It helps to impose a structure on your solutions, and avoids rambling. When you have finished your attempt, make notes of any mistakes you made, or any areas that you failed to cover or covered only skimpily.
6. Make notes as you study, and discover the techniques that work best for you. Your notes may be in the form of lists, bullet points, diagrams, summaries, 'mind maps', or the written word, but remember that you will need to refer back to them at a later date, so they must be intelligible. If you are on a taught course, make sure you highlight any issues you would like to follow up with your lecturer.
7. Organise your paperwork. There are now numerous paper storage systems available to ensure that all your notes, calculations and articles can be effectively filed and easily retrieved later.

Paper E1 – Enterprise Operations

Syllabus Overview

This paper addresses several functional areas of business, as well as introducing candidates to the economic, social and political context of international business. For each of the sections dealing with information systems, operations, marketing and managing human capital, the learning requirements alert students to major developments in the field as well as tools and techniques important to each functional area.

Syllabus Structure

The syllabus comprises the following topics and study weightings:

A	The Global Business Environment	20%
B	Information Systems	20%
C	Operations Management	20%
D	Marketing	20%
E	Managing Human Capital	20%

Assessment Strategy

There will be a written examination paper of 3 hours, plus 20 minutes of pre-examination question paper reading time. The examination paper will have the following sections:

Section A – 20 marks
A variety of compulsory objective test questions, each worth between 2 and 4 marks. Mini scenarios may be given, to which a group of questions relate.

Section B – 30 marks
Six compulsory short answer questions, each worth 5 marks. A short scenario may be given, to which some or all questions relate.

Section C – 50 marks
One or two compulsory questions. Short scenarios may be given, to which questions relate.

Learning Outcomes and Indicative Syllabus Content

E1 – A. The Global Business Environment (20%)

Learning Outcomes		Content
Lead	**Component**	
1. Explain the social, political and economic context of business. (2)	(a) Explain the emergence of major economies in Asia and Latin America. (b) Explain the emergence and importance of outsourcing and offshoring. (c) Explain the impact of international macroeconomic developments (e.g. long-term shifts in trade balances), on the firm's organisation's competitive environment.	• Liberalisation and economic nationalism. (A, C) • Cross-cultural management and different forms of business organisation. (A) • Emerging market multinationals. (A) • Liberalisation and economic nationalism. (A, C) • Outsourcing and offshoring. (B) • Major economic systems including US, European and transition economies. (C) • National account balances (especially from international trade), monetary policy and their impact on markets. (C)
2. Analyse the relationship between the internal governance of the firm and external sources of governance and regulation. (4)	(a) Explain the principles and purpose of corporate social responsibility and the principles of good corporate governance in an international context. (b) Analyse relationships among business, society and government in national and regional contexts. (c) Apply tools of country and political risk analysis. (d) Discuss the nature of regulation and its impact on the firm.	• Corporate governance, including stakeholders and the role of government. (A) • Principles of corporate social responsibility and the scope for international variation, e.g. between developed and developing economies. (A, B) • Business–government relations in developed and developing economies. (A, B, C) • Regulation in the national and international context and its impact on the firm. (A, B, D) • Role of institutions and governance in economic growth. (B) • Corporate political activity in developed and developing markets. (B, C) • Country and political risk. (B, C)

E1 – B. Information Systems (20%)

Learning Outcomes		
Lead	**Component**	**Content**
1. Discuss the wider business context within which information systems operate. (4)	(a) Identify the value of information and information systems in organisations. (b) Discuss the reasons for organisations' increased dependence on information systems. (c) Discuss the transformation of organisations through technology.	• The role of information systems in organisations. (A, B, C) • Emerging information system trends in organisations (e.g. enterprise-wide systems; knowledge management systems; customer relationship management systems, e.g. e-business, Web 2.0 tools). (A, B, C) • Information technology – enabled transformation; the emergence of new forms of organisation. (B) • Geographically dispersed (virtual) teams; role of information systems in virtual teams and challenges for virtual collaboration. (B)
2. Analyse how information systems can be implemented in support of the organisation's strategy. (4)	(a) Discuss ways for overcoming problems in information system implementation. (b) Discuss ways of organising and managing information system activities in the context of the wider organisation.	• Assessing the costs and benefits of information systems; criteria for evaluating information systems. (A) • Privacy and security. (A) • System changeover methods (i.e. direct, parallel, pilot and phased). (A) • Information system implementation as a change management process; avoiding problems of non-usage and resistance. (A) • Information system outsourcing (different types of sourcing strategies; client–vendor relationships). (B) • Aligning information systems with business strategy (e.g. strategic importance of information systems; information systems for competitive advantage; information systems for competitive necessity). (B)

E1 – C. Operations Management (20%)

Learning Outcomes		
Lead	**Component**	**Content**
1. Explain the relationship of operations management to other aspects of the organisation's operations. (2)	(a) Explain the shift from price-based to relational procurement and operations. (b) Explain the relationship of operations and supply management to the competitiveness of the firm. (c) Explain the particular issues surrounding operations management in services. (d) Explain the importance of sustainability in operations management.	• Supply chain management as a strategic process. (A, D) • An overview of operations strategy and its importance to the firm. (B) • Supply chains in competition with each other; role of supply networks; demand networks as an evolution of supply chains. (B) • Design of products/services and processes and how this relates to operations and supply. (C) • The concept of sustainability in operations management. (D)
2. Apply tools and techniques of operations management. (3)	(a) Apply contemporary thinking in quality management. (b) Explain process design. (c) Apply tools and concepts of lean management. (d) Illustrate a plan for the implementation of a quality programme. (e) Describe ways to manage relationships with suppliers.	• Different methods of quality measurement (e.g. Servqual). (A) • Approaches to quality management, including Total Quality Management (TQM), various British and European Union systems as well as statistical control processes. (A) • External quality standards. (A) • Systems used in operations management: Manufacturing Resource Planning II (MRPII); Optimized Production Techniques (OPT); and Enterprise Resource Planning (ERP). (B) • Use of process maps to present the flow of information and product across supply chains and networks. (B) • Methods for managing inventory, including continuous inventory systems (e.g. Economic Order Quantity, EOQ), periodic inventory systems and the ABC system (Note: ABC is not an acronym; A refers to high value, B to medium and C to low value inventory). (B, C) • Methods of managing operational capacity in product and service delivery (e.g. use of queuing theory, forecasting, flexible manufacturing systems). (B, C) • Application of lean techniques to services. (C) • Practices of continuous improvement (e.g. Quality circles, Kaizen, 5S, 6 Sigma). (C, D) • The characteristics of lean production. (C) • Criticisms and limitations of lean production. (C, D) • Developing relationships with suppliers, including the use of supply portfolios. (E)

E1 – D. Marketing (20%)

Learning Outcomes

Lead	Component	Content
1. Explain developments in marketing. (2)	(a) Explain the marketing concept, and the alternatives to it. (b) Describe the marketing environment of a range of organisations. (c) Explain marketing in a not-for-profit context. (d) Explain the social context of marketing behaviour. (e) Describe theories of consumer behaviour.	• The marketing concept as a business philosophy. (A) • The marketing environment, including societal, economic, technological, political and legal factors affecting marketing. (A, B) • Marketing in not-for-profit organisations (i.e. charities, non-governmental organisations; the public sector). (C) • Theories of consumer behaviour (e.g. social interaction theory), as well as factors affecting buying decisions, types of buying behaviour and stages in the buying process. (D, E) • Social marketing and corporate social responsibility. (D)
2. Apply tools and techniques used in support of the organisation's marketing. (3)	(a) Explain the relationships between market research, market segmentation, targeting and positioning. (b) Apply tools within each area of the marketing mix. (c) Describe the business contexts within which marketing principles can be applied. (d) Describe the market planning process (e) Explain the role of branding and brand equity.	• Market research, including data gathering techniques and methods of analysis. (A, D) • Segmentation and targeting of markets, and positioning of products within markets. (A) • How business-to-business (B2B) marketing differs from business-to-consumer (B2C) marketing in its different forms (i.e. consumer marketing, services marketing, direct marketing, interactive marketing, e-marketing, internal marketing). (C) • Promotional tools and the promotion mix. (B) • The 'service extension' to the marketing mix. (B) • Devising and implementing a pricing strategy. (B) • Experiential marketing. (B) • Marketing communications, including viral, guerrilla and other indirect forms of marketing. (B) • The role of marketing in the business plan of the organisation. (B) • Brand image and brand value. (A, B, E) • Product development and product/service life-cycles. (B) • Internal marketing as the process of training and motivating employees so as to support the firm's external marketing activities. (C) • The differences and similarities in the marketing of products, services and experiences. (B, C) • Product portfolios and the product mix. (B, D)

E1 – E. Managing Human Capital (20%)

Learning Outcomes		Indicative Syllabus Content
Lead	**Component**	
1. Explain the relationship of Human Resource (HR) to the organisation's operations. (2)	(a) Explain how HR theories and activities can contribute to the success of the organisation. (b) Explain the importance of ethical behaviour in business generally and for the line manager and their activities.	• Theories of Human Resource Management relating to ability, motivation and opportunity. (A) • The psychological contract and its importance to retention. (A) • The relationship of the employee to other elements of the business. (A) • Personal business ethics and the fundamental principles (Part A) of the CIMA Code of Ethics for Professional Accountants. (B)
2. Discuss the activities associated with the management of human capital. (4)	(a) Explain the HR activities associated with developing the ability of employees. (b) Discuss the HR activities associated with the motivation of employees. (c) Describe the HR activities associated with improving the opportunities for employees to contribute to the firm. (d) Discuss the importance of the line manager in the implementation of HR practices. (e) Prepare an HR plan appropriate to a team.	• Practices associated with recruiting and developing appropriate abilities including recruitment and selection of staff using different recruitment channels (i.e. interviews, assessment centres, intelligence tests, aptitude tests, psychometric tests). (A) • Issues relating to fair and legal employment practices (e.g. recruitment, dismissal, redundancy, and ways of managing these). (A) • The distinction between development and training and the tools available to develop and train staff. (A, B) • The design and implementation of induction programmes. (A, B) • Practices related to motivation including Issues in the design of reward systems (e.g. the role of incentives, the utility of performance-related pay, arrangements for knowledge workers, flexible work arrangements). (B) • The importance of appraisals, their conduct and their relationship to the reward system. (A, B) • Practices related to the creation of opportunities for employees to contribute to the organisation including job design, communications, involvement procedures and appropriate elements of negotiating and bargaining. (C) • Problems in implementing an HR plan appropriate to a unit or team and ways to manage this. (D) • HR in different organisational forms (e.g. project–based, virtual or networked firms) and different organisational contexts. (B, C, D) • Preparation of an HR plan (e.g. forecasting personnel requirements; retention, absence and leave, wastage). (E)

1

The Global Business Environment

The Global Business Environment

LEARNING OUTCOMES

This part of the syllabus attracts a 20 per cent weighting and covers recent trends in the global business environment. By completing this chapter you should be assisted in your studies and better able to:

- explain the emergence of major economies in Asia and Latin America;
- explain the emergence and importance of outsourcing and offshoring;
- explain the impact of international macroeconomic developments (e.g. long-term shifts in trade balances), on the firm's organisation's competitive environment;
- explain the principles and purpose of corporate social responsibility and the principles of good corporate governance in an international context;
- analyse relationships among business, society and government in national and regional contexts;
- apply tools of country and political risk analysis;
- discuss the nature of regulation and its impact on the firm.

1.1 Introduction

Today's global managers are expected to possess entrepreneurial qualities beyond those of judgement, perseverance and knowledge of business. Above all, global managers must have an understanding of the complexities of the modern world and how to deal with people from a wide range of backgrounds and cultures.

Enormous changes are taking place in the world of business, whether it is the rise of China and India or the decline of Europe. International finance has become more complex. Not only do global managers have to contend with the technicalities of raising and managing global finance, but they have to work with a huge range of labour, environmental, legal, ethical, social and governance issues for which many are ill equipped.

The real issue facing many of today's global leaders is what to say about corporate governance when the rules and expectations of society are changing so quickly. What do you teach managers about the global competitive landscape, when countries like China and India are fundamentally changing the rules of the game?

1.2 Free trade and economic nationalism/protectionism

1.2.1 International trade

The global economy is not a new concept, and international or global companies have existed for many years. The British East India Company, founded in 1600, is popularly cited as the world's first international and global company though, hundreds of years earlier, China was trading extensively with Europe by means of the 'silk route'. Today, however, it is no longer the case that international business means Western multinational companies selling to or operating in world markets.

1.2.2 Liberalisation – free trade

> **Free trade:** The movement of goods, services, labour and capital without tariffs, quotas, subsides, taxation, or other barriers likely to distort the exchange.

The concept of Free trade has been debated extensively for many years with advocates arguing that:

- Free trade will make society richer, since the free movement of goods and services allows for local specialisation.
- Free trade will mean that nations can develop their resources to gain a competitive advantage.
- The fact that countries trade and communicate should reduce conflict.
- Free trade will lead to dramatic increases in the well being of one population, as the exposure to the higher standards of another nation are more rapidly adopted.
- The quality of the goods will be better in absolute terms, and this will lead to a better quality of life generally.
- Since the trade is a voluntary exchange it will necessarily be for the mutual benefit of both parties.
- Allowing entrepreneurship and investment a free rein will lead to more rapid growth in the economy.
- The fact that trade can be reciprocal will encourage both sides to export.
- Free trade is considered to be a fundamental right.
- Free trade is often encouraged for political reasons – the US actively supported the free trade in flowers with Colombia so that farmers would grow carnations rather than cocaine.

However, there are criticism of free trade:

- Countries get locked in to supplying a particular set of products or services, and do not develop alternative products. The Middle East dependence on oil exports was always given as an example of this.

- Less developed countries are disadvantaged in some product groups, notably those with high technology content. The case of life saving pharmaceuticals is often quoted where developed countries charge premium prices and fiercely protect their intellectual property.
- Free trade undermines national culture. France has resisted the import of American culture through cinema and radio for a number of years and has media legislation in place restricting the amount of broadcasts in languages other than French.
- The influence of multinationals is often so strong in the country in which they operate that it can be used to corrupt the political system.
- The impact of outsourcing abroad, known as offshoring, is damaging both to the nation from which the jobs are exported but also to the host country. Whilst the labour rates are lower in the host country quite often the safety standards are as well. There may well be a lack of basic human rights and other considerations which the people of the country outsourcing the work take for granted.
- Free trade reduces national security by reducing border controls.
- International free trade is inefficient, as consumer expectations are increased. Many people in the developed world are no longer satisfied with seasonal produce and the cost of shipping out of season fruit and vegetables around the world, usually by air, is high to the consumer and damaging to the environment.
- Protectionism may actually be good for young firms in emerging industries.

There are a number of alternatives to Free Trade policies. In some instances two countries will attempt a policy of 'balanced trade', whereby they will try to maintain a fairly even relationship between their respective imports and exports so that neither country runs a large trade deficit. Another approach is to actually try to protect the local market by restricting imports. This is known as economic nationalism or, more commonly, protectionism.

1.2.3 Economic nationalism

> Protectionism: Where one country, or trade bloc, attempts to restrict trade with another, to protect their producers from competition.

Traditionally, protectionism meant the imposition of taxation on imported goods, much the same as a purchase tax. This would have the effect of making those goods more expensive than locally produced goods, and would discourage their purchase. Where the goods continued to be purchased the tax would be a source of revenue for the government that could, in theory, be invested to make local production more effective. This approach was common in the United States immediately after World War II, allowing the country to maintain a low rate of income tax and encourage high growth in the economy, often using capital borrowed from the countries from which they restricted imports.

There are a number of ways in which markets can be protected without the use of tariffs:

- Quota systems. A quota will restrict the imports to a particular level, and locally produced goods will become more expensive. The government will receive reduced tariff income.

- Buy national campaigns. Sometimes a country will encourage its citizens to buy locally produced goods – on other occasions it will enforce this with regulations. A government may say that a particular product must have a certain percentage of locally produced components or labour (as is often the case in car manufacture) or will require firms to report quarterly the sources of any purchases over a certain value, and tax them if the proportion of foreign goods is too high.
- Customs valuations. This approach is not so common now but in the past some governments have insisted that customs duty be paid on invoice cost plus a percentage, effectively increasing the cost to the importer.
- Technical barriers. Some countries insist on over stringent standards of quality, health and safety, packaging or size to restrict what may be imported. At one point in time, as environmental legislation, Germany insisted that foreign firms importing goods into Germany were responsible for collecting and removing packaging from the country. This increased transport costs to such a level as to make many such goods no longer economically viable. Similarly North America introduced standards for cars requiring the bumpers to be a particular height which was impractical for imported sub-compact cars made by Toyota and Honda.
- Subsidies for local manufacturers. This is particularly prevalent for agricultural products in North America and also in the EU, where the Common Agricultural Policy protects small farmers in the European countries. There has been an ongoing battle between Airbus and Boeing whose respective governments have supported the development of each new airliner with which the companies have sought to dominate the market.

Most developed nations have agreed to abolish protectionism, and policies that favour free trade are encouraged through organisations such as the World Trade Organisation. (http://www.wto.org)

1.3 Comparative and competitive advantage

1.3.1 Comparative advantage

Adam Smith realised that international trade would allow each country to specialise in what they could do best and without import tariffs and quotas, the nations of the world could all benefit by producing and selling the goods and services at which they had 'absolute advantage'. With all nations trading freely together, without the intervention of governments, the 'invisible hand' of the market mechanism would ensure that everyone gained. The problem was that this might create problems. If an established industry within one country loses its absolute advantage, it is often not easy to switch from one activity to another, especially if large investments have been made to establish the industry in the first place. In addition, skilled workers cannot or do not want to change to another activity.

Developments were made to the theory that Adam Smith had formulated and these were introduced by David Ricardo, who focussed on the availability and skills of the labour force. Two Swedish economists, Hecksher and Ohlin, elaborated on Ricardo's version by also bringing the availability of the other factors of production, land and capital, into the analysis. Both theories suggested that even if a country could produce a product, it could be better to import the goods from abroad. This would mean that their local industry could focus all their attention on the production of the goods at which they had the greatest advantages. This meant that if they could produce oil but the same quality imported from Saudi Arabia was cheaper, then they should import their requirements and focus their attention on the production of motor vehicles or electronic goods. This was the theory of Comparative Advantage.

Factors such as climate, which would allow certain crops to be cultivated or natural resources, such oil reserves did prescribe what products could be produced. But the theory of comparative advantage provided an explanation of why tea, oil and products that needed high levels of technological knowledge and skill were produced in specific countries. However, it did not explain the patterns by which a country such as Germany would export chemicals, motor vehicles and machinery.

1.3.2 Competitive advantage – Porter's Diamond

> Porter's Diamond is very examinable, and is also covered by later papers in the CIMA qualification. Make sure you understand it.

The internationalisation and globalisation of markets raises issues concerning the national sources of competitive advantages that can be substantial and difficult to imitate. Porter, in his book *The Competitive Advantage of Nations* (1992), explored why some nations tend to produces firms with sustained competitive advantage in some industry more than others. He set out to provide answers to:

1. Why do certain nations host so many successful international firms?
2. How do these firms sustain superior performance in a global market?
3. What are the implications of this for government policy and competitive strategy?

Porter concludes that entire nations do not have particular competitive advantages. Rather, he argues, it is specific industries or firms within them that seem able to use their national backgrounds to lever world-class competitive advantages.

Porter's answer is that countries produce successful firms mainly because of the following four reasons, as illustrated in Figure 1.1.

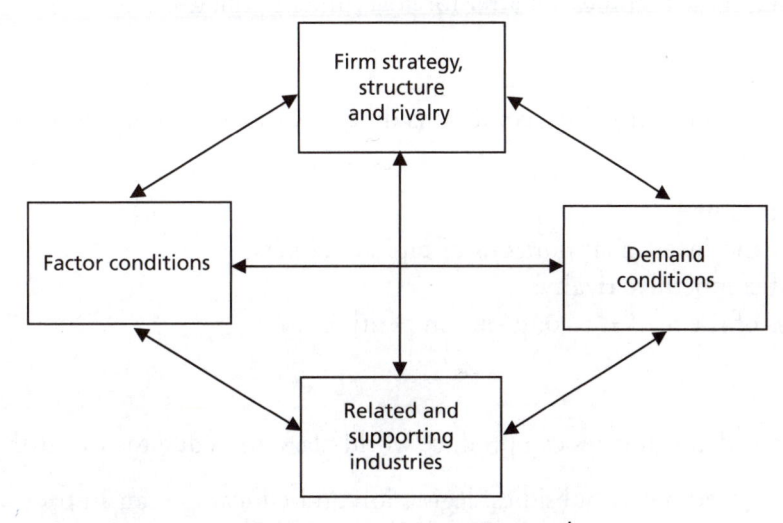

Figure 1.1 Porter's Diamond

Demand conditions

The demand conditions in the home market are important for three reasons:

1. If the demand is substantial it enables the firm to obtain the economies of scale and experience effects it will need to compete globally.
2. The experience the firm gets from supplying domestic consumers will give it an information advantage in global markets, provided that:
    (a) its customers are varied enough to permit segmentation into groups similar to those found in the global market as a whole;
    (b) its customers are critical and demanding enough to force the firm to produce at world-class levels of quality in its chosen products;
    (c) its customers are innovative in their purchasing behaviour and hence encourage the firm to develop new and sophisticated products.
3. If the maturity stage of the plc is reached quickly (say, due to rapid adoption), this will give the firm the incentive to enter export markets before others do. (Product life cycles (plc) are covered in 4.9.2. later)

Related and supporting industries

The internationally competitive firm must have, initially at least, enjoyed the support of world-class producers of components and related products. Moreover success in a related industry may be due to expertise accumulated elsewhere (e.g. the development of the Swiss precision engineering tools industry owes much to the requirements and growth of the country's watch industry).

Factor conditions

These are the basic factor endowments referred to in economic theory as the source of so-called comparative advantage. Factors may be of two sorts:

1. Basic factors such as raw materials, semi-skilled or unskilled labour and initial capital availability. These are largely 'natural' and not created as a matter of policy or strategy.
2. Advanced factors such as infrastructure (particularly digital telecommunications), levels of training and skill, R&D experience, etc.

Porter argues that only the advanced factors are the roots of sustainable competitive success. Developing these becomes a matter for government policy.

Firm structure, strategy and rivalry

National cultures and competitive conditions do create distinctive business focusses. These can be influenced by:

- ownership structure;
- the attitudes and investment horizons of capital markets;
- the extent of competitive rivalry;
- the openness of the market to outside competition.

Other events

Porter points out that countries can produce world-class firms due to two further factors:

1. The role of government. Subsidies, legislation and education can impact on the other four elements of the diamond to the benefit of the industrial base of the country.

2. The role of chance events. Wars, civil unrest, chance factor discoveries, etc. can also change the four elements of the diamond unpredictably.

National competitive advantage

Successful firms from a particular country tend to have linkages between them; a phenomenon that Porter calls clustering.

Clustering allows for the development of competitive advantage for several reasons:

- transfer of expertise, for example, through staff movement and contracts;
- concentration of advanced factors (e.g. telecommunications, training, workforce);
- better supplier/customer relations within the value chain (i.e. vertical integration).

Clustering may take place in two ways:

1. common geographical location (e.g. Silicon Valley, City of London);
2. expertise in key industry (e.g. Sweden in timber, wood pulp, wood-handling machinery, particleboard furniture).

1.4 Outsourcing and offshoring

1.4.1 The growth of outsourcing

This section looks at key 'boundary of the firm' decisions. These are the decisions a firm makes over whether to make components (or perform activities) itself, or whether to subcontract or outsource such production (or processes) to a supplier.

> A competence: An activity or process through which an organisation deploys or utilises its resources. It is something the organisation does, rather than something it has.

Strategic competences can be classified as follows:

- Threshold competence is the level of competence necessary for an organisation to compete and survive in a given industry and market. For example, an online bookseller must have a logistics system that allows books to be delivered as promised, to the customers who have bought them.
- A core competence is something the organisation does that underpins a source of competitive advantage. For example, if an online bookseller is able to deliver books a day or two earlier than its rivals, this represents a core competence.

Cox has developed a different way of looking at competences in terms of strategic supply chain management. He suggests that competences come in three types, as follows:

1. Core competences. These are areas where the organisation should never consider outsourcing, as they are those competences that give a competitive advantage. In this case, the decision should always be to make or do.
2. Complementary competences. In this case, the firm should outsource, but only to trusted key suppliers who have the skills to supply as required. The firm would also enter into a strategic relationship with the supplier.

3. Residual competencies. In these areas, the organisation should outsource by means of an 'arms length' relationship – a simple 'buy' decision.

Thus, when making strategic 'make/do or buy' decisions, the organisation should determine what type of competence is being considered.

Quinn and Hilmer put forward three tests for whether any non-core activity should be outsourced:

1. What is the potential for gaining competitive advantage from this activity, taking account of transaction costs? The lower the potential, the more sensible it is to outsource.
2. What is the potential vulnerability to market failure that could arise if the activity was outsourced? Once again, the lower the risk, the more sensible it is to outsource.
3. What can be done to reduce these risks by structuring arrangements with suppliers in such a way as to protect ourselves? In this case, the more we can protect ourselves, the more sensible it is to outsource.

1.4.2 Advantages of outsourcing

The main advantages of outsourcing are thought to include the following:

- That it allows more accurate prediction of costs and, hopefully, improves budgetary control.
- That, due to the specialist nature of the external provider, the services received will be of a higher standard.
- The supplier should be able to provide a cheaper service, due to economies of scale from specialisation.
- The organisation will be relieved of the burden of managing specialist staff in an area that the organisation does not really understand.
- It supports the concept of the 'flexible firm'.

1.4.3 Drawbacks of outsourcing

The main disadvantages of outsourcing are:

- The difficulty of agreeing and managing a 'service level agreement' (SLA).
- The rigidity of the SLA and the contract with the supplier might prevent the organisation from exploiting new developments.
- It is almost impossible to change outsourcing supplier or to revert to in-house provision.

1.4.4 Offshoring

> **Offshoring:** Transferring some part of the organisation's activities to another country, in order (generally) to exploit differentials in wage rates.

Strictly speaking, the term includes both having a subsidiary or department in the other country, and contracting out (or outsourcing) the supply of services to a foreign firm. These two approaches are often differentiated by referring to the latter as 'offshore outsourcing'.

Whether offshoring is done 'in-house' or by means of an outsourcing agreement, the motivation is usually to exploit lower labour costs in the other country. Although such differentials in wage rates can be significant (often in the order of one tenth the level of the 'home' country) there are a number of issues, other than cost, that should be considered. Managing operations (or outsourcing agreements) across national borders can lead significant to issues in areas such as:

- Language barriers
- Time differences
- Exchange rate effects
- Cultural differences (see later in this chapter)
- Real (or perceived) service levels

Despite all these concerns, the significant economic benefits of offshoring mean its growth continues. A recent estimate of the Indian offshoring market, for example, estimated total annual revenues at US$35 billion, two-thirds of which was from the provision of IT-related services. This figure represented an increase of $10 billion over the previous year.

1.5 Emerging market multinationals

1.5.1 Globalisation

> Globalisation: The growing economic interdependence of countries worldwide through increased volume and variety of cross border trade in goods and service, freer international capital flows, and more rapid and widespread diffusion of technology. (Source: IMF)

> Globalisation: The freedom and ability of individuals and firms to initiate voluntary economic transactions with residents of other countries. (Source: World Bank)

We can see from these definitions that there are significant elements of political, cultural, economic and technological factors in globalisation. In fact, globalisation has been considered to consist of five monopolies based on; technology, finance, natural resources, mass media and weapons of mass destruction.

The features of globalisation are:

- the ability of multinational organisations to exploit arbitrage opportunities across different tax jurisdictions,
- the lowering of transaction costs by developments in communications and transport,
- the rise of the financial service industries,
- the reduction of the importance of manufacturing industry,
- the rise of the newly industrialised nations by the exploitation of cheaper labour, and
- the increasing importance of global economic policy over national sovereignty.

Most of the emphasis of globalisation relates to the ability of larger and larger multinational organisations to operate globally, taking advantage of local specialisms. They may do this, for instance, by outsourcing their IT operations to India where the expertise is as high and the costs are significantly lower than in, say, the United States.

Effectively the division of labour has become global. The capacity of these corporations to offshore has been greatly increased by the recent advances in information technology which have made the speed of transactions so much faster, particularly in the area of financial resources. This has led to an increase in the importance of these activities globally, and 24-hour trading is possible since there is always a stock market open somewhere in the world. As one market closes, another opens, and the security of transactions via the Internet means that they are working ever closer together and at significantly reduced transactions costs. Billions of dollars of assets and currencies are traded around the world on a daily basis by electronic means at virtually no cost other than the commission.

Most people are affected by globalisation in a number of ways and are aware of global brands either through personal experience or via the media. Thinking about what you are doing at the moment, it is quite possible that:

- You are reading a book written in the UK
- Using software developed in North America
- Which was typeset in India
- Printed locally wherever you live
- Bought using a credit card issued by an international bank
- You are drinking a coffee made from Columbian beans
- Wearing trainers made in Vietnam
- Clothes made in China
- Or possibly from Egyptian cotton
- You may be listening to music recorded locally
- But playing on equipment made in Japan
- You may even be studying in a foreign country where you have gone to work

Exercise 1.1

How global is your world, right now?

Not all examples of globalisation relate to commercial organisations. For example, you may decide to make a charitable donation to Médecins sans Frontières, Amnesty International or Greenpeace, all of which are global organisations.

Since all of these elements have an impact upon the lives of people there are bound to be serious debates about the relevance, and importance, of advancing globalisation.

The power afforded the multinationals compared to nation states is often a source of criticism. Bill Gates, the founder of Microsoft, has a personal income from his involvement in the company greater than the combined GDP of a number of African countries. George Soros, the international financier, has in his financial trading affected the economies of a number of countries. He was one of the speculators whose dealings helped cause Italy and the UK to leave the ERM in the 1980s. Many protestors see this as a bad thing suggesting that the interests of ordinary people are being subsumed under the interests of the corporations.

1.5.2 How transition economies change

As countries seek to become more competitive, they will attract investment from overseas firms, eager to share in the growth of the country. The investment that those companies make is known as foreign direct investment (FDI).

The firms that make these investments are known as multinational enterprises (MNEs), and retain control of the entity in which they have invested. This is often met with mixed feelings by the population, who are grateful for the creation of wealth and jobs but resentful of the country being 'bought by foreigners'. Similarly there can be resentment in countries whose firms invest abroad, particularly when there is domestic unemployment.

The current trend to offshore call centres and computing services has been a hotly debated issue since it began, but it is a phenomenon that has been occurring for many years. Originally the preserve of OECD countries is now a truly global feature of the world economy.

There are two main types of FDI:

1. Acquisitions, where the MNE acquires the shares of the local company and control of the assets and markets of the acquired firm are transferred to the new parent. The local form becomes a division of the new parent. Sometimes the acquiring firm will 'collect' companies in adjacent countries and a cross border merger results in the production of a whole geographical region being coordinated. Unless the acquired company was in danger of imminent collapse, and was rescued by the new parent, there is no long term benefit to the local economy, as all future profits are likely to be exported to the parent group.
2. Greenfield investment occurs where a company creates new facilities in the host country to take advantage of local conditions. These are better for the host country, since they are likely to create jobs, productive capacity, knowledge transfer and access to the global economy. Although the profits that the parent makes are still exported to head office, the domestic economy should benefit from the wages earned by the workforce and the income earned by any local firms that supply the new facilities.

Many countries are seeing their economy boosted by the arrival of foreign firms, as is the case of Russia, where growth in the domestic economy is being fuelled by the arrival of multinational retailers who have established bases in the country. In 2005 Russia attracted $16.7 billion of FDI, with Coca Cola acquiring a fruit juice maker, Heineken acquiring local brewers and both Toyota and Volkswagen establishing automobile factories. Other companies establishing factories include Carlsberg, Nestle and Whirlpool (the domestic appliance manufacturer) in partnership with the Turkish company, Vestel Group.

FDI is often the 'trigger' to an economy, and can lead to rapid growth in wealth and skills. Countries that are beginning to benefit from FDI are known as 'transition' economies, and they sometimes develop significant domestic economic infrastructure as a result. Other transition economies are triggered into growth by offshoring, and the economic gain can lead to the development of a local pool of highly skilled labour. Some local organisations grow, until they too are ready to enter the world stage.

1.5.3 Emerging market multinationals and international influence

So, what are the emerging markets and changes in patterns of activity, and how are these creating new challenges and interdependencies? Many business commentators place great emphasis on the four emerging world economies: Brazil, Russia, India and China (the 'BRIC' economies).

Although located in different regions, with different political climates, the sheer size of the BRIC countries, combined with robust growth rates, sets them apart from other emerging markets. All the emerging BRIC nations display one similar characteristic: they all have large and rapid growth rates. The growth has been initiated by, and is typically dominated by, the development of large metropolitan areas where increasing middle-class populations are driving economic demand through increased consumer spending on a range of domestic goods. However, all four countries also have large rural regions and populations, where this change is slower to develop but wage rates remain low.

Consequently, all four areas have large and increasing wealth disparities between rich and poor. As consumer habits and demand expand from the metropolitan areas into the less developed rural areas, growth continues to expand into the longer term but drives new and different ways to access and market products.

A second tier of emerging markets, which demonstrates some similar characteristics to those of the BRIC nations, is Indonesia, Vietnam, Colombia and Ukraine. Economic growth in these countries is beginning to drive consumer spending on domestic goods. The size of their populations means there is unlikely to be any reversal of this trend.

The rise of Asian and South American economies means that economic flows have become increasingly complex. Hans Ulrich Maerki of IBM observed, in 2007, that both capital and trade flows are now increasingly multidirectional: 'the deepening of global trade, capital and information flows, enabled by a flat world, is changing where and how business value is created'.

He cites a number of examples, including:

- Global investment banks send derivatives processing to Dublin.
- US radiologists send X-rays to Australia for analysis.
- Asian chipmakers use US engineers for expertise.
- Asian clothing manufacturers outsource design to Italian designers.
- Customer service centres in Nova Scotia handle warranty enquiries for US shoppers.

Between 2000 and 2003, foreign firms built 60,000 manufacturing plants in China. However, China is no longer just a recipient of FDI. FDI is now truly a global issue, with export of capital and acquisitions now coming from the emergent BRIC nations. For example, the acquisition of the UK's Corus Steel by India's Tata Group in 2006 was followed by a move into automotives through the acquisition of UK-based Jaguar and Land Rover.

There is now a strong move in China to export capital and make foreign acquisitions, driven in part by state-backed strategies to secure access to increasingly scarce mineral and energy sources essential to continued growth. The involvement of Chinese state owned organisations in the mining and refining industry of Australia is an example of this. Much of this trend represents the use of large capital assets by cash-rich Chinese businesses to acquire stakes in the European and US financial sectors. In November 2007, for example, China's second-largest life assurance group paid £1.3 billion to become the top shareholder in Fortis, the Belgian-Dutch banking and insurance group. Similarly, China holds significant deposits in American government bonds (T-bonds).

These examples indicate how much more complex and multidirectional the flows of the world economy have become.

Consumer-led growth in the BRIC and other emergent economies is creating powerfully resourced organisations which are moving from being trading partners to owners of, and investors in, major Western businesses. The Eastern economies are beginning to take a large and direct stake in the markets and businesses of the West. This major socio-economic shift is leading to an increasing and inexorable interdependence between business managers and owners from different cultures.

Working with different cultures is moving from the need to have an understanding in order to promote your business abroad to dealing with a truly global economy where the balance of resource power is shifting and the web of relationships is becoming more complex.

Exercise 1.2

Look at your organisation, or one with which you are familiar, and see how 'global' it is. Even quite small organisations can have global aspects.

1.6 National account balances and monetary policy

1.6.1 Fiscal policy

There will always be decisions that a government must make, and legislation they must enact to ensure those decisions are carried through. At every level, be it local, national or supranational, there will be a department of government which will have the unenviable job of balancing a number of economic factors by the use of both fiscal and monetary policy. Ultimately a government is no different to you and I – we must run a balanced budget. Just as we can spend no more than we can earn (and borrow) nor can they.

There are factors will be of importance to any company that trades with, or within, that particular market. The factors that companies need to consider include:

- The size and growth of the economy as a whole.
- The rate of inflation in the market and how it compares to that of other markets.
- The exchange rate of the currency compared to others.
- The level of unemployment in the market.
- The balance of payments with other trading blocs, whether this area is a net importer or a net exporter. This might be further subdivided between manufacturing and consumer goods (visibles) and service goods (invisibles).

These are not the only factors about a trading area that an organisation will be interested in; there will be others depending on the specific nature of their industry. As an example, the Financial Services Industry will be concerned with the propensity to save and the propensity to borrow.

Governments raise revenue from individuals and businesses via a variety of taxes. The way they spend that money can have a significant effect of the strength of the economy. There are two ways we can look at taxation; we can consider taxation to be direct (in which case it deducted from earnings, either individual or corporate), or indirect, in which case it is levied on expenditure.

Direct tax is normally a percentage deducted from either earnings or profits. Invariably for businesses it is based on profits. Not all direct tax is levied on earned income and an individual may pay income tax on their salary but also a tax on dividends that they hold in a company unrelated to their work. This would be described as a tax on unearned income. Sometimes a special tax on individuals will be designated for a particular purpose, for instance a tax to provide for old age pensions.

Indirect taxes, sometimes called taxes on consumption, are levied on expenditure. This means that when we buy something the cost will have been inflated by a percentage which when the vendor receives it must be paid to the government. One of the advantages of this type of tax for the government is that they have to collect tax from fewer sources – there are fewer vendors in most economies than there are earners. Types of indirect tax include;

- A value added tax – which can be levied on all goods, although a government may decide to apply different rates to different products to encourage (or discourage) patterns of consumption. For instance there is unlikely to be any VAT on this book – the government may want to encourage study – but if you have some chocolate whilst you are reading it that will carry VAT since it is a luxury.
- Hydrocarbon tax – a tax on the fuel that people use in their vehicles. Again there is a motivation for government over and above the mere raising of revenue; they may wish to discourage the use of cars and so tax fuel heavily. We shall discuss that again when we discuss the environment.
- Tobacco tax – aside from the revenue raised the higher the tax the more people are discouraged from smoking which will be good for the nation's health and, possibly, reduce the demands on the health provision in the country.
- Import duties – again governments will use this form of taxation to encourage or discourage particular patterns of consumption as we discussed earlier in the chapter.

For a government there are two further decisions to be made other than those implied in the decisions described above.

1. Firstly they will need to decide whether the majority of the tax revenue should come from individuals or from companies. Obviously businesses will consider the environment more favourable if there is a low level of corporate tax. If it isn't they may decide to relocate to a country with a more favourable tax regime. Tax havens such as the Bahamas or Bermuda will have exceptionally low, or even no, income tax to attract foreign companies to set up branches there. Governments may decide to have a threshold of income below which taxation is not paid by individuals, effectively helping the low waged to live. In the case of companies they may have a system of tax credits for particular industries to encourage investment in those areas.

    The population would prefer the income tax levels to be low since they would prefer to keep the majority of their earnings to use as they see fit. Too high a level of taxation will not encourage people to work harder to raise their income levels.
2. Secondly they will need to decide whether how much they wish to raise by taxing earnings compared to the amount the wish to raise via indirect taxation.

1.6.2 International trade

Since Adam Smith published *The Wealth of Nations*, there have been many important developments that have brought us to the present position. It is now possible to obtain goods that have been produced in many parts of the world and are purchased and used after travelling thousands of miles. This allows people in the UK to enjoy tuna from the Seychelles in the Indian Ocean, pineapples from Africa and clothing from Bangladesh and China.

Industrial production began in Europe. In many instances, the other parts of the world supplied the raw materials that enabled European industries to add value and although most of the finished products would be consumed in Europe, the finished products were sometimes exported back to the colonies.

The spectacular success of the USA meant that, by the beginning of the twentieth century, it was the largest participant in world trade. With a large population and without any major conflicts at home, the US flourished and dominated both world trade and foreign direct investment, with American firms becoming multinational organisations with investments in plants in many countries around the world.

An estimate of the value of the exports of merchandise has been produced by the World Trade Organisation. In 2007, the total value was $13,618 billion. The value of the main elements and share of the total trade were:

	Value ($ billion)	Share of world merchandise trade (%)
Agriculture	1128	8.3
Fuels	2038	15.0
Mining	621	4.5
Manufactures	9500	69.8
Other	331	2.4

Some of the major developments that have allowed international trade to expand and dominate the economic lives of most people are:

- The development of industrial production processes has been affected by the introduction of machines and this has decreased the importance of labour as the prime source of skills and expertise.
- Transportation systems, especially rail, shipping and air travel have improved and the goods can now be moved relatively easily and quickly from where they have been produced to the place where the products are consumed. In particular, the introduction of cold storage facilities and handling has made a significant difference to the extent of international trade.
- The efficient and safe transfer of funds from the buyer to the seller was essential and so improvements in the financial systems have been important in developing international trade. In addition, the growth of international financial institutions has enabled capital to be obtained in the cheapest markets and this would enable large projects to be undertaken in most countries and enable the countries to exploit their natural resources and skills.
- Advances in technology over the period have contributed greatly to the development of international trade as it is possible for people to communicate with each other instantaneously and meet regularly, despite living and working in different parts of the world.

1.6.3 Monetary policy

Whereas fiscal policy relates to the level of taxation and spending that a government decides, monetary policy relates to the supply and price of money. By varying the price of money, a government or central bank can have a significant effect on the spending habits of companies and individuals. The price of money only relates to borrowed money – the price is the interest we have to pay on it. Since the government is normally known as the 'lender of last resort' it is the primary source of funds in a country.

When you go to the bank to borrow money with an overdraft that bank will have borrowed money from another lender who, after a number of other intermediaries will have borrowed money from the government. At each stage from the central bank onwards the interest rate will have increased. If the central bank wish to encourage businesses, or even consumers, to spend more money they will reduce the rate of interest they charge so that the bank will, hopefully, charge you a lower rate of interest for your overdraft. Not all of the money that the bank have available to lend is borrowed from the central bank in this way. It is quite possible that whilst you are in the bank borrowing money, someone else is in there investing their money and expecting interest to be paid to them. Naturally, they will be concerned about the interest rate, but they will want it to move in a different direction to you! So, the central bank can encourage people to save by raising the interest rates, but run the risk of discouraging companies from borrowing money to invest in the future.

When we talk about the money supply we need to consider not only the amount of money in the system but also the speed with which the money moves around. The cycle of money at its simplest level is as follows; a consumer draws money from their current account at the bank, they spend it with a retailer who pays it into the bank. If the central bank decides to restrict the money supply by destroying more notes than it prints then we might expect the level of spending to go down, but that is not necessarily the case. If the central bank is running short of money they may ask retailers to deposit their takings for the day a bit sooner (not every retailer makes deposits every day). Effectively the money is going around faster.

This assumes that the money supply is a closed system which, of course, it isn't. There are a number of ways in which the money supply can be increased, only some of which are under the control of the central bank.

- The consumer uses some of their savings.
- Foreign currency is changed into the local currency. This might happen because a tourist visits or because a company has exported goods or services.
- Businesses or individuals borrow money to invest and keep their free cash for consumption.
- The government itself may release reserves into the economy by spending money by building roads, hospitals or other aspects of the country's infrastructure. Or it may just employ more civil servants.

Similarly there are a number of ways in which the money supply can be reduced, or money can 'leak' out of the system:

- Consumers decide not to buy but to save.
- People make investments using cash, shares in companies or even government savings bonds.
- Goods are imported, or people go on foreign holidays, and money leaves the country.
- People pay tax to the government.

So a central bank cannot control the money supply completely. We might ask why they would want to. The central bank (and other bodies) will have the responsibility for maintaining the monetary stability and financial stability of a country and its currency.

The integrity and value of a currency are important to the economy as whole, since it means there will be sustained and steady growth without significant price inflation. This will be another balancing act for the central bank since, as we mentioned earlier, if interest rates (for instance) are set at just the 'right' level they will encourage people to spend in such a way that demand matches supply.

If the interest rates are too low then there will be too much money in the system and people will borrow money cheaply to buy many of the things that could not ordinarily afford.

If the productive capacity of the country cannot match that demand then the vendors will put up their prices and we will see price inflation.

If the interest rates are too high then there will be no encouragement for people to buy and production will slow down to match the reduced demand. Ideally governments will want to achieve non-inflationary growth since it means there will be real growth in the economy as a whole.

Real growth can be defined as the rate of increase in the economy's output minus the prevailing rate of inflation over the same period. This tends to be measured by two figures:

1. The Gross Domestic Product. The concept of the total economic activity of a country. It can be measured as incomes earned, as expenditures made or as the level of production.
2. The Gross National Product. This is the gross domestic product plus any net overseas earnings. As such it is a better reflection of the wealth of a developed nation since, as we shall see shortly, when we talk about foreign direct investment, a number of countries earn a lot of money from their investments abroad.

1.6.4 Impact on business and markets

Even if you have only the vaguest interest in World event, you cannot have failed to notice the current (2009) global recession. To what extent this situation is a consequence of government economic policy is debatable, but regardless of cause the impact of macroeconomic variables on the environment of organisations can clearly be seen.

Exercise 1.3

Read some reviews, in a good business newspaper, of world economic affairs.

1.7 Cross-cultural management

1.7.1 Managing across cultures

In a twenty-first century economy, intercultural awareness is the key to international business success. It is estimated that international trade has increased from $136 billion in 1960 to approximately $9 trillion at the beginning of this century.

Increasing migration and more business opportunities have also produced greater interaction across cultures. In a world where global brands dominate all retail environments, it is very evident that we now live in a global economy. Any visitor to an African city is greeted by the sight of people wearing English football shirts, billboards advertising European designer-label fashions, people driving Japanese or Korean cars and local families queuing up for a McDonalds meal. The global economy has become one not only of trade but also one where cultures and identities are merging.

Managers are increasingly exposed to working with, or within, many different business cultures. This involves working in other countries, working in organisations that have operations in other cultural environments, or working with colleagues from a wide range of cultures.

This presents three key interdependent challenges for managers:

- The need to become more inter-culturally competent in order to operate in an increasingly diversified business world.
- The need to understand and develop business models that will be suitable to this changing context.
- The need to create organisational models and structures which will reflect the new circumstances and gain maximum benefit and opportunity.

David Foster writes about what constitutes cross-cultural management:

"It is a shorthand term which summarises a number of different elements. First, it describes the range of organisational behaviour which exists within both countries and cultures. Second, it compares and contrasts organisational behaviour across countries and cultures. Third, it seeks to understand to understand and improve the interaction of co-workers, clients, suppliers and partners from different countries and cultures."

The purposes of cross-cultural education and training are threefold:

1. It is designed to encourage people to study and evaluate the components of their own culture so that they become more aware of their own hidden cultural assumptions which interfere with effective intercultural action.
2. It seeks to expand people's repertoire of culturally appropriate behaviours so that they can operate more effectively in cross-cultural encounters in the workplace.
3. It tries to evaluate the impact of cultural factors on job performance. It can be argued that cultural traits and differences are so ingrained that it is hard for individuals even to understand they are there or that they have an influence on behaviour. There is a large body of opinion supporting the idea that different cultural traits between countries can be understood to play a part in the behaviours and ways of working prevalent among individual managers. These traits influence individual action, how relationships are formed and maintained, how products are perceived and located in markets and the success of communication.

1.7.2 Hofstede

> This theory is very examinable – make sure that you understand it, and have plenty of examples to illustrate Hofstede's arguments.

Geert Hofstede researched the role of national culture within the organisation and identified five dimensions which he argued largely accounted for cross-cultural differences in people's belief systems and values. These he termed 'uncertainty avoidance', 'masculinity', 'individualism', 'power-distance' and 'Confucian dynamism'.

Individualism versus collectivism

(Examples: Individualistic=United States, Great Britain; Collectivistic=Pakistan, Taiwan)

Is the individual the basis of society or does society give meaning to the individual? The United States is the best example of a society in which individualistic traits are most pronounced. For example, differences are admired and the cult of individuals prospers most.

Perhaps in direct contrast is the Chinese culture, where society's rights and responsibilities are dominant and individual needs are subservient. Here conformity is generally considered the norm.

Masculinity versus femininity
(Examples: Masculine=Japan, Italy; Feminine=Denmark, Sweden)

Masculine cultures emphasise 'assertiveness' compared to 'nurturance' for feminine cultures.

High masculine societies, whether individualistic like United States or collectivist like Japan, provide weaker people with, on average, less support whether from within the organisation or from society at large. People learn to admire the strong and to have a relatively negative view of the weak and dependent.

Power-distance
(Examples: Low=Denmark, Austria; High=France, India)

Measures the extent to which individuals (society) tolerate an unequal distribution of power in organisations and in society as a whole. In high power-distance organisations, superiors display their power and exercise it. Subordinates expect this behaviour and feel uncomfortable if they do not personally experience their superiors displaying their status and power.

In high power-distance cultures, subordinates feel separated from one another: it is not easy to talk with higher-ranking people and real power tends to be concentrated at the top. In low power-distance societies, members of organisations, and of society, tend to feel equal and relatively close to each other at work. Power is much more likely to be delegated in low power-distance cultures.

Uncertainty avoidance
(Examples: Low=Denmark, Sweden; High=Japan, France)

Measures the extent to which people tend to feel threatened by uncertain, ambiguous, risky or undefined situations.

In cultures where uncertainty avoidance is high, organisations promote stable careers and produce rules and procedures, which staff must follow (and which staff find comforting to follow). Hofstede argues that uncertainty avoidance is about reducing ambiguity and should not be confused with risk avoidance.

Confucian dynamism
(Examples: Low=United States, Australia; High=China, Japan)

Measures the extent to which conformity according to 'position' is stable and elicits predictable behaviour between individuals.

Behavioural attributes that are valued highly include obedience, deference, maintaining the status quo within organisational and social hierarchies and trouble-free social relations. Where you are in an organisational hierarchy predetermines the way you are expected to treat others and in turn the way you should be treated. Behaviour is much more predictable in Confucian cultures that exhibit high levels of Confucian dynamism.

1.7.3 Other models

Trompenaars, and subsequently writing with Hamden-Turner, follows a functional approach, like Hofstede, in which the premise is that culture can systematically cause differences in behaviour between people from different countries.

Trompenaars and Hamden Turner developed the 'Seven Dimensions of Culture Model' to analyse cultural differences and this also provides managers with some insight into the complexity of managing international teams.

Trompenaars' basic premise is that an understanding of the underlying values of different cultures leads to greater respect for diverse ways of operating and to the desire and skills for reconciling cultural differences to achieve business performance. Each one of the seven dimensions is presented below along with a summary definition.

Relationships with other people

- Universalism versus particularism – Cultures with a universalistic tendency emphasis rules and drawing up of detailed contracts, eg of employment, where particularistic cultures focus on the relationship between people. Here there is consideration of the rules versus relationships. Does the cultural emphasis on living by the rules – respect for law, and so on – take precedence over personal relationships or vice versa?
- Collectivism (Communitarianism) versus individualism – Consideration of groups versus individuals. Cultures, for a variety of reasons, either tend to value self-orientation or group orientation. This can affect the decision-making process and the extent to which authority resides in an individual to make decisions. This can have a profound effect on working practice with widespread consultation favoured by a common orientation culture. There is a danger, for example, that this might be perceived as procrastination by those from an individualistic background. It is this type of understanding that can help support the development of co-operative relationships inside and between organisations where one or both individuals are inexperienced in working with multi cultural teams.
- Neutral versus emotional (affective) – This reflects the range of emotions that people are able to express openly. This could have a considerable impact upon the way in which products are promoted, and how relationships are established with customers and the organisations in which they operate.
- Specific versus diffuse – reflects how people will adjust their behaviour in different settings (specific). However, diffuse reflects the consistency of a person's relationships regardless of their situation. This has implications for managing staff, that is 'once the boss, always the boss', as opposed to specific where 'the boss is the boss in work and friend out of work'. This has a number of complexities, particularly for international working relationships.
- Achievement versus ascription – This relates to how status is accorded. Status is achieved via years of experience, service, education and age. In other words the 'respect your elders' scenario.

Orientation in time and attitudes towards the environment.

- Sequential time versus synchronic time – This is essentially the difference between a sequence of events or simultaneous events. It is a question of being able to juggle a lot of balls in respect of time, or needing to operate in a sequence to differentiate activities. This can indicate a lot about an individual's ability to work individually, within a team, on a self-motivated basis, or on a delegated activity basis.
- High context and low context – High context behaviour will have a form of ritual behaviour in everyday life. Priorities, status, and so on will be important. Low context will see little in the way of ritual behaviour and can generally cope with a number of events happening at any one time.

Trompenaars and Hampden Turner (2001) interviewed 15,000 managers in 28 countries to explore the cultural differences between universalist societies and particularist societies.

In universalist societies, people follow the rules and assume that the standards they support are the correct ones. Further, they believe that society works better if everyone conforms to them. Particularist societies believe that particular circumstances are more important than general rules, and that people's responses depend on circumstances and on the particular people involved.

In universalist countries written contracts are taken seriously. Teams of lawyers are employed to make sure that a contract is correctly drafted, and once signed it must be policed to ensure it is kept. Particularist countries think that the relationship is more important than the contract and that a written contract is not always necessary – the particular people and the particular situation matter more than the universal rules.

Further attempts at categorisation have clustered individual countries into groupings based on observed shared characteristics and affinities. For example, Ronen and Shenkar (1985) created a set of clusters based on an analysis of four key characteristics:

- the importance of work goals,
- job satisfaction,
- the impact of managerial and organisational variables,
- work roles and interpersonal orientations.

As a result they proposed eight main groupings that display shared characteristics on these dimensions.

1. The Nordic states – Finland, Norway, Denmark and Sweden.
2. The Germanic states – Austria, Germany and Switzerland.
3. The Latin European states – France, Belgium, Portugal, Italy and Spain.
4. The Latin American states – Mexico, Peru, Argentina, Chile and Venezuela.
5. The Arab states – Bahrain, Abu Dhabi, Saudi Arabia, United Arab Emirates, Oman and Kuwait.
6. The Near Eastern states – Turkey, Iran and Greece.
7. The Anglo states – the USA, Canada, New Zealand, Australia, the UK, Ireland and South Africa.
8. The Far Eastern states – Singapore, Malaysia, Hong Kong, the Philippines, Vietnam, Indonesia, Taiwan and Thailand.

Brazil, India, China and Russia are notable absentees from this list due to the date these studies were produced. Recent years have seen a flurry of research into China since the country has increasingly opened up both politically and economically. It is possible to place China in an Asian cluster, as it displays many of the characteristics of strong family ties and tendency to collective acceptance of authority structures. However, the relationship between state control and enterprise is complex and worthy of a separate discussion later.

Different cultures have different ways of coping with life, a different set of responses to the same underlying dilemmas. In Far Eastern cultures, books start 'at the back' and are read from right to left in vertical columns. To Westerners, this seems a reversal of normal practice.

Managers need to display cross-cultural competence and reconcile cultural differences. Successful leaders are those who are flexible, sensitive and skilled enough to be able to ride what they call 'the waves of culture'.

1.8 Stakeholders: society and government

1.8.1 Stakeholders

There are a number of different individual and interest groups both inside and outside the organisation who will have views of the strategic development of the organisation and who can affect or is affected by the performance of the organisation. These groups or individuals are referred to as stakeholders.

> Stakeholders: Those persons and organisations that have an interest in the strategy of an organisation. (Source: CIMA)

They include:

- shareholders and owners
- management
- employees
- customers/clients
- suppliers
- local community
- local and national governments
- trade unions
- media
- regulatory bodies
- pressure groups.

There are different classifications of the above stakeholders, for example internal stakeholders (employees and management); connected stakeholders (shareholders, customer and suppliers); and external stakeholders (governments, community, pressure groups).

Strategic decision-making requires managers to consider stakeholders when setting the mission and objectives of the firm. This is for two broad groups of reasons:

1. Issues of stakeholder power. This view observes that, like it or not, management must recognise that stakeholders can affect the success of a strategy, depending on whether they support or oppose it. For example, customers refusing to buy products, shareholders selling their shares or staff striking would disrupt any strategy. The view concludes that management should consider stakeholders before setting strategic objectives.
2. Issues of organisational legitimacy. This more radical view suggests that firms are required to be good citizens because they are only permitted to exist by society on sufferance of not abusing their power. Consequently, although working primarily for the shareholders, management must ensure that its decisions do not ignore the interests of other stakeholders.

1.8.2 The role of society

The most obvious, and originally the only, role of 'society' as a stakeholder is as the ultimate producer and consumer of an organisation's goods or services. Indeed, until the development of stakeholder theory in the 1950s, few if any firms though much about society at all.

During the 1950s and 60s, many authors began writing about the organisation's responsibilities outside of its immediate stakeholder group (customers, suppliers, staff and shareholders). The era of 'stakeholder-driven' strategy had arrived.

By the 1970s, most organisations recognised that they owed some sort of 'duty of care' to society at large. They also saw that being a 'responsible' organisation could lead to a payback in terms of staff, customer and investor relations. The concept of 'corporate social responsibility' had arrived (see later in this chapter).

1.8.3 The role of government

Similarly, until the 1970s, government was treated by most organisations as a regulator and taxation-levying body. Although some organisations, such as public sector bodies and defence contractors, saw government as a customer and/or supplier, a very simplistic approach to business-government relations was pursued.

Public 'scandals' of the 1980s and 1990s (such as Maxwell and Polly Peck) led to governments recognising a new role – one of protecting other stakeholder bodies from over-aggressive, negligent or even fraudulent directors and managers. This led to the development of corporate governance (see later).

1.9 Corporate social responsibility

1.9.1 General principles of CSR

Social responsibility can be defined as 'taking more than just the immediate interests of the shareholders into account when making a business decision'.

Issues commonly associated with social responsibility include:

- environmental pollution from production or consumption of products,
- standards of factory and product safety,
- non-discrimination in employment and marketing practices,
- avoidance of the use of non-renewable resources,
- non-production of socially undesirable goods,
- production of non-degradable packaging or products.

In business decisions, a conflict may be encountered between what furthers the firm's interests and what satisfies society. Corporate social responsibility (CSR) is a key element in the management of the organisations relationships with governments and regulatory agencies, NGOs and civil society.

At this point we can distinguish between business ethics and CSR which, although the two are often used interchangeably, have distinct meanings. Business ethics comprises principles and standards that govern behaviour in the world of business. Actions can be judged to be right or wrong, ethical or unethical, individuals inside or outside the organisation. These judgements will influence society's acceptance or rejection of the actions taken. CSR, however, refers to a firm's obligation to maximise its positive impacts upon stakeholders whilst minimising the negative effects. As such, ethics is just one dimension of social responsibility.

The extent to which stakeholders judge that businesses meet, legal, ethical, economic and philanthropic responsibilities placed on them by their various stakeholders will determine the degree of corporate citizenship exhibited by the firm.

CSR has been defined as having four dimensions: economic, legal, ethical and philanthropic. As such society can:

- require business to discharge its economic and legal duties,
- expect business to fulfil its ethical duties,
- desire business to meet its philanthropic responsibilities.

1.9.2 The scope for international variation: developed and developing economies

CSR has also been defined as: '… the continuing commitment to business to behave ethically and contribute to economic development while improving the quality of life of the workforce and their families as well as of the local community and society at large' by representatives of the World Business Council for Sustainable Development.

From the same source perceptions of CSR from different societies and cultures were given as:

- 'CSR is about capacity building for sustainable livelihoods. It respects cultural differences and finds the business opportunities in building the skills of employees, the community and the government' (Ghana).
- 'CSR is about business giving back to society' (Philippines).

In America there is more emphasis on the philanthropic approach to CSR, where companies will make charitable donations to society or its representatives.

We can contrast the European approach where the emphasis is on business processes which are more socially responsible, complemented by investment in communities for reasons which are supported by good business cases.

It is argued, by Mallen Baker, that the European approach is more sustainable since social responsibility becomes an integral part of the wealth creation process which should enhance the competitiveness of the business and maximise the wealth created from both the business and the society. With a more philanthropic approach when times are hard and the bottom line is under pressure it becomes very easy to cut the size of the donation.

We can see that there is no one definition, or theory, of corporate social responsibility. We can consider an 'ethical conception' which is concerned with corporate self-restraint, expansive public policy and corporate altruism which can be contrasted with an 'economic conception' involving fiduciary responsibility, minimalist public policy and customary ethics. In short the former is about general welfare and the latter about private wealth. The third conception that of corporate citizenship, concerned with corporate reputation, strategic philanthropy, political influence and multiple jurisdictions sits, uncomfortably, somewhere between the two.

It is certain that there will be increasing pressure on organisations to play an increasing role in the solution to social issues. This will be particularly true of those that have a global presence. This means that multinationals and NGOs will increasingly be looked to take a lead in addressing those issues where a national government or local firm has not been able, or willing, to arrive at a solution. With increasing globalisation, which we discussed earlier in this chapter, the power of the institutions attached to the nation state (national governments, judiciary and police for example) is declining.

1.10 Corporate governance

This section is based on extracts from the CIMA working party report, Corporate Governance: History, Practice and Future, published by CIMA Publishing and reproduced with permission.

> These principles are very examinable, but you do not need to know the specific requirements of the UK Combined Code, or any other Corporate Governance regime.

1.10.1 Why corporate governance?

According to the Cadbury report, corporate governance is the system by which companies are directed and controlled. A number of high profile scandals over the last few decades have highlighted the need for guidance to confront the problems that can arise in organisations' systems of governance. Whilst usually associated with large quoted companies, governance is an issue for all organisations – profit making and not-for-profit.

Some of the earliest considerations of corporate governance come from the US. The Treadway Commission issued a report on fraudulent financial reporting in 1987, which confirmed the role and status of audit committees. The Treadway Report prompted the Securities and Exchange Commission (SEC) to incorporate in its listing requirements, from 1988, that all SEC-regulated companies should have an audit committee with a majority of non-executive directors. Further work by a subgroup of the Treadway Commission, COSO, developed a framework for internal control, providing detailed criteria for management to assess internal control systems, and gave guidance for reporting publicly on internal control.

In the UK, the corporate governance debate was stimulated by a series of corporate scandals and unexpected corporate collapses in the late 1980s and early 1990s.

Press coverage of BCCI, Polly Peck and the pension funds of the Maxwell Communications Group caused much public questioning about how effective the boards of these companies had been in monitoring the actions of their executive management, and about the difficulties that non-executive directors and auditors faced in 'standing up' to dominant chairmen or chief executives.

1.10.2 Stakeholders and government

The primary reason for corporate governance is to protect stakeholders such as shareholders, employees and pensioners. As can be seen from the examples cited above, many of the 'scandals' that led to the development of different corporate governance regimes were a direct result of directors abusing the power of their positions. Corporate governance regulation is therefore primarily intended to remind directors of the limitations of their power, and to enforce the primary agency relationship of business – that directors work *on behalf of* the shareholders.

One of the main debates surrounding corporate governance regulation is whether it should be a legal requirement (as in the US) or a set of best practice guidance (as in the UK). Individual governments around the World have to choose which approach is most appropriate, according to the culture and situation in their countries.

1.10.3 General principles (The Combined Code)

The Combined Code was first published in June 1998 and comprised Principles of Good Governance and a Code of Best Practice, which set out Code Provisions for each of these principles. The code was revised in 2003, and now reflects the work done by Turnbull, Smith and Higgs. Only the 'purpose and principles' of corporate governance are examinable in the Integrated management paper, and the principles of the code are divided into the broad areas listed below.

- Directors. Listed companies should be led by an effective board, with a balance of executive and non-executive directors such that no individuals or small groups can dominate decision-making. There should be a clear division of responsibilities of the two key tasks of running the board (Chairman) and running the business (Chief Executive) so that no individual has unfettered powers. Appointments to the Board should be made in a formal, rigorous and transparent manner. To enable it to discharge its duties, the board should be supplied in a timely manner with good quality information. Directors should receive an induction, on joining the company, and should regularly update and refresh their skills. The Board should evaluate its own performance, and that of its committees, on an annual basis. The directors should offer themselves for re-election at regular intervals, and should plan for the Board to be 'progressively refreshed' by bringing in new members.
- Directors' remuneration. Without paying more than is necessary, the level of remuneration should be that which is necessary to recruit and retain directors of the right calibre. A significant proportion of executive directors' pay should be performance-related in such a way as to encourage the achievement of corporate objectives and to reward individual performance. Policy on executive remuneration should be clear, and no director should be involved in determining his/her own remuneration.
- Accountability and audit. The Board is responsible for presenting a balanced and understandable assessment of the company's financial position and prospects. It is also responsible for maintaining a sound system of internal controls to safeguard the company's assets and the shareholders' investments in the company. It should establish formal and transparent arrangements for considering how to apply the principles of financial reporting and internal control and for maintaining an effective relationship with external auditors.
- Relations with shareholders. There should be a dialogue with shareholders based on the mutual understanding of objectives. The Board as a whole is responsible for ensuring that this dialogue takes place. The Board should use the annual general meeting (AGM) of the company as a vehicle for communication with investors, and a tool to encourage them to participate.

The Combined Code requires listed companies to include in their accounts a narrative statement of how they applied the principles set out in the Combined Code and a statement as to whether or not they complied throughout the accounting period with the provisions set out in the Combined Code. Listed companies which do not comply must give reasons for non-compliance.

The Combined Code includes Code Principles and Provisions for institutional shareholders, covering matters such as voting, communication between investor and company, and the investor organisation's responsibilities to evaluate the company's corporate governance arrangements. In a section titled 'Related Guidance and Good Practice Suggestions', the code also provides guidance relating to internal control (the 'Turnbull guidance') and audit committees (the 'Smith guidance').

1.10.4 The benefits of corporate governance

Good corporate governance:

- Reduces risk. It helps to ensure that the personal objectives of the board and the company's strategic objectives are brought into line with those of stakeholders. It can help to reduce the risk of fraud. It can provide a mechanism to review risk, and it can provide a framework for reviewing and assessing projects.
- Stimulates performance. It institutes clear accountability and effective links between performance and rewards which can encourage the organisation to improve its performance.
- Improves access to capital markets. It reduces the level of risk as perceived by outsiders, including investors. In particular, corporate governance can be seen as protecting shareholders' rights, and thus makes it easier for companies to raise finance.
- Enhances the marketability of goods and services. It creates confidence among other stakeholders, including employees, customers, suppliers and partners in joint ventures.
- Improves leadership. It allows increased expertise to be brought to bear on strategic decision-making, through the influence of non-executive directors (NEDs), and because all board members are encouraged to examine board decisions critically. The wider pool of knowledge and experience available to the board, through the inclusion of external members, helps the board to identify opportunities more readily.
- Demonstrates transparency and social accountability. This in turn can foster political support for, and public confidence in, the organisation.

1.11 The impact of regulation on the firm

1.11.1 The legal environment

All markets are controlled to some extent. That degree of control is exercised by regulation. The intention of regulation is to produce, prevent or modify a particular outcome.

Common examples of regulation will govern; prices, wages, market entry, the size of firms in an industry and the control they can exercise, employment conditions, pollution, and standards of production and quality. Since there will always be a conflict between the maximisation of profit, and the interests of those people using the products or services, this is obviously necessary. In general, the existence of regulations means that some parties will incur costs whilst others will accrue benefits.

Effective regulation will ensure that a safe and effective product or service is delivered, whilst not inhibiting the effective functioning and development of businesses and other organisations. Efficient regulation is said to exist if the total benefit to the nation is greater than the total cost.

Regulation can have a number of elements:

- Standards and statements of expectations and public statutes.
- A process of registration or licensing to permit and approve the service or provision of the product.
- A process of inspection to ensure compliance to standards.

There are also schemes of voluntary regulation, and we will talk about these later when we talk about corporate governance.

Regulation can occur at a number of different levels and, for example, in North America this could mean that a company was regulated by the local government, state government and the federal government. A similar number of layers would exist in most European countries as well.

The term deregulation must be used carefully in this context since it is often, incorrectly, used to describe the privatisation or liberalisation of some markets. For instance, whilst many countries still have a national airline owned and operated by the government, the USA, Europe, Australia and Japan have liberalised their markets. Whereas the nationalised airlines are subject to a wealth of regulation on safety, economic and political matters, in the liberalised countries only the political and economic control is removed. The airlines concerned are still regulated in terms of safety, amongst other things, but they are free to negotiate their own arrangements with airports, supply whatever routes they wish, and charge whatever fares they wish.

1.11.2 The impact of regulation

The forces that shape business are in many respects tied to government policy and regulation.

Studies conducted in Germany highlight that inappropriate regulation makes firms less likely to innovate and adapt the quality and mix of goods and services to changing consumer needs. In recognition of the adverse effects that regulation can have on markets, many of the multinational firms that operate within the OECD (and in other countries such as China and India) have devised strategies and business practices that enable cross-border transactions to take place under conditions that minimise bureaucracy and bureaucratic interventions.

The increasing volume of cross-border transactions, and interdependence of trade flows, investment, technology and capital, creates the need for greater coordination and integration of policies relating to them. There is also a requirement for trade (and industry) associations and national governments to work at a higher level of integration which is mutually reinforcing.

1.12 Corporate political activity

1.12.1 Business and politics

> Corporate Political Activity (CPA): The involvement firms in the political process, with the aim of securing particular policy preferences.

Though scholars disagree over the precise extent of corporate influence over the policy process, in the US overt political activity by firms was essentially unheard of until the 1970s. This changed when amended campaign financing legislation paved the way for the creation of Political Action Committees (PACs). PACs were a way that politicians seeking re-election could raise money in excess of limits on party-specific expenditures.

The 1980s saw dramatically increased CPA by firms, including new activity at the international level. For example, American and European firms were key players in the development of international regulations for intellectual property at the World Trade Organisation (WTO).

Lobbying scandals in the US most notably the arrest of Jack Abramoff in 2006, have also raised the profile of corporate involvement in the policy process among the wider public. As the US economy becomes more integrated into the world economy, CPA extends further: foreign firms are now seeking to influence US public policy. Indeed, restrictions on political activity by non-US multinationals were relaxed during the Clinton Administration and several foreign firms have taken advantage of this opportunity.

Non-market strategies are receiving increasing interest amongst strategic management scholars as a mean of improving firm performance. Ring comments that:

Non-market strategies can be employed to create and/or maintain a firm's source(s) of competitive advantage or to erode or destroy the sources of competitive advantages of its competitors.

In pursuing non-market strategies, firms may engage – directly or indirectly – in activity with one or more of a number of institutions such as the WTO, domestic and international courts, legislative and regulatory bodies, as well as the media.

Corporate political activity (CPA) can be an important element in any firm's effort to gain competitive advantage. This has been particularly true in the area of international trade, where domestic producers seek to bar or disadvantage foreign competitors in the home market though the imposition of trade protection.

CPA can benefit firms on the revenue side, such as a firm's sales to the federal government or amount of defence contracts, or the cost burden imposed from regulation. Firms that receive a significant portion of their revenues or face elevated levels of regulatory scrutiny have high motivation to manage that dependency through CPA.

There are two basic types of corporate political behaviour: buffering and bridging. Political 'buffering' behaviours include proactive political actions on the part of firms, such as informing government decision makers about the impact of possible legislation, trying to actively reduce government regulation of the firm, and working alone or in trade associations to make campaign contributions, lobby, or otherwise influence legislative/regulatory processes. 'Bridging', on the other hand, is a more reactive form of behaviour. It includes such activities as tracking the development of legislation/regulation, so to have compliance in place when legislation is passed, or exceeding compliance levels for regulation.

Some authors define 'relational' approaches to CPA as long term and issue spanning relationships, while 'transactional' approaches are more ad-hoc and issue specific.

1.12.2 Developed markets

In the US, the interests of businesses influencing public policy are well documented. For example, research has shown that firms employ 41% of all Washington lobbyists, and trade associations a further 22%. Business interests are major contributors to political action committees (PACs), and three firms (Saban Capital Group, Newsweb Corporation, and Shangri-La Entertainment) topped the list of 'soft money' campaign contributors in the 2001–2002 election cycle. Corporate executives also have a place in influential policy-making circles, including seats on the US President's Energy Task Force and the Department of Commerce-led Advisory Committee on Trade Policy Negotiations.

While the US Congress controls a budget of over $2 trillion, the amount spent by firms in support of PACs in the 1999–2000 election cycle was a relatively paltry $200 million. The British defence contractor, BAE Systems, gave some $650,000 to various congressional campaigns in 2005, though its US-based subsidiaries have over $40 billion worth of DoD contracts.

Though one explanation may be that US politicians are easily swayed by donors, a deeper and ultimately more compelling explanation is that firms have other mechanisms for presenting their policy preferences. It also reflects the fact that in a complex society like the United States, legislators seeking re-election are only part of the government apparatus. Regulatory agencies, whose members are not usually directly elected, are key players in many developed states. Lobbying regulators cannot be easily done through the electoral process, so other means and other instruments must be employed.

1.12.3 Developing markets

The ubiquitous nature of political participation by business firms, not only in the US, but also in the European Union, Japan, South Korea, Russia, Jordan and Kuwait has been noted by researchers. It is indisputable that business firms spend considerable money and are among the most prominent political players not only in Washington, DC but in capitals across the globe.

In many developing markets, CPA is far more overt in its nature than in the US or Europe. Politicians, or even whole governments, can be persuaded to introduce, modify or remove legislation fairly cheaply. Policy-making bodies can be threatened or bribed, and political opponents removed.

1.13 Country and political risk

1.13.1 Country and political risk

As we have already discussed, an analysis using Porter's diamond will ignore the environmental factors in the target country. It is important, therefore, that as well as conducting a PESTLE analysis for the home country of a company a similar analysis is conducted for any country within which a firm is currently operating or considering operating (see Table 4.1 later). Particular emphasis should be placed on determining any political and cultural differences.

1.13.2 Political risk analysis

Political risk can be considered to arise at the macro or micro level. Macro-political risks will affect all foreign firms in the same general way. Expropriation, the seizure of private businesses with little or no compensation to the owners would be an example as would indigenisation laws which require that national citizens hold a majority share in all enterprises. In recent years with the liberalisation of trade in Eastern Europe, the entry of China to the WTO and the negotiation of a trade agreement between Vietnam and the US macro-political risk has diminished somewhat but still needs to be monitored by multinationals.

Micro-political risk tends to affect selected sectors of the economy or specific foreign companies and is often driven by the dominance of those firms. These risks often take the form of industry regulation, taxes on specific types of business activity and local content laws.

Rugman and Hodgetts have produced a useful summary:
Sources of risk:

- political philosophies that are changing or are in competition with each other,
- changing economic conditions,
- social unrest,

- armed conflict or terrorism,
- rising nationalism,
- impending or recent political independence,
- vested interests of local business people,
- competing religious groups,
- newly created international alliances.

Groups that can generate political risk:

- current government and its various departments and agencies;
- opposition groups in the government that are not in power but have political influence;
- organised interest groups such as teachers, students, workers, retired persons, etc;
- terrorist or anarchist groups operating in the country;
- international organisations such as the World Bank or United Nations;
- foreign governments that have entered into international alliances with the country or that are supporting the opposition within the country.

Effects of political risk:

- expropriation of assets (with or without compensation);
- indigenisation laws;
- restriction of operating freedom concerning, for example, hiring policies and product manufacturing;
- cancellation or revision of contracts;
- damage to property and/or personnel from terrorism, riots, etc.;
- loss of financial freedom such as the ability to repatriate profits;
- increased taxes and other financial penalties.

When forecasting political risk whether the company does this on a formal or ad hoc basis, it is usual to focus on two areas:

1. the political system in which the company is doing business;
2. the goods/services to be produced and the operations to be carried out.

As regards the political system the major concerns would be the prospect of political upheaval in the country, the likelihood of the government giving preference to local firms or the prospect of a government acting on a totalitarian fashion. They would also consider the strength of lobby groups within the target country. For instance, within the US, lobby groups have considerable strength in the areas of steel, textiles, softwood timber and semiconductors and have been able to bring considerable pressure to bear on their government to bring about favourable decisions.

Products and operations also face an element of political risk. For instance where a government requires a joint venture to exist with a local partner there is both a limit to control and the risk of theft of product knowledge or technology. Where local laws do not offer patent protection this can be a significant risk. Similarly a requirement to source a fixed percentage of components locally can be a source of risk as can the government's approach to monopolies, cartels and price fixing.

Exercise 1.4

Assess the political risk in three or four different countries, for an organisation that might be considering doing business there.

1.14 Summary

If any one thing characterises the last decade, it has been a time when leaders of big multinational firms thought about the governance of the global economy – the principle being that there was no such thing as world government, and national governments in the main were particularly focused on their own jurisdictions when creating the rules of trade and finance or environmental protection of labour. Just a few years ago, it was thought that firms were moving into this vacuum tentatively, but that the world would soon be run more according to business and market principles. Over the past decade, most global managers have decided this idea is not to their liking; in turn they have created a vacuum into which governments are moving, for better or worse.

References and further reading

Bartlett, C.A. and Ghoshal, S. (1989) *Managing Across Borders*. Boston, MA: Harvard Business School Press.

Bridgewater, S. (2000) 'Strategic management in emerging markets', in M. Tayeb (ed.) *International Business*. London: Financial Times/Prentice-Hall, pp. 340–53.

Dicken, P. (1998) *Global Shift*. London: Paul Chapman.

Drucker, P.F. (1992) *Managing for the Future*. New York: Butterworth-Heinemann.

Foster, D. (1998) *Managing Across Cultures*. Lincoln: University of Lincolnshire and Humberside.

Hecksher, E. and Bertil, O. (1991) H. Flam and M. J. Flanders (eds), *Hecksher – Ohlin Trade Theory*. Cambridge: MIT Press

Hofstede, G. (1980) *Culture's Consequences: International Differences in Work Related Values*. London: Sage Publications.

Hofstede, G. (1991) *Cultures and Organizations: Software for the Mind*. New York: McGraw-Hill.

Huijser, M. (2006) *The Cultural Advantage: A New Model for Succeeding with Global Teams*. Boston, MA: Intercultural Press.

Levitt, T. (1983) The globalization of markets. *Harvard Business Review*, May–June: 92–102.

Mintzberg, H. (1994) *The Rise and Fall of Strategic Planning*. Hemel Hempstead: Prentice-Hall International.

OECD (2006) *Science and Engineering Indicators 2006*. Arlington, VA: National Science Foundation.

Ohmae, K. (1990) *The Borderless World*. New York: Harper Business.

Porter, M. E. (1990) *The Competitive Advantage of Nations*. New York: Free Press.

Quinn, J.B. and Hilmer, F.G. (1994) Strategic outsourcing. *Sloan Management Review* 35: 43–55

Ricardo, D. (1817) *On the Principles of Political Economy and Taxation*.

Smith, A. (1776) *An Inquiry into the Nature and Causes of the Wealth of Nations*.

World Bank (2005) *Overview: World Development Report 2005. A Better Investment Climate for Everyone*. Washington, DC: World Bank.

World Trade Organization (2004) *World Trade Report 2004: Exploring the Linkage between the Domestic Policy Environment and International Trade*. Geneva: WTO.

World Trade Organization (2005) *World Trade Report 2005: Exploring the Links between Trade, Standards and the WTO*. Geneva: WTO.

Revision Questions

Question 1

Each of the sub-questions below requires a brief written response and is worth 5 marks. This response can be in note form and should not exceed 50 words.

1.1 Explain the differences between free trade and protectionism. **(5 marks)**

1.2 Explain how 'demand conditions' in a company's home country might lead to a competitive advantage. **(5 marks)**

1.3 Explain why organisations choose to outsource services. **(5 marks)**

1.4 Explain what Hofstede meant by a 'masculine' culture. **(5 marks)**

1.5 Explain what general principles of corporate governance apply to the Board of Directors. **(5 marks)**

Question 2

2.1 Porter's 'diamond' is a model that explains

(A) how an organisation gains competitive advantage
(B) how a country gains competitive advantage
(C) how a product gains competitive advantage
(D) how an organisation can assess risk in a country **(2 marks)**

2.2 Offshoring is…

(A) gaining a competitive advantage by virtue of being based in a particular country.
(B) a form of outsourcing.
(C) having processes carried out in a different country.
(D) a way of avoiding tax. **(2 marks)**

2.3 A country that is moving from being a recipient of Foreign Direct Investment, to being a provider of it, is said to have

(A) a developed economy.
(B) a transition economy.
(C) a balanced economy.
(D) a command economy. **(2 marks)**

2.4 If interest rates are high…

    (A) there will be an incentive to borrow.
    (B) exports will increase.
    (C) output will increase, to satisfy increased demand.
    (D) the country's currency will strengthen. **(2 marks)**

2.5 Gross Domestic Product is…

    (A) a measure of the volume of goods produced.
    (B) a measure of the wealth of a country.
    (C) a measure of inflation rates.
    (D) a source of competitive advantage. **(2 marks)**

Solutions to Revision Questions

✓ Solution 1

Note: for the purpose of clarity, these answers are not in note form, and therefore exceed the word limit. In the exam, you should use the form directed by the questions.

1.1

- Free trade is the movement of goods, services, labour and capital without tariffs, quotas, subsides, taxation, or other barriers likely to distort the exchange.
- Protectionism is where one country, or trade bloc, attempts to restrict trade with another, to protect their producers from competition.

1.2

The demand conditions in the home market are important for three reasons:

1. If the demand is substantial it enables the firm to obtain the economies of scale and experience effects it will need to compete globally.
2. The experience the firm gets from supplying domestic consumers will give it an information advantage in global markets, provided that:
   (a) its customers are varied enough to permit segmentation into groups similar to those found in the global market as a whole;
   (b) its customers are critical and demanding enough to force the firm to produce at world-class levels of quality in its chosen products;
   (c) its customers are innovative in their purchasing behaviour and hence encourage the firm to develop new and sophisticated products.
3. If the maturity stage of the plc is reached quickly (say, due to rapid adoption), this will give the firm the incentive to enter export markets before others do.

1.3

The main advantages of outsourcing are thought to include the following:

- That it allows more accurate prediction of costs and, hopefully, improves budgetary control.
- That, due to the specialist nature of the external provider, the services received will be of a higher standard.
- The supplier should be able to provide a cheaper service, due to economies of scale from specialisation.
- The organisation will be relieved of the burden of managing specialist staff in an area that the organisation does not really understand.
- It supports the concept of the 'flexible firm'.

1.4

Masculine cultures emphasise 'assertiveness' compared to 'nurturance' for feminine cultures.

High masculine societies, whether individualistic like United States or collectivist like Japan, provide weaker people with, on average, less support whether from within the organisation or from society at large. People learn to admire the strong and to have a relatively negative view of the weak and dependent.

1.5

Listed companies should be led by an effective board, with a balance of executive and non-executive directors such that no individuals or small groups can dominate decision-making. There should be a clear division of responsibilities of the two key tasks of running the board (Chairman) and running the business (Chief Executive) so that no individual has unfettered powers. Appointments to the Board should be made in a formal, rigorous and transparent manner. To enable it to discharge its duties, the board should be supplied in a timely manner with good quality information. Directors should receive an induction, on joining the company, and should regularly update and refresh their skills. The Board should evaluate its own performance, and that of its committees, on an annual basis. The directors should offer themselves for re-election at regular intervals, and should plan for the Board to be 'progressively refreshed' by bringing in new members.

✓ Solution 2

2.1 (A)

2.2 (C)

2.3 (B)

2.4 (D)

2.5 (B)

2

Information Systems

Information Systems

2

LEARNING OUTCOMES

This part of the syllabus attracts a 20% weighting and covers a variety of areas associated with information systems. This chapter addresses information systems as a significant functional area of business, outlines major developments and introduces some important tools and techniques. By completing this chapter you should be assisted in your studies and be better able to discuss the wider business context within which information systems operate. You should also be able to analyse how information systems can be implemented in support of the organisation's strategy. Specifically you should be able to:

- identify the value of information and information systems in today's organisations,
- discuss the reasons for organisations' increased dependence on information systems,
- discuss the transformation of organisations through technology,
- discuss ways for overcoming problems in IS implementation,
- discuss ways of organising and managing IS activities in the context of the wider organisation.

2.1 Information and information systems

The hunger for information has never been greater than for today's organisations, likewise the value of information systems that deliver this information has never been more keenly felt. The dependence of modern day organisations on information and information systems is underlined by Hellriegel and Slocum (1992) as follows:

Today's organizations store and process vast amounts of data, which managers and other employees must turn into useful information. In turn, this information enables them to perform their jobs better.

Pesola's (2004) explains:

businesses increasingly run their databases over office-wide networks, link employees' computers via office-wide wireless-LAN (local area network) connections, sell goods and run support services over the internet and rely on receiving customer commissions by email

The increase in more sophisticated information and technological solutions has led to the emergence of the automated office, teleworking and the 'information superhighway' as facts of organisational life. It follows that information technology (IT) and information systems (IS) assume increasing managerial importance within the modern organisation.

It is at this stage worthwhile explaining the relationship between data, information technology (IT) and information systems (IS).

Data are facts or figures in a raw, unprocessed format. To become useful to a decision-maker, data must be transformed into *information*. Information is data presented in a form that is useful for decision-making, adding value to the decision-maker by reducing uncertainty and increasing knowledge.

The process of turning data into information may include the following stages:

- *Data collection*: raw data is collected from both the internal and the external environment.
- *Data evaluation*: collected data is filtered for relevance.
- *Data analysis*: different dimensions of the data are analysed, e.g. comparison with budget, with the historical record, with industry best.
- *Data interpretation*: meaning added to the data.
- *Data reporting*: information is disseminated to users.

Hellriegel and Slocum (1992) explain that IT involves:

> any devices or systems that help individuals or organisations assemble, store, transmit, process and retrieve data (raw facts and figures) or information

Information technology allows organisations to operate a number of different types of organisational *information systems* each designed with a specific purpose in mind. Information Systems are therefore products of Information Technology and normally take the form of software programs. Clegg (2003) explains that technology is just a delivery option and it may be feasible to have a viable IS strategy without computers, because the 'quality of information is more important than technology.' Despite Clegg's comments it is difficult to imagine an organisation of any *size* operating effectively without IT.

Within the factory, computer aided design (CAD) and computer aided (or automated) manufacturing (CAM) offer integrated solutions in product design and control of machinery. This allows flexibility and the elimination of waste factors integral to a 'lean philosophy' and constant improvement. An integrated approach combining both CAD and CAM can lead to the use of robots and computerised inventory management. The problems of economic machine loading and provision of customer and stockists' requirements is one of the most complex in modern factory management but can be easily facilitated through IS.

The office, like the factory before it, has been subject to huge technological advancements in recent years. 'Office automation' is a term that refers to the use of computers, communications and network technology in managing the organisation's operations and information resources. In recent years this has resulted in the combination of data, text, image and sound into office-built multimedia systems. Many organisations have made use of network technology, specifically *electronic data interchange* (EDI). EDI is the computer-to-computer transmission of data contained in standard business documents and reports, such as customer invoices and purchase orders. EDI replaces conventional business documentation with structured data transmitted electronically over networks ('paperless trading'). Obvious advantages of EDI include saving cost and speeding of transactions, potentially reducing lead times for material purchases (and stock holding) better customer service and improved responsiveness to changes in customer demands.

Many forms of automation and other technology are commonly found in most office environments. Some are reflected in Table 2.1.

Table 2.1 Examples of office automation

Application	Description	Comments
Teleconferencing	The ability to conduct meetings, business negotiations and presentations without the participants having to be at the same location.	Relatively inexpensive means of communication, allowing a number of telephone participants to hold multiple-way communication. One potential difficulty is the lack of visible identification and recognition of participants.
Videoconferencing	As above.	Videoconferencing overcomes the problems cited above by screening images of participants. It is still relatively expensive and requires special equipment. Advantages include savings in cost and time for participants, fast communication and timelier decision-making.
The Internet	A virtual network that links millions of computers all over the world.	Many organisations now use the Internet to advertise, trade and search for information about competitors, customers and suppliers. The World Wide Web exists on the Internet and consists of pages of information that can be found at websites, which can be accessed through the use of a web browser by using a unique address called a universal resource locator (URL). The flexibility and accessibility makes it a particularly useful tool for business.
e-mail	Electronic mail.	The primary form of organisational communication. It offers speed, versatility, the elimination of distance as an impediment, and the potential for an immediate response. It can significantly reduce the volume of paper. A potential difficulty of e-mail is the risk of computer viruses being transmitted through the opening of rogue messages.
Fax	Facsimile image transmission. Messages are digitally coded then transmitted, recorded and composed by the receiver's equipment.	e-mails popularity may have eclipsed the fax. Fax transmissions allows the sending of an exact copy of a document.

2.1.1 The role of information systems in organisations

An organisation's information system serves two important purposes. First, the information system records and monitors actions in the operational system, by processing, storing and reporting day-to-day transactions. The second major function of the organisation's information system is to support managerial activities, such as decision-making, planning and control. Information systems play a vital role in modern day organisations at a number of levels, whether:

- improving operations and manufacturing,
- contributing to enhanced products and services,

- offering the opportunity for cost reduction,
- improving communication, or
- allowing managers to make better informed decisions.

Decision-making is an important aspect of any organisation. The process of decision-making includes three stages: identifying decision problems, developing decision alternatives and making appropriate choices. Each level of the organisation has different types of decisions to make and therefore requires different types of information. Classically, three levels of decision-making are normally identified, strategic, tactical and operational, each resulting in different informational requirements and information sources:

Information attribute	Strategic	Tactical	Operational
Orientation	Mainly externally oriented	Internal and external	Internal
Planning time	Long term	Short to medium term	Immediate
Performance focus	Predictive rather than historical performance	Historical and current activities	Current activities
Coverage	Whole organisation	Groups of activities within departments/functions	Specific activities
Level of detail	Highly summarised	Some detail/some summarised	Very detailed
Uncertainty	High due to the long-term focus	Moderate levels	Low levels
Objectivity	High levels of subjectivity	Combination of subjective and objective information	Objectively measured data
Accuracy	Less critical	Moderate accuracy	High accuracy

Decisions may be defined in terms of frequency (e.g. volume) and their significance on the organisation. Operational (low-level) decisions occur most frequently in an organisation (e.g. on a daily basis). Strategic decisions are less frequently made. On the other hand, strategic decisions are potentially more significant and far-reaching for the whole organisation, whereas operational decisions are likely to have a lesser impact on the organisation as a whole, but are likely to have a significant impact on the particular operational function in which they are made. (It is important to recognise that there is unlikely to be a clear distinction of levels in practice, the distinction between operational and tactical decisions and between strategic and tactical decisions is often a matter of judgement and interpretation).

As good decision-making is at the heart of good management the hierarchy of systems available to support managers are worthy of consideration at this stage. They range from straightforward data processing systems to highly sophisticated expert systems. The hierarchy of potential systems and their uses are reflected in Table 2.2.

Table 2.2 Decision-based systems

Type	Description	Usefulness
Data processing system (DPS) or transaction processing system (TPS)	The processing of repetitive tasks using well-defined and structured information that is relatively easy to capture and store in large volumes.	Provides first line managers with vital day-to-day information about efficiency of operations and activities, but is limited due to the inflexible nature of information produced. Examples: payroll systems, purchase/sales order entry systems and stock control systems
Management information systems (MIS)	Report-producing packages that use information from the same source as the DPS.	Provides middle managers with information to monitor and control the organisation's activities and to report this to the senior-level managers. Useful for decision-making, planning, programme implementation and control. Examples: forecasting, reporting, budgeting and control information (exception reports, variance reports, etc.)
Executive information system (EIS)	Powerful software for supporting the types of high-risk, unstructured decisions that are made by strategic-level managers. EIS combines information from within the organisation and from its external environment, then organises, analyses and presents it.	Provides senior-level managers with strategic-level information to help them make strategic decisions. Presents output using text and graphics (e.g. bar charts and histograms), which can be tailored and customised. Examples: key performance indicators (KPIs) through user-friendly interface graphical user interface (GUI)
Decision support systems (DSS)	Possesses interactive capabilities, assists in solving 'ad hoc' queries and provides data-modelling facilities.	Provides managers with information to support unstructured, one-off decisions by retrieving and analysing data. The complex mathematical models used are designed to simulate the behaviour of an organisational activity in an unpredictable situation. DSS generate a number of potential solutions, enabling managers to carry out 'what if?' analysis.
Expert systems (ES).	A system that simulates the problem-solving techniques of human experts, by applying human expertise and knowledge to a range of specific problems about a particular area of expertise.	Higher degree of support than that provided by the EIS or DSS. The major benefits of expert systems include a preservation of knowledge and its distribution. Examples: investment appraisal decisions

Exercise 2.1

Identify the benefits of having good MIS and good EIS.

Solution

The value of having good MIS includes:

- Potentially more effective operations and improved management control;
- More complete information available to managers to improve decision-making;
- Improved satisfaction and motivation amongst managers;
- Better information leading to improved budgetary control, stock control, improved forecasting, etc.

The value of having good EIS includes:

- Ability to make informed, potentially significant decisions of strategic significance;
- Maintaining a competitive advantage over rival companies who do not make this investment;
- Improved ability to recognise opportunities or external challenges;
- Ability to track key performance indicators (KPIs) meaning that monitoring and control at strategic level is more effective.

Information systems should possess a number of important features in order that they fulfill a useful role within the organisation. These include:

- *Relevance*. Relevant information is capable of making a difference in a decision by reducing uncertainty and increasing knowledge about that decision. For example, making a decision about offering credit to a new customer might include an analysis of the customer's financial statements or previous credit history. An analysis of the customer's staff levels would not be relevant.
- *Timeliness*. Information must be provided to the decision-maker in sufficient time for it to be used in the decision-making process. Information that is presented to the decision-maker before it loses its influence on the decision being taken has timeliness. Information has to be available in order to be timely.
- *Understandability*. Understandable information is presented in a form that permits the user to apply it effectively to a decision-making situation. Information needs to be clear so that the user can recognise how important the information is to a particular decision.
- *Comparability*. This is the quality of information that enables users to identify the similarities and differences in various pieces of information. If we can compare information about the same object or event collected at two or more points in time, then the information is also *consistent*. Consistency aids comparability in decision-making.
- *Accuracy*. This is the degree to which there is agreement between the information and the events or activities that the information is meant to represent. Information must be sufficiently accurate for it to be relied upon by the manager, and for the purpose for which it is intended. It is important to assess the level of accuracy required by managers before providing the information, as the accuracy requirements will differ between decisions.
- *Completeness*. This is the degree to which information includes data about every relevant event necessary to make the decision.
- *Neutrality*. This means that information is not biased towards one particular perspective or from one particular source or location. Biased information is likely to lead the decision-maker to the wrong decision or an incomplete decision.
- *Meaningful*. The content of information, particularly, if the information is provided to managers, should be of strategic importance, meaningful and actionable. Meaningful information is synthesised from various pieces of data and is usually interpreted.
- *Effectiveness*. Effective information is that which is relevant and pertinent to the business process, as well as being delivered in a timely, correct and consistent manner.
- *Efficiency*. Efficient information is provided through the optimal use of resources.

2.2 Organisational dependence on information systems

Many organisations cannot function adequately without their information systems, e.g. airlines, travel agents, banks, insurance companies, even supermarkets. It has become difficult for firms to survive on domestic business alone. To achieve scale economies, firms need to develop new markets and e-marketing has allowed organisations to trade more easily globally and seek out and exploit new markets. This trend is evidenced by the fact that the last 20 years has seen world trade has grown at twice the rate of world GNP.

The competitive advantage to be gained from adept use of this potential to create new business models is easily apparent. Philips (2000) for instance cites the strategic implications of e-business as including the death of distance as a communication impediment and the reality of virtual organisations able to make savings and operate differently.

2.2.1 Emerging IS trends in organisations

This section explores emerging IS trends in organisations including:

- enterprise-wide systems such as area networks and databases,
- knowledge management systems,
- customer relationship management systems such as e-business and Web 2.0 tools.

Enterprise-wide systems. In early computer systems many organisations consolidated their information systems into one centralised data processing system. However, as companies become more diverse and distributed across large geographical areas, it was recognised that information systems were required that could meet the specific processing requirements of these distributed locations, but still retain communication to a central computer facility. This is known as distributed data processing (DDP), where the individual processing centres are linked to a centralised computer but have individual processing capabilities at each location. The use of DDP in the modern business environment is increasing and, as a result, large volumes of data transmission over wide area networks (WANs) are increasingly common.

A network is where a number of computers and other devices are linked in such a way that any one device can communicate with any other so enabling resource sharing between a number of users. Many organisations adopt a computer systems configuration that utilises a data communications network. Networks may link computers in different organisations and can involve widely distributed geographical sites (known as wide area networks or WAN), or computers within the same local site (known as local area networks or LAN). Where the WAN uses dedicated links it is called a physical network. Where a WAN uses a combination of links that are 'transparent' to the user, the network is called a virtual network.

Databases. Data needs to be stored, managed and retrieved. One method of simplifying matters is by means of an integrated dataset, whereby one set of data can be used by the enterprise as a whole. Traditional approaches to file management have taken an applications approach to data structure. For example, files based around accounting transactions, such as stock records, sales invoices and purchase orders, would be collected and stored in an accounting application. Under this approach each application collects and manages its own files and data, normally within separate files for each application. The accounting department may keep files relating to customers, as might the marketing department, but these records are likely to be kept separately within different departmental applications. One outcome of this type of file structure is 'data redundancy', a duplication of data in two or more files, leading to inconsistencies of the same data and an increased storage costs.

A database is a collection of data structured completely independent of any one application. A database could be described as a collection of data files that are integrated to provide one single file system. The main aim of a database file structure is to provide one common dataset for a wide variety of users and their information needs. A database management system (DBMS) is a set of integrated programs designed to organise and simplify the creation, management and access of data held within a database structure. A DBMS represents the way in

Table 2.3 Features of databases

Aims	Advantages	Disadvantages
Provide data for a number of users and meet their individual information requirements.	Data independence: allows multiple applications to use the same data at the same time. The data can be accessed in a number of different ways according to what the user is doing (e.g. preparing a report, performing a query or through basic applications processing, etc.).	Privacy. A requirement is for sophisticated security features to protect the database from unauthorised access, alteration or data destruction. (These are to be found in a DBMS)
Allow multiple users to have shared access to the database to carry out their own processing.	Reduction of data redundancy. In a database structure, data is only stored once. Any application that requires an item of data can access and retrieve it from a central store.	Data ownership. A dispute over who 'owns' the data within the database may result in problems over who should carry out file maintenance.
Maintain the integrity of the data (as there is only one dataset).	Reduced storage costs. Potential file storage requirements are reduced, resulting in file storage savings. Data integrity by keeping only one version of each data item within the database, inconsistencies in data between applications are eliminated.	It is important to restrict users from making unauthorised changes that could spoil the data for all other database users. However, users must be able to have access to the data so that they can update it when necessary. *Database failure*, should the power or the database fail, no processing or access to files is possible anywhere within the organisation. *Contingency planning*. As all files are held in one location the risks of loss is an increased concern. Contingency planning is significantly more important, which may be costly and time-consuming.
Advance corporate objectives.	An ability to develop as the organisation's information needs evolve.	Some organisations may implement databases without considering the benefits to their specific situation.

which an organisation coordinates the complex activities carried out by its department into one data location. A DBMS should enhance the organisation's ability to provide reliable, relevant information to decision makers easily, efficiently and effectively.

Exercise 2.2

Your organisation is considering changing to a database system. List the issues it would need to consider.

Solution

- Specialist staff required (in implementing and running the new system, such as a database manager and administrators).
- Set-up costs of new software and possibly new hardware.

- Training costs.
- Security features.
- Possible disruption.
- Responsibilities.
- Contingency and back-up facilities.

When a database is connected to a web server by a database connectivity component, (e.g. Microsoft ADO and Open Database Connectivity) visitors from outside the organisation (such as potential customers) can make enquiries about product and price information, and make orders and view shopping cart items from a web browser.

Exercise 2.3
Reflection

Think about the way in which you and your organisation use the World Wide Web. Take a few minutes to consider how it is used:

- to trade
- to network
- for entertainment
- for information
- for marketing.

What are the trends in web-based technology?

Undeniably sharing information within an organisation can lead to more effective operations and innovation, however this becomes difficult where the organisation grows in size and complexity. Often knowledge is contained in pockets within the organisation. *Knowledge Management Systems* (KM Systems) as its name implies is a system for managing knowledge. The software allows the collection, storage, organising and dissemination of various kinds of information for future use as part of internal ideas generation, collaboration, or operational efficiency, etc. Mind maps, diagrams, notes, reports, contracts, policy documents, e-Learning materials, e-mails, messages and training manuals might be managed by the software. Knowledge management solutions range from small software individual packages, such as brainstorming (thought shower) software, to highly sophisticated tailored software suitable for shared use. The philosophy that underpins KM systems is consistent with other trends such as knowledge workers, the learning organisation and collaborative team working. Organisations clearly believe in the importance of KM systems as evidenced by growing corporate expenditure on software of several pound billion per year.

The Internet is a public and global communication network that provides direct connection to anyone over a local area network (LAN) and represents an example of a virtual network. Access is potentially open to all, which arguably has resulted in an unruly proliferation of information of varying standards of reliability. Common Internet tools include e-mail, World Wide Web (www), social networking, shopping online, newsgroups, blogging and electronic conferencing.

Exercise 2.4

What significant benefits can the Internet bring to modern day organisations?

Solution

- online survey and market research,
- access to competitors' information and intelligence,
- improved communication,
- enhanced relationships with business partners,
- improvements to the supply chain,
- the potential to access new customers and markets,
- online customer services leading to enhanced customer loyalty,
- innovation in new products and services offered,
- online contract tendering,
- the potential for home working,
- a platform for doing business and Internet shopping.

According to the UK Government's Office of Fair Trading internet shopping market in the UK is estimated to be worth over £21.4bn, and over 20 million people shop online.

Using the Internet as a platform a rapid growth in so-called 'dot.com companies' took place about a decade ago, most taking advance of e-marketing. Although not all of these start-up companies survived more established organisations have since invested in this technology to enhance their operations.

Berens (2006) explains:

The dot-com boom was led by start-up companies that had unproven records, but the latest growth is being led by established retailers who understand their customers, have brands that people trust and see the web as a bolt-on', says Nick Gladding, senior retail analyst at Verdict Research. 'Lots of businesses that were sitting on the sidelines have now taken the plunge. It has been a difficult time for the retail industry, but there seems to be more confidence now and e-retailing is one area that has a lot of potential for attracting new business.

Grocery shopping has become one of the key interests for UK consumers. Tesco's and Asda's online services have had a dramatic impact, the former controlling two-thirds of the Internet groceries market. Other

Table 2.4 Practical advice for building a commercial website

Ensure that the site works across all platforms (e.g. Apple Mac, PCs, Linux) and across browsers (e.g. Internet Explorer, Firefox and Opera).
Inform users how secure their transactions are. Winning your customers' trust is vital.
Take account of any Consumer Protection and privacy legislation.
Draw up a privacy policy and terms of use for the site.
Do not collect too much information from site users in case it deters them.
Stay in contact with your customers, (e.g. by sending e-mail newsletters).
Get advice from experts sponsored by the government

Source: Berens (2006)

big names among the country's top 20 Web retailers include Argos, B&Q, Comet, Currys, John Lewis, Marks & Spencer and Next……………………..

Conventional retailers must also adjust to the fact that the Web has redefined how people shop. It's enabling consumers to choose goods that meet their requirements precisely, empowering them to find the lowest-priced product and allowing them to go shopping at any time that suits them.

So what are the keys to successful online trading? 'You have to provide something extra in terms of the product, the service and the price,' Gladding says. 'With the advent of comparison sites such as Kelkoo, prices are very visible online, particularly those of electrical goods. But established retailers still have the edge, because customers find that a reputable brand provides a lot of reassurance.'

With the incredible uptake of use of the Internet a number of benefits present themselves in marketing term (for example, in terms of data collection and providing enhanced value to customers and suppliers). It should, however, be noted that there are potentially a number of drawbacks of internet trading (e.g. financial security issues, computer disruptions, and a possibility of organisations ceasing trading).

Early e-business pioneers claimed a 20% reduction in costs. Berens (2006) highlights the online auction house of eBay that has become one of the largest UK marketplaces. The UK population now spends 10% of its web-surfing time on buying and selling goods. This seems to emphasise a new technology-enabled retail marketplace, and

> … most retailers can't afford not to trade on the internet, particularly those based in the UK. According to analysts, online shoppers in the UK will spend £1,170 per head on the Web this year, compared with their US counterparts' £987. One of the factors behind this growth is thought to be the rapid take-up of domestic broadband services.

The Internet has transformed our environment presenting a global canvas and in the process has reshaped the business world. The electronic business phenomenon has seen phrases such as 'e-commerce', 'e-business', 'digital economy', 'Internet commerce' and other besides becoming mainstream language. Phillips (2000) believes that they all mean similar things, drawing a slight distinction whereby:

- e-commerce (electronic commerce) represents the means by which companies communicate via digital transactions, but
- e-business (electronic business) also incorporates doing business throughout the value chain (with suppliers and customers).

An *Intranet* is an internal organisational network that is based on the Internet technologies, and can be accessed only by authorised employees. While the Internet has open access to the public, an Intranet is private and is protected by a 'firewall' (an access control system consisting of hardware and software that is placed between an organisation's internal network and external networks). One of the main advantages of an Intranet is that it allows confidential internal information sharing (e.g. corporate policies, document sharing, telephone directories, training programmes, etc). An *Extranet* refers to an extended Intranet of an organisation that links to its business partners (such as customers, suppliers or other trade organisations). Only authorised users are allowed access. One of the main advantages of an Extranet is to connect dispersed networks together. It has great potential in enhancing inter-organisational communication, facilitating electronic data interchange (Internet-based EDI) and e-procurement.

Web 2.0 is a category of Internet tools that effectively turn users into media contributors. The technology allows virtual communities to be built and opinion, knowledge and ideas can be shared. The potential for this has clear implications for not only social computing but also education, government and business. Wikis, second life, blogs and RSS feeds are examples of facilities offered by Web 2.0. (RSS involves subscribing to syndicated feeds and get publication updates every time there's new information (such as news headlines) in a variety of visual and audio formats).

The following short article describes the way in which some organisations are exploring the potential for what is known as 'blogging':

> ....Blogger.com began offering free blogs – short for weblogs, or online journals – in 1999. One is now created every second. According to Technorati, a website that monitors online activity, the 'blogosphere' now comprises 27 million blogs, peddling opinions on anything from bubblegum ice cream to censorship in China. Does anyone care? Well, yes. Boing Boing, a directory ranked by Technorati as the world's most linked-to blog, has an audience of 1.7 million and commands up to $8,000 a week for ad space; AOL last year bought blog hub Weblogs for $25 million; and the BBC and Guardian's websites now endorse blogosphere musings, giving credence to talk of 'citizen journalism'.
>
> But the anti-establishment heyday of the blog could be over. The corporates have themselves begun blogging. GM's vice-chairman Bob Lutz uses his Fastlane blog to talk product development, while Microsoft lets employee Robert Scoble criticise its products in his popular Scobleizer blog.
>
> *Source:* It'll never fly: Blogging, *Management Today*, April 2006, p. 12

2.2.2 IT – enabled transformation

When considering the issue of organisational transformation Carnall (2007) points to the vital requirement to capture and convert knowledge:

this point can be illustrated by looking at the retail sector. Here , large out of town stores sell groceries and electronics. Stores like Toys R Us, PC World and Waterstones dominate particular niches….Telephone banking becomes more important and who knows how huge internet commerce will become. All the above has required increasingly sophisticated IT.

He continues by listing what the technology has offered in order to transform these businesses, including:

- advanced logistics,
- real time inventory control,
- just in time (JIT) restocking, and
- analysis of sales patterns to identify product for the Christmas period.

Lynch (2009) makes the point that the increased information that comes from the adoption of new systems means that we are in a third industrial revolution: the information age:

…the information is global, not just local or national. For example, a major UK company now has a permanent three way telecommunications link between its engineering design teams in the USA, UK and India. The communications use the specialist engineering knowledge of the US team, the skills but low labour costs of their Indian colleagues, and the overall coordination and marketing skills of the UK headquarters. Such activity was simply not possible some years ago. New information technology has also opened up the possibility of greater strategic control in companies. Again, the possibilities from such technological innovations will provide continued strategic opportunities for companies.

Scase (1999) postures that:

Organisations of the future will be heavily dependent on information management. Supply chains will be characterised by cooperative relations between companies through joint ventures, strategic alliances and partnerships

In short IT has enabled, and continues to enable complete organisational transformation. Complete organisational restructuring might accompany changes to take full advantage of technology. The need to respond to a fast moving environment has led to organisations moving from traditional hierarchies to adopting more flexible organisational structures including more fluid matrix or project-based firms. Alongside these structures, virtual or networked firms have grown up. Inevitably these non-traditional structures have presented new challenges and required managers to adapt traditional approaches to these local contexts.

One significant development has been the increase in staff working from home, rather than being based in an office. By utilising a combination of communications technology such as e-mail and the web staff now have the ability to communicate with colleagues, customers and suppliers from their own homes. There are a number of clear advantages of teleworking not least reducing commuting to and from a fixed place of work. This means that less fuel is consumed and the environment is subject to less vehicle pollution. From the organisation's point of view time savings, together with the reduction in office distractions and disruptions, should lead to improved productivity. Operating costs are also reduced (through lower facilities costs). For the employee there is greater flexibility over precise working times and geographical proximity to colleagues is rendered less relevant.

Exercise 2.5

What are the disadvantages of teleworking?

Solution

- A potential loss of team cohesion and a sense of belonging.
- Potential control difficulties.
- The need to provide and maintain adequate levels of office equipment in a domestic setting.

Despite the obvious potential offered by IT, many organisations have yet to fully seize the opportunities. Carnall (2007) reports findings of a survey of the role of IT which suggest a number of barriers, for instance 60% of respondents felt that staff prefer structured organisations, and 50% saw control of homeworkers as an issue. Carnall stresses the need for leadership to overcome these barriers and seize the IT capability.

2.2.3 Teams: dispersed and virtual

Johnson, Scholes and Whittington (2008) observe that the Internet remains a major strategic issue for many organisations, and it allows formal organisational structures to be '...*dismantled and replaced with well functioning networks supported by this information infrastructure*'.

IS provides an opportunity for work teams to be geographically dispersed, even virtual and whilst there are challenges associated with virtual collaboration the flexibility and potential are easily apparent.

Senior and Fleming (2006) report a rapid move to '*a more dispersed workforce that is using technology to link workers and their functions together*' including virtual organisations and virtual teams. Whilst identifying considerable savings, organisations need in the view of the authors to bring team together at regular periods to socialise and to reinforce a shared culture.

Skyrme (1997) is clear that:

There is no a priori evidence with today's travel and electronic network that a geographically dispersed network is any less effective than one based at a single location. On the contrary, there is some evidence that people put more effort into making remote linkages and communication work, because there is less opportunity to meet face to face. In my experience the biggest causes of failure are:

- not having a compelling shared vision
- not clearly identifying network participants and their respective roles
- having team missions and goals incompatible with individual's aspirations
- having dominant nodes (i.e. a competitive or pressure relationship rather than truly collaborative one)
- not communicating sufficiently and clearly enough.

Skyrme (1997) also proposes certain principles for creating and maintaining innovative networked structures, grouped as prerequisites, attitudes and behaviour, team composition, norms and relationships, activity sequencing and communication. Some of the main principles are reflected here:

- high levels of trust,
- being mutually supportive,
- giving as much as you get, in terms of support, transfer of information and knowledge,
- teams that are small and multi-disciplinary,
- every worker should belong to at least two teams,
- every team must have a sense of purpose,
- frequent communication,
- accept that decision-making will often be ambiguous,
- use one e-mail per topic, especially when multiple recipients are involved,
- if face-to-face conversations take place summarise the meeting by e-mail,
- e-mails are conversations, so insert a level of informality.

The piecemeal harnessing of new IS by organisations of all shapes and sizes has however left many with a mixture of disparate and disconnected systems that do little to improve their efficiency or effectiveness. Meall (2004) reports that the accounting profession has been particularly hard hit, and the growing burden of bureaucracy threatens many:

....increased automation, and improved integration, could offer a non-merger route to survival.

By using integrated applications, and taking advantage of broadband technology, Bevan & Buckland has been able to improve communications between the 5 partners and 60 team members in its five offices across Wales, and enhance the service it offers clients.

As all of the firm's offices are now linked by a broadband-based wide area network, it has benefited from faster and cheaper access to applications. Partners can also dial in remotely from either a client's office or from home working from the same screens they would have in the office.

2.3 Information technology, contexts and change

Addressing the 2008 CIMA Lecturers' Conference, Dr. Melodie de Jager profiled what she believed to be new generation (generation Y) of potential student emerging in many Western countries. Born between 1980 and 2001, the Y generation are technology savvy (well used to ipods, facebook, blogs and youtube) but have poor grammar and spelling due to over reliance of text, mms and sms. 95% of the generation own a computer and cell phone, and 76% own an instant messaging service. 34% use websites as the primary source of news, 28% author blogs, 44% read blogs and approximately one in two share and download with peers. The implication of this is that a generation is emerging that is being actively shaped by current technology, possibly more than any other before it. This generation will not only be future customers of existing businesses but also form the workforce. Ignoring technology is not an option for any organisation.

The altering socio-technical context of information technology and the dynamics of change are hugely significant. Effective use of technology can help support as well as transform business organisations to enable them to operate effectively and competitively in increasingly hostile environments. There is an essential role to be played in automating business processes, finding networking business and providing information for management decision-making and planning. It is interesting to note that just as change management thinking can be successfully applied to an IS situation so the use of information systems can assist in change management ('IT-enabled transformation'). This is particularly so where technological change can form a focus for a significant organisational change including its culture.

Change is often necessary because of external 'triggers'. It is clear that there are a number of external factors that organisations must come to terms with. Ultimately these factors become triggers for change. The 'general' environment within which an organisation exists can usually be categorised under a 'PESTEL' framework which includes technological changes. Johnson, Scholes and Whittington (2008) include within this category innovations (e.g. the Internet), nanotechnology, inventions and developments in both products and processes. (For the airline industry, by way of example the technological influences that could trigger change might include fuel efficient engines, security check technologies and teleconferencing for business).

Exercise 2.6

Conduct a similar analysis for an organisation you are familiar with.

Internal drivers for change from within an organisation may be due to a continuing search for organisational effectiveness. For the organisation, an important issue is the interrelationships between the key internal subsystems, including tasks, people, structure, management and *technology*. It follows that change in response to the triggers and drivers for change might involve organisations adjusting these subsystems.

In short, technological trends represent a trigger to organisational change. Technology itself is one of the variables that can be adjusted by the organisational to cope with either trends in the external environment or an internal desire for effectiveness.

2.4 Challenges in IS implementation

Many information system projects have been reported failure. Failure can be measured by anything that is not delivered as agreed and within scope. This will involve the challenges of implementation not being properly addressed. The symptoms of failure include overrun timescales and budget, scope creep, not meeting user requirements, system function and interface are not as expected or specified. A number of factors can contribute to the failure of information systems project, including:

- poor project planning and definition,
- a lack of management support,
- poor project organisation,
- faulty resource planning and allocation,
- a lack of progress monitoring mechanism,
- inadequate user participation and involvement,
- ineffective communication and coordination, and
- inadequate attention given to education and training.

It should at this stage be recognised that implementation forms part of a fuller cycle of systems development involving:

- a feasibility study,
- systems analysis,
- systems design,
- implementation, and
- systems review and maintenance.

This can be viewed as a serial process, whereby each stage produces an output which in turn becomes the input for the next stage forming a systems development life cycle (SDLC). The SDLC is characterised by a number of key elements:

- The project is divided into a number of identifiable processes, made up of several activities. This aids project planning and control.
- Specific reports and documentation, known as *deliverables*, must be produced throughout the stages of the life cycle. These are used to control and monitor procedures.
- Users and managers participate throughout the project.
- The system must be thoroughly tested prior to implementation.
- Training plans are developed for those who will operate and manage the system.
- A post-implementation review is carried out to assess the effectiveness of the new system once in operation.

This section considers some of the challenges associated with IS implementation.

2.4.1 Evaluating information systems

One straightforward method of evaluating information systems would be to conduct a formal cost benefit analysis (CBA) whereby all costs and benefits both quantifiable and non-quantifiable are gathered and ultimately 'weighed' against one another. Another approach would be for an individual organisation to establish criteria which constitute a good information system and then audit the existing system to determine how well it 'measures up'.

Denton (2002) makes the point that when IS is introduced the process should begin with a full justification for the expenditure involved. After implementation a thorough review of the new system should be conducted in order to establish whether it is operating as expected and whether the previously stated development objectives have been met. Table 2.5 indicates the features of a post-implementation review.

Table 2.5 The features of a post-implementation review

Review area	Recommendations
Establish whether the new system satisfies user needs.	Make recommendations for improvement if necessary.
Evaluate the actual performance of the new system compared with anticipated performance.	Recommend improvements to the systems development procedures if necessary.
Ascertain the quality of project management of the system implementation.	Examine project costs and project team activities and recommend improvements to project planning procedures.
Review original cost–benefit analysis to ascertain if costs have been met/exceeded and whether perceived benefits have been achieved.	Suggest any other changes that might improve systems development and systems project management in the future.

2.4.2 Privacy and security

Various controls can be established to safeguard privacy and security measures might be established. There are two categories of control, classified as *general* and *application*.

General controls are designed to ensure the completeness and effectiveness of the organisation's overall control environment over its information systems. These controls concern the overall transaction processing environment and include:

- Personnel controls, including the appropriate segregation of duties.
- Access controls such as password systems, or the more sophisticated 'retina recognition' which is being used in some high-risk areas.
- Computer equipment controls to protect equipment from destruction, damage (deliberate or accidental) or theft.
- Business continuity planning which involves a risk assessment to establish which activities/systems will have a critical impact on the ability of the organisation to continue its business activities. In particular, it includes disaster recovery planning for the organisation's information systems.

Application controls are specific to individual applications and can be categorised into input, processing and output controls (corresponding to the basic steps in the data processing cycle). These controls are designed to detect, prevent and correct errors occurring within IT enabled transaction processing.

Exercise 2.7

Data integrity and security is a particular issue in a database. For data to have integrity, it must be accurate, consistent and free from accidental corruption. Data should also be secure with the prevention of unauthorised access, modification or destruction of data in the database. What controls are required in a database to ensure that data integrity and data security are maintained?

Solution

- control of access to workstations,
- user identification required for access by individual passwords,

- restrictions on external scheme contents,
- users only see the icons for the functions where they have access rights,
- restrictions on access to certain aspects of the database,
- users only to have access to those aspects that they need to do their job,
- restrictions on use of functions or programs (e.g. writing off debts as bad debts),
- transaction logs maintained automatically for checking and for back-up purposes.

A computer virus can cause damage to business organisations by infecting documents, file directory, storage, software and even hardware (through alteration, duplication, deletion and spreading). Organisations can proactively minimise the likelihood and impact of infection by taking a number of security measures such as:

- virus detection and protection software packages installed on individual computers and networks which are regularly updated,
- establishing formal security policy and procedures for users,
- regular audits to check for unauthorised software,
- frequent back-ups made of data and programs to allow recovery if all else fails.

Sadly viruses are not the only privacy and security risks that organisations face. Others include:

- unauthorised access from outside to the network files by "hackers",
- electronic eavesdropping (including users accessing personal privacy or information not intended for them),
- data integrity(information may be accidentally or maliciously altered or destroyed during transmission),
- computer hardware and software malfunction,
- unintentional human errors in using computer and networks,
- natural disasters, including fire, flood, earthquakes, etc.

As the opportunities of new technology present themselves so do the risks. Businesses typically spent between 2% and 4% of their IT budgets on contingency planning, others more. Such expenditure is easily justified. An hour of IT down time preventing a bank from trading can cost (in US dollars) $6.5 million or a travel agent $90,000 in lost airline bookings (Pesola, 2004).

There are a number of controls that can be built into computer networks such as:

- *Data encryption*, whereby data is converted (scrambled) prior to transmission and is reconverted into a readable format once transmission is complete. The encrypted data can only be read by a receiver with a matching decryption key. Data encryption is relatively inexpensive and is a useful and effective method of preventing electronic eavesdropping.
- *Authentication* of a buyer's identity through password and user ID control.
- Using a *Firewall* which allow only those external authorised users to access a protected network. A firewall is a device consisting of hardware and software that is placed between a company's private network (including Intranet) and the public network.
- *Digital envelope* a 'key' used to encrypt the message is sent to the receiver separately from the encrypted message.
- *Network design* to cope with periods of high volumes and peak processing activity.
- *Checkpoint controls,* periodically the network system temporarily stops processing new data, and instead completes the processing of partially completed transactions and then

creates a full and exact copy of all data values and information required to continue processing. Should a systems failure occur the system may be started by using the last checkpoint file.

2.4.3 Changeover approaches

When a new Information System is introduced there are four main methods of system changeover.

- The *Parallel approach* is probably the most common, whereby old and new systems operate together for a period of time, processing the same current data. The outputs of the two systems are compared to determine whether the new system is operating as expected and that no processing errors occurred. This approach allows for greater control, as the new system is not fully operational on its own until the organisation is satisfied that it is working correctly. The problem is that new system implementation is delayed, possibly indicating a lack of confidence in it, and a requirement for greater resources to operate two systems instead of one. It is important that if this approach is taken the organisation decides upon a time limit for final changeover so that continual delays do not occur.
- The *Direct approach* has the highest risk, as at a predetermined point in time the old system simply ceases to operate. There is no opportunity to validate the new system's output with the old, so management must have complete confidence in the new system. This kind of changeover should be carried out during a slack period, such as a weekend or bank holiday, when minimum disruption is likely.
- The *Pilot approach* can be implemented in two ways. A restricted data pilot involves taking one whole part of the complete system and running it as the new system. If this operates correctly, then remaining elements of the system can be transferred gradually (e.g. one group of stock records could be transferred and run on the new system as a first stage). A retrospective pilot, by comparison, involves operating the new system with old data already processed by the existing system. The results produced by the new system can be readily cross-checked with the results already processed by the existing system.
- The *Phased* or *Modular* approach involves gradual implementation and is often used in large systems projects or in organisations that are geographically dispersed. To illustrate an organisation may implement a new accounting information system by first converting the sales order subsystem, then the customer accounts subsystem, then the purchase order subsystem, etc. Alternatively, an organisation may implement a complete system, but in one geographical location at a time. (For example the implementation of a new banking customer enquiry system branch by branch). A modular approach allows pilot testing to be carried out on a system or subsystem prior to full implementation.

2.4.4 Managing systems implementation

This section considers IS implementation as a change management process and addresses problems of non-usage and resistance. Hellriegel and Slocum (1992) identify seven factors vital to effective implementation of an information system:

- user involvement,
- top management support,
- evaluation of time and cost,
- gradual implementation,

- thorough testing,
- training and documentation, and
- system backup.

Of these seven, the involvement of users 'through all of the stages' is highlighted as the single most important element.

The implementation of Information System technologies can be highly disruptive. Poorly supervised projects may, without care, lead to the organisation operating in an ineffective manner. Managers must (collectively) ensure that disruptions are kept to a minimum. Alternatively one manager may need to supervise a major IS project to ensure its smooth implementation. Systems implementation is sometimes treated as a separate project involving formal project management techniques and the designation of a named project manager. An implementation schedule needs to be created, and the activities required for successful implementation carefully planned. Tools such as critical path analysis might usefully be deployed.

Denton (2002) makes the point that while the process of implementing a piece of software may vary in terms of time, resource and general upheaval depending on the type of system and the size and complexity of the organisation. The steps that need to be followed however are common, and if they are properly executed there will be successful implementation, namely:

Justification, definition and planning of the project

Requirement analysis: The degree of customisation of the software in order to meet business requirements, and the change of business process due to introducing the new system.

Implementation: A number of factors could be critical during the implementation stage, these include top level support, engagement of users and managers, behavioural issues, aligning the new system and business process, training, systems changeover and user support.

Support: Monitoring system performance and supporting users followed by system evaluation.

A critical activity prior to changeover is testing the new system to ensure that it is working correctly before going live. Ultimate users should be involved in conducting tests of several kinds, possibly in a sequence indicated in Table 2.6.

Decisions will need to be made over the training needs of system users and their managers. The requirements of the new system users are likely to involve training in basic computer literacy and user skills if the system is a move from manual to computerised one. If the move is from one computerised system to another training will emphasise learning how to use specific applications quickly. This training might be delivered through structured sessions, on-the-job training, or involve frequent training updates as the users become more familiar with the system.

Middle management is also likely to require training on those elements of the system for which they are responsible. It is unlikely that they will require detailed user knowledge but they will need an understanding of the particular business issues and security and control features related to a particular system.

The post-implementation review should identify whether the user's needs are being satisfied. Systems maintenance can be performed in response to specific user needs identified as part of this review or as a result of ongoing process. Systems maintenance is the

Table 2.6 System testing

Type	Description	Purpose
Realistic tests	Presents the system with a realistic example of the environment in which the system is to operate.	Tests the system and the understanding and effectiveness of training of users. It also gives users confidence before they take over the system.
Contrived tests	Presents the system with as many unusual and unexpected events as possible, such as incorrect codes, wrong amounts, inappropriate commands, and so on.	To see how the system reacts, and whether all conceivable anomalies have been catered for in the system.
Volume tests	Presents the system with a large volume of transactions.	To see how it reacts, particularly in operating and response times.
Acceptance tests	The users undertake acceptance testing after all other systems testing is complete.	To test the complete system, and to ensure that it is satisfactory from the users' point of view.

repair, correction or further enhancement of systems once in operation and can take several forms:

- *Corrective maintenance* remedies errors within the existing system, normally identified as a result of some problem occurring. Corrective maintenance is reactive by nature and its main function is to ensure that the system can continue to operate. It has been estimated that this represents 20% of all maintenance time.
- *Adaptive (or adaptative) maintenance* is carried out in order to adjust applications to reflect changing business operations or the wider environment. This type of maintenance is likely to be more of a mid- to long-term maintenance process. It has been estimated that typically this also represents 20% of all maintenance time.
- *Perfective (or preventative) maintenance* aims to prevent possible failures in the future or to make the system nearer perfect, so improving efficiency.

Occasionally implementation produces difficulties and challenges for the manager of a human rather than technical kind! Implementation may be met with employee resistance, either direct or passive. Inevitably there may be a variety of reasons for this and every individual case is unique. Reasonable speculation of the likely reasons can however be made in the most general of terms. These reasons could be:

- the chosen methods of implementation may be felt to be inappropriate,
- there may have been faulty communication,
- there may have been a lack of adequate training.

Exercise 2.8

Suggest potential problems that might arise if there is either inadequate or inappropriate user training following the introduction of a new system.

Solution

- Fear of new system's effect on jobs
- Fear of the unknown

- Reluctance to use the new system
- Errors in processing (either deliberate or accidental)
- Slower processing due to a lack of confidence, unfamiliarity or covert sabotage
- Staff turnover or absence arising from avoidance of the new system.

Resistance in the wake of the implementation of an IS system should be acknowledged as little different by nature to the resistance met by implementation of any form of organisational change. Obviously anticipation of problems beforehand to avoid conflict is preferable. Nevertheless, should conflict arise tactics can be evolved to deal with the situation. Kotter, Schlesinger and Sathe (1992) identified six main methods of exercising influence to overcome resistance, namely:

- education and communication,
- participation and involvement,
- facilitation and support,
- negotiation and agreement,
- manipulation and co-optation,
- explicit and/or implicit coercion.

The final two methods raise ethical and legal problems as well as involving considerable risk of making the situation worse. These six approaches are not mutually exclusive and managers may find it effective to use a combination of them. The most appropriate approach in each instance will depend on a variety of factors, including the goals of the change programme and the likely reactions of the people involved. One of the problems of choosing the 'right' approach is that people will not always openly admit the *real* reasons for opposing change. In particular, those reasons relating to self-interest are likely to be disguised as technical objections, arguing that the proposed system will not work. Attempts to deal with these technical objections will not get to the root cause of the resistance to change. Only in a climate in which individuals feel free to discuss their objections and fears openly will it be possible for managers to understand and deal with the underlying reasons for resistance.

Exercise 2.9

If a manager discovers that there are instances of non-usage of the systems how might this be interpreted?

Solution

It may be as being a result of a number of reasons, including:

- An expression of resistance. In this case appropriate influencing measures should be applied (see above).
- A lack of confidence in the new system, in which case enhanced communication is required and system modification should be applied where appropriate.
- A lack confidence in their own abilities to cope with the new system. In this case training and other support mechanisms should be addressed.

Exercise 2.10

Review Kotter and Schlesinger's listing and identify the conditions under which each of these methods might 'work'.

✅ Solution

There is no right or wrong answer, and your thinking is likely to be as valid so long as it is based on commonsense and your own experience.

Education and communication	• Useful when the problem is a lack of information about the need for, or the nature of, the planned change of system. • Can be very time-consuming and will not work by itself if there are reasons other than misunderstanding for resisting the change.
Participation and involvement	• Increases the probability that people will be committed to the system and if their views are taken into account, this may enhance the effectiveness of implementation. • Appropriate when the individuals initiating the change do not have all the necessary information and when the people affected by the change have considerable power to resist it. • Can be time-consuming.
Facilitation and support	• Involves the use of techniques such as training and group discussions designed to reduce fear and anxiety. • Particularly appropriate where the main reason for resistance is based on insecurity and adjustment problems.
Negotiation and agreement	• May be necessary where an individual or a group stands to lose out in some way because of the change, particularly if they also have the power to resist the change. • May help to avoid major problems. • Disadvantages are that it can be expensive and also it can encourage others to negotiate to 'buy' their compliance.
Manipulation and co-optation	• Relies on presenting partial or misleading information to the people resisting the change. Co-optation involves identifying key individuals resisting changes and 'buying them off' by giving them positions of authority to help implement the change. • A quick and relatively inexpensive approach, it will probably result in future problems if the people involved realise they have been manipulated.
Explicit and implicit coercion	• Involves the use of force, or the threat of it, to bring about change. • May be necessary as a very last resort if the parties involved are operating from fixed positions and there are fundamental disagreements over objectives and/or methods.

2.5 Organising and managing IS activities within a corporate framework

IS should not be considered in isolation, it must complement and support other areas including marketing, finance, human resourcing and operations.

✋ Exercise 2.11

Identify examples of the way in which IS can support other functional areas.

✅ Solution

Examples of IS supporting other organisational roles includes:

- The development of a DBMS to support all functional areas.
- Use of the Intranet in supporting operations and meeting customer support needs.

- Use of the Internet to support marketing activity and providing enhanced value to customers and suppliers.
- Online technology-supported learning as part of HR training and development efforts.

The relationship between IS and other management functions within an organisation should be apparent.

2.5.1 IS outsourcing

The scope of IS outsourcing can range from single system development to complete facilities management. The use of contracted expertise raises the issue of establishing and maintaining strong client–vendor relationships. Boomer (2007) reflects on the need for organisational abilities to manage IS and muses the potential for outsourcing as follows:

Over the past 10 years, technology has become more ubiquitous, as well as more complex…..
….The breadth of knowledge required to support and integrate these systems has grown to the point where it's time for firms to assess the talent required and whether to employ professional IT personnel, outsource or settle on a combination of strategies.

The organisation corporately holds certain values and broad policy ideas. For some there may be an enthusiasm for outsourcing while others may feel strongly that services should be retained in-house. Advocates of outsourcing may point to cost savings whilst proponents may argue that additional monitoring mechanisms might be costly in themselves.

Systems development does not necessarily have to be carried out by in-house development staff and could be outsourced. The problem with 'outsourcing' is that the external vendor may not understand the business process, and the organisation may lose control over its information systems. It also runs the risk that cost could be high, as the vendors may charge extra services to keep updating technology. Therefore careful planning, tight contract specifications and systems of monitoring will be required to ensure that systems development objectives are achieved by the external organisation.

Differing management problems are associated with in-house and vendor solutions. In-house, the difficulties tend to centre on the assembly and maintenance of an adequately skilled and motivated workforce to deliver IS solutions. The emphasis for outsourced facilities tends to focus on contract compliance and adherence to predetermined standards.

Boomer (2007) acknowledges outside resources and consulting as invaluable because, 'it is what you don't know you don't know that will cost you time and money.'

When choosing a vendor careful evaluation and selection processes should be followed including background reviews of vendor financial performance, references, litigation history, etc. Vendors should be chosen in accordance with predetermined selection criteria. Relationships should be built on trust and reasonable mutual expectation to this end it is helpful to:

- Make clear the organisation's vendor arrangements within formal planning documents, and communicate mutual roles and relationships within the organisation.
- Ensure the vendor understands and will comply with organisational ethical policies, procedures and practices.
- Ensure easy contact with the vendor by establishing a series of relationships at various levels (e.g. key account manager, operators, executives, etc.).
- Put in place mechanisms to periodically review performance, evaluate customer satisfaction and agree remedial action if necessary.

Table 2.7 Internal versus external hardware and software options

	Internal	External
Software features		
Quality	Must manage development effectively	Contract must specify quality standards and performance criteria
Cost	Often costly	Usually less costly than internal
	Difficult to estimate if new software	More easy to determine final cost
Time	Need to wait for software to be developed – requires significant planning	If amendments not required – availability immediate
Compatibility	Should be completely compatible	May require amendments to fit in with current system
Support	Organisation must provide and perform training and maintenance programme	Vendor likely to support both own training and maintenance (built into contract)
Satisfaction of user needs	Maximum satisfaction as designed specifically for users	May not satisfy needs exactly – may require further tailoring to do so
Nature of development	Develop in-house if unique requirement	Purchase if industry standard
Hardware features		
Management	Organisation/user responsible for management	Managed by outside party
Support	Internal (IT department)	Available externally (for a fee)
Cost	Mostly fixed	Mostly variable
Satisfaction of user needs	Tailored – maximum satisfaction (within budget)	Less flexibility (more determined by cost budget)

2.5.2 Aligning information systems with business strategy

When taking a management perspective of the IS function, one should remember that the main customers IS normally interfaces with directly are internal. This means that the function should take trouble to understand the needs of their colleagues and seek to satisfy these through their policies, practices and developments.

Undoubtedly, effective information management can be a source of organisational strength. This can be built upon as a competence in order to gain a advantage over an organisation's competitors. It is apparent from the preceding sections in this chapter that IS is a competitive necessity. If an organisation's IS are a source of strategic weakness this could prove disastrous resulting in a failure of quality and unfulfilled customer expectations.

Cohesive IS strategies are developed in many organisations and these should be consistent with and contribute to the achievement of corporate aspirations. In terms of overall corporate performance, above all the benefits of systems should outweigh the costs associated with them.

Clegg (2003) offers a number of insights into strategy development. He makes the point that an IS strategy is a plan for ensuring that information is effective (appropriate, accurate, available and timely). Strategy development might begin by either:

- reviewing all the information currently in the organisation, and then overcoming duplication and inaccuracies, or alternatively,

- taking the starting point as the organisation as a whole, and then deciding upon the information it needs to operate effectively.

Secondly, strategy should not be left to IS experts; managers themselves know what type of information they need.

Boomer (2007) offers a checklist of issues to address in planning IS at both a strategic and tactical level as follows:

Strategic	Tactical
What are the organisation's priorities (as expressed in the corporate plan)?	What HR resources do we have, and what are their unique abilities?
How might technology help meet corporate objectives?	How are our IS and IT resources currently managed? Should we outsource or staff internally?
What are the latest trends in and outside of our industry?	What is the timeline and budget and other resources?

Source: Based on Boomer, G. (2007)

2.6 Summary

A managerial perspective has been taken throughout this chapter when covering a number of IS topic areas. The wider business context within which information systems operate should be apparent as should the ways in which systems can be implemented in support of the organisation's corporate objectives.

References and further reading

Anon (2006) It'll never fly: Blogging. *Management Today*, April, p. 12.

Berens, C. (2006) Windows of opportunity. *Financial Management* (UK), November, Vol. 12, No. 5.

Boomer, G. (2007) IT Strategies and tactics. *Accounting Today*, August 20.

Carnall, C. (2007) *Managing Change in Organisations*. 5th edition. FT Prentice Hall

Clegg, B. (2003) Deciding factors? *Professional Manager*, September.

de Jager, M. (2008) *Shaping the future new generation. Generation y and what makes them tick.* CIMA Lecturers' Conference (unpublished)

Denton, A. (2002) Stepping out – a four-step guide to implementing new financial systems. *Conspectus*, April.

Hellriegel, D. and Slocum, J. W.,Jr. (1992) *Management* (6th edn). Addison Wesley.

Kotter, J. P., Schlesinger, L. A. and Sathe, V. (1992) *Organization: Text, Cases, and Readings on the Management of Organizational Design and Change* (3rd edn). Homewood, IL: Irwin.

Lynch, R. (2009) *Strategic Management* (5th edn). FT Prentice Hall.

Johnson, G., Scholes, K. and Whittington, R. (2008) *Exploring Corporate Strategy: Text and Cases* (8th edn). Financial Times, Prentice Hall.

Meall, L. (2004) Automation Nation. *Accountancy*, March, pp. 74–75.

Phillips, P. (2000) E-business: what is it and does it matter to accountants? *Management Accounting*, February.

Pesola, M. (2004) Network protection is a key stroke. *Financial Times*, March 8.
Scase, R. (1999) Britain Towards 2010: The changing business environment, DTi, August.
Senior, B. and Fleming, J. (2006) *Organisational Change* (3rd edn). FT Prentice Hall.
Skyrme, D.J. (1997) Virtual Teaming and Virtual Organizations: 25 Principles of Proven Practice. Update http://dev.skyrme.com/updates/u11.htm

Revision Questions 2

Question 1
Describe the most important properties that a database system should have in order to be successful. **(10 marks)**

Question 2
The R company is about to implement a new management information system. This MIS will replace an existing system, although this provides little more than a daily summary of the information maintained on the transaction processing system. The new MIS will still access the TPS data, but will provide more comprehensive analysis including historical statistics and limited comparison to prices charged by competitors.

The system will be implemented by direct changeover, because the network servers have insufficient capacity to maintain both systems on the hard disks. The installation will also take place over a weekend to minimise disruption to managers. The system developers believe that the new MIS is so intuitive that managers will be able to use it straight away.

Requirement
Identify and discuss the risks with the implementation of the new MIS. **(10 marks)**

Question 3

3.1 Local area networking is used for:

   (A) communication between computers within a limited geographical area
   (B) structuring an organisation within a division or business unit
   (C) exchange of information through a trade association or region
   (D) managing a complex operational issue by global interface with trade associations and professional bodies. **(2 marks)**

3.2 Many large organisations have established a computer Intranet for the purpose of:

   (A) providing quick, effective and improved communication amongst staff using chat rooms
   (B) providing quick, effective and improved communication to staff
   (C) providing quick, effective and improved communication to customers
   (D) providing quick, effective and improved ordering procedures in real time. **(2 marks)**

3.3 The main advantages of a database management system include:

(A) the development of separate data sources
(B) unlimited access and open communication
(C) end user flexibility and a devolution of responsibility
(D) data integrity and elimination of duplication. **(2 marks)**

3.4 An expert system describes:

(A) a database built upon past knowledge and experience
(B) a powerful off-the-shelf software solution
(C) an online library of operating advice and handy hints
(D) an electronic version of working papers assembled by the research and development department. **(2 marks)**

Each of the sub-questions below require a brief written response and are worth 4 marks each. This response can be in note form and should not exceed 50 words.

3.5 Explain why a phased system change-over for a computer development might help employees cope better with technological change. **(4 marks)**

3.6 Describe the main benefits of in-house developed information systems. **(4 marks)**

Question 4

TF7 is a progressive manufacturing company, which is open to new approaches and willing to learn from good ideas wherever they are practiced. One of the first within its industry to invest heavily in new technology, TF7 runs its database over office-wide networks and links employees' computers by wireless local area network (LAN) connections.

TF7 has, in the past, only dealt with wholesalers but, thanks to e-mail links from a new Internet home page, it now receives a substantial number of enquiries from ultimate consumers of its products. TF7 feels that this will represent the majority of its business in the future.

In response to employees spending more time communicating with potential customers by e-mail, TF7 is considering expanding its technology, including the connection of its database to a web server. This would enable potential customers to search for product specifications, availability, and delivery and price information for themselves. It would also allow customers to place orders and view shopping cart items through a browser facility. Before making such an investment, TF7 has commissioned management consultants to conduct an organisational review.

The consultants have produced a draft report in which they outline a number of interim findings, including the following:

- TF7 should gain significant benefits over its rivals through its existing database operations.
- TF7 should consider developing further the interconnection of applications so long as contingency plans are made for the potential of systems failure.
- Although there has been considerable expenditure on hardware, TF7 now needs to invest in software applications.
- TF7's management information systems and executive information systems are undeveloped to the detriment of the company both operationally and strategically.

You work in TF7's technical department and report directly to the Chief Executive, who has asked for a series of brief notes so that he is prepared when discussing the draft report with the management consultants.

Requirements

Provide appropriate briefing notes for the Chief Executive for each of the following issues:

(a) Describe the benefits TF7 should be enjoying as part of its current database operations. **(5 marks)**

(b) Explain the value of good management information systems and executive information systems. **(5 marks)**

Question 5

K1S is a fast growing chain of hair and beauty salons (shops) located throughout the prosperous north of the country. The company is due to expand from 30 to 35 salons within the next year. K1S's policy is to buy existing salons in fashionable city centre shopping malls which it believes are 'underperforming' by offering too limited a range of treatments and charging too low prices. (All K1S's salons charge 'top' prices but provide excellent customer care. In addition to hairdressing services, K1S offer pedicures and manicures, teeth whitening, neck and facial massages, botox treatment and lip enhancements). K1S also plan to sell own-brand hair styling products and treatments at premium prices from its premises. K1S's managing director (MD) sees training as critical to 'keeping our service sophisticated, slick and professional: with a distinctive K1S style'. K1S now operates its own hairdressing training academy from purpose built premises.

The MD has however identified a number of areas which need to be addressed if K1S is to continue to prosper.

- The opportunities for the use of information technology (IT) needs to grasped, particularly in the implementation and running of the information system network and in support of management operations.
- Information systems (IS) need to be developed primarily based upon the needs of the company as a whole but also mindful of the need to support salon management operations locally.
- The threat posed by competitors who are copying K1S's approach.

The MD has appointed a management consultancy team to conduct a complete organisational review. Their report identifies a number of issues, some of which are highlighted below.

- Systems are generally weak and the benefits of modern software applications lacking. The accuracy and completeness of information received from branches needs to improve, and there needs to be better coordination of activities. Several different systems are used and some are very inefficient. (For example over 40% of salon receptionist/administrators time is spent manually analysing and searching for information). Through its acquisition policy K1S has 'inherited' a series of salons operating independent systems of varying sophistication and effectiveness. Some still use manual systems, others use stand-alone computers, but none take full advantage of software capabilities and most only use basic software functions. It seems that the more complex a system a salon has the more the staff resistance to its full use seems to be. Internet possibilities are being missed and there

is no virtual network. Common computerised stock records will also be required when hair styling products and treatments are sold.
- Brand development and management is crucial to competing successfully. A more recognisable K1S brand should be supported by consistent shop style, uniforms, paperwork, etc. and a user-friendly website needs to be developed.
- There is a need to strengthen management locally. Salons are currently managed by senior stylists who have much industry knowledge but little management training or experience. These senior stylists are assisted by a receptionist/administrator. Each salon keeps its own set of accounts and makes its own staffing arrangements including recruitment, selection, rotas, holiday cover and remuneration, etc. Managers should be appointed with responsibility for a few salons each (so leaving senior stylists to concentrate full-time on hairdressing) and a centralised HR and Finance function should be established to support salons. Staff flexibility between salons would also lead to more efficient operations.

You are part of the management consultancy team responsible for the report and have been asked to prepare for a discussion with the MD a series of notes on key themes.

(a) Explain how information systems (IS) should be developed to serve K1S's management operations both centrally and within salons. **(5 marks)**
(b) Explain how KIS's operations can be improved through the use of information technology generally and a wide area network (WAN) specifically. **(5 marks)**
(c) Discuss the likely training implications associated with the installation of a new computer system for K1S. **(5 marks)**

Solutions to Revision Questions

✓ Solution 1

The essential feature of a database approach is that data is regarded as a central resource of a company. Data, like other assets, should be owned and maintained for the use and benefit of the business as a whole. To be successful, a database system must have the following properties:

- Data independence – the data must be defined and exist independently of the programs that use it. The logical definition of data in the database is different from the physical organisation and storage on the disks – physical independence. The logical data in an application is viewed from the perspective of that application, this is, different from the logical definition of data in the database – logical independence. As the data and programs are independent of each other, either can be amended without changing the other.
- The database must be capable of being shared. Different users, using different application programs, must be able to access the same data, often at the same time.
- Duplication of data and data redundancy can be reduced as only one entry per record or transaction is needed in the database. Data inputs may also be reduced as data is only required to be input once to update all files.
- Integrity of the data in the database must be maintained. Controls need to be implemented to ensure that the data remains accurate at all times.
- The database should be flexible and able to develop or evolve with the organisation. The database needs to change and develop to meet the future needs of the company.
- The database should be able to connect to web server to support dynamic e-commerce transaction.

✓ Solution 2

The risks associated with implementing the new MIS will include:

Lack of user acceptance testing. There is no indication that users have actually been involved with the system development or even seen the new system prior to installation. If users have not been part of the system development testing, then they may not accept it when it goes online. (People like to be involved in the development process rather than have new systems imposed on them.) Lack of user involvement also carries the problem that the system may not meet user requirements, which will add to the temptation for users to reject it.

At the very least, some user representatives should review the system to make sure it does meet their requirements and provides information in a format that they can understand.

No parallel run. The changeover between the old and new MIS will be direct; that is, one system will no longer be used and the new is made available immediately, so there is no time when both systems are available. While this approach has some benefits in terms of staff time and costs, there are risks that errors may occur in transferring data between the two systems. The errors will be difficult to identify because the output from the systems cannot be compared. This may have significant effects for R, for example transferring the price of a product incorrectly will give a wrong comparison with another company. An incorrect price adjustment could be made to R's product causing it to be sold below cost.

Providing a parallel run will be appropriate to ensure that data is completely and accurately transferred.

Direct implementation. It is not clear from the question whether there has been any testing on the company's hardware systems. If this has not been carried out, then stopping one system and implementing another may have a significant negative impact on the company if the new system does not work.

If there is insufficient server space, then R must consider purchasing or hiring a duplicate server to test the new MIS in parallel with the old to confirm that it does work correctly.

Lack of training and user documentation. The suggestion that the new system is easy to use may be correct. However, even if this is the case, it is quite possible that users will not be aware of the most effective or efficient method of using the system. Significant amounts of time can be lost through 'trial and error' as managers attempt to obtain information without detailed guidance on how to do this.

Some form of training, or at least provision of user documentation, is advisable. This will show to users that their requirements have been considered and will enforce good system use from the beginning. Trying to amend work methods at a later date will be difficult as managers will tend to see training at this stage as a waste of time.

✓ Solution 3

3.1 (A)
3.2 (B)
3.3 (D)
3.4 (A)
3.5 A phased system changeover:
- allows employees time to adjust
- appears less pressured and stressful
- appears less extreme potentially reducing resistance
- allows time for retraining & staff displacement, and so on to be addressed.

3.6 In-house development benefits:
- Information system is likely to match the needs of users more closely (greater staff acceptance/involvement?).
- Development team is local and immediately available.
- Greater focus on progress/success?
- Development team gets user acceptance more readily?

✓ Solution 4

Requirement (a)

Background

Apparently TF7 is levering significant benefits through its database operation compared with its rivals. A database is a collection of structured data held in data files and completely independent of any one application, meaning that when data is integrated a single file system emerges. The main aim of a database is to provide one common dataset for a wide variety of users and their information needs.

Likely benefits

The main benefits are likely to include:

Basis of new ways of operating
TF7's database experience represents a 'stepping stone' to web-based operations. Such operations will allow both customer and supplier easy access and free staff to work from flexible locations (for example home or at the premises of potential customers). Without the cultural acceptance and knowledge of databases such a development might be more problematic.

Increased trading potential
By moving to database operations the potential for introducing web database technology is readily apparent, so potentially opening up facilities for customer searches and, in turn, increased trading possibilities.

Cost reduction
There should be reduced net data storage costs. This will only apply however, so long as these cost savings outweigh the additional costs of operating a database management system (DBMS). (Rather than reduce the overall budget, it is more likely that these savings will take the form of released staff time that can be put to other activities.)

Waste elimination
Data is only stored once. The database operations will prohibit data being duplicated. This will involve the elimination of data redundancy and the potential for inconsistencies of the same data are eliminated.

Data reliability
Without database operations, data integrity can be compromised in a number of ways (for example human error, software bugs, natural disasters, errors arising from data being transmitted from one computer to another and so on.). These difficulties are eliminated.

Meet user needs
User needs can be catered for under a database operation, specifically:

- Data independence. A single data source can be accessed by a number of different users at the same time. Without database operations, it is down to individual users to generate the necessary data.

- Privacy can be provided by DBMS software through sophisticated security so preventing unauthorised access and data alteration or destruction. It may be that access and privacy can be enhanced under such an approach.

Requirement (b)

Management information systems (MIS)

MIS provide managers with information to monitor and control the organisation's activities. MIS collect and process data to produce management reports to a range of managers (typically middle managers) who can use it for decision-making, planning, programme implementation and control.

Such systems support operations and managerial decision-making. This enables middle managers to report matters of significance more appropriately to senior level managers.

MIS can be manual but in this case are likely to be computer generated and are often based upon report-producing packages that use information from the same source as the data processing systems.

The value of having good MIS includes:

- Potentially more effective operations and improved management control.
- More complete information available to managers to improve decision-making.
- Improved satisfaction and motivation amongst managers.
- Better information leading to improved budgetary control, stock control, improved forecasting and so on.
- Maintaining a competitive advantage over rival companies who do not make this investment.

Executive information systems (EIS)

EIS is a computer-based system intended to support the information and decision needs of top-level executives through easy access to both internal and external strategic information. An EIS will contain powerful software for supporting the types of high-risk, unstructured decisions that are made by strategic-level managers. EIS help analyse, compare and highlight trends in important areas so identifying strengths, weaknesses and external opportunities and threats.

The value of having good EIS includes:

- Ability to make informed, potentially significant decisions of strategic significance.
- Maintaining a competitive advantage over rival companies who do not make this investment.
- Improved ability to recognise opportunities or external challenges.
- Ability to track key performance indicators (KPIs) meaning that monitoring and control at strategic level is more effective.

✓ Solution 5

Requirement (a)

A staged approach to developing IS to support K1S's management both centrally and within salons should be adopted taking account of both 'human' factors and supporting technology:

- *Problem definition.* Utilising the consultants' report, business goals should be clarified. K1S's MD needs to consider the overall business and its information needs. This will arise from K1S's corporate plan, and include information that is essential to the company. IS should complement and support other aspects of K1S's functioning including marketing, finance, HR, operations within salons and salon business plans.

- *Feasibility study.* Alternative solutions might be considered including the costs and benefits associated with different approaches (manual, commercial 'off the shelf' or bespoke software). Consideration also needs to be given to the scope of the system. Data processing systems (DPS) process repetitive tasks and can provide day-to-day monitoring information about efficiency of operations and activities. In this case DPSs can offer unified payroll, HR, cash and receipting, and (bearing in mind K1S's plans) stock purchasing and control systems. Management information systems (MISs) are based upon report-producing packages that use information from data processing sources. MIS's can provide salon managers with information to monitor and control the salons' activities and to report to the MD and central staff. Executive Information Systems (EIS) are a further option; these represent a potentially sophisticated software package that manipulates data (both internal and external) to inform management at a strategic HQ level.
- *Project planning.* Once the chosen solution is identified a project team led by someone with project management and leadership abilities should be selected. The project team will be responsible for the stages of system development and could report to a steering group comprising representatives of head office, salon and IT staff. An implementation plan should be drawn up and agreed involving clearly identified key dates and designated responsibilities. All relevant staff should be consulted. The benefits need to be 'sold' to staff. Communicating the need for such a development and the potential benefits should help avoid resistance.
- *System analysis.* A detailed understanding of the current system should be gained by liaising with staff and management. This can be captured using dataflow diagrams (DFD) and data storage explained through entity relationship diagrams. A mature understanding of the requirements of users in fulfilling K1S's management operations should be gained. This will culminate in a requirement report.
- *IS solution purchase or design.* It is highly likely that a commercial package will exist to meet K1S's needs and potential packages should be checked against the requirement report. If a bespoke solution is favoured, system design will need to be undertaken.
- *Adjustment and coding.* The software package may require the addition of an e-commerce website. This may mean modification of the package. This stage might be outsourced.
- *Data build up including validating accuracy of existing data.* There are doubts about the accuracy and completeness of information received from salons. Without complete, accurate information K1S could be operating 'blind' with potentially disastrous consequences.
- *System testing.* Possibly the most appropriate approach would be a period of parallel running. It is important that information is appropriate, accurate, available and timely.
- *Training and staff communication and involvement.* People need to be motivated to enter accurate information. If a need is seen the chances are that accuracy will be improved.

Requirement (b)

Use of information technology

The MD recognises the opportunities that IT offers:

- *Strengthening current operating and managing systems.* K1S's systems are generally weak and clearly these need to be improved upon and developed. In theory it would be possible to have effective information systems without using information technology (IT). The size and complexity of the company however, means that IT is the only practical delivery option for meeting K1S's expanding information needs arising from an expanding product range and 35 geographically diverse salons.

- *Standardising operations.* It would allow K1S to operate a number of different types of system each designed to assist management, coordination and decision-making. This will involve a move from the current stand-alone applications to a common integrated system.
- *Increasing operating efficiencies.* Currently receptionist/administrators spend over 40% of their time searching for and analysing information. IT can offer the platform to perform these functions in a less time-hungry fashion including an online diary and booking form and printed appointment cards. The time released should enable more value adding activities to be conducted and allow for a speedier answering of telephone queries.
- *Simplifying procedures.* Each salon keeps its own set of accounts and makes its own staffing arrangements including recruitment, selection, rotas, holiday cover and remuneration, etc. IT allows these processes to be computerised making them easier and less time intensive to operate.

Operating a WAN

A network is where a number of computers and devices are linked. As K1S operates throughout the north of the country the most appropriate computer systems configuration would be through a wide area network (WAN). Operations can be improved through the use of such a network in the following ways:

- *Speeding up communication* between K1S's central management function and individual salons.
- *Improving inter-salon collaboration.* A WAN would provide e-mail access and easier inter-salon communication and cooperation. This would allow resource and information sharing between users in this case in every salon.
- *Making more timely returns to the centre.* The installation of internet access in all salons would allow e-mail systems which offer speed and versatility, allowing easy communication, and the facility to send electronic attachments so making returns to K1S's head office more efficient.
- *Maximising the benefits of a website.* Many organisations now use the potential offered by websites. K1S could use it as a means of advertising and staying in touch with customers. It would be possible to develop an online booking system. A user-friendly website would be a vital component in establishing a single recognisable K1S brand and would reflect useful information, convey K1S's core values and exhibit sophistication, a slick and professional approach and reinforce K1S's logos and corporate colours, etc.

Requirement (c)

Nature of staff involved

K1S has inherited a series of salons each operating independent systems of varying sophistication and effectiveness:

- Some still operate manual systems
- Some use stand-alone computers
- None takes full advantage of software capabilities and only use basic functions.

This means that staff are at different levels of competence, experience and understanding. A breadth of training will be required.

Level of training
Some salons still operate manual systems and there is no use of e-mail, etc. As a consequence, some training might need to be quite basic. Training in basic computer literacy and user skills for salons will be necessary where the system is a move from manual to computerised one. It will be necessary to explain to staff how to use specific programs and how to e-mail.

Who gets trained?
Decisions will need to be made over who will operate the systems and who manages those individuals. It is likely that the prime users will be the receptionist/administrators, salon managers, and central HQ staff (if centralised functions are to be developed for HR, finance, purchasing, etc.). In summary, staff will have application specific training needs and provision will need to be made accordingly.

Cost of training
Initial/one off training can be treated as a capital cost, (and so be written off over a number of years). Ongoing training and refresher training should in future be a charge to revenue costs. Budgets will need to be agreed.

Method
There are potentially endless possibilities for delivering training ranging from on-the-job training, (training while staff are actively using the new system) to DVD or web-based demonstrations to seminars and courses. There is a need, therefore, to identify and access the most suitable, acceptable, feasible and effective training mechanisms necessary within the budget allocated.

Reaction
Consultants have identified that the more complex a system available to a salon the more the resistance to its full use seems to be. There needs to be an anticipation of difficulties such as this beforehand, and tactics evolved to deal with these problems. Famously, Kotter and Schlesinger identified certain methods of exercising influence to overcome resistance to change including education and communication. As part of the training, the benefits of new technology and the advantages of the particular systems will need to be 'sold'.

3

Operations Management

Operations Management 3

> ## LEARNING OUTCOMES
>
> Operations Management, which includes management of quality, accounts for 20 per cent of the overall syllabus. This chapter addresses operations as a functional area of business, explains the relationship of operations management to other aspects of the organisation's operations and describes relevant tools and techniques. By completing this chapter, including the exercises and questions you should be able to:
>
> ▸ Explain the shift from price-based to relational procurement and operations
> ▸ Explain the relationship of operations and supply management to the competitiveness of the firm
> ▸ Explain the particular issues surrounding operations management in services
> ▸ Explain the importance of sustainability in operations management
> ▸ Apply contemporary thinking in quality management
> ▸ Explain process design
> ▸ Apply tools and concepts of lean management
> ▸ Illustrate a plan for the implementation of a quality programme
> ▸ Describe ways to manage relationships with suppliers.

During the eighteenth century the UK experienced dramatic change through what became known as the industrial revolution. It was during this period that the economy was transformed from agricultural to industrial and population migrated to towns from the countryside. Key features of the newly formed organisations included:

- the introduction of machines used to mass produce items,
- effective means of warehousing stocks of raw and finished products, and
- effective distribution of finished products.

F.W. Taylor and others developed work measurement and applied 'scientific' methods to production from the 1890s onwards. These studies clearly showed that the productivity of organisations depended both on the technology available and how the effective management of key resources were managed. 'Good' management constituted an application of knowledge and skills of a 'scientific' nature, rather than intuition and guesswork. This thinking laid the foundations for the study of an area later referred to as operations management. At its simplest operations management tries to ensure that organisations are run as efficiently as possible.

Brown et al. (2001) point out that all organisations have an operations function whether it is explicitly called that or not. Galloway (1998: 2) described operations as 'those activities concerned with the acquisition of raw materials, their conversion into finished product and the supply of that finished product to the customer'.

Most contemporary thinkers would broaden this definition as 'what the company does' so involving service as well as manufacturing organisations. McDonald (2008) explains:

Operations management is mainly concerned with how resources are used to produce goods or services. Depending on the nature of the organisation, the transformed resources could be materials, information or even customers. For example, changing the physical properties of a metal is a fundamental part of car manufacturing; information processing is one of the business practices of a marketing company; and customer processing could be achieved by a beauty treatment. In addition, a company needs to have facilities, such as buildings and equipment, as well as people who maintain, plan and manage operations.

Using this thinking examples of operations are provided in Table 3.1.

Exercise 3.1

Develop a similar analysis for your organisation.

As operations turn various kinds of inputs into useful outputs, organisations can be viewed as 'transformers' by taking either raw materials, money, people, machine time, etc. and then either manufacturing, assembling or packing, etc. to produce goods or services.

Operations management is concerned with the planning, direction and control of the vital operations that link the business of the organisation with the needs and wants of the organisation's customers. It is important to emphasise, that 'products' can be either goods or services, and 'operations' are the processes by which either of these are produced.

> Note: Much of this thinking originated in manufacturing firms but, increasingly it is seen as relevant to all types of organisation. There will be times within this chapter that the word 'product' is used within the context of operations management. This may signify services as well as products.

Table 3.1 Examples of operations

Organisation	Operations function	Operation
McDonalds	Kitchen and serving staff	Selling fast food
Vauxhall/Opel	Production lines	Making cars
Dell Computers	Production lines, internet	Making and selling computers
Real Madrid	Football coaches, training facilities	Playing football
Schools	Teachers	Teaching children

Although all organisational operations have similar transforming properties there are organisational differences according to volume, variety, variation and visibility (McDonald, 2008):

- *volume*, the degree to which the organisation can standardise work, the greater the standardisation the lower the unit cost
- *variety*, the degree of flexibility required to match services with customer demands (e.g. most prominently in the fashion industry)
- *variation*, how seasonal demand for products presents issues of capacity management for the particular organisation
- *visibility*, the exposure of operations to the customer which will vary from encounters with the customer online to personal discussions in an office or shop.

3.1 Shifting perspectives

It is clear from this brief introduction that operations and the development of an associated strategy is of vital importance to any organisation. For many enlightened contemporary organisations effective operations is viewed as a strategically significant issue and a vital means of gaining a competitive advantage. This section explains the shift from price-based operations to relational procurement and operations and emphasises supply chain management as a strategic process. (Price-based operations grew from the mass production methods of the industrial revolution whereby economies of scale allowed unit costs to be driven down.)

3.1.1 Procurement and operations

Recently purchasing has become a strategic issue for firms as techniques such as just-in-time (JIT) operations have taken root in a diversity of industries (initially from successes in motor manufacturing). JIT purchasing involves a system whereby 'material purchases are contracted so that the receipt and usage of material, to the maximum extent possible, coincide' (CIMA, 2005). Put simply the stock of raw materials is reduced to near-zero levels. Financial savings are easily apparent as is the requirement to foster an effective working relationship with suppliers.

The purchasing department has always been responsible for the majority of some company's expenditure. (Most manufacturing firms spend more than 60% of total expenditure on purchasing.) Some of the large buyers, for example in the automobile companies, have become highly sophisticated materials managers and fully integrate design and purchasing especially as JIT requires exact specifications and materials handling to achieve low inventory levels. Purchasing experts are also now involved with the design and development department with the responsibility of finding suppliers for materials that are to the specifications required by designers.

Manufacturers are increasingly recognising that buying is as important as selling, and that excellent selling cannot make up for a mediocre buying specification. Savings from economies of scale can be gained by centralising procurement to include not along raw materials but also supplies and capital equipment for offices (e.g. computers, cars, telephone systems, office furniture, paper and other stationery items, etc.).

Those responsible for purchasing discuss prices, discounts, delivery lead times and specifications with suppliers, chase late deliveries and sanction payments. They monitor quality, seek out competitive sources and maximise quantity discount opportunities where several sources are buying from the same supplier.

Gargan (2004) underlines the crucial significance of an organisation's procurement operation by reporting that improved purchasing has saved the UK government more than £1.6 billion on an annual spend of £15 billion, and that in the manufacturing industry, each 5% reduction of purchasing costs increases profitability by 35% on average.

3.1.2 Strategic issues

Rudzki (2006) makes a case for strategic purchasing and seees it as a lever to world class performance:

During the last 20 years, procurement departments around the world have adopted some new and very powerful processes and tools. Done well, advanced procurement and supply management can trigger a compounding positive effect on a company's lifeblood–its return on invested capital.

If you could reduce your product development cycle time by 50 per cent and beat competitors to market, while also reducing costs, would that be meaningful to your business? For most companies, that would be a huge plus. That is why world-class competitors involve their procurement group and other internal functions, plus suppliers, in an aligned effort to increase competitive advantage..............

Rudzki (2006) also draws attention to more than 30 critical factors that produce exceptional supply management performance, categorised under the headings of:

- procurement strategy
- objectives
- leadership
- optimised organisation
- best practices
- innovation and technology.

Purchasing deals with day-to-day buying of goods and services, ensuring they conform to the quality demanded, are priced appropriately and delivered to a suitable time scale. *Supply* by comparison involves strategic considerations including planning and implementing a strategy and managing the overall supply process.

One way of assessing whether supply chain management is being approached strategically is by applying Reck and Long's (1988) strategic positioning tool. This identifies the purchasing stage an organisation has reached on a continuum as described in Table 3.2.

Cousins' (2000) strategic supply wheel depicts the corporate supply strategy at the hub of a wheel and underlines the need for an integrated approach to supply strategy involving a balancing of all five 'spokes' in the wheel, namely:

- *Organisational structure* affects interactions with the rest of the organisation and the way in which control is exercised, the three main options are centralised, decentralised or some combination (a hybrid).
- *Relationships* with suppliers and their nature impact on the strategic success of the organisation. These relationships may be based on driving deals on price and can be quite adversarial. Alternatively, they may be more collaborative where there is a joint quest to reduce costs and a sharing of technology and innovations (known as 'partnership sourcing').
- *Cost/benefit analysis* is at the heart of rational decisions over the most appropriate strategic approach to follow.

Table 3.2 Reck and Long's strategic positioning

Passive	Purchasing acts on requests from other departments, some departments may get involved in the detail.
Independent	A more professional approach to purchasing including enhanced IT and communication.
Supportive	Purchasing is corporately recognised as essential. The function provides timely information about price and availability.
Integrative	Purchasing is integral to competitive strategies and management gets involved in strategy development.

- Appropriate *skills and competencies* are vital in order to implement a chosen strategy. Long-term relationships with suppliers might (for instance) lead to a need to re-orientate and train key personnel.
- *Performance measures*, both internal and external aligned with the strategy are necessary for monitoring and control.

From a strategic point of view cohesion between these five elements needs to be achieved, and each factor should be supportive of the other.

Exercise 3.2

What potential performance measures can be used to assess suppliers?

Solution

- Capability
- Delivery performance
- Price competitiveness
- Quality (defect rates)
- Timeliness (which will vary dependent upon the value and volume of the item purchased, e.g. a piece of computer hardware versus nuts and bolts).

Sourcing strategies refer to the way an organisation organises its supply process and clearly these have strategic implications. There are four main sourcing options:

1. *Single.* The buyer chooses one source of supply. This may be because of a scarcity of suppliers and under these circumstances the supplier is potentially powerful. One advantage of this option is that it is easier to develop a relationship with a single supplier.
2. *Multiple.* The buyer chooses several source of supply. Suppliers are rendered less powerful and prices can be driven down as a result. This is a traditional price-based strategy but it may not be conducive to good working relationships, or developing meaningful supplier relationships.
3. *Delegated.* The buyer chooses one (first tier) supplier who is responsible for the delivery of for example a complete sub assembly. Using the example of car manufacture, rather than deal with several suppliers to complete a dashboard one first tier supplier would assume this responsibility and deliver a completed dashboard through dealing with a range of other suppliers. This approach allows for a collaborative partnership approach

to develop including in some cases 'open book' accounting where savings are shared between both parties. One downside is of course that the first tier supplier becomes powerful so the supplier partners must be chosen with great care.
4. *Parallel.* A complicated approach that involves mixing all three approaches in order to maximise the benefits of each.

Operations is no different from other functional areas in that it can be approached from a strategic viewpoint. Brown et al. (2001: 39) stress the significance of this thinking as follows:

Operations capabilities are at the heart of the success of companies such as Dell, Nokia and Sony ... Although other areas such as marketing and human resource (HR) management are also important, even with the best marketing or HR plans in the world, without operations capabilities an organisation will flounder because it cannot deliver on its promises to customers. Organisations can no longer compete on a single dimension such as low cost, high quality, or delivery, but must provide all of these (and more!) simultaneously.

The process of strategy formulation including external and internal scanning and the generation and choice of strategies applies equally to this area. Operations must be central to the development of an overall corporate strategy.

Brown et al. (2001) include six items that as a minimum should be addressed as part of the operations strategy:

1. the capability required by the organisation,
2. the range and location of operations,
3. investment in technology, both product and process,
4. strategic buyer–supplier relationships,
5. new products or services, and
6. the organisational structure of operations.

Another term often used to describe the fundamental changes required in operations management is 'world-class manufacturing' which is generally concerned with achieving significant improvements in quality, lead times, flexibility and customer satisfaction. By making these improvements, an organisation might realistically become globally competitive. The concept and practice of world-class manufacturing is wide ranging and the term is not always used consistently. However, the core features of most approaches to world-class manufacturing include a *strong customer focus* which ensures that customer requirements are fully understood and can be satisfied with short lead time and *flexibility* to respond to changing customer requirements. This represents a significant shift from price-based operations.

3.2 Operations and organisational competitiveness

This section explains the relationship of operations and supply management to the competitiveness of the firm.

3.2.1 Operations strategy and the organisation

Two well known management models are presented here in order to illustrate the significance of operations to an organisation.

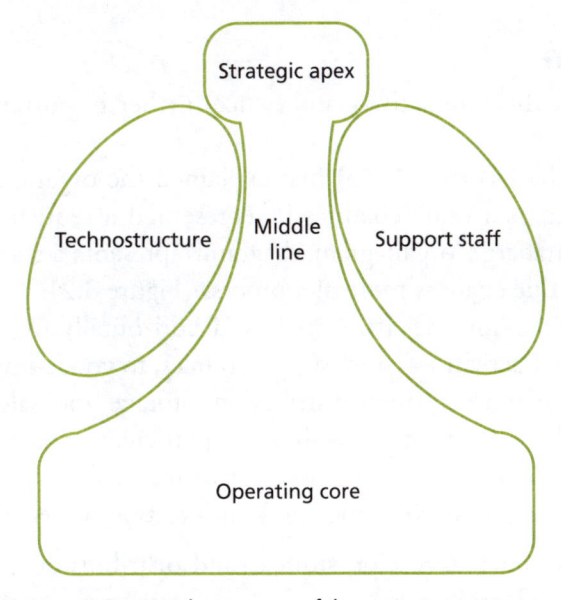

Figure 3.1 Five basic parts of the organisation

From Structures in Fives: Designing Effective Organisations by H. Mintzberg. Reprinted by permission of Pearson Education Inc., Upper Saddle River, NJ.

'Operations' is a term covering the central core of an organisation. Famously this central core has been used as a springboard for the development of theory by academics such as Henry Mintzberg (1983) who referred to it as 'the operating core'. Mintzberg suggested that it is useful to view organisations as being made up of five parts (Figure 3.1). It is important that organisations consider the relative balance of these elements in order to achieve their organisational goals and secure optimal competitiveness.

The *operating core* consists of those people who perform the work of rendering the services or producing products. In a small organisation this operating core may represent nearly all of the organisation, but larger organisations will require more complex arrangements. There will be a requirement to formulate and implement strategy so that the organisation serves its mission in an effective way. This is the role of the *strategic apex* which may in some circumstances also be responsible for linking the organisation to the needs of those who own or control it. The *middle line* represents the hierarchy of authority from senior managers to first-line supervisors linking the strategic apex to the operating core. As an organisation continues to grow and develop it is likely to include within its structure specialist staff outside the central line positions (i.e. strategic apex, middle line and operating core). Specialist staff are placed into two categories by Mintzberg. The *technostructure* is concerned with co-ordinating work by standardising work processes, outputs and skills, and will be made up of people such as management accountants, work–study engineers, HR managers, etc. *Support staff* exist to provide assistance to the organisation outside its operating work flow. Examples would be catering services, legal advice and press relations.

Clearly operations management is focussed upon the operating core and specialists who form part of the technostructure.

Exercise 3.3

Many organisations are now actively seeking flatter hierarchies, better quality and ways of contracting out of non-core activities. What are the implications of these developments for the five basic parts of the organisation identified by Mintzberg?

✓ Solution

A clearer focus on the core activity and hence further importance attached to operations management.

Economist Michael Porter (1985) first explained the organisation as a business system, which he described as a value chain as it represented a sequence of value-creating activities. Whereas Mintzberg's 'organagram' diagram represents a static description of a vertical organisation the value chain is more of a process (Figure 3.2).

Porter depicted the 'line' departments linked horizontally together in a chain of sequentially-interdependent activities – from supply sources, to goods-inward inspection, operations (the 'transformation process') then distribution, storage and sales. Organisations structure these activities differently to cope with their particular external environments. Typically departments or divisions are created to interact with specific sectors of the environment. Five primary activities are directly concerned with the creation or delivery of a product:

- Inbound logistics refer to receipt, storage, and distribution. They include material handling, stock control, etc.
- Operations convert these inputs into the final product.
- Outbound logistics involves the distribution to consumers. (For example, if sales take place in stores, checkout tills are important. For on-line sales, assembling and transporting customer orders are also included.)
- Marketing and sales is the mechanism whereby the customer is made aware of the product.
- Service can include installation, training and spares. This would also include customer enquiry/returns/complaints desk and maintenance of an organisation's web page.

Operations management is directly concerned with four of these five primary activities. (Marketing and sales are dealt with separately within this Learning System.) Support activities help to improve the efficiency and effectiveness of all primary activities, specifically:

- Procurement processes at all stages including product purchases.
- Technology development including 'know-how'.
- Human resource management embracing all primary activities and covers recruitment, selection, training, development and reward policies, etc.
- Infrastructure or systems, structures and routines.

Operations management is directly concerned with procurement and elements of technology and infrastructure. Arising from this thinking Table 3.3 illustrates some key issues associated with operations management within a fictional organisation.

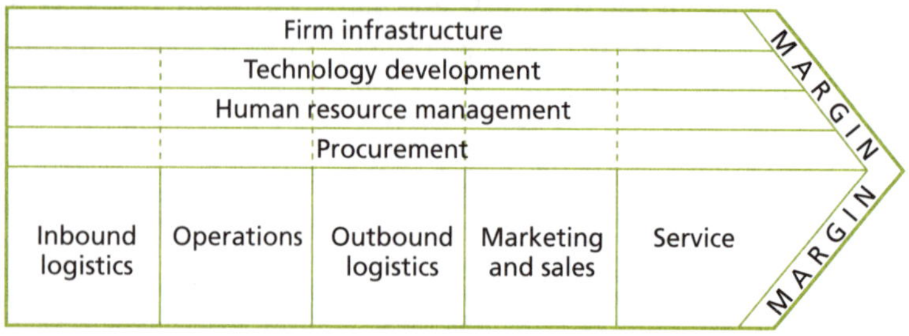

Figure 3.2 Porter's value chain. Reprinted with the permission of The Free Press, a division of Simon & Schuster Adult Publishing Group, from *Competitive Advantage: Creating and Sustaining Superior Performance* by Michael E. Porter. © 1985, 1998 by Michael E. Porter. All rights reserved

Table 3.3 Example operations management: issues

Purchasing activity capable of buying the raw material, components, tools and equipment necessary for efficient high-quality minimum-cost manufacture.

The provision of economic and efficient storage of consumable goods, raw materials and components for further fabrication. Records capable of ensuring that quantities held in stock are within the predetermined budgets.

Production engineering capability to plan manufacturing methods, use of tools, design of machine tools, assembly, fixtures, etc.

Production control department with the capability of translating customer orders and stockists' requirements into orders in the factory.

The organisation and operation of the manufacturing department and assembly department. Economical and competitive cost of manufacture.

Quality control department with the capability of ensuring adequate quality commensurate with cost, by inspection at various stages of manufacture and assembly and 'bench testing' of final products.

The efficiency of the company's facilities, plant, buildings, tools, etc.

Supplier's value chain → Firm's value chain → Channel's value chain → Customer's value chain

Competitor's value chain

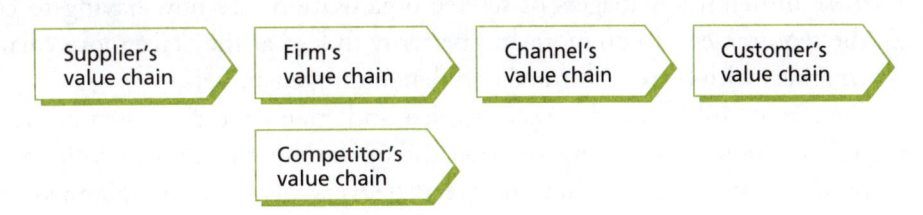

Figure 3.3 Porter's value system. Reprinted with the permission of The Free Press, a division of Simon & Schuster Adult Publishing Group, from *Competitive Advantage: Creating and Sustaining Superior Performance* by Michael E. Porter. © 1985, 1998 by Michael E. Porter. All rights reserved

3.2.2 The supply chain

The implications of the value chain and the wider value system have encouraged organisations to consider supply chain partnerships as part of a wider value system. The value system extends to suppliers, distributors and customers' own value chains. Competitive advantage through linkages between the organisation and its value system components can be achieved by examining supplier specifications, common merchandising, applying total quality management principles or by collaborating with other organisations in the form of strategic alliances or joint ventures.

Porter uses the concept of the value system to describe the position of the firm relative to the firms upstream and downstream of it. Figure 3.3 shows the firm at a point in the value system between suppliers and customers. The supply chain and the organisations that are partners within it is considered in more detail later in this chapter.

3.3 Operations and service organisations

The new approaches to operations management and quality discussed in this chapter have been most widely applied in manufacturing firms. However, modern advanced economies are now dominated by service organisations and future economic growth also depend heavily on this sector. For service organisations to maintain their competitive advantage they need to embrace management philosophies and techniques that have proven successful in other sectors. Service industries however have certain distinguishing features that may make it difficult to reduce costs and increase quality.

Exercise 3.4

List five distinctive features of a service not found in a product.

Solution

- Services are intangible and it is more difficult to measure their quality than it is for a physical product.
- Services are consumed immediately and cannot be stored.
- Customers participate directly in the delivery process (in contrast to a manufacturing organisation where production and purchase are usually physically separated).
- The customer when evaluating the quality of the service will take into account the face-to-face contact and the social skills of those providing the service.
- Service organisations tend to be labour intensive.

Despite these difficulties managers of service organisations are now having to come to terms with the requirement 'to do more and better with less' as they face more volatile and competitive markets with better informed and demanding customers.

Some believe that differences between service and manufacturing organisations may be over played. For both types of organisation the operations function provides an agreed volume of products or services within an agreed delivery plan at a pre-planned cost and level of quality. Manufacturing firms also have to achieve targets such as planned return on assets employed, and some of these measures are now starting to take on relevance for service organisations due to changing technologies.

Exercise 3.5

Identify a service that you use and analyse the way in which it has altered over the past ten years.

Solution

You may have identified factors such as:

- being less labour intensive
- extensive use of IT
- being more centralised and global
- communication via the Internet
- trading via the Internet
- other online services.

3.4 Sustainability in operations management

Sustainability is a long-term programme involving a series of sustainable development practices, aimed at improving organisational efficiency, stakeholder support and market edge (Goldsmith and Samson, 2004).

- *Efficiency:* Practices could include reducing waste, energy usage, water consumption and the sale of bye-products that were previously a cost of disposal. Practices to improve efficiency ultimately contribute to improved long-term financial performance.

Table 3.4 Examples of sustainable development practices

Organisation	Actions	Outcomes
A pet food manufacturer de-bones chickens as part of the production process	Rather than pay to have the waste taken to a landfill site, find a business that can use this waste in their production (e.g. glue manufacturer)	• environmentally sound practice • new income stream • helps create value for someone else
Factory	Installing a TV and exercise video in the staff room	• encourage good health of employees • less sickness • greater productivity
All organisations	Flexible working hours or teleworking for employees with young families	• less sickness • greater productivity • less turnover
All organisations	Child care and health and fitness provisions for employees, programmes such as matching staff donations to charity	• improve industrial relations

Source: Based on Goldsmith and Samson (2004).

- *Stakeholder support*: Reductions in greenhouse gas emissions would undoubtedly strengthen the relationship between the organisation and environmentalists. Other practices could be aimed at addressing the agendas of other stakeholder groups such as employees, shareholders, customers and suppliers, etc.
- *Market edge*: Practices could include research and development, innovation and supply chain improvements. Ultimately these practices will help an organisation gain a competitive advantage by exploiting new business opportunities, so increasing market share and profitability.

Table 3.4 gives examples of sustainable development practices provided by Goldsmith and Samson (2004).

3.5 Quality management thinking

Quality is one of the most important and far-reaching issues in modern organisations. The term is difficult to define precisely and often mean different things to different organisations. Table 3.5 shows some of the many definitions of quality.

Notably, the need to satisfy the customer's needs is critical to most definitions of quality. Therefore, it is vital that organisations are able to identify and deliver the needs of its customers.

Table 3.5 Definitions of quality

'The totality of features and characteristics of a product or service that bears on its ability to meet a stated or implied need' (ISO 9000)
'Fitness for use' (Juran)
'Quality, meaning getting everyone to do what they have agreed to do and do it right the first time, is the consistent conformance to customer requirements skeletal structure of an organisation, finance is the nourishment, and relationships are the soul' (Crosby)

Exercise 3.6

Make a list of some of the quality problems that could be encountered in your own organisation.

Solution

It is likely that you have come up with a number of specific examples. The following list provides a few more examples that you may not have identified (this list is not intended to be exhaustive):

- Billing errors
- Down-time due to equipment/computer failure
- Stock shortages
- Incorrect stock delivered
- Faulty data entry and calculation
- Scrap and rework
- Returned goods
- Late management reports
- Contract errors.

The growth of global competition has resulted in dramatic improvements in the quality and efficiency of products and services. Much of this impetus can be attributed to the efforts of Japanese manufacturing companies who developed systems of management that have produced higher standards of quality and efficiency. Others have now adopted many of these methods and large Western companies are increasingly keen to 'benchmark' themselves against the best in the world. In Figure 3.4 Glass (1991) contrasts traditional Western approaches and Japanese approaches to quality issues.

Ironically, much of the success of Japanese businesses has been because of the application of techniques first developed in the West. In particular, Edward Deming and Joseph

Quality issues	The West	Japan
Concept of quality	Static	Continuous improvement
Focus of activity	Volume/profit	Quality/customer satisfaction
Quality responsibility	Quality control department	Mainly workers
Quality training	For QC staff	For all workers
Solving quality problems	QC staff & engineering	Employees, supervisors and managers
Quality targets	Set by QC staff	Set by top managers
Role of QC experts	Inspection	Helping workers

Figure 3.4 Comparison of Western and Japanese approaches to quality
Source: Based on Glass (1991, p. 190)

Juran spent a good deal of time in Japan in the 1950s and 1960s promoting their thinking, which was largely ignored elsewhere. Initially, many of these ideas were to do with the application of statistical techniques to problems of quality control, but they soon began to cover a much wider philosophy of quality management. Deming, Juran and other renowned experts had been pleading the case for quality for decades. The uptake of this advice by the Japanese in the 1950s onwards only began to take root in the West thirty years later. The essence of the argument was indisputable: quality pays. Famously companies like Hewlett-Packard, Xerox, and Motorola, demonstrated that quality could translate into reduced costs that could be reinvested in IT for further product improvements.

Much of the research into quality in the last half-century has arrived at broadly similar conclusions in terms of what organisationally is required:

- *Commitment* to a quality philosophy within an organisation with senior management 'buy-in'. If senior management is not fully committed, it is unlikely that customer requirements of quality will be met.
- *Competence*: quality can only be achieved by competence in the job or activity undertaken. Without competence it is difficult to create quality in a product or service. Competence can only be gained with continual training and development of skills and experience.
- *Communication* of the importance of quality throughout all levels of the organisation. Poor communication will lead to lack of clear customer specifications, poor feedback and a lack of understanding. Communication improves the understanding of the purpose and benefits of quality, and ensures that the whole organisation (i.e. from strategic to operational levels) clearly understands the concept of quality and its importance.
- *Continuous improvement* or Kaizen, signifies continuous improvement in all aspects of an organisation's performance at every level over a period (CIMA, 2005).

W. Edward Deming

Deming was an experienced statistician who believed that management should concentrate on setting up and then continuously improve the systems in which people work. He emphasised the importance of managers working with other employees, because the best feedback is from those who actually do the jobs. Unlike the scientific management approach, which involves managers setting work standards and methods, Deming stressed the need to train workers in methods of statistical process control and work analysis. This enables the workers to identify for themselves what needs changing and how.

Joseph M. Juran

Juran worked at the Hawthorne Electricity Plant in Chicago in the 1920s. He visited Japan in the early 1950s and drawing on the Pareto principle, he explained the concept of the 'vital few and the trivial many'. Juran suggested that typically 80–85% of quality problems at work are the result of the systems that employees work within and, therefore, there is little point in trying to solve them by seeking to increase worker motivation. His prescription was for managers, with their employees, to identify the main quality problems, highlight the key ones which if solved will produce the most benefits, and set up projects to deal with them. Juran also believed that anyone affected by the product is considered a customer, so introducing the idea of internal as well as external customers.

Philip P. Crosby

Crosby, is best known for popularising the Zero Defects concept that originated at a company he once worked for. Eventually, Crosby became Director of Quality and Corporate

Vice-President of the ITT Corporation. Crosby's mantra was 'Quality is Free'. Additionally quality is not an issue of degree: it is either present or not present. Management must measure quality by continually tracking the cost of doing things wrong (the price of non-conformance). Crosby (1980) suggested that conformance to requirements was key, and championed a quality improvement process, based on four criteria:

1. Quality can be defined as conformance to customer specifications.
2. A quality system should focus on prevention, not appraisal and detection.
3. The quality standard must be set at zero defects.
4. The measurement of quality is the price of non-conformance (the costs incurred from undertaking quality management measures).

This process should be used to ensure that the suppliers, customers and internal staff all understand the quality process.

3.5.1 Methods of quality measurement

For the manufacturing sector quality failures are easily apparent through the amount of scrap material, faulty batches or returned products. These costs, which are internal to the organisation, are referred to as 'internal failure costs'. Some manufacturing companies have attempting to measure quality. Measures might include parts per million defects rates, ratio of 'good' items produced to items entering the process and levels of waste and scrap (Bowhill, 2008). Poor quality will for any organisation also have a cost of lost sales and customers switching to competitor products or services (Bowhill, 2008). Kaplan and Norton (1996) cite the example of a manufacturing company that discovered that they were reworking 84% of their products. By reducing this figure to 40% in six months they were able to reduce their overall workforce by a quarter. (One hundred people had been employed inspecting, detecting and rectifying defects.)

Despite Crosby's mantra there are four types of quality cost (including internal failure) as illustrated in Table 3.6.

Internal failure and external failure costs are the cost of non-conformance, whilst the other two, prevention and appraisal are conformance costs.

Table 3.6 Types of quality costs

Type of cost	Description	Examples
Internal failure	Costs associated with the detection and rectification of items that do not conform to quality requirements. Goods have not yet been passed to the customer.	Waste, scrap, rework, lost time
External failure	Costs associated with the rectification of items that do not conform to quality requirements and have been passed to the customer.	Dealing with customer complaints, warranty claims, product recalls and returns
Appraisal	Costs incurred while conducting quality tests and inspections in order to determine whether products or services conform to quality requirements.	Inspection costs (of raw materials, WIP and finished), quality control audits
Prevention	Costs of activities undertaken to prevent defects occurring in the design and development phase of a product or service	Staff training, preventative maintenance, quality circles and quality planning

The maintenance of factory buildings, machinery, plant power and lighting are crucial to prevention of quality errors. Total productive maintenance (TPM) is a contemporary idea aimed at increasing the productivity of the organisation's equipment. The fundamental objective of TPM is to prevent quality failures caused by equipment failure or degradation so TPM might usefully contribute a quality management programme. It involves identifying equipment in every division, including planning, manufacturing and maintenance, and then planning and implementing a maintenance programme that covers their entire useful life.

Exercise 3.7

What do you think the major factors that need to be considered in order to implement TPM?

Solution

- Training
- Equipment maintenance
- Planning
- An adequate budget

TPM should reduce equipment breakdowns, enhance equipment capability and improve safety and environmental factors.

Servqual is a customer attitude measurement scale developed to assess quality in service and retail businesses (Parasuraman et al., 1988; Parasuraman et al., 1991). The concept is widely used in areas such as healthcare, banking, finance and education. Servqual indicates differences between a customer's expectations for a service and their feelings of how the service was received. To do this customers answer questions about both their initial expectations and their perceptions of the actual service delivered. A scale captures service quality under the acronym RATER:

- Responsiveness (a willingness to help and respond to customer needs)
- Assurance (the abilities of staff to inspire confidence and trust)
- Tangible factors (physical facilities, equipment, staff appearance, etc.)
- Empathy (the extent to which caring personalised service is delivered)
- Reliability (an ability to perform service dependably and accurately.

Servqual may be complex to administer, subjective and statistically unreliable but it is built on a straightforward concept, and is easily explained and understood.

3.5.2 Approaches to quality management

Some key approaches to quality management are explored in this section.

Use of Total Quality Management. Continuous improvement (or kaizen) is a philosophy to continually improve the quality of goods/services of an organisation, it involves the continual analysis of organisational processes to ensure continued improvement in performance and quality. Total Quality Management (TQM) builds on the kaizen concept and can be defined as an all encompassing organisational philosophy that encourages and fosters continuous improvement. The fundamental features of TQM are as follows:

- prevention of errors and defects before they occur
- the importance of total quality in design of products/services and systems.

By breaking TQM down into its constituent elements, the meaning and methodology behind the philosophy can be better understood:

Total	Everyone linked to the organisation (staff, customers and suppliers) is involved in the process. The concept of viewing every business activity as a process that can be improved is shared.
Quality	The requirements of customers are achieved.
Management	Senior managers must be fully committed to continuous improvement if all other parties are to help achieve it.

Importantly, TQM focusses on quality from a customer perspective, using a systematic, integrated, organisation-wide approach. TQM encourages the full involvement of all people, at all levels, working within multi-disciplinary teams to suggest and implement improvements from within the organisation. Then the principles of TQM can be implemented throughout the organisation.

There are several approaches to developing a TQM philosophy, however there are some common features:

- Those departments not directly involved in satisfying the needs of external customers must serve the needs of their internal customers – that is, the departments which use their services within the organisation.
- Open, honest communication is to be encouraged throughout the organisation.
- An investment in employee training and education to equip them with the skills required for TQM and to enable them to realise their potential.
- An emphasis on teamwork and collaboration (some initiatives make use of 'quality circles', in which the employees involved in a process meet at regular intervals to discuss problems and implement improvements).
- Involvement of customers and suppliers as an integral part of the improvement process.

Table 3.7 summarises organisational pre-requisites for TQM.

Use of Quality control is an approach involving:

- establishing quality standards for a service or product
- designing a process to deliver the service or product to the required quality
- measuring the quality of the service or product
- comparing actual quality with planned quality
- taking remedial action where quality does not meet standard
- reviewing the standard originally set and adjust if necessary.

Table 3.7 Prerequisites for TQM

Prerequisite	Feature
Leadership	Senior management commitment
Methodology	Zero-tolerance philosophy
Objective	100% customer satisfaction and competitive advantage
Performance measurement	Quality costs: prevention, appraisal, internal and external failure
	Customer retention and market share
Scope	Total organisation and external stakeholders (suppliers and customers)
Nature	Continuous improvement
Skills	Continuous training
Communication	Quality circles
	Management reporting

Table 3.8 Quality control: a worked example of a roadside breakdown service such as the RAC or AA

Action	Detail
Set standard	98% of breakdowns to be attended to within one hour of the call being received, 75% of breakdowns to be repaired at the roadside.
Organise resources	For example, breakdown vehicles, call centres, trained mechanics, to deliver the service (of the standard) from work records and customer surveys
Measure achievement	The results with the standard.
Compare	
Take remedial action	For example, if the target of 98% attended within 1 hour standard is not met it may be necessary to increase the numbers of vehicles and drivers; or if the target of 75% of repairs at the roadside is not met it may be necessary to retrain mechanics or improve their equipment.
Review	If the standards are easily met consider revising standards to improve service further.

A quality control mechanism would be used mainly in technical production processes and consists of identifying an element of the production process that is critical to the quality of production, then establishing warning limits and tolerances to measure any unacceptable variances. The process is monitored closely (possibly using advanced technology) to ensure that immediate action is taken to remedy any breach of the tolerance. A worked example is provided in Table 3.8.

The quality control system can be organisation-wide and could include the design process, quality assurance of suppliers of raw materials, production, warehousing, distribution, or after-sales service, etc.

Use of Quality assurance (QA) systems are in certain ways superior to quality control systems in that they attempt to *create* quality rather than *control* it. According to Campbell (1997) QA must account for:

- design of products and services
- materials of a consistently appropriate standard
- suppliers who are reliable and consistent in the supply of materials
- plant and machinery that is reliable
- staff that benefit from training development so reducing the potential for human error
- operations procedures and the way in which they are planned, managed and carried out.

Use of European Quality Foundation model. Self-assessment models for business improvement have become widespread. One of the most common is the European Quality Foundation model. This provides a structured methodology for organisations to measure their own performance in areas that are critical to businesses. The model allows strengths and areas for improvement to be identified through self-assessment and thereby contributes significantly to the business planning cycle. It is a non-prescriptive framework based on nine criteria. The assessment looks at an entire organisation. The nine criteria are divided into what the organisation achieves (results) and how results are achieved (enabler). *Results*, that is, customer results, people results, society results, key performance results. *Enablers* involve leadership, policy and strategy, people, partnerships and resources, processes. An explanation of how this was introduced in one organisation is reflected in the following web page extract:

> Thames Valley, in common with the National Probation Directorate and the other 41 local areas, under- took its first self-assessment under the model in the summer of 2001 and published the results in the autumn.
>
> Aided by a consultant from TQMI (sponsored by the British Quality Foundation), a cross-grade group of staff gathered evidence throughout the organisation over a period of several weeks. This culminated in a consensus workshop in which the validity and weight of each piece of evidence was analysed. This in turn led to a self-assessment score, and a report to Senior Managers and the Board.
>
> The report contributed significantly to the Area's Business Plan. . . . and also heavily influenced a restructure of the Area's management arrangements and priorities.'
>
> *Source*: Thames Valley probation board www.thamesvalleyprobation.gov.uk/about/about_eem.html

Use of British and European systems. The ISO 9000:2000 series quality award is a form of a quality system standard which according to CIMA (2005):

requires complying organisations to operate in accordance with a structure of written policies and procedures that are designed to ensure consistent delivery of a product or service to meet customer requirements

The forerunner of this series of quality standards was the British Standards Institution (BSI) BS 5750 series of quality standards. To qualify for accreditation an organisation defines a standard for quality and the processes needed to achieve it. Registration under the standard requires the submission and approval of documentation, including a quality manual, procedures manuals and work instructions. There is an initial external inspection before accreditation is awarded and then regular reappraisal visits. The key feature of the ISO 9000:2000 series is the underlying assurance that customer satisfaction and fulfilment of customer requirements are achieved. The series of quality standards are designed to:

- provide a clear system of quality management which includes establishing processes, their interactions, the resources required and how to manage and improve the processes
- gain total company involvement and commitment
- obtain a nationally accepted standard of quality, ensure commitment to quality and customer requirements of quality.

Benefits of implementing ISO 9000:2000 are listed in Table 3.9.

Table 3.9 Benefits of ISO 9000:2000 implementation

Recognised standard of quality.
Excellent marketing tool.
Better quality will improve customer satisfaction, leading to more sales, competitiveness and profitability. Customers are less likely to conduct an independent quality audit on the supplier, thus saving costs and time.
Increasingly useful in export markets.

Accreditation of ISO 14001 is closely allied to the ISO 9000:2000 series. It specifies a process for controlling and improving a company's environmental performance. It covers:

- environmental policy
- planning
- implementation and operation
- checking and corrective action
- management review.

Environmental management systems focus on the environmental practices in organisations, including use and source of raw materials, use of energy, waste, emissions to air, water and soil, noise, aesthetic impact and use of hazardous substances.

The organisation identifies elements of its business that impact on the environment, sets objectives for improvement and implements a management programme for achievement. This programme is regularly reviewed for continual improvement.

Exercise 3.8

What are the main benefits of this accreditation?

Solution

Benefits of this accreditation are:

- enhancement of environmental awareness within the organisation
- cost savings and reduction in use of resources
- improved compliance with legislation
- potential competitive advantage over companies without accreditation
- demonstration of environmental commitment to stakeholders.

To ensure quality throughout the value chain, some organisations insist that their suppliers produce and deliver using a certified quality system.

There are, however, inevitably critics of these types of quality approaches. Managers of some small- and medium-sized organisations are unhappy at being required to develop apparently expensive and bureaucratic procedures that are not consistent with their organisation's culture and ways of working. Other critics claim that registration under the standards does not guarantee quality products and services, and that this approach might even make it more difficult to obtain the levels of employee support and involvement required.

3.6 Process design

Bowhill (2008) explains the value of process design in the following terms:

Measuring process costs, quality and time can help highlight areas where inefficiencies are present and corrective action is required. In order to compete, it is necessary for the workforce to improve the processes that lead to customer satisfaction.

Processes might be improved by

- the operation of TQM and/or kaizen
- reorganisation to reflect processes not functions

- supply chain management with the aim of improving links with suppliers and customers
- business process re-engineering (BPR).

'Business Process Re-engineering' is the term for reconfiguring organisational processes and structures to bring about radical process changes in a short time. BPR challenges managers and staff to fundamentally rethink the way they do things in order to maximise organisational effectiveness. It has been described as:

'... the fundamental rethinking and radical redesign of business processes to achieve dramatic improvements in critical, contemporary measures of performance, such as cost, quality, service and speed'

(Hammer and Champy, 2001)

and

'... areas of business activity in which repeatable and repeated sets of activities are undertaken, and the development of improvement understanding of how they operate and of the scope for radical redesign with a view to creating and delivering better customer value'

(CIMA, 2005)

As the improvement of an organisation's business processes is an integral part of a quality approach, BPR might be used as part of a TQM philosophy. Hammer and Champy identify four themes of BPR:

- Process reorientation, a focus on jobs, tasks, constraints, resources, etc.
- Creative use of IT (The impetus for doing this might be the introduction of new information technologies.)
- Ambition
- Rule breaking.

BPR demands five phases: planning, internal learning, external learning, redesign and implementation.

Although hailed as the biggest innovation of the 1990s its effectiveness in bringing about lasting improvement has been questioned more recently. BPR has also been stigmatised because it has been seen as a device to down size organisations and shed jobs.

3.6.1 Process maps

It has been suggested that the workforce spend between 20% and 40% of their time dealing with 'waste' issues. This might involve an individual doing things which have either not been done or were done badly. This duplication of effort, the requirement to complete unnecessary paperwork, dealing with misdirected queries or encountering bottlenecks that hold up production are waste. To regain control and drive out waste management must first understand the basic processes that are undertaken. One straightforward way of getting this overview is through the use of process maps. (If you have been involved in systems-based auditing it is likely that you will have encountered process mapping.) Process maps provide a visual flowchart representation of:

- processes that show how a product or transaction is processed
- workflow either within a process or within the organisation
- flows of information or products across supply chains and networks.

In certain ways process maps capture the entire operations process by demonstrating the activities that transform inputs into pre-defined sets of outputs. (Flowcharting might be

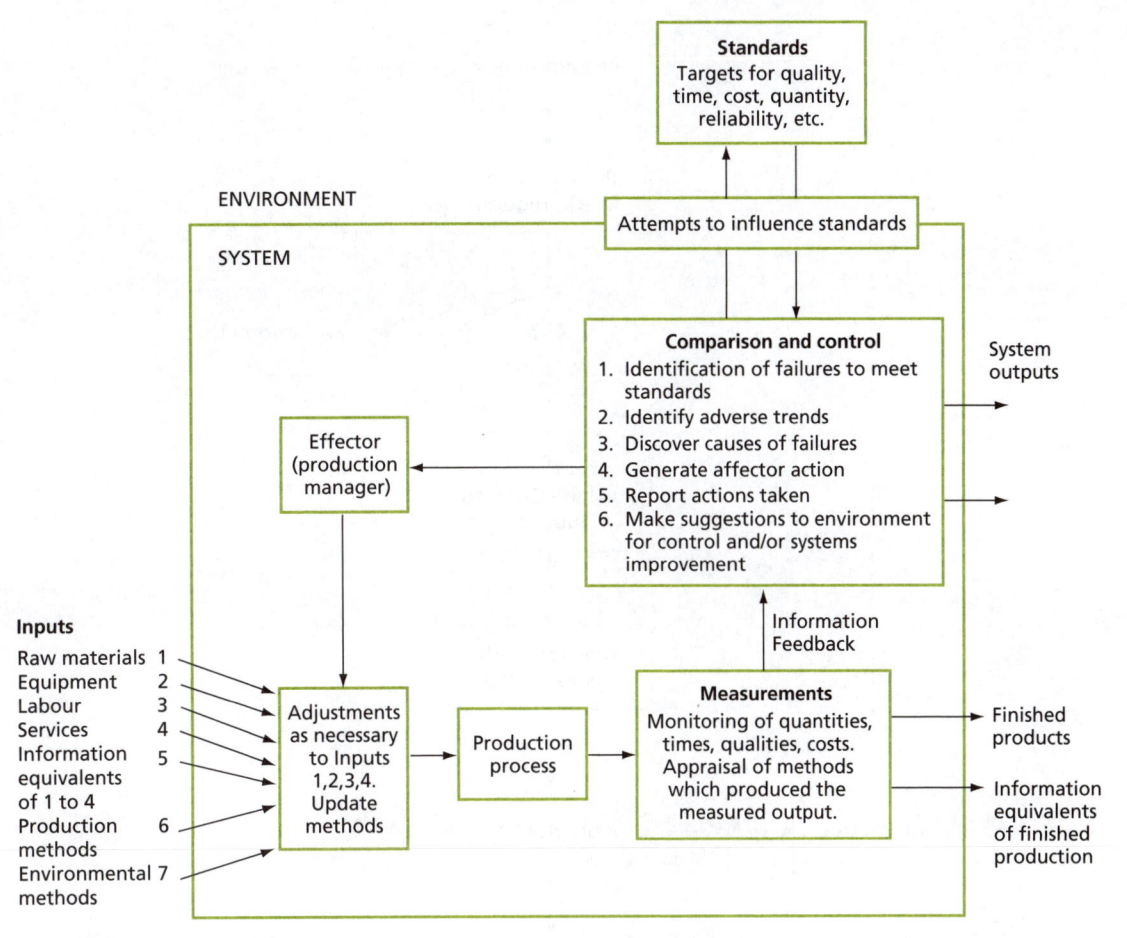

Figure 3.5 Production system example of GST. T. Lucey, Management Information Systems, 8th edition. Reprinted with permission of Taylor and Francis.

used as part of ISO registration.) An example of a typical production system is shown in Figure 3.5.

There are potentially many types of chart each with its own conventions and symbols, the two most popular are featured here.

Outline Process Map (flowchart). This map gives an overview of all actions undertaken, highlighting the sequence of activities and key points within the process. An example of a typical process outline map is shown in Figure 3.6.

Deployment Chart. This chart depicts a process with the added detail of matters such as in which section, department or organisation actions are performed. An example is shown in Figure 3.7.

Charting has many advantages:

- it provides management with a convenient overview demonstrating responsibilities and key stages in the supply chain
- it indicates the efficiency of a process, where waste exists and the impact on customers
- it can act as springboard to critical examination and improved processes
- it might be used as a trigger for change
- it allows everyone to understand what their job is and how their work fits into the whole process.

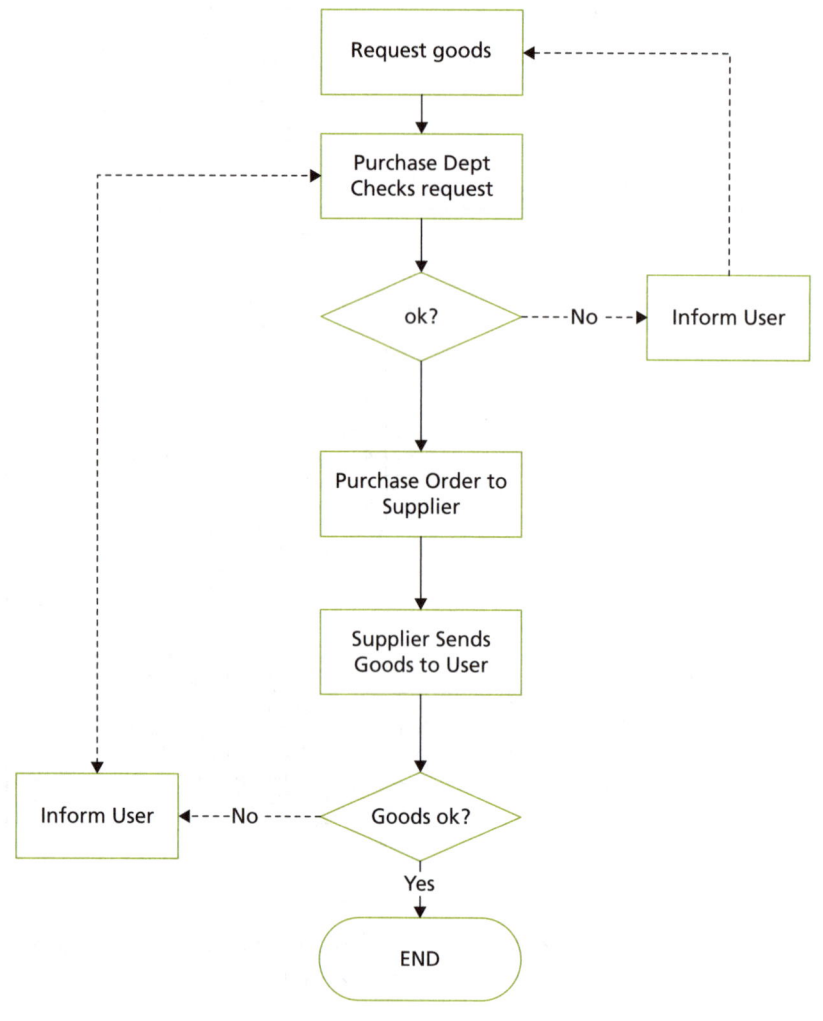

```
                    ┌─────────────────┐
                    │  Request goods  │◄─────────┐
                    └────────┬────────┘          │
                             ▼                   │
                    ┌─────────────────┐          │
            ┌──────►│  Purchase Dept  │          │
            │       │  Checks request │          │
            │       └────────┬────────┘          │
            │                ▼                   │
            │             ╱ ok? ╲ ----No---►┌──────────┐
            │             ╲    ╱            │Inform User│
            │                │              └──────────┘
            │               Yes
            │                ▼
            │       ┌─────────────────┐
            │       │Purchase Order to│
            │       │    Supplier     │
            │       └────────┬────────┘
            │                ▼
            │       ┌─────────────────┐
            │       │ Supplier Sends  │
            │       │  Goods to User  │
            │       └────────┬────────┘
            │                ▼
    ┌──────────┐         ╱Goods ╲
    │Inform User│◄--No---╲ ok? ╱
    └──────────┘            │
                           Yes
                            ▼
                         ( END )
```

Simple process flow chart

Figure 3.6 Crown Prosecution Service outline process map

(*Source:* Crown Prosecution Service (2004) http://www.cps.gov.uk/Publications/finance/process_mapping.html)

3.6.2 Systems used in operations management

One important aspect of operations management is to ensure that materials are ready when they are needed. A number of systems are used in improving flows, some from the application of sophisticated information systems, others the adoption of Japanese inspired approaches.

Manufacturing Resource Planning (MRP) is a planning and control system designed for organisations that engage in mass production. MRP is a push-based system, pushing work through the system. The computer system MRP II is a form of inventory control matching supply and demand with sophisticated features such as:

- shop floor control
- production planning
- financial analysis
- capacity planning
- customer order entry
- purchasing
- forecasting.

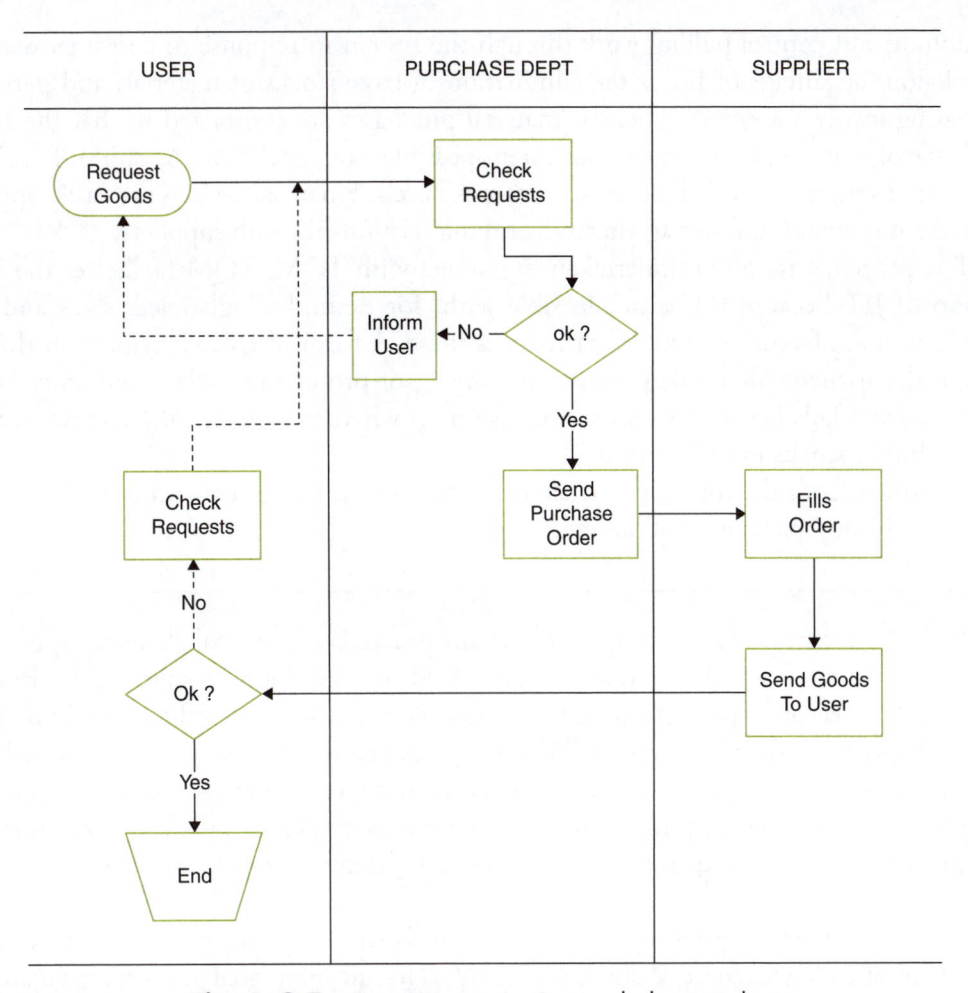

Figure 3.7 Crown Prosecution Service deployment chart

(*Source*: Crown Prosecution Service (2004) http://www.cps.gov.uk/Publications/finance/process_mapping.html)

Brown et al. (2001) cite the benefits of MRP as potentially providing:

- reduced stock holding and stock turnover
- increased customer service (fewer delays through materials shortage)
- swift, reliable quotations of delivery times
- improved facilities utilisation
- less time spent on hurrying emergency orders
- better relationships with suppliers by identifying clear lead times.

Enterprise Resource Planning (ERP) combines internal processes such as MRP II with external processes. ERP is a management system that integrates all aspects of business, including planning, manufacturing and sales. As ERP has become more popular certain software applications have emerged to help implement activities such as inventory control, order tracking, customer service, finance and human resources. It may be costly and time hungry to implement but it does cohesively link the supply chain.

Optimised Production Technologies is a production improvement method based on bottleneck improvements. It concentrates on constraints and seeks to identify and then remove obstructions that hinder the flow of a system.

Just-in-time (JIT) systems have an objective of producing or procuring products or components as they are required by a customer or for use (CIMA, 2005). JIT is a pull-based system of planning and control pulling work through the system in response to customer demand. The obvious advantage of JIT is the elimination of large stocks of materials and parts. JIT purchasing involves a system whereby 'material purchases are contracted so that the receipt and usage of material, to the maximum extent possible, coincide' (CIMA, 2005). Put simply the stock of raw materials is reduced to near-zero levels. Financial savings are easily apparent as is the requirement to foster an effective working relationship with suppliers.

JIT approaches are often undertaken in parallel with TQM. TQM facilitates the introduction of JIT because JIT is not feasible with, for example, high reject rates and high wastage in manufacturing, and TQM reduces these. A form of risk assessment in the production department often takes place. The impact of production delays and stock-outs if the JIT system fails has implications. A decision on whether to accept the risk or, perhaps, to carry buffer stocks must be made.

The extract from the following article explains how crucial just-in-time (JIT) deliveries are to optimising space in retail outlets.

For all the attention focused on supply chain processes, from global sourcing to the end consumer, very little discussion is dedicated to how shipments are received into stores. The reason is perhaps quite pragmatic: Few retailers are willing to talk about what happens in their back rooms. When approached for this story, most declined to comment. However, there is a clear consensus among retailer expectations: Inventory should flow from the back room to the store floor as quickly as possibly. Back rooms, kept to a minimum footprint, are for processing shipments, not for storage.

....

Reliance on transportation carriers and third-party logistics providers for store-level logistics has become a dominant trend. The ultimate goal is to manage store deliveries so that store resources, specifically back-room space and labour, are utilised most efficiently and in-stock positioning is optimised.

....

Pharmacies in traditional drug stores as well as in grocery and super-store formats have some of the most stringent requirements for JIT deliveries. Every inch of every footprint is at a premium, and neither the pharmacist nor technicians has time to receive shipments.

'A pharmacy retailer may need to receive deliveries before 6 a.m. to replenish stock or at a defined time slot when they have scheduled clerks specifically for receiving deliveries.' noted Drew Kronick, executive VP of business development and supply chain solutions for Velocity Express.

A national home-accessories and lifestyle retailer began using Velocity Express for furniture replenishment about 18 months ago. In a targeted Northeastern market where the retailer operates approximately 30 stores, Velocity Express makes daily deliveries to the stores, and in some cases may deliver multiple times to a single store. Valuable square footage that was once dedicated to back-room storage has been converted to selling space, and replenishment inventory of large furnishings is held in a centralised location. When furniture sells from the store floor, Velocity Express picks up at the central warehouse and delivers to the store that same day.

The JIT service is designed to deliver to whatever parameters the retailers set. In markets where there is a critical mass of stores, a fleet of trucks and drivers may be dedicated to a specific retailer.

Source: Robbins Gentry, C. (2007) Back-room secrets. *Chain Store Age*, March.

Exercise 3.9

What is the main principle difference between MRP and JIT?

Solution

JIT is a pull-based system which responds to demand. In contrast MRP is a push-based system which tends to use stock as buffers between the different elements of the system such as purchasing, production and sales (CIMA, 2005).

3.7 Lean management

Lean production and its management involves a consolidation of improvement systems into a single coherent process for continuous improvement. The concept was born from the experience of Western firms competing with Japanese businesses with their emphasis on quality. For some firms this new type of competition proved fatal whilst others realised that if they were to survive they would have to radically change the ways in which they transformed their inputs into outputs. Consequently, 'operations management' has been elevated from being viewed in the West as a largely mundane and unimportant aspect of management to being seen as the key to revitalising organisations. Womack et al. (1990) famously traced the impact of new approaches to manufacturing in the automobile industry.

Henry Ford's adoption of assembly line production methods early in the twentieth century transformed the way cars and many other products were made. An alternative way of making things pioneered by the Japanese is now making mass production obsolete. Lean producers are thought to achieve a 2:1 advantage over non-lean producers. This method involves bringing together the activities of managers, employees and suppliers into a tightly integrated system that can respond extremely quickly to changing customer demands. The result is what is called a 'lean production' system which focusses on a removal of all forms of waste from the system, whether parts, people or processes and is explained by Dankbaar (cited in Brown et al., 2001) as:

- making use of the workforce by giving them more than one task
- cross-functional management and employee involvement
- integrating direct and indirect work
- taking advantage of quality circles.

Cross-functional teamwork involves active project-based communication and problem solving. Inevitably this demands a change of organisational culture in order to overcome damaging inter-departmental rivalry, conflict and politics. Often the only way in this can be facilitated is by organisational restructuring and different specialists working together in the same physical location on common problems (the use of quality circles).

Flexible manufacturing is only achieved where 'economies of scope' make it economical to produce small batches of a variety of products with the same machines. This represents a stark contrast to the inflexibility of traditional mass production assembly lines with their emphasis on 'economies of scale'. This leads to the manufacture of a larger variety of products at lower cost and higher quality. For Womack et al. (1990) the position of the customer should be taken whereby six lean principles need to be observed:

1. Solve my problem completely.
2. Don't waste my time.
3. Provide exactly what I want.

4. Deliver value where I want it.
5. Deliver value when I want it.
6. Reduce the number of decisions I must make to solve my problems.

All six principles will provide a definition of value for the customer. Womack et al. describe waste as any human activity that absorbs resources but creates no value. They quote a Toyota executive who categorised waste as:

- product defects
- over-production of goods not needed
- stocks of goods awaiting further processing or consumption
- unnecessary processing
- unnecessary movement of people
- unnecessary transport of goods
- employees waiting for process equipment to finish its work or an upstream activity to be completed.

Coote and Gould (2006) evaluated the work of Womack and applied it to the latter day finance function. They suggest that a further category of waste is the design of goods and services that do not meet the needs of the customer. In the context of finance they suggest ways of delivering customer value without waste, including:

- focussing on products where benchmarking shows high costs for relatively little value
- talking to customers to establish their definition of value
- assigning process ownership, responsibilities and power
- establishing clear and frequent measurement of the process's effectiveness and efficiency
- building a culture of continuous improvement, and using this as a foundation for more transformational change.

From these explanations it is clear that the main characteristics of lean production include flexible workforce practices and high-commitment human resource policies. It will also require a commitment to continuous improvement through the organisation whether inventory management, capacity management or performance enhancement methods.

Despite the obvious advantages of lean production it does have certain limitations and has at times been criticised. For instance, Brown et al. (2001) suggest that it ignores four critical areas of operations:

1. manufacturing's contribution to corporate planning
2. manufacturing strategy
3. the seniority of operations staff
4. potential alliances.

In addition it may not empower employees, indeed it could be seen as a top-down approach forcing employees to devise ways of doing more for less resource.

3.7.1 Managing inventory

From the Toyota listing of 'waste' (specifically over-production of goods not needed, stocks of goods awaiting further processing or consumption) it is clear that lean thinking can be applied to methods for managing inventory. Managing inventory is a major contributor to improving material, customer and information flows from the business to satisfy the needs and wants of the customer. All those studying accountancy will readily recognise that inventory can exist in several forms (raw materials, work in progress, finished goods, etc.). They will also know that stock holding has costs attached to it and such costs may ultimately contribute to an organisation becoming uncompetitive.

Brown et al. (2001) point out that different organisations hold inventory in different places. For example, some sandwich shops only sell pre-packaged food (finished) while others make on site at a special location, and others still hold a combination of raw materials (salads, etc.) and allow customers to customise their basic sandwiches (work in progress). Decisions such as these leads to the concept of 'make-to-order' approaches where inventory is only taken and assembled on receipt of an order or 'make-to-stock' where items are held in anticipation of an order.

There are of course several methods for managing inventory (summarised in Table 3.10) the challenge for organisations is to determine which supports their 'lean' efforts best.

3.7.2 Managing operational capacity

Methods of 'balancing' demand and productive capacity is a key challenge in operations, because in the short term all organisations are capacity-constrained, demand fluctuations impact on inventory management and operations, and demand may exceed supply leading to a reduction in quality.

Table 3.10 Methods for managing inventory

System	Explanation	Usage
Continuous inventory	Levels are continually monitored, and when stock drops below a predetermined level a fixed amount is ordered to 'top up' levels.	The tinned food in person's home or the cleaning materials held are domestic examples. Continuous inventory can be operated using a fixed order quantity replacement system or an Economic Order Quantity system (EOQ), which takes into account variable costs associated with ordering the item and holding the item. The system encourages buffer stocks and reflect 'just in case' rather than 'just in time'.
Periodic inventory (or bin)	Stock levels are checked after a specific time and this leads to variable ordering of new stock.	Commonly used in retail outlets such as a supermarket at the end of a day's trading.
ABC system	ABC is not an acronym, ABC is a classification based on the Pareto 80/20 rule which suggests that 20% of the items are likely to account for 80% of the annual expenditure. ABC focuses on those items that are most important and therefore need careful monitoring.	A: items of high value, close monitoring needed including managing the supplier/buyer relationship. B: medium items less tightly managed. C: low value inventory requiring little management (e.g. nails, screws, tacks, etc.).

There are issues when demand is high. Problems might be avoided by either managing capacity and/or managing levels of demand (usually by applying marketing practices). Supply is inevitably fixed by factors largely internal to the organisation such as facilities, systems, technology, human resources and capability. Demand is by comparison an external force. Inevitably there will be fluctuations between these two dimensions. Three main means are used for balancing capacity and demand, namely: level capacity, chase and demand management strategies.

1. *Level capacity strategies* involve the organisation building inventory levels so that these excess stores can be used to deal with increases in demand beyond capacity. Clearly this has cost implications and will not apply to service organisations where excesses of demand over capacity will result in queues (a good example being waiting lists for operations in the UK's National Health Service).
2. *Chase strategies involve* constantly adjusting organisational activity levels to shadow fluctuations in demand. This is difficult for a fixed workforce operating under rigid conditions.
3. *Demand management strategies* involve attempts to influence demand to smooth variations above or below capacity. For example a football club that has to maximise attendance for an upcoming fixture against 'unattractive' opposition in a minor competition might introduce a two people for one ticket price scheme or a 'kids go free' with an adult initiative. Table 3.11 summarises the main approaches available to service organisations.

McDonald (2008) explains that in reality most organisations combine several approaches when managing capacity. She cites the example of Ikea stores with:

- large warehouses containing goods that have yet to be ordered
- extended opening times over Christmas periods in order to cater for extra demand
- price cutting in order to shift products that have gone out of fashion.

In terms of supply of goods, most modern manufacturing processes now utilise the *computer-aided design* (CAD) and *computer-aided manufacturing* (CAM) operations. CAD and CAM are also the keys to flexible manufacturing as they enable computerised machines to perform a variety of functions. Computer-aided design and computer-aided manufacturing (CAM) can help an organisation:

- provide flexibility to meet customer requirements more fully
- eliminate mistakes
- reduce material wastage.

These advances work towards world class manufacturing performance. When CAD and CAM are integrated it is possible to achieve *computer-integrated manufacturing* (CIM)

Table 3.11 Main approaches for managing service capacity

Through managing demand	Through managing supply
• Complementary services	• Sharing capacity
• Reservations	• Cross-training employees (multi-skilling)
• Price incentives	• Part-time employees
• Off-peak demand	• Flexible working patterns

Source: Based on Fitzsimmons and Fitzsimmons (2004)

whereby a system directs data flow whilst also directing the processing and movements of material.

These IT developments may be allied to production techniques such as *Just In Time* (JIT) methods of production which according to CIMA (2004) 'is driven by demand for finished products whereby each component on a production line is produced only when needed for the next stage'.

A systems' ability to accommodate significant changes in volume, capacity or capability can prove an invaluable source of organisational competitive advantage. *Flexible Manufacturing Systems* (FMS) react to both predicted and unpredicted changes. This might take the form of machine flexibility to produce new product types and change the order of operations conducted on a part.

Exercise 3.10

What measurements of performance might be developed for a production department?

Solution

- Degree of flexibility
- Time taken to acknowledge an order to the customer
- Time taken to process orders into a form acceptable to the factory
- Speed of dispatch to the customer
- Quality achieved.

Queuing theory is the study of waiting times through mathematical analysis of related processes. The theory enables performance measures to be calculated including:

- average waiting times for a product or service
- the expected number of customers (or clients or patients) waiting at a particular time
- the probability of encountering the system that is either empty or full (e.g. such as arriving at a hospital department).

Within the operations system itself recent approaches such as cellular manufacturing have had the effect of altering traditional plant layouts by creating a U-shaped flow of work in which different machines assisted by CAD technology are grouped to make products with similar machining requirements.

The relationship between manufacturing and engineering and maintenance should be acknowledged. *Engineering* is responsible for providing the methods of manufacture. While they work with design engineers, their task is to provide the most economical way of *manufacturing* the product, to pre-agreed quality levels, at pre-planned costs, and in respect of forecast quantities. The *maintenance* function is responsible for the maintenance of the factory buildings, machinery, plant and for power and lighting.

3.7.3 Practices of continuous improvement

There are several practices of quality management that an organisation might operate, some are discussed here.

Quality Circles. Prof. Kaoru Ishikawa, pioneered quality management processes in the Kawasaki shipyards following the Second World War. One concept he introduced was that of the Quality Circle (QC). QCs are small groups of staff that meet on a regular basis to identify quality issues and attempt to formulate solutions. QCs are normally multidisciplinary, and are given a brief to work as a team to identify, investigate, analyse and solve work-related problems or tasks. The basic concept is that QCs form part of an organisation-wide quality control activity.

QCs can help the quality process in a number of ways by:

- using interdisciplinary quality teams to help staff gain a better perspective of the whole organisation and their part within it
- strengthening linkages between functional areas
- devolving authority and responsibility for quality down to the operational level
- fostering commitment and ownership of problems.

Kaizen involves continuous improvement by small incremental steps over a long period. This Japanese concept emphasises providing the workforce with the tools and techniques for improving operations. Maurer (2005) stresses Kaizen's impact in setting and achieving higher standards, and the value of Kaizen events in:

- bringing people together to face up to technical and quality challenges
- encouraging stakeholder involvement and interaction
- allowing participants to leave with a plan in hand.

Some of the most commonly used kaizen tools are reflected in Table 3.12.

Table 3.12 Kaizen tools

Tool	Explanation	Use
PDCA	Use of a plan-do-check-act operating sequence.	A cycle that encourages the key stages to continuous improvement.
The fishbone diagram	A cause and effect diagram used to analyse all contributory causes (or inputs) that result in a single effect (or output). For example, lost sales because of temporarily stock outs would frustrate quality. The cause, however, might be difficult to pin down and may not be due to a single reason. A line is drawn indicating a route to continuous improvement and off this line 'fish bones' will splinter indicating problems that may be encountered. Causes can be arranged into categories (typically systems, technology, people and resources).	A map in the form of a fishbone illustrates all the difficulties and so focusses effort.
The Pareto rule	Vilfredo Pareto identified that 80% of the country's wealth was held by 20% of the population. Similarly 80/20 classifications occurred regularly in most other areas.	The 'rule' encourages a focus of effort on the important 20% in order to be effective.
The five why process	Examine issues by constantly asking 'why' until the real issue is identified.	First developed at Toyota; it encourages employee problem solving.

5-S practice is a technique used to improve both the physical and the thinking environment of the organisation. It encourages standardisation of procedures, and is devised to improve the clarity of management processes. 5-S is based upon five Japanese terms 'seiri, seiton, seiso, seiktsu and shitsuke' or 'organisation, neatness, cleanliness, standardised cleanup and discipline' (interpreted below):

S-word	Meaning	Example
Structurise	Organise	Delete old information, throw away unwanted items
Systematise	Neatness	Clear organisation of documents and filing system
Sanitise	Cleanliness	Individual responsibility for own tidiness and cleaning
Standardise	Standardise	Transparency of storage and filing systems
Self-discipline	Discipline	Do the above daily

Six Sigma reduces variation in a product offering. It is a methodology that strives for near perfection. It is a data-driven approach for eliminating defects (aiming towards six standard deviations between the mean and the nearest specification limit) in any process. To achieve Six Sigma, a process must not exceed 3.4 defects per million opportunities (where a defect is anything outside of customer specifications).

Exercise 3.11

What does an organisation need to adopt the Six Sigma philosophy?

Solution

According to The British Quality Foundation an organisation needs:

- the tools
- the methodology
- training
- metrics
- total commitment from executive level
- significant culture change.

3.8 Planning quality programmes

The British Quality Foundation (2005) observe that:

Successful programmes require tenacity and dedication to the pursuit of perfection

Lynch (1999) reflecting on organisational difficulties in getting quality initiatives successfully implemented observes that:

Quality is a symptom, an expression of healthy management in an organisation, a reflection of personal responsibility taken by staff. If staff think too much about their delivery of quality, they may ignore the customer – consequently it is not important to 'think quality'. Staff need to 'think customer' and as a result 'be quality'.

Lynch's argument is that generally organisations exist to provide a consistency of goods or services to their customers or clients. Achieving consistency means setting customer expectations at an achievable level, and comprises delivery at the right time, meeting expectations of the customer and differentiating the organisation from competitors.

Exercise 3.12

What suggestions can you give to a car manufacturer that wants to begin thinking about how to improve its quality?

Solution

The first step for an organisation wishing to move towards the Japanese concept of quality management is to clarify the meaning of 'quality' in its particular sphere of operations. It might be looked at in terms of 'fitness for purpose' from the viewpoint of the customers. The focus of quality is to satisfy customer expectations and anticipate their needs. From this viewpoint, there can be no automatic assumption that a luxury car, such as a Rolls-Royce, is better than a mass-produced vehicle. The issue of respective quality has to be defined in terms of customer expectations of the product and its price.

3.8.1 Implementing TQM

Total Quality Management should involve embedding shared beliefs and standards permanently. It should not be considered a one-off, quick-fix exercise, as implementation requires thorough planning and a clear implementation strategy if it is to succeed. The decision to implement a TQM programme is a long-term commitment for an organisation and early TQM pioneers expected it to take up to 20 years before the full benefits were realised. (Current thinking suggests that the quest for quality may never be finished but it is still a worthwhile journey.)

One of the first stages of a quality implementation programme is education and training. In order for staff to understand the processes and benefits of a TQM approach, it is important to consult and communicate organisational objectives of introducing TQM. This may involve the following phases:

- *Senior management consultancy.* Senior managers must first be trained at the strategic level, in order to be able to lead and drive the quality programme.
- *Establishment of a quality steering committee/council.* Team members should be drawn from all levels of the organisation, and all disciplines. The quality team/council must also be trained in the TQM philosophy so that they can participate in the training programme as it is cascaded through the organisation.
- *Carry out organisation-wide presentations/training sessions.* This will be general training in the quality philosophy and its long-term benefits, followed by more specific quality-training sessions on an ongoing basis. It is critical that clear communication of the quality message is carried out at an early stage and is then reinforced on a regular basis. As already stated, poor communication will lead to lack of understanding of the purpose and benefits, mistrust and poor feedback.
- *Establish quality circles.* The next stage is to get key personnel actively involved in the process. This will involve establishing a number of quality circles and training in problem-solving and quality-related data collection.
- *Documentation.* It is important that the processes, procedures and activities undertaken throughout the implementation of a quality programme is thoroughly and clearly documented and evidenced. This will help to ensure continuity as the programme develops, and from an important aspect of quality auditing. It will also aid communication of quality procedures and successes.

- *Monitor and report back.* Feedback is also crucial. Quality targets need to be set and actual results monitored against these targets and standards on a regular basis. The successes (and failures) of the approach must be reported.

The successful implementation of TQM is a long-term process and problems are almost inevitable at some points because of the radical nature of the changes involved. In some ways managing the introduction of TQM is like any major organisational change, but common reasons for failure in TQM programmes include:

- *Tail-off.* After an initial burst of enthusiasm, top management fails to maintain interest and support.
- *Deflection.* Other initiatives or problems deflect attention from TQM.
- *Lack of buy-in.* Management pays only lip service to the principle of worker involvement and open communication.
- *Rejection.* TQM is not compatible with the organisation's wider culture and ways of doing things. For example the cultural emphasis does not change from punishing mistakes to encouragement and rewards.

3.9 Supplier relationships

Three key factors contributing to world-class manufacturing in the Japanese organisations seemed to be:

1. operations processes being highly integrated so that parts travel the minimum distance and the production flow is free of interruptions
2. team leaders involving employees, maintaining concern for quality and developing problem-solving skills
3. the existence of tightly integrated value chains.

Relationships between the firms in the value system matter. A firm might maximise returns by striking good deals with suppliers (low prices) and customers (high prices) to take as much of the available 'value' (difference between the revenue received and costs) for itself. Alternatively, the firm might collaborate with others in the system to increase total value. This would involve increasing the ability of the final product to generate satisfaction (reflected in the price) by working together to reduce the total costs in the value system. Critically, the role of the supply chain and strategic supply networks could be key in gaining competitive advantage, including the development and maintenance of supplier relationships. Viewed in this way, supply chain management assumes the significance of a strategic process.

Contemporary developments reflect a strategic redefinition of the boundaries of organisations. Some organisations are rethinking what should be researched, designed, made or assembled under direct control which in turn involves long-term alliances in a supply chain.

Networks have been described as a link between supplier and purchaser in the supply chain but a more accurate and useful division is between different suppliers, and the co-ordination methods employed within the firms. Savings based on mutual learning and experience can become a competitive advantage. Ody (2000) observed:

The supply chain used to be simple, serial and linear, with raw materials moving slowly through manufacturing production and onward via the distribution system to retailers and end-consumers.

Today, talk is of 'supply networks', 'parallel chains', 'enhanced concurrent activities', and 'synchronised supply models', with information technology set to cut both inventory and lead times throughout the pipeline still further.

The new supply chain model demands seamless integration of software and systems and 'visibility' throughout the network so that all trading partners are singing from the same 'available-to-promise' song sheet.

Information sharing is crucial to gaining mutual advantages with suppliers through outlining future requirements so allowing the supplier to plan ahead or collaborating with partners for example to develop improvements in packaging design by sharing knowledge of the latest technologies available (Goldsmith and Samson, 2004).

It is important that quality implementation is monitored and audited on a regular basis, in order to continually assess and improve processes. A quality audit should be a systematic inspection to appraise whether quality activities achieve the planned objectives, and whether the activities have been carried out effectively.

3.9.1 Supply chain management

Supply chain management, and hence supplier relationships, are often explained with reference to Porter's value chain and value systems (see earlier). According to Christopher (2005):

> The supply chain is the network of organisations that are involved, through upstream and downstream linkages, in the different processes and activities that produce value in the form of products and services in the hands of the ultimate consumer.

Supply chain management is the entire chain leading to the end customer in which the firm concerned will be only one link.

Logistics management is most well known in its military application: the development of procurement, storage and supply lines to support battlefield troops. Both Napoleon and Hitler lost armies and eventually campaigns when their logistic chains into Russia became too long to maintain and defend. However, very similar concerns face burger bars, retail stores, car manufacturers and airlines as they attempt geographical expansion. Logistics management deals with issues such as:

- procurement management
- materials movement and storage
- finished inventory
- moving of finished goods through distribution channels.

Supply chain management considers logistics but also relationships between members of the supply chain, identification of end-customer benefit and the organisational consequences of greater inter-firm integration to form 'network organisations'. According to Christopher (2005), several forces have led to this radical rethink:

> *The customer service explosion.* Customers have come to expect service excellence and will leave any firm that does not provide it. This increasingly means reliable availability and on-time delivery of the final product. This demands that all links in the supply chain can provide the same to their downstream customers.
>
> *Time compression.* Short product life cycles and rapid new product development are the norm. Thus the supply pipeline must be short to avoid slow response and lots of obsolete product and inventory.
>
> *Globalisation of industry.* Many organisations operate globally and depend on a complex web of international transfers of materials, components and finished product. Many

seek to use logistics to combine the benefits of the economies of scale from volume production with the potential to customise products to the needs of local markets.

Organisational integration. Classical organisation theory believed in chopping businesses up into departments and divisions. This puts barriers up to the sorts of communication and information flows that are essential to meet the fast-changing needs of customers and challenges of competition. Consequently teams are the norm, backed up by partnerships between suppliers and their customers.

Supply chain management has three themes:

1. *Responsiveness.* Firms must be able to supply their customers quickly. This has led systems such as JIT.
2. *Reliability.* These deliveries must be reliable. This means that there must be transparency in the supply chain such that upstream firms can 'see the order coming' from the customer well in advance.
3. *Relationships.* Responsiveness demands that members of the supply chain develop a high degree of mutual understanding of each other's methods and trust in each other's ability to supply. This cannot be sustained if the former confrontational model of customer/supplier relations is used where each constantly looks for better deals elsewhere. Single sourcing and long-term contracts are the norm in modern supply chain management.

Effective supply chain management can be achieved through:

- *Creating a logistics vision.* This is deciding how relative strengths can be used to deliver customer value. It will require the firm to identify which activities it excels at and which it should contract out. For example, a national retail and wholesale newsagents found that it excelled at the shop and warehouse elements of the supply chain from publisher to reader. However, its attempts to manage a delivery company and lorry fleet were abandoned and contracted out. Trying to do it all leaves the entire supply chain only as good as its weakest link, which may not be good enough in a competitive world.
- *Develop the logistics organisation.* Traditional organisational structures are divisionalised into separate business functions (marketing, production, sales, etc.), and each is arranged hierarchically. This impedes information flows and leads to inventory being built up at the interfaces. This should be replaced with a 'horizontal organisation' that focusses the key processes of supply chain management on the customer.
- *Increase integration.* The organisation and its upstream and downstream partners should be linked by information. This necessitates the following supply chain policies:
  (a) Supply base rationalisation: That is, cut the number of suppliers and let each supply more of the final assemblies or components. This enables closer relationships to be built.
  (b) Supplier development programmes: Cross-functional specialists work with supplier organisations to improve quality and ensure process improvement.
  (c) Early supplier involvement in design: Let the supplier help design cost-effective components for the finished product.
  (d) Integrated information systems, replacing paper orders and instructions to suppliers with information networks. For example, by using computer-aided design (CAD), suppliers can have access to the firm's designs and so get working on designing components quicker. Similarly, electronic data interchange (EDI) is much quicker and more accurate than oral or paper orders. If these EDI orders originate from the point at which the customer orders the product, then suppliers can fine-tune their supply better.

(e) Centralisation of inventory: The final sales point carries a minimum of inventory but instead is able to gain access to the supply chain database to specify products on a 'cook to order' basis.

- *Manage the supply chain as a network*. This replaces the 'us and them' mentality of the conventional buyer/seller relationship with one based on collaboration and common interest. Elements of this include:

(a) Collective strategy development: All members of the network share their strategic thinking.

(b) Win-win thinking: An end to thinking that the only way to increase the firm's profits is to strike harder bargains with upstream and downstream partners. All partners come to believe they are better off by collaboration.

(c) Open communication: This involves EDI links but also *open book accounting* in which cost data is shared with upstream and downstream partners to ensure that all partners are paid reasonable fees and there are no suspicions of excessive profits being enjoyed by one member of the network.

3.9.2 The lean supply chain

The main objective of developing a lean supply chain is the complete removal of waste in order to achieve a competitive advantage. That advantage can be achieved by both the reduction of costs and the improvement of quality (whether product or service). Other benefits of lean supply are claimed to be:

- reduced inventories (and thus improved cash flow and profit)
- shorter lead-times, and thus faster delivery to consumers
- fewer bottlenecks, so better utilisation of resources, and further improvements to profit
- fewer quality problems, so less re-work, lower costs of quality failure, and happier consumers.

These obvious advantages should to a degree be balanced against the possible disadvantages of the lean chain approach, including the potential for large, powerful customers dominating lean supply chains. In addition, there may be a concentration on reducing cost rather than improving quality. Any resulting savings may be kept as increased margins, rather than being passed on to the customer. Too much concentration on cost reduction may, in fact, worsen quality or at least increase the risk of quality failure.

3.10 Summary

This chapter has described the nature and significance of operations and demonstrated how it supports other aspects of the organisation, both manufacturing and service. It has then considered certain key dimensions of operations and its strategic importance. The influence of Japanese thinking on Western organisations to bring about fundamental changes in quality has been explored and concepts of quality and the accompanying changes required to organisational approaches and systems have also been dealt with.

References and further reading

Bowhill, B. (2008) *Business Planning and Control*. Sussex: John Wiley & sons.
Brown, S., Blackmon, K., Cousins, P. and Maylor, H. (2001) *Operations Management. Policy, Practice and Performance Improvement*. Butterworth-Heinemann.

Christopher, M. (2005) *Logistics and Supply Chain Management* (3rd edn). London: Harlow : Financial Times Prentice Hall.

CIMA (2005) *CIMA Official Terminology*. CIMA publishing, Elsevier.

Coote, P. and Gould, S. (2006) Lean management. *Financial Management*, March, p. 31(3).

Cousins, P. D. (2000) An investigation into supply base restructuring. *European Journal Purchasing Supply Management*, Vol. 5, No. 2, pp. 143–155.

Crosby, P. B. (1979) *Quality is Free: The Art of Quality Certain*. New York: McGraw-Hill.

Galloway, L. (1998) *Principles of Operations Management* (2nd edn). Thompson.

Gargan, J. (2004) Hello, good buys. *Financial Management*, November.

Glass, N. M. (1991) *Pro-active Management*. New York: Continuum International Publishing.

Goldsmith, S. and Samson, D. (2004) Sustainable *Development and Business Success: Reaching beyond the Rhetoric to Superior Performance* Foundation for Sustainable Economic Development in the Department of Management, University of Melbourne, March, 2004.

Hammer, M. and Champy, J. (2001) *Reengineering the Corporation: A Manifesto for Business Revolution* (3rd edn). London: Nicholas Brearley.

Kaplan, R. S. and D. P. Norton. (1996) *The Balanced Scorecard: Translating Strategy into Action*. Boston: Harvard Business School Press.

Lynch, D. (1999) Focus on quality. *Management Accounting*, September.

McDonald, I. (2008) Organisational Management and Information Systems, study notes. *Financial Management*, December, pp. 54–55.

Maurer, R. (2005) Stop me before I Kaizen again. *Journal for Quality & Participation*, Summer, Vol. 28, No. 2, p. 37.

Mintzberg, H. (1990) *The Structuring of Organisations: A Synthesis of the Research*. Englewood Cliffs, NJ: Prentice Hall International.

Mintzberg, H. (1983) *Structures in Fives: Designing Effective Organizations*. Englewood Cliffs, NJ: Prentice Hall International.

Ody, P. (2000) Working towards a total, visible network. *Financial Times Survey,* October 25, Times Newspapers Limited, London.

Ouchi, W. (1982) *Theory Z: How American Businesses can Meet the Japanese Challenge*. Reading, MA: Addison-Wesley Pub Co.

Parasuraman, A., Berry, L. and Zeithaml, V. A. (1988) SERVQUAL: A multiple-item scale for measuring consumer perceptions of service quality, *Journal of Retailing,* 64(1) pp. 12–40.

Parasuraman, A., Berry, L. and Zeithaml, V. A., (1991) Refinement and reassessment of the SERVQUAL scale. *Journal of Retailing*, pp. 420–450.

Porter, M. E. (1985) *Competitive Advantage: Creating and Sustaining Superior'Performance*. London, New York: Free Press, Collier Macmillan.

Reck, R. F. and Long, B. G. (1988) Purchasing: a competitive weapon. *International Journal Purchasing Materials Manual*, Fall, pp. 2–8.

Robbins Gentry, C. (2007) Back-room secrets. *Chain Store Age*, March, Vol. 83, No. 3, p. 66.

Rudzki, R. A. (2006) World-class supply practices boost shareholder value. *Financial Executive 22.3*, April 2006, Vol. 56, No. 3.

Womack, J. P., Jones, D. T. and Roos, D. (1990) *The Machine that Changed the World*. New York: Simon & Schuster.

Also:

Crown Prosecution Service
www.cps.gov.uk/Publications/finance/process_mapping.html

Thames Valley Probation Service
www.thamesvalleyprobation.gov.uk/about/about_eem.html

The British Quality Foundation
www.quality-foundation.co.uk/pi_sixsigmaservice.htm

Revision Questions 3

❓ Question 1

1.1 According to Porter's value chain the final primary activity is referred to as

   (A) Marketing and sales
   (B) Outbound logistics
   (C) Procurement
   (D) Service **(2 marks)**

1.2 Approval of documentation, procedures manuals and work instructions are associated with

   (A) registration under the standards required for quality certification
   (B) total quality management (TQM)
   (C) appraisal costs
   (D) job evaluation **(2 marks)**

1.3 Compare and contrast Kaizen and Business Process Re-engineering (BPR) (50 word limit) **(4 marks)**

❓ Question 2

YO employs buyers, designers, machinists and tailors to produce coats, jackets, trousers, dresses and skirts that its sales team sells. YO has a long-standing relationship with MX which sells directly to the public from a chain of out-of-town stores. Over 80% of YO's sales are to MX whose approach has been to sell clothing in great volumes at lower prices than the high street stores. It expects its suppliers (including YO) to 'take account of' new fashion designs and manufacture its clothes at competitive prices.

MX is rethinking its strategy and wishes to move more 'up market' by introducing a better quality clothing range, which it believes that its customers will be prepared to pay a little more for. Already YO has noticed that MX has started to be more demanding and has sent back any batches they feel are in the slightest way unsuitable.

MX want to work with fewer suppliers but develop a better relationship with each of them. MX wants to renegotiate its contract with YO (which expires soon in any case). MX are prepared to talk with YO about the need to improve the quality of their products and has indicated that if it receives the right assurances it would be prepared to pay a slightly higher unit cost per item. They also propose to work more closely with YO's designers to maximise production of the type of clothing that they feel their customers want.

If these talks are unsuccessful MX will use one of their other suppliers when the existing contract expires. (YO is aware that MX has experimented by using a few trusted overseas suppliers who have managed to achieving both relatively low price and superior quality through the adoption of total quality management (TQM) techniques).

Anxious to maintain their relationship with MX, YO recognises that it must change from its present focus on price to one that includes quality considerations.

Requirements
(a) Evaluate the way in which MX is proposing to manage its suppliers as part of a value system or network. **(10 marks)**
(b) Explain the term 'total quality' and the requirements of achieving it within YO. **(10 marks)**

(Total = 20 marks)

Question 3

The divisional managing director of the organisation that you work for has proposed a total quality management (TQM) programme to help change prevailing attitudes and improve results. You have been asked to prepare a report for the next management board meeting as a basis for constructive discussion as to how the TQM programme should be implemented.

Requirements
(a) Explain the critical success factors for the implementation of a programme of total quality management. **(7 marks)**
(b) Explain the categorisation of quality costs and how such a categorisation could be of assistance in the establishment of a TQM programme. **(6 marks)**

(Total = 13 marks)

Question 4

4.1 Quality management thinker J. M. Juran once suggested that 85% of the organisation's quality problems are

   (A) a result of ineffective control by supervisors and managers
   (B) a result of ineffective systems
   (C) a result of ineffective workers
   (D) a result of ineffective incentive bonus schemes **(2 marks)**

4.2 The five S (5-S) practice is a technique aimed at

   (A) effective investment of resources in training and recruitment
   (B) standardised procedures to improve the physical and thinking organisational environments
   (C) excellence in strategy, style, skills, staff and structure
   (D) diversity of activity and independence of thought in order to achieve closeness to the customer **(2 marks)**

Each of the sub-questions below require a brief written response. This response can be in note form and should not exceed 50 words. Each of these sub-questions are worth 4 marks each.

4.3 Explain the relationship between a JIT system and cash flow management. **(4 marks)**

4.4 Explain how computer software can assist in achieving quality in a manufacturing organisation. **(4 marks)**

4.5 Distinguish quality control from quality circles. **(4 marks)**

Solutions to Revision Questions 3

✓ Solution 1

1.1 (D)

1.2 (A)

1.3

Both:
- Associated with quality
- Aim for beneficial change and enhanced performance
- Customer-focused
- Involve learning.

Kaizen	BPR
Continuous improvement	One-off exercise
Small incremental steps	Radical changes
Longer term	Short term
Providing workforce with tools & techniques	About business processes and structures & creative use of IT

✓ Solution 2

(a) Evaluate the way in which MX is proposing to manage its suppliers as part of a value system or network.

Most products arise through several organisations combining and trading with one another from sourcing raw materials, to design, development, manufacture and then bringing the final product to market. In these circumstances relationships between several organisations combine to create a value network comprising of a series of value chains.

Both MX and YO form part of a wider value network with YO undertaking the design and manufacture stages. In this example YO represents the supplier value chain whilst MX's own value chain interacts with the final customer. (YO presumably also has a supplier or suppliers of cloth that it makes designs for and then manufactures clothing from).

Michael Porter's work in this area stresses the need for good management of the value network in order to gain competitive advantage and 'create and sustain superior performance'.

In Porter's terms relationships between the firms in the value system matter. The overall value system describes the position of a firm relative to the firms upstream and downstream of it:

- MX is upstream (nearer the ultimate customer) of YO
- YO along with MX's other suppliers are downstream of MX
- YO's suppliers of cloth are downstream of YO.

When viewing supply strategically the nature of relationships with suppliers becomes key. When relationships are based on driving down price they can be quite adversarial. Alternatively, more collaborative arrangements operate where there is a joint quest to reduce costs and a sharing of technology and innovations (known as 'partnership sourcing').

The way an organisation manages its supply process is known as its 'sourcing strategies' and the success of these clearly has strategic implications. MX in the past appeared to favour a traditional strategy known as the 'multiple' option. Here MX as the buyer chooses several sources of supply (both home and abroad). Individual suppliers under this arrangement become less powerful and prices can be driven down as a result. It is fairly obvious that YO is far more dependent upon MX (as its number one customer with 80% of its sales) than MX is on YO. MX seems to have realised however that this may not be necessarily conducive to good working relationships. Meaningful supplier relationships and reliance on trusted suppliers is necessary in order to achieve a quality product. In the past MX have relied on low prices in order to make sales but now it is rethinking its strategy and wishes to move more 'up market' by introducing a better quality clothing range, which it believes its customers will be prepared to pay a little more for.

MX propose to work more closely with YO's designers to maximise production of the type of clothing that they feel their customers want. Both organisations have a long-standing relationship with one another, and assuming that YO is prepared to change its approach to one more akin to TQM it will become one of MX's preferred suppliers. This means that with less suppliers MX will be able to concentrate on developing their relationship more fully.

Consistent with Porter's thinking both MX and YO as firms in the value system now have an opportunity to collaborate more fully in order to increase total value. (By increasing the ability of the final product to generate maximum customer satisfaction). In this case it will be through making a better quality product including taking more care to ensure that the design is 'right' (appropriate). Competitive advantage through linkages between the organisation and its value system components is being attempted in this case by applying TQM principles.

(b) Explain the term 'total quality' and the requirements of achieving it within YO.

The underlying concepts of quality
Organisations that compete on the basis of price must ensure low-cost operations to be successful. Cost containment in material sourcing, production, and distribution is important. Resultant cost savings from these activities can (in part) be passed on to their

customers. These organisations believe that their customers value the relatively low cost of the product (commensurate with a certain level of quality). By comparison, a company competing on the basis of quality will try to achieve a better quality product that will appeal to less price-sensitive consumers. In these circumstances quality rather than price will be the key consideration in bringing goods to the market. It is apparent that MX is altering its view of what it believes its customers value most (namely improved quality rather than low cost). This is unsurprising, as quality is increasingly being recognised as a critical issue for modern organisations operating in sometimes hostile environments with intense competition and demanding customers.

MX is said to want to move more 'up market' by introducing an altogether better quality clothing range. This change in strategy will require less of an emphasis on price in favour of approaches that achieve quality. The need to satisfy customers' needs is central to most understandings of quality. Quality should in fact be best understood from the perspective of the customer, including their expectations and specific requirements. MX is by far YO's biggest customer with in excess of 80% of total sales and has made their requirements quite clearly. Given its dependence on MX, YO has little option but to adopt a quality approach in order to satisfy its major customer.

'Total quality'

There are many definitions of quality. Quality guru Philip P Crosby is known for his emphasis on achieving Zero Defects (no faulty products) and maintaining that *Quality is Free*. He explained quality as meaning getting everyone to deliver what he or she has agreed and *getting it right the first time*.

There are a number of approaches to ensuring total quality, most popularly TQM. MX's overseas suppliers apparently are able to achieve relatively low prices and superior quality through the adoption of TQM. This involves developing an organisational culture founded on a belief in quality so that:

- Everyone (including customers and suppliers) is involved in this continuous process.
- The quality requirements of customers are central.
- There is the full commitment of senior management.

Requirements for achieving quality in YO

There are certain fundamental concepts that any organisation wishing to establish a quality ethos must adhere to including:

- *Commitment from the top*. If management is not fully committed, it is unlikely that customer requirements of quality will be met. (In YO's case the commitment is obvious: M is its most significant customer and it must change in order to survive at its present level of operation.)
- *Competence*. Quality is achieved through competence in whatever activity is undertaken. Competence can only be gained through continuous training, skill development and experience. YO needs to commit funds to training, recruitment and people development, etc.
- *Communication*. The importance of quality must be effectively communicated throughout the organisation in order to improve understanding of its purpose and benefits. YO needs to develop a communication strategy that includes briefings, written reminders and visible symbols. The key message for YO is to change practice in order to retain its most important customer: MX.

- *Continuous improvement.* The *Kaizen* philosophy will involve the continual analysis of processes to allow continued improvement in performance and quality. YO will need to develop a non-threatening culture, possibly involving quality circles and training facilitators to ensure that this takes place.

✓ Solution 3

(a) Total quality management (TQM) is defined by CIMA (Official Terminology, 2000):

An integrated and comprehensive system of planning and controlling all business functions so that products or services are produced which meet or exceed customer expectations. TQM is a philosophy of business behaviour, embracing principles such as employee involvement, continuous improvement at all levels and customer focus, as well as being a collection of related techniques aimed at improving quality such as full documentation of activities, clear goalsetting and performance measurement from the customer perspective.

The key factors in the success of TQM:

- There is a concentration on continuous improvement. This means that small improvements are as important as large leaps in technology. Such improvements may be changes in production flow, product specification or manufacturing methods.
- There needs to be widespread commitment to improvement in quality. All those involved in the company are part of the TQM environment: from board to shop floor.
- TQM should focus on the customer, not on just a single area of a business. This customer focus means the perspective of the company changes from its present obvious production/sales/research one. Within the company, all sections may see themselves as potential customers of other sections and potential suppliers to other sections. This refocussing is vital in this company.
- TQM is about designing quality into the product and the production process. This means there must be a close working relationship between sales, production, distribution and research.
- Concentration on short-term profit needs to be abandoned in favour of long-term quality improvement, which will itself lead to long-term profit improvement. This implies being prepared to invest in changes for the future.
- There is a need for a fundamental culture change. Management, in particular, needs to use feedback and appraisal to find better ways of doing things. Failure to meet targets is probably inevitable, but needs to be met with positive, rather than negative, comment.
- There needs to be a clear willingness to discuss and measure quality. This may involve setting standards and gathering information that perhaps has previously been ignored. Feedback information, which need not be quantitative or financial, must be fed back quickly and in an intelligible way.
- Reward systems need to be reorganised to enable and encourage quality, rather than to prevent it happening. Thus, incentive schemes based on improvement suggestions would be a very rapid way of improving quality.

Other factors that might have been identified, though these are by no means always vital:

- Training in areas where the company is felt to be weak. The TQM programme should identify these. Training possibly needs to be external.

- The establishment of project teams to change procedures.
- The establishment of quality circles.
- The establishment of regular reporting of key indicators of quality.

It is difficult to select factors that are more crucial than others: the particular ones of importance will depend on the company and the areas of shortfall. The most crucial overall area, especially in the company quoted, appears to be the building up of teamwork.

(b) Quality cost is normally defined as the 'cost of ensuring and assuring quality, as well as the loss incurred when quality is not achieved' and may be measured in four ways. These four methods have often been called the 'cost of not achieving quality':

1. Prevention cost: The cost of ensuring that poor quality does not happen, e.g. training, planning and administration, checking design is adequate and so on.
2. Appraisal cost: The cost of discovering poor-quality items. This would include quality control, inspections, etc.
3. Internal failure cost: The cost, internal to the company, caused by poor quality. Costs include rework costs, scrap, re-engineering, retooling, etc.
4. External failure cost: The cost of poor quality incurred outside the company: this includes direct costs, such as warranties, repair and after-sales service, and indirect costs such as lost customer goodwill.

These costs are very difficult to isolate and judge. In each area, there is often a need to apportion costs (e.g. training, planning and administration) and there are many areas, especially the external failure cost, where costs cannot be calculated, for example, the opportunity cost of lost sales as a result of poor-quality service.

Nevertheless, striving towards measuring quality costs keeps this issue on the management's agenda. The presence of multiple measures of quality can be helpful in presenting a balanced approach to control and the identification of the key areas for an individual organisation.

Some writers regard the cost of quality as zero, because if TQM is achieved, then none of the costs above will be incurred and so cost is actually reduced. Others see the above costs of quality as being avoidable non-value-adding and therefore costs that might be reduced. This latter view is central to the understanding of how the cost of quality can assist TQM: discovering the cost of wasted resources we have been using to meet current customer standards. It is these costs that need to be reduced and doing so is central to a programme of cost reduction.

Solution 4

4.1 (B)

4.2 (B)

4.3 JIT system:

- purchase and production of goods only when needed
- aim to eliminate unnecessary stock of material/parts.

As less money is tied up in stock, organisational cash flow should improve.

4.4 Software such as computer-aided design (CAD) and computer-aided manufacturing (CAM):

- Provide flexibility to meet customer requirements more fully
- Eliminate mistakes
- Reduce material wastage.

These advances work towards world class manufacturing performance.

4.5

Quality control	Quality circles
Traditionally western approach to production	Associated with Japanese production
Involves inspection of work by third party	Involves collaborative effort
Rejects defective work that is sampled	Allows idea sharing, problem solving and ongoing quality improvement

4

Marketing

Marketing

4

LEARNING OUTCOMES

Marketing accounts for 20 per cent of the overall syllabus. This chapter introduces this important functional area of business, explores major developments in the field and outlines some important marketing tools and techniques. By completing this chapter and the associated readings and questions it should help you to:

- Explain the marketing concept, and the alternatives to it
- Describe the marketing environment of a range of organisations
- Explain marketing in a not-for-profit context
- Explain the social context of marketing behaviour
- Describe theories of consumer behaviour
- Explain the relationships between market research, market segmentation, targeting and positioning
- Apply tools within each area of the marketing mix
- Describe the business contexts within which marketing principles can be applied
- Describe the Market Planning Process
- Explain the role of branding and brand equity.

This chapter provides some basic frameworks and ideas to help appreciate the importance of marketing within the business environment. It describes the marketing tools an organisation will need to compete successfully in contemporary, dynamic and often chaotic markets.

4.1 The marketing concept

Newspapers and other media tend to use 'marketing' as an alternative word to selling, advertising or retailing. Marketing is however a much broader concept embracing all these areas plus many others besides. Marketing is in evidence all around us, from the packaging on the products we buy, to our recognition of companies through their logos and symbols, or the television advertisements we watch. The choices we make as consumers are likely to be shaped in some way by marketing. So what exactly is marketing?

The UK's Chartered Institute of Marketing (CIM) when answering this question suggest that many organisations either knowingly or unknowingly engage in marketing to some degree:

Think about what you do. You probably make a particular effort to know your customers well. Your instincts tell you that getting to know what your customers want on an individual basis and giving it to them is what will keep you in business. You know that you can't stand still, and that you need to improve and extend existing products and sometimes develop new ones. If this description rings true, then your marketing activity closely fits the classical definition of marketing.

CIM defines marketing as:

> the management process responsible for identifying, anticipating and satisfying customer requirements profitably.

This definition acknowledges the importance of the customer, their requirements and the careful planning processes needed to achieve the organisations goals. It follows that marketing is a business activity that should be at the core of any organisation. Marketing is relevant to any organisation irrespective of its size or nature of operation.

Kotler and Armstrong (1994) link the marketing concept with organisational performance maintaining that success "depends on determining the needs and wants of target markets and delivering ... satisfactions more effectively and efficiently than competitors do"

As CIM point out

It is all about getting the right product or service to the customer at the right price, in the right place, at the right time. Business history and current practice both remind us that without proper marketing, companies cannot get close to customers and satisfy their needs. And if they don't, a competitor surely will.

Satisfying customers is at the heart of marketing. Who then assumes responsibility for this important function? Possibly the marketing department or the sales force? True, such personnel can have an influence on customer satisfaction, but marketing as a philosophy is wider than this narrow group of employees. Employees outside the marketing department or sales force can also play an important role in determining customer satisfaction.

Marketing is more than a range of techniques that enables the company to determine customer requirements. It can be better understood as a shared business ethos. The marketing concept is a philosophy that places customers central to all organisational activities. The long-term strategies of an organisation might be centred on profit maximisation, market share growth, or growth in real terms but none of this can be achieved without satisfying customers. Without customers there would be no business.

4.1.1 Differing business philosophies

Organisations that put customer needs first and provide products and services that meet these needs in this way are said to be 'market orientated'. Some organisations however still reject or ignore such a philosophy. For these organisations making products assumes prime concern followed by an attempt to 'get customers'.

Boddy and Paton (2002) distinguish four alternative organisational philosophies. These are given here with the main advantages and disadvantages of each:

- *Product-orientated* organisations have a main focus of product features. This could result in the production of goods with high quality features. Little or no research to identify a demand for the product beforehand means that the organisation risks their products not selling in sufficient numbers.
- *Production-orientated* organisations have a main focus of production efficiency and low costs. Production levels and process changes have no regard to the customer. This means that either too much may be produced (and left unsold) or customers might associate low cost with low quality leading to lower sales.
- *Sales-orientated* organisations have a main aim of selling their goods or service. This implies the need for a keen sales force with clear targets and a focus on short-term cash flow. Ethically questionable, high-pressure sales techniques might not be sustainable longer term as there may be adverse publicity and past customers may be left feeling dissatisfied.
- *Marketing-orientated* organisations have a main focus of the customer and their demands. The benefit is that products offered are determined by consumer demands. Although this may seem preferable it should be conceded that there might be a need for a heavy initial investment of time and effort in achieving such an orientation. To be market (or marketing) orientated is an effective way of implementing the marketing concept.

Exercise 4.1
Reflection
Under which market conditions could product-orientated organisations best succeed?

Solution
Where demand far exceeds supply and the consumer is not discerning due to the shortage of this product or service. Thirty years or so ago this was particularly true within the former Eastern bloc countries where queues formed to buy food and goods irrespective of quality. In some cases those queuing did not know the precise goods they were queuing for!

Stages in the evolution of marketing within the UK can be identified and linked to periods in history:

- *The production era*. The rapid growth in production from factories towards the end of the Industrial Revolution gave rise to this thinking. Rising standards of living fuelled demand, but customer preferences were not accounted for, instead output was maximised wherever possible.
- *The sales era*. 'The depression' due to the downturn in the world economy through to the immediate post-Second World War period provided a background. In order to stay competitive firms needed to *sell* goods rather than just *produce* them. A growing expertise in sales techniques developed including more attention being paid to advertising.
- *The marketing era*. When in the early 1960s demand for goods was matched by supply, organisations began to try to better understand their customer base, and the use of segmentation and differentiation strategies heralded a new era. (Segmentation and differentiation as topics are dealt with later in this chapter.)

Exercise 4.2
For reflection

Does the pace of technological change and heightened customer demand mean another marketing era is about to unfold?

More recently the relevance of the marketing concept as being universally applicable to all organisations in all situations has been questioned. The concept was first articulated in stable markets during a period of post-Second World War growth. With more turbulent environments some thinkers believe that a concentration on the nature of competitive forces is perhaps of greater significance. Houston (1986) controversially suggested that the marketing concept rather than actually leading to improved performance, may cause reduced performance where the costs associated with gathering, disseminating and integrating market information can outweigh the competitive benefits associated with such activities. An organisation adopting a market orientation might be unhelpful when demand for a particular good is lacking.

4.2 The marketing environment

The marketing environment is the surroundings of an organisation. Such factors can impact upon it considerably. The environment has been described as existing at three levels the macro environment, the micro environment and the internal environment.

The macro environment includes all factors that can influence the organisation, but are realistically out of the organisation's control. It might therefore include the laws of a country that the organisation is required to comply with or the aggressive strategies of its competitors. This environment can be quite dynamic and volatile and this will call for organisations to adopt flexible marketing practices in response to changes in culture, politics, economics and technology, etc.

The micro environment includes all factors that can influence the organisation, but the organisation has some opportunity to exercise influence. It consists of the organisation's stakeholders such as suppliers and customers.

The internal environment includes all factors that are internal to the organisation, and are therefore potentially all controllable including its human resource, finance available and assets.

Exercise 4.3

The factors in the macro environment are realistically out of the organisation's control, however is there any way an organisation might seek to exercise some influence?

Solution

An organisation may seek to influence laws through political lobbying or be part of a trade organisation.

Exercise 4.4

An analysis of the dominant forces in the environment of a fast food outlet is suggested below. Perform a similar analysis for your organisation.

	Fast food outlet	**Your organisation**
Macro environment	Food and hygiene legislation, substitute products, competitor pricing policy.	
Micro environment	Suppliers of food, logistical partners, customers, local government officials.	
Internal environment	Workforce, premises, plant and equipment.	

Within the external business environment Johnson, Scholes and Whittington (2008) identify three layers of influence: competitors and markets; industry or sector; and the macro environment (comprising PESTLE factors, see Table 4.1).

4.3 Marketing in a not-for-profit context

There is a vast array of not-for-profit (NFP) organisations including social, health care, political parties, educational, cultural, religious and social cause. Some are extremely large and impact on millions of lives. Whilst private sector organisations may try to communicate with their customers NFPs need to reach several groups with their marketing efforts, including:

- contributors (of money, time, etc.),
- customers (often referred to in a different way such as client or patient, etc.), and
- volunteers and other supporters.

Although the CIM definition of marketing stresses 'profitability' marketing guru Philip Kotler was the first to propose the relevance of marketing to NFP organisations including

Table 4.1 The PESTLE factors framework

Political	**Technological**
Government stability	Spending on research
Regulations (e.g. concerning foreign trade)	Industry focus on technological effort
Taxation policies	New discoveries/developments
	Speed of technology transfer
	Rates of obsolescence
Economic	**Legal**
Inflation	Competition laws
Unemployment	Employment laws
Trade cycles	Health and safety laws
Interest rates	Product safety
Levels of disposable income	
Sociocultural	**Environmental**
Demographic trends	Environmental protection laws
Income distribution	Waste disposal
Life-style changes	Energy consumption
Attitudes to work, leisure, consumption, etc.	
Consumerism	
Social mobility	

Source: Based on Johnson, Scholes and Whittington (2008)

charities, hospitals, political parties and universities and local authorities. Indeed marketing has been embraced with varying degrees of enthusiasm and success within this sector. Many NFP have not adopted the marketing concept at all. It is at this stage worthwhile perhaps highlighting the particular features associated with NFP organisations, namely:

- NFPs are subject to tighter legislative requirements,
- heightened issues of achieving value for money often arise, and
- customers may be a different grouping from those paying for the service to be provided.

These factors dictate that marketing practices adopted by other sectors may need to be adapted and modified by an NFP organisation.

4.3.1 Marketing for Charities

Bruce (2005) believes that charities have to improve their focus on the needs and wants of all different customer groups:

- beneficiaries (users, clients, members, etc.),
- supporters, and
- regulators.

He goes on to argue that commercial marketing concepts can be adapted to suit voluntary and community organisations through relationship marketing, partnership marketing, and cause marketing. (Cause marketing involves the cooperative efforts of a business and a charity for mutual benefit and so goes much further than the organisation merely making a charitable donation.)

With thousands of charities world wide (there are over 200,000 registered charities in the UK alone), competition for voluntary giving is intense. Those charities employing the most appropriate marketing practices are most likely to lever the generosity of peoples' time and money for their particular cause. Branding in particular is important in communicating a particular charity's core values, and distinguishing it from another.

4.3.2 Marketing for non-governmental organisations

Non-governmental organisations (NGOs) were first conceived as part of a United Nations Charter as a non-profit making international organisation made by members of two or more states. Although development-orientated NGOs predate the UN charter they have grown in number over the past 50 years and there are in excess of 20,000 international NGOs. NGOs are above politics and dedicated to a common cause. (Amnesty International and the International Committee of the Red Cross are examples of NGOs). NGOs play an important role in international development directing development funds from donors and agencies to the point of need, while setting aside profit or politics. NGOs use marketing to:

- to find a position for themselves within the market
- to distinguish client and donors needs
- to formulate and communicate NGO requirements
- to gain new supporters.

4.3.3 Marketing for the public sector

The public sector is a broad category for many different sorts of organisation and functions. Within local government for instance there are very many differing services each

Table 4.2 Public sector/customer exchanges

Public sector organisation	Organisation exchanges	Customers exchange
Museum	Culture	Time
	Education	Interest
	Entertainment	Donations
		Entry Fee
University	Education	Fees
	Qualifications	Time
	Career	Commitment
Local Authority	Local services	Payments through taxation
	Lifestyle	Votes

Source: adapted from Lancaster and Withey (2006)

using marketing techniques in different ways for leisure, culture and the arts, to regeneration, education and social services, etc.

Lancaster and Withey (2006) draw reference to the exchange that takes place between the public sector and its customers (see Table 4.2).

Proctor (2007) examines the role of marketing in public organisations, and views it from the perspective of creating value for different organisational stakeholders through a philosophy based on setting a vision, creating and communicating values and establishing a shared culture.

Within the UK, political reforms have pushed the public sector into a more commercial and managerial style meaning some managers need to make marketing decisions. A considerable amount of market research has in any case carried out on behalf of public sector bodies such as the national or local government. Social problems concerning (say) the elderly or disabled may call for information about their opinions and circumstances to help inform policy decisions. The possible disadvantage of market research for smaller public sector bodies is the cost of conducting a 'professional' research project. There might be a temptation for an organisation to use its own staff to do research, with the result that the findings might be incomplete, biased or misleading.

4.4 The social context of marketing behaviour

4.4.1 Social marketing

Social marketing uses commercial marketing practices to achieve non-commercial goals. The term social marketing refers to the application of marketing to the solution of social and health problems (Kotler and Zaltman, 1971). Social marketing is based on the logic that if marketing techniques can encourage people to buy products such as a fizzy drink brand or a particular telephone handset then it can also encourage people to adopt 'beneficial' behaviours for their own good and the good of others (see Table 4.3).

Merit goods are commodities that an individual or society think they should have on the basis that it is 'good' for them. Governments often provide merit goods 'free at the point of use' and then finances them through general taxation (e.g. in the UK access to health care through the National Health Service). Demerit goods are the exact opposite of merit goods and negative consequences can arise from their consumption for society as a whole. It is human behaviour that causes many of society's problems (e.g. the spread of sexually transmitted diseases, road traffic accidents, smoking tobacco, unwanted pregnancies, etc.).

Table 4.3 Social marketing definitions

Social marketing	The systematic application of marketing, alongside other concepts and techniques, to achieve specific behavioural goals for a social good
Health related social marketing	The systematic application of marketing, alongside other concepts and techniques, to achieve specific behavioural goals, to improve health and reduce inequalities

Source: National Social Marketing Centre (2008)

Social marketing can be applied to promote merit goods and encourage society to avoid demerit goods. Social marketing involves the systematic application of marketing along with other concepts and techniques to achieve specific behavioural goals for the wider good of society. This may include persuading people (for instance) refraining from smoking in public places, reducing the speed at which they travel in cars or practice 'safe sex'.

According to the National Social Marketing Centre (2008) the following features and concepts are key to understanding social marketing:

- A strong customer orientation with importance attached to understanding where the customer is starting from, their knowledge, attitudes and beliefs, along with the social context in which they live and work.
- A clear focus on understanding existing behaviour and key influences upon it, and developing clear behavioural goals.
- Using a mix of different methods to achieve a particular behavioural goal.
- Audience segmentation to target efforts more effectively.
- Use of the 'exchange' concept (understanding what is being expected of an individual, and the real cost to them).
- Use of the 'competition' concept (understanding factors that impact on people and that compete for their attention and time).

4.4.2 Corporate social responsibility in a marketing context

Holme and Watts (2000) define Corporate Social Responsibility (CSR) as:

> the continuing commitment by business to behave ethically and contribute to economic development while improving the quality of life of the workforce and their families as well as of the local community and society at large

It should be acknowledged that there are many alternative definitions and that interpretations of the concept vary throughout the world. The European interpretation is focussed on operating the core business in a socially responsible way, complemented by investment in communities for sound business reasons.

Accountability can be viewed as a corporate concept, in this case the organisation being accountable to society at large. As with all areas of business, ethics and responsibility to society is a relevant issue. Certain questions naturally arise in relation to marketing including:

- To whom do we sell?
- Are our products of an appropriate standard, safe and produced to environmental standards?
- How do we advertise: is it fair balanced and truthful?
- Do we have policies that address the concerns of dissatisfied customers?
- Is our pricing or advertising policy exploitive of any groups in society, etc.?

The basis of social responsibility is the premise that an organisation enjoys certain benefits of society and in return should engage in practices that supports rather than exploits society. The following article extract illustrates an interesting dilemma for the fast food giant McDonald's as it considers whether it should adjust one aspect of its marketing mix (the product) or not in the USA.

Exercise 4.5

As you read this short passage make notes on the significant factors in the macro environment (PESTLE factors) and the ethical issues arising.

Why McD's hasn't cut the fat. Fast-food leader fears oil change will leave bad taste among its fry fans

When McDonald's Corp. announced it would move to a trans-fat-free oil, the impact was immediate as consumers flooded the fast feeder with complaints that its fries didn't taste as good. But in actuality the taste was the same, the company hadn't yet switched oils, and some four years later it still hasn't.

Now the share leader is still struggling to make good on its 2002 vow as the pressure mounts from rivals such as Wendy's and KFC, which have cut trans fats from their menus and Burger King, which will start testing new oil within 90 days. McDonald's, meanwhile, has yet to put an end date on its super-secret tests.

It's understandable that McDonald's would be ambivalent about changing its signature fried potatoes, which helped shape the Golden Arches. Fries rank second only to beverages as the chain's margin-leading item and are the undisputed leader in quality and taste among McDonald's peers, said executives close to the marketer.

'In a category where there are low quality ratings of food, the fries are always rated high, and they are inexorably linked to the brand, perhaps more than any other product', said one executive, comparing McDonald's trans-fat conundrum to New Coke. 'That would be the one thing you wouldn't want to mess with if you didn't have to.'

Yet McDonald's has to, unless it wants to go toe-to-toe with municipalities mandating that it has to go trans-fat-free.

And that raises the specter of a public-relations nightmare, no matter what McDonald's does. If it changes its oil, the company will likely encounter the same kind of consumer push back it felt in 2002. If it keeps trans-fat oil, the chain could get lambasted by health advocates.

Source: Extracted from *Why McD's hasn't cut the fat*, by MacArthur, Kate, Advertising Age, 11/6/2006

☑ Solution

You could have made notes in the following areas:

- *Socio-cultural trends*. A desire for fast food as part of a busy lifestyle. Fast food has become an American way of life. There is still a taste by customers for full fat fries (chips). In society generally there are concerns over healthy eating and fears of obesity which is being led by a vocal health lobby.
- *Political*. The desire by governments for trans-fat-free oil to be used.
- *Legal*. Possible legislation over the use of trans-fat-free oil.
- Ethical issues:
    - McDonald's announced it would move to a trans-fat-free oil in 2002. Does this make it honour bound to keep its public promise? Is the delay ethical?
    - Is it ethically defensible that McDonald's should continue to sell food that it knows is unhealthy? Is it right that vulnerable groups (children, those in a hurry) should have easy access to food that may lead them into having health difficulties?
    - Do McDonald's sell the customer what they want even if it is harmful to them?
    - If legislation is brought in are McDonald's prepared to break the law and continue with production of fries (chips) as present?

4.5 Consumer behaviour

The marketing concept means that organisations need to understand their customers before marketing plans can be developed, or attempts made to improve customer satisfaction. Combining many strands and elements from sociology, anthropology and economics the study of consumer behaviour is highly relevant because it gives insights into:

- who buys (individuals or groups)
- how people buy
- what they buy
- when they buy
- why they buy

4.5.1 Factors affecting buying decisions

There are many factors that influence the purchasing decision. It is felt that the major factors influencing consumer behaviour are as follows:

- Cultural: the national, or organisational culture, and factors such as social class of the consumer.
- Personality: age, gender, occupation, economic circumstances, lifestyle, personality and the consumer's self perception.
- Social: the consumers reference groups (e.g. family) and their own role and status within these groups.
- Psychological: the consumer's motives, perceptions, beliefs and attitudes.

Naturally organisations also hope that the marketing mix (of product, price, promotion and place) will provide a powerful additional influence. Social interaction theory states that an individual's behaviour may depend on what he or she perceives others in society to be doing. The social influence of others therefore impacts on a person's buying habits. So social stigma associated with purchasing a particular product or service may deter consumption. Conversely a feeling that others are acquiring a particular service of good might create a 'me too' attitude amongst consumers.

Business-to-business (B2B) marketing differs from business-to-consumer (B2C) marketing in a number of key respects, not least the fact that the purchaser makes buying decisions for organisational rather than personal reasons. In addition several individuals and groups are involved in the B2B buying decision including:

- *Initiators* who start the buying process. (It might be for instance a department who identify a need to replace a piece of equipment.)
- *Influencers* who affect the buying decision often based on their particular technical expertise.
- *Buyers* who raise orders and sanction payment and although they may enter into negotiation they may be guided heavily by others in the organisation.
- *Users* who ultimately operate the equipment (using the earlier example).

There may be others (dependent upon the organisation) who will have further roles such as Deciders, Approvers and Gatekeepers.

Exercise 4.6

On what basis are B2B (where B2B means business to business) purchasing decisions made?

Solution

- Economic/task factors (price, delivery, location, quality, reliability, customer care, after care, etc.)
- Non-task factors (personal risk or gain, previous decisions, politics, those influencing the purchaser, perception, etc.)

or probably some combination of both.

Significant B2B marketing mix features include quality assurance, reliability, delivery, price and after sales service.

4.5.2 The buying process

Lancaster and Withey (2006) identify a consumer decision buying process as having five stages:

1. *Problem recognition* (as purchasing is a problem solving process). It is important to understand that consumers do not buy so much goods or services as to satisfy a demand or need through the purchase. The consumer identifies the need or problem. The organisation must attempt to convince the consumer that the product could be the answer.
2. *Information searching*. The consumer may perform this search informally in terms of memory of past experiences or by talking with others. Here the marketing implication is the nature of information provided to prospective consumers.
3. *Evaluation of alternatives by the consumer*. The consumer compares various brands and products in order that a choice might be made. The organisation needs to understand on what basis this choice is made (e.g. price, weight, value for money, packaging, etc.).
4. *Purchasing decision*. This stage is where the customer actually makes a purchase choice. The marketer will be keen to learn how they might assist in this process. The choice

might only be altered if for instance there is a stock out or further information emerges about alternatives.

5. *Post purchase evaluation.* The consumer will assess whether they are satisfied with their purchase decision. Increasingly consumers are written to or telephoned to determine this information.

4.5.3 Buyer behaviour

Rationally, consumer behaviour can be understood in terms of:

- *Relevance*: If a product or service is being purchased for the first time the consumer will be highly involved. The consumer will take more time and effort to make a choice as a way of compensating for their inexperience or minimising the risk. Consumers will also spend more time gathering and processing information for decisions that are important to them.
- *Frequency*: If by comparison the consumption is repetitive by nature, possibly purchased frequently, and low priced the consumer will give the purchase little conscious attention and have low involvement in the process. (The purchaser will, after all have experienced the good or service many times previously).
- *Freedom*: A less voluntary or involuntary consumption. It may be seen as something unavoidable possibly if there is little choice between brands, for instance the purchasing process in refilling a car with fuel.
- *Influence*: Here the issue is the susceptibility of the consumer to influence by others because the consumer might be purchasing on behalf of the family as a whole or the business they work for.

Exercise 4.7

Using these four headings think of different examples of purchases that illustrate buyer behaviour.

One solution

	Example
Relevance	Purchasing a wedding dress
Frequency	Purchasing household cleaning liquid
Freedom	Energy consumption
Influence	(Family) purchase of a particular breakfast cereal

Sometimes these ideas might not apply for a variety of reasons, not least too much choice can create information overload and confuse the consumer. In addition decisions are not always made on rational grounds and often they are emotion-driven possibly because of the impact of a brand name.

4.5.4 Theories of consumer behaviour

Theories of consumer behaviour help guide marketing practices by offering insights into issues such as:

- the effectiveness of pricing incentives (the likely impact on sales, behaviour when the price cut ends, etc.)

- the effectiveness of promotion (the likely impact on sales, loyalty, the duration of the impact of promotion, etc.)
- efforts to strengthen a brand image (the likely impact on new products, old products and the reasons for this, etc.)

The main theories of consumer behaviour are briefly outlined here.

The cognitive paradigm. This theory is based on the idea that a purchase is an outcome of problem-solving. Thus consumer behaviour can be explained as a decision-making process. The consumer is believed to be able to receive and make sense of considerable quantities of information, to engage in comparative evaluation of alternative products and brands, and to make a rational selection. The theory falls down when the consumer has insufficient time or motivation to the search for information and evaluation alternatives.

The learned behaviour theory. Consumers learn from past experiences either through satisfaction or dissatisfaction with a product or service. Consumers take short cuts when purchases are of a routine or habitual nature.

Habitual decision-making. Consumers make decisions based on either loyalty to a particular brand, inertia (the need is satisfied, but there is no special interest in the product) or 'satisfying behaviour', accepting the first solution that is good enough to satisfy your need, even if a better solution may exist. Buyer behaviour can become established and habits may be deeply embedded.

Influencing peoples' actions in their consumption patterns is an important issue in marketing. Consumer behaviour can be influenced by a potentially diverse series of factors including the social and physical environment.

4.6 Market research, segmentation, targeting and positioning

Market research should be distinguished from marketing research. Market research is a concentration on one of the market alone while the wider brief of marketing research involves investigating all marketing activities (see later).

Success often depends on organisations understanding and attempting to exercise control over markets or market segments. Many management decisions are made under conditions of uncertainty and risk, hence the need for good research. Market research concentrates on quantifying information about potential sales and based on the use of respected mathematical and statistical techniques.

Segmentation, targeting and positioning are marketing tools used by an organisation to achieve a competitive advantage. Market research is a foundation stone upon which these tools are built. They help an organisation differentiate its services or products from those of its competitors and reaches an exact part of the market.

Market segmentation is the process of dividing the market into similar groups with common characteristics. *Targeting* is the process of selecting the most lucrative market segments for its service product. *Positioning* involves developing a marketing 'mix' for aligning services and products to the target market.

4.6.1 Market research

To be comprehensive, market research must show an awareness of the PESTLE factors (see earlier) that may affect supply and demand for a product. Changes in these influences should wherever possible be anticipated. Typically, these research studies include investigation of demand in a particular market segment or geographical area, through the cyclical or seasonal pattern of demand by analysis of sub-segments by age, gender, etc. When undertaking market research there is a need to:

- define the problem
- establish the type and amount of information needed
- decide on the type of data (secondary or primary)
- determine the collection method to be used (postal questionnaire, personal interview, etc.)
- identify an appropriate organisational resource or select a research agency
- determine the sample
- collect the data
- interpret the data
- report.

In terms of data gathering technological advances and the potential offered by IT have assisted the process considerably. The Internet can access *secondary* research data sources, and universities typically have effective databases allowing for research and analysis of customer behaviour. *Primary* research that is generated by the organisation itself (because such data does not currently exist) can emanate from a number of sources. Leading research companies can be employed for the purpose and methods of data collection and analysis are again helped by technology (for example the use of scanners, observational equipment and sophisticated databases all may have a role to play).

Forecasting turnover for new products might be based on information already provided by a market research survey into the sales potential of existing products (at given prices and with given levels of expenditure on advertising and sales promotion).

Sales forecasting can be based on statistical techniques using historical sales data from the previous years or months. These techniques are not described in detail here, but include extrapolation by judgment, linear regression analysis, trend line analysis with adjustments for seasonal variations in sales, and exponential smoothing. The focus of market forecasting current demand for products and services, includes:

- total market potential
- (geographical) area market potential
- total industry sales
- relative market share between main competitors.

Market forecasting methods of future demand for products and services include:

- surveys of buyers' intentions
- a composite of sales force estimates
- obtaining estimates of future sales from 'experts'
- estimates based on past-sales analysis
- estimates based on other factors (e.g. monthly house sale figures can be correlated to purchases in DIY stores).

Sales potential is an estimate of the part of the market that is within the possible reach of a product. The potential will vary according to:

- the price of the product
- the amount spent on sales promotion

- how essential the product is to consumers
- whether it is a durable commodity whose purchase is postponable
- the overall size of the possible market
- competition.

Whether sales potential is worth exploiting will depend on the cost of sales promotion and selling that must be incurred to realise the potential. Sales potential will influence the decisions by a company on how much of each product to make (its production mix). The market situation is dynamic, and market research should reveal changing situations. A company might decide, for example, that maximum profits will be earned by concentrating all its production and sales promotion efforts on one segment of a market. Action by competitors might then adversely affect sales, and so market research might reveal that another market segment has become relatively more lucrative. The company might therefore decide to divert some production capacity and sales promotion spending to the new segment in order to revive its profits. Estimates of sales potential are required in deciding whether to invest money in the development of a new or improved product.

4.6.2 Market segmentation

'Market segmentation' is a technique based on the recognition that every market consists of potential buyers with different needs, and different buying behaviour. These different attitudes may be grouped into segments and a different marketing approach may be taken by an organisation for each market segment.

Market segmentation may therefore involve subdividing a market into distinct subgroups of customers, where any subgroup can be selected as a target market to be met with a distinct marketing mix.

The important point is that although within the total market widely different groups of consumers may exist, each group consists of people (or organisations) with common needs and preferences, who perhaps react to a market mix in a similar way. For example, the market for hats might be segmented according to the gender as women and men prefer hats of different styles. The men's market might be further subdivided into age or occupation (e.g. professional classes, commuters, golfers). Each sub-division of the market (or sub-segment of a market segment) will show increasingly common traits (e.g. golfers buy baseball caps).

Any market segment can become a target market for a firm, requiring a unique marketing mix if the firm is to exploit it successfully. Recognition of segmentation will enable a company to adopt a more refined approach to selling to a given group of potential customers.

Exercise 4.8

When might market segmentation prove difficult or inappropriate?

Solution

- If the total market is so small as to make segmentation unprofitable.
- Sometimes consumer differences may exist, but it may be difficult to analyse them into segments.
- A total market may occasionally be homogeneous but this is likely to occur only rarely.

Table 4.4 Typical segments within a market

Basis	Example
Geographical area	A regional newspaper
End use	Some types of paper are specially made for drawing offices
Age	Market for classical or pop music
Gender	Clothes
Family size or family life cycle	The market for housing
Income	The market for luxury goods
Occupation	The market for briefcases
Education	The marketing of magazines
Religion or religious sect	Marketing by mail-order by religious booksellers
Nationality, race, and culture	The market for food
Lifestyle	A general category based on differences in personality, peer social class, groups, etc.
Social class	Magazines

Kotler and Lane Keller (2006) suggest that since the purpose of segmentation is to identify target markets, segments must be:

- *measurable* (segmentation by 'personality' for example, might be difficult to measure)
- *accessible* (the market must be easily reached by the organisation)
- *substantial* (the costs of reaching the target market must be weighed against potential demand for the uniquely-marketed product).

Table 4.4 indicates typical segments within a total market.

Segmentation may to some extent be a matter of subjective analysis, and may be quite complex. There are many different bases on which segments can be analysed; one basis will not be appropriate in every market, and sometimes two or more bases might be valid at the same time. One basis or 'segmentation variable' might be 'superior' to another in the hierarchy of variables; for example, market segments may exist on the basis of gender sub-segments may then be age group within gender, and sub-sub-segments may be geographical region within age group within gender. On the other hand, if a market can be segmented both by marital status (unmarried, married) and by religion (say, Protestant and Catholic) then the market might be divisible into two at times; with separate segments (married Protestants, unmarried Protestants, married Catholics and unmarried Catholics, etc.).

The following extract from an article illustrates the increasing significance of a market segmented on the basis of age within the UK and the way in which products might be promoted to appeal to a mature age group:

> She's back. Isabella Rossellini, the actress and model who was allegedly dropped as the face of cosmetics brand Lancôme because she was too old at the age of 40, is making a new foray into the world of celebrity endorsements. Now 52, the elegant Italian will act as brand ambassador for Silversea Cruises and is to feature in print ads and brochures for the company as well as making appearances aboard the line's ships 'to create a photographic journal of her travels'.
>
> Silversea says Rossellini was hired for her 'timeless beauty' and ability to represent the brand's Italian heritage. But a spokesman admits that her mature years will strike a chord with people aged over 50 who make up the bulk of the market for cruises.

> The issue of how to promote brands to the burgeoning mature market is set to become a major concern for marketers over the next 20 years.
>
> Cruises, coach tours, financial products and medicaments are age-specific and can be directly targeted at the senior market. But the bigger question is how best to promote products such as packaged groceries, new media, cars and clothes, which are bought by people across the age spectrum, when declining childbirth and increased longevity mean there are fewer consumers under 35 and more over 50.
>
> The population is rapidly ageing. In 2020, there will be 5.2 million more people in the 45-to-74 age-group than there are today..........By 2041, the over-75 s will outnumber those aged between 55 and 74.
>
> The Government is being forced to grapple with the demographic time-bomb as it addresses the pensions crisis and the realisation that many people will be heading into retirement with insufficient provision for their old age. One important question will be how to unlock the enormous spending power in retired people's homes. Another will be how marketers should tap into this income.
>
> *Source*: Extracted from Marketing's age concern by David Benady, *Marketing Week*, October 28, 2004. Reproduced with Permission.

Identifying the significant bases for segmentation in any particular market is a matter of judgment. A new company entering a market may be able to identify a potentially profitable target market segment that existing firms may have 'missed'.

4.6.3 Targeting and positioning

If the company wants a market leadership position, but is unable to achieve it in an entire market, it can attempt to gain leadership in a single segment or in several segments. In addition to measurability, accessibility and being substantial the market segments selected for a leadership position would ideally:

- have potential for future growth
- show a distinctive customer need for 'exploitation'
- be without a direct competitor of similar size.

Taking the last of these, it would be unusual to enter a market segment where there is no direct competitor. This being the case a firm will probably need to make its product 'different' by creating some form of differentiated feature (real or imagined) as part of the marketing mix. This competitive positioning requires a firm to understand of what kind of offer it will make to the target market in relation to what the competitors are offering. The alternative strategies are:

- *Undifferentiated positioning* involves a targeting of the entire market with a single marketing mix. The undifferentiated policy is based on the hope that as many customers as possible to buy it. (In essence this approach ignores segmentation possibilities entirely). 'Mass' marketing may be 'sufficient' if the market is largely homogeneous (e.g. the market for safety matches).
- *Differentiated targeting* involves targeting certain market segments and then applying distinct marketing mix to each. This can be complex and time consuming but should

be ultimately rewarding. The company may attempt to introduce several product versions, each aimed at a different group of potential customers (e.g. the manufacture of different styles of the some article of clothing adapted to different world climates and national cultural tastes). The major disadvantage of a differentiated marketing strategy is the additional costs of marketing and production (more product design and development costs, the loss of economies of scale in production and storage, additional promotion costs and administrative costs, etc.). When the costs of further differentiation of the market exceed the benefits, a firm is said to have 'lower differentiated'. Some firms have tried to overcome this problem by selling the same product to two market segments. (For example, Johnson's baby powder and Heinz baby apple food is sold to many adults for their own use). The company's resources must not be over-extended by differentiated marketing. Small firms may succeed better by concentrating on one segment only.

- *Concentrated positioning* involves a targeting of a single market segment with an ideal product for that one segment of the market (e.g. Rolls-Royce cars). This would possibly be the best approach for a small player within the market place. The major disadvantage of concentrated marketing is the business risk of relying on a single segment of a single market. On the other hand, specialisation in a particular market segment can give a firm a profitable, although perhaps temporary, competitive edge over rival firms.

Decisions are generally made on:

- the relative attractiveness of segments
- the capability of the organisation itself
- the positioning of competitors
- the product must be sufficiently advanced in its 'life cycle' to have attracted a substantial total market. Without such a substantial market, segmentation and target marketing is unlikely to be profitable.

4.7 The marketing mix

It is obvious from the preceding sections that successful marketing strategies and plans can only be crafted with a clear focus on satisfying (meeting) customer needs and wants. Customers must be central to everything an organisation does.

Approximately 30 years ago it became accepted that in this quest for a customer driven approach, organisations had four basic marketing dimensions. These became known more commonly as known as the four Ps;

- Product (or service)
- Price
- Promotion
- Place (or distribution).

The term 'marketing mix' was first applied at the Harvard Business School, USA to explain the range of marketing decisions and elements that must be balanced to achieve maximum impact. The marketing mix represents the 'tool kit' for marketing practitioners to 'blend' the four Ps. The apportionment of effort, the precise combination, and the integration of all four elements to achieve organisational objectives represent an organisation's own marketing programme or 'mix'. The marketer therefore is a mixer of these ingredients of procedures and policies to produce a profitable outcome.

Table 4.5 The variables of the marketing mix

Variable	Examples
Product	Features, quality, durability, design, brand name, packaging, range, after-sales service, optional extras, guarantees, warranties
Place	Distribution channels, distribution coverage, the types of transportation vehicle, locations of sales outlets, the arrangements of sales areas, stock levels, ware house locations
Promotion	Advertising, personal selling, publicity, sales promotion
Price	Levels, discounts, allowances, payment terms, credit policy, etc.

Kotler and Lane Keller (2006) define the marketing mix (Table 4.5) as:

> '… the set of controllable variables and their levels that the firm uses to influence the target market.'

For the majority of private sector organisations the aim of marketing is, generally speaking, synonymous with the overall purpose of maximising financial returns. There are clearly a wide variety of possible combinations of marketing variables which management can select. Inevitably some combinations will earn greater financial returns than others. The crucial combination of factors comprising the marketing mix is therefore of high significance.

The 'design' of the marketing mix will normally be decided on the basis of management intuition and judgment, together with information provided by market research. There are number of different considerations when formulating the marketing mix. For instance:

- The time of year might be relevant to the manufacturers of seasonal products (most products are seasonal to some extent).
- Altering one component impacts upon another, for instance the quality of advertising may need to be raised if the selling price of products is increased.
- The mix will change as the marketing environment changes. (The popularity of Internet buying has persuaded some booksellers to switch to an Internet café approach in some of its stores.)
- The image of the product in the eyes of the customer.

The 'Four Ps' are now discussed in more detail including the specific tools and techniques associated with each.

4.7.1 The product mix

Product embraces quality, durability, design, brand name, logo, packaging, the product range, after-sales service, optional extras, guarantees and warranties, etc. Marketing a product involves product design, concept testing and product launch. For service rather than product-based organisations this category includes the nature of the service including its key features.

The starting point should be of course begin not with the product, but instead with the customer. By understanding their needs and wants an appropriate product or service can be developed. Potential customers need to be satisfied with an organisation's product or service or they are unlikely to buy it. The product or service must fulfil their need and should clearly be of a quality that fits its purpose. The organisation therefore needs systems to monitor customer perceptions of the product or service. Furthermore, product quality must meet the 'fitness for purpose' test. (For example, developing a sophisticated software package with many applications might be inappropriate for a market that just wants to write business letters when an electronic typewriter might suffice.)

It is worth recalling that the customer does not buy so much a product as satisfies a need or a want. It is therefore important that organisations concentrate on the *benefits* of its product rather than its *features*. Useful questions from a marketing point of view include:

- Are customers satisfied with existing products and services?
- Do these products or services fulfil their future needs?
- How are competitors addressing themselves to the same questions?
- Can competitors fulfil customers' future needs?

Exercise 4.9
For reflection

As customers buy the benefits of a product not its features identify a recent purchase you have made and make a note of both its features and benefits.

In terms of generic competitive strategy, Porter (1980) argued that an organisation could compete on the basis of price or by differentiating its product from the competition in some way. It might then choose to address itself to the whole market or just a narrower part (segment) of that total market. If the chosen competitive strategy is differentiation clearly the features of the product assume added significance as part of the marketing mix. If the chosen strategy is price then production costs should be reduced as far as possible and savings should be passed on to the customer.

4.7.2 Place

Getting 'place' right in marketing terms means effective distribution: getting the right products to the right places at the right time. The movement of goods from production to consumption points is key. Place therefore refers to distribution channels, distribution coverage, the types of transportation vehicle, locations of sales outlets, the arrangements of sales areas, stock levels, warehouse locations, etc. Research indicates that delivery performance is one of the main criteria for businesses choosing a particular supplier. Questions from a marketing point of view include:

- Is the place of purchase convenient to customers and does it fulfil their needs?
- Is the means of distribution appropriate?
- Is the product available in the right quantities?

Contemporary developments have dictated that there is a changing emphasis for 'place' within the marketing mix with advances in direct marketing and interactive marketing (see later).

4.7.3 Promotional tools and the promotional mix

Promotion includes the tools available to communicate with customers and potential customers about a product or service. A clear focus on communication as well as customers is central to modern marketing. Increasingly organisations attempt to understand customers before tailoring their communications. Marketing communications are the messages and media used to promote an organisation, initiative, product or service to its target market and encouraging potential customers to interact. Once the organisation has determined what they believe the customers see as the main benefits of their product or service these aspects are focussed upon when promotion takes place. Communications can take many forms and generally operates at one of three levels:

1. non-personal and mass, typically aimed at a market segment at large (e.g. advertising)
2. personal and direct, typically one way communication with a potential customer (e.g. communicating by letter)
3. personal and interactive, involving some one-to-one dialogue between a salesperson and the potential customer.

Promotion (irrespective of form) involves persuasion: ways of convincingly communicating the benefits of an organisation's products or services to customers and potential customers. There are many individual promotional tools available and possibly these constitute the most visible dimension of marketing. These communication mechanisms need 'blending' by an organisation to develop its own promotional mix. The features of the main promotional tools are summarised in Table 4.6.

Table 4.6 Promotional tools

Tool	Explanation	Example
Advertising	Non-personal presentation and promotion of ideas, goods, or services but targeted at a specific market through some media channel.	Media: TV, press, radio or newspapers. Traditional: posters, billboards and fliers. Contemporary: on line. (See more on advertising later in this section)
Sales promotion	Impersonal and short term involving the offering of incentives to encourage sales by stimulating consumer purchasing.	Examples: coupons, offers, giveaways, discounts, competitions, BOGOFs (buy one get one free) products. Promotional events: displays, exhibitions, demonstrations, and product sponsorship.
Publicity and public relations	Non-personal stimulation of demand by planting commercially significant news items in the media, or obtaining favourable presentation on e.g. radio or TV. Not paid for in the way that media time or space is paid for advertising.	Company open days, press releases and conferences.
Personal selling	Direct, often one-to-one contact with potential customers. The salesperson verbally presents the benefits of the product or service in the hope of making a sale.	Examples: Telesales, travelling sales representatives, 'cold' calling by knocking on doors.
Direct mailing	Posting out promotional literature and brochures. Databases allow messages to be personalised to include the prospective customer's name.	Traditional mail systems (often referred to as junk mail) or the e-mail (often referred to as SPAM mail).
Product packaging	(If the packaging contributes to the communication of the products benefits).	Package, label and description design. This might also form part of brand (see later).

In terms of advertising, it is estimated that within Western Europe every adult has up to 3,000 'advertising encounters' every day. With so much expenditure on advertising it is perhaps surprising that there is any controversy over whether a company advertises or not. Lancaster and Withey (2005) articulate the diverse opinions surrounding the value of advertising as part of an organisation's promotional mix. Although most marketers agree that advertising has a role to play, some believe that it is an ineffective way of getting customers to purchase products. Two polar opposite positions can be identified as follows:

- Advertising is ineffective and a waste of money, only adding to company (and hence eventually customer) costs. Brands such as Body Shop and Pizza Express do not see a need to use advertising in their promotional campaigns relying instead on other sources of information in order to form positive attitudes towards their products. In any case some might think that advertising demeans a particular product or company. In some cases advertising may seem unethical. Lancaster and Withey (2005) conclude that some brands may be strong enough to sell on their own merits only if they are long-established and have strong brand-loyal users.
- Advertising is so powerful and effective as to be essential. Consumers, it could be argued, will rarely purchase unadvertised brands so by not advertising a company will be at a serious disadvantage compared to competitors. The results of advertising campaigns have been undeniably successful including for brands such as Walkers Crisps, Strongbow cider and French Connection.

For advertising to be successful it needs to be:

- well planned and executed
- part of an effective promotional mix
- effective as a communication tool
- consistent with the values and mission of the organisation.

Exercise 4.10
For reflection

You may wish to reflect on why two of the companies cited, Body Shop and Pizza Express can afford not to advertise. Hint: (Think of the other compensating aspects associated with their operation such as PR within the promotional mix and place visibility.)

Direct marketing involves taking an active role in the selling process (e.g. by advertising in a trade journal). Indirect marketing is a more passive, less aggressive approach and might not be explicitly linked to a specific product or service or goal. Indirect strategies involve performing a series of related activities, such as:

- participating in community events
- writing articles for publication (in practitioner journals for instance)
- taking part in public speaking events
- posting Internet blogs

In the same way, existing satisfied customers can also contribute to an organisation's indirect marketing through their 'word of mouth' recommendation. When positive messages and information sharing occurs using the Internet as a platform it is referred to *viral marketing*. Viral marketing encourages individuals to pass on a marketing message to others, so creating exponential growth in the message's exposure in the same way that computer viruses grow. A good example is a Nike video of footballer Ronaldinho putting on a new pair of boots and then ball juggling for three minutes. The video was posted on YouTube and to date nearly 26 million people have got to know about the video and so have been exposed to Nike's promotion of their products.

Activity

Watch Ronaldinho: Touch of Gold using the link http://uk.youtube.com/watch?v=lsO6D1rwrKc

You have now been exposed to viral marketing (pass it on!)

The stages involved in developing and running a *marketing campaign* are clearly outlined in the article below:

> **How to Develop and Run a Marketing Campaign**
>
> ….Successful campaigns tend to be carefully researched, well-thought-out and focused on details and execution, rather than resting on a single, grand idea. Planning a marketing campaign starts with understanding your position in the marketplace and ends with details such as the wording of an advertisement. You may also want to include decisions about uniforms, stationery, office decor and the like in your marketing plan.............
>
> First, you need to redefine your product or service. Describe your product or service and its features and benefits in detail. Focus on how it differs from the competition. Concentrate on key features of your offering, including pricing, service, distribution and placement. In other words, know what you are going to be selling more of and why more people are going to buy it.
>
> Second, look at the various market segments into which you hope to introduce or expand demand for your product. Decide what type of buyer is most likely to purchase it. Now describe your target customer in detail in terms of demographics: age, sex, family composition, earnings, geographical location, lifestyle, purchasing patterns, buying objections, and the like. Know exactly who will be driving your growth.
>
> Third, create a strategy for communicating the message that will produce growth. Find out what your target customers read and listen to, and spell out your promotional objectives. Do you want people to recognize your name or know where you're located? Decide how often you'll need to and can afford to expose customers to your message to create the growth you desire.
>
> *Source*: Entrepreneur.com http://smallbusiness.aol.com/grow/marketing/article/_a/how-to-develop-and-run-a-marketing/20051213184009990005

The following extract illustrates the way in which new media is challenging traditional forms and the different views on how best a promotional budget might be spent:

> At the conference (of the Association of National Advertisers), execs from some of the most traditional companies (who control some of the biggest marketing budgets) described big shifts away from traditional media. Wachovia Chief Marketing

> Officer Jim Garrity said his research on ad effectiveness would sadden broadcast TV execs but gladden employees of Yahoo! and – yup – Google. Joseph V. Tripodi, a good-humored old-school salesman, is Allstate's chief marketing officer. He told me Allstate's spending on 'nontraditional media' – from the Internet to sponsorships – increased from 5 to 25 per cent of its marketing budget in recent years.
>
> Titans of traditional media are all too aware of this shift. Vanity Fair Editor-in-Chief Graydon Carter last month told an audience of advertisers that while he often used Google, he never remembered the ads. Schmidt countered by using Vanity Fair as Exhibit A: Its circulation is around 1 million, he said, and a full-page ad for a Prada bag costs around $100,000. So that ad in Vanity Fair costs 10 cents per impression. How about paying about 20 cents per impression, he offered, for a link to a Web site where you can buy the bag?
>
> In truth, Vanity Fair's ad is cheaper per impression if you measure by the magazine's total audience, but Schmidt's point is nonetheless clear: Which gets you closer to commerce, and how much do you pay for that?
>
> *Source*: Extracted from Hard Questions from Google; Asking advertisers: What's the right amount to spend? By Jon Fine, *Business Week*, October 24, 2005 i3956 p. 28 The McGraw-Hill Companies, Inc.

During the 1980s Jay Conrad Levinson came up with the phrase *guerrilla marketing* as an approach for smaller organisations with limited marketing budgets. Like guerrilla warfare the approach relies on well thought out, highly focussed and often unconventional attacks on key targets. The aim is to get maximum impact from minimal resources. Levinson (1983) identifies certain key principles:

- it is aimed at entrepreneurs and small businesses
- it should involve human psychology not experience, judgment and guesswork
- it calls for an investment of time, energy and imagination rather than money
- measurements should be of profits, not sales
- how many new relationships are made each month should be a metric
- focus on a few products or services
- instead of 'chasing' new customers concentrate on more referrals, more business with existing customers, and larger transactions
- collaborate with other businesses not competition
- use a combination of marketing methods
- use existing organisational technology.

Just as promotional tools need to be blended to form a promotional or communication mix, so promotion itself needs to be blended with the other Ps comprising the marketing mix. For instance, a reduction in promotional activity may be possible if a wider range or larger number of sales outlets is developed. (This implies a heavier mix of place at the expense of promotion.)

Lancaster and Withey (2005) differentiate promotion according to uses and types as follows:

- products and services (e.g. Ford cars)
- ideas and issues (e.g. Greenpeace)
- people (e.g. David Beckham)

- trade type (e.g. C&Q: 'warehouses for professional decorators')
- consumer type (e.g. Robinson Barley Water: 'refresh your ideas')
- corporate type (e.g. Shell: 'the caring company').

Procter and Gamble has been active in supermarkets assisting in the merchandising (displaying) and just-in-time supply of their goods. This effort is linked to EFTPOS (electronic funds transfer at the point of sale) and manufacturing scheduling at the Procter and Gamble factories. This had led to lower inventories at both locations, and greater team working resulting in shared ideas for point-of-sale promotions. As a result, Procter and Gamble managers are now more involved in the entire supply process.

Gray (2004) illustrates the advantages of IT in promotional campaigns by citing the example of the Carlson Marketing Group, which apparently:

- Plans campaigns using desk research including the Internet and reference guides.
- Maintains a database for all the venues visited, including demographic and volume details.
- Uses geographical information software to give detailed local marketing targets including customer profiles to pinpoint areas of the country that have a high concentration of the customer profile looked for.

The effect is to reach the targeted segment more effectively and accurately, so improving response rates and sales.

4.7.4 Price

Of the four Ps comprising the marketing mix, price is the one most directly linked to revenue levels. Price setting is all-important especially for a financially orientated firm. Pricing includes basic price levels, discounts and allowances, payment terms and credit policy, etc.

The accountant within us may force us to view price from a mathematical viewpoint and culminate in fixing a product price based on 'cost plus'. Undeniably the need to recover total costs plus necessary profit is a powerful and legitimate consideration. However, customers need to see price as 'fair' (not necessarily cheap). Pricing, therefore, needs to meet both the organisation's financial and marketing aspirations. It is perhaps illuminating to consider the issue from three perspectives (Lancaster and Withey, 2005):

- *The economic view.* Suppliers are in the business of profit maximisation. A market is a place where supply and demand comes into contact. Price is the mechanism whereby demand and supply are brought into equilibrium.
- *The accountancy view.* Price is set to recover costs and make profit. Pricing should be guided by the use of ratios and techniques such as breakeven analysis.
- *The marketing view.* Price is the only one factor influencing demand, it does however have an impact on an organisations competitive market position, including sales, and market share. A good price measure might be what 'the market will bear'.

In practice all these viewpoints should be considered to some degree. In addition an appropriate blending of the three other factors of the marketing mix (place, product, promotion) will also help establish the price. Table 4.7 summarises the range of approaches that can help determine selling price.

Customers' feelings about a product or service are reflected in what they are prepared to pay, so getting pricing 'right' is crucial. Ultimately the organisation must address the issue of whether customers believe the price is fair commensurate with the quality of the product or service.

Table 4.7 Approaches to pricing

Competitive	Setting a price by reference to the prices of competitive products
Cost plus	Adding a mark-up to costs of production which may incorporate desired return on investment
Market based	(or perceived value). Setting a price based on the value of the product in the perception of the customer
Penetration	Setting a low selling price in order to gain market share
Predatory	Setting a low selling price in order to damage competition
Premium	Achieving a 'high' price due to differentiation of the product
Price skimming	Setting a high price in order to maximize short-term profitability (e.g. the introduction of a novel product)
Selective	Setting different prices for the same product maybe in different markets
Selective: category	Cosmetic modifications to allow variations to take place
Selective: consumer Group	Modifying the price to take account of certain groups (e.g. junior or OAP area)
Selective: peak	Setting a price which varies according to level of demand (e.g. happy hours, premium rate calls, etc.)

Source: Based on CIMA *Official Terminology* (2005)

CIM make the point that existing customers are generally less price sensitive than new ones. (This is one reason why it is vital to retain existing customers. A truism is that it is preferable to retain existing customers rather than having to find new ones.)

For the prospective purchaser price can imply quality. Pricing that is too low can have a detrimental effect on purchasing decisions and overall sales levels. Conversely, the higher the price, the more customers will expect in terms of product and service (whether packaging, the shopping environment, or promotional material, etc.)

4.7.5 Extending the marketing mix

The co-ordination of the four elements of the marketing mix is crucial to the success of the overall marketing strategy. Some thinkers believe that other factors could also usefully be considered. The factors augmenting this basic categorisation arise mainly as recognition that service organisations are 'different' to production organisations in marketing terms. These additional factors might be viewed as 'the service extension' to the marketing mix.

People include both staff and customers. An organisation's people come into contact with customers and can have a massive impact on customer satisfaction levels. In the customers' eyes, staff are generally inseparable from the total service. This implies the need for well-trained, motivated workforce mindful of the adage 'the customer is always right'. It is important therefore that every member of staff contribute to the marketing philosophy and support the firm's external marketing activities. As organisations introduce streamlined hierarchies and more flexible working practices, marketing offers the opportunity for their employees to operate in interdisciplinary teams furthering an overall marketing philosophy. Corporate investment in their most valuable asset, employees, through training and development supports the processes of creating and defending competitive advantages gained from successful marketing. In addition to workers people might be viewed as individual customers, and good research should reveal vital, personal, cultural, social and psychological profiles of potential customers. This data can be exploited when applying other aspects of the marketing mix. Many supermarket chains offer regular customers 'loyalty cards'.

Table 4.8 An example of a client testimonial appearing on a website of an HR consultancy practice

'I have been very impressed with the service provided by Reed Consulting's strategic research team. Our account manager took the time to gain a thorough understanding of the issues we face, and designed and delivered research which has fully met our requirements. The analysis report was clearly presented and has been influential in driving our strategic decision-making.'

Source: www.reedconsulting.co.uk

These cards allow sophisticated databases to record purchasing profiles of customer groups and enable better targeting of their products.

Processes refer to systems involved in providing a service focussed upon 'identifying, anticipating and satisfying customer requirements'. So for instance, useful considerations might include the processes implied by the following questions:

- Do customers have to queue or wait to be dealt with?
- How are customers kept informed?
- Is the service conducted efficiently?

Processes assume greater significance in certain sectors such as banking and financial institutions.

Physical evidence. As one of the features of a service is that it is intangible by nature it cannot (unlike a product) be experienced before it is delivered. This means that potential customers may perceive greater risk. To overcome these feelings service organisations can give reassurance by way of testimonials and references from past satisfied customers as a substitute for physical evidence (See Table 4.8).

4.8 Marketing contexts

Hopefully, the organisational contexts within which marketing principles can be usefully applied are apparent. A few of these contexts are discussed here in order to give a flavour of the particular marketing considerations.

4.8.1 Consumer marketing

Consumer goods can take two forms, namely durable goods and fast-moving consumer goods (FMCGs). The decision to purchase high cost durable goods such as televisions, computers, cars and furniture and the frequency of repurchase will be influenced by changing technical features, fashions and wearing-out of the old product. FMCGs are by comparison purchased for personal reasons and generally involve relatively low financial outlays. For FMCGs like canned foods, soft drinks and confectionery there may be habitual purchasing but products tend to have short life cycles. It follows therefore that the marketing mix will differ considerably between both types of consumer good. Of particular relevance to FMCG is advertising, branding and packaging.

In the following extracts Simms (2007) discusses the value of the UK's stellar FMCG brands in the light of health concerns. The article underlines the value of branding to FMCG and the way in which societal attitudes towards healthy eating are being responded to by food producers.

> Health and indulgence have been two of the most important trends in the grocery market since the turn of the millennium. But over the past 12 months, they have made a bigger impact than ever before. With brands such as Walkers and Coca-Cola – both demonised by the health lobby – climbing onto the health bandwagon, the value of the top 50 brands rose by 4 per cent to more than £77billion last year. 'The rate at which people are trading up to something a bit nicer, different or healthier has accelerated,' says Chris Longbottom, a director of TNS Worldpanel.
>
> ....
> Walkers became the third biggest supermarket brand this year, growing its sales 5 per cent by emphasising the reduced levels of fat and salt in its crisps. It has also enjoyed great success with its Potato Heads brand for children, which has 33 per cent less fat than ordinary Walkers crisps, and the launch of its Lights (less than 115 calories in a bag) and Baked (70 per cent less fat than the standard product) lines. Its new Sensations Corn Chips, which are billed as 'light and crispy', exemplify the blurring of the health and premium trends.
>
> Coca-Cola's launch of sugar-free variant Coke Zero, aimed at men, has similarly boosted its sales. 'Coca-Cola knows it will lose consumers unless it provides healthier alternatives that are also aimed at people who wouldn't traditionally have considered Coke,' says Longbottom 'Coca-Cola and Walkers are great examples of brands making "debatable" products more permissible, without ditching the core brand values.'
>
> *Source*: Simms, J. (2007) Biggest brands. *Marketing*, August 22nd.

4.8.2 Business-to-business marketing

For organisations that market goods and services to other intermediary organisations (rather than direct to ultimate consumers), the implication of buyer behaviour, the assessment of marketing opportunities and industrial market segmentation take on heightened significance. A manufacturer may need a marketing mix for the end consumer, and an additional mix for the retailers who they actually sell the product to.

Business-to-business (B2B) marketing differs from business-to-consumer (B2C) marketing in a number of key respects, not least the purchaser makes purchasing decisions for organisational rather than personal reasons. In addition many people are involved in the B2B buying decision (see earlier). Other differences include:

- *Customer focus.* The customer requirement differs. B2C involves individual customer transactions, B2B has other businesses as consumer meaning that different IT applications will be needed to accommodate their needs. It also means that customer relationships are extremely valuable and need to be managed. A company's brand identity most likely will be created based upon the personal relationship developed.
- *Sales pattern.* The types of order will differ. B2B orders tend to be repeat orders usually the same products in the same quantities at regular intervals.
- *Credit terms apply for B2B customers.* While a credit card might be used for B2C purchases company to company trading involves the use of invoices and credit periods. This will form part of the pricing mix.

4.8.3 Services marketing

The extension of the basic four factor marketing mix acknowledges that there are fundamental differences between products and services and the marketing of a service assumes a different emphasis to product marketing. Mullins (2007) identified the main differentiating features as:

- The consumer is a participant in the service process.
- Services are perishable. If there is no sale on monday it cannot (unlike a tin of fruit) be sold on tuesday: that sale is lost forever. Pricing will be mindful of persishability of the service.
- Services are intangible, so communication is made more difficult when explaining the benefits.
- Services are people orientated and the characteristics of the workforce determine the effectiveness of the service. Promotion might emphasise personal selling.
- Output measurement is less easy to evidence.

Exercise 4.11

Using the above features identify examples of services and the implications this has on service marketing.

One Solution

- The consumer is a participant in the service process. Environmental surroundings of the service operation need attention, for example, the décor of a hairdressers, the cleanliness of the hospital ward, etc.
- Services are perishable therefore consideration might be given to differential pricing, for example, seats left unsold on airplanes one hour before flight might have to be heavily discounted.
- Services are intangible, communication might recognise that feelings and emotions are important (e.g. for instance for an insurance company the strap line 'sleep safely with our house cover').
- Services from accountancy or legal firms are people orientated and the characteristics of the workforce determine the effectiveness of the service. The implication is that attention must be paid to key human resourcing issues such as recruitment and training.
- Output measurement is less easy to evidence, therefore multiple indicators might be stressed, for example, length of hospital stay, cost of operation, post-operation support, etc.

For service organisations it is worth noting the heightened emphasis on the augmentation of 'four Ps' already identified namely

People. As employees interface with customers and can have a massive impact on customer satisfaction levels.

Processes. Systems involved in providing a service.

Physical evidence. Organisations can give reassurance by way of testimonials and references from past satisfied customers as a substitute for physical evidence.

It is true to say that some services are more like manufacturing organisations than others, as illustrated in Table 4.9.

Table 4.9 Overlaps between service organisations and manufacturing organisations

Service	Overlap	Manufacturing
Simultaneous production and consumption		Goods stored for later consumption
Customised output		Standardised output
Customer participation		Technical core buffered from customer
Intangible output		Tangible output
Labour intensive		Capital intensive
Examples	Overlap	Examples
Airlines	Fast food outlets	Drinks
Hotels	Banks	Steel
Consultancy	Cosmetics	Cars
Teaching/training	Estate agents	Mining
Health	Retailing	

Lancaster and Withey (2005) explain that the banking industry took a long time to wake up to the need to be customer oriented and the benefits of using the marketing tools and techniques in the same way that fast-moving consumer goods did. They identify a dramatic change over the past decade concluding that 'the global banking sector is one of the success stories in recent years of the application and implementation of the marketing concept'. Some of the changes include:

- market research and analysis designed to keep in touch with customer needs and customer satisfaction levels
- organisational and marketing structures based around customer requirements
- marketing planning and control systems including market segmentation and targeting
- a need for increased quality, service and customer care
- an awareness of wider environmental factors, including its ethical and social responsibilities towards customers.

4.8.4 Direct marketing and distribution channels

Distribution involves getting products to the right people at the right time. Distribution channels take a number of forms which are briefly outlined here.

One level channel. The links in a distribution channel involve the manufacturer selling to retailers who then act as an intermediary to the final customer or consumer. Under this model the customer would have no direct dealings with the manufacturer. Where there is only one intermediary link in the chain the activity is referred to as a one level channel. This generally applies to most consumer goods such as branded foodstuff and clothing.

Two level channel. Often there are several intermediaries in the chain making manufacturer and ultimate customer contact even more unlikely. The links in such a distribution channel involves a producer selling to a wholesaler to a retailer to the consumer or more extended involving a producer selling to an agent who in turn sells to a wholesaler. The greater the market an organisation wishes to access the longer and more complicated the distribution channel. The further the manufacturer is from the final customer the less control the manufacturer has over marketing effort.

Zero level channel. Direct marketing is a 'zero level channel' where the manufacturer interacts directly with the customer. It is common for small businesses to sell directly from their premises to members of the public, or through direct mailing. The Chartered Institute of Marketing (2004) comment that direct marketing 'is becoming increasingly important, particularly as technology advances'. Under these conditions 'place' translates as cyberspace. Examples include the web-based company Amazon.com and the direct booking of air travel on line.

Some products such as fresh foodstuff clearly benefit from short distribution channels. In the countryside it is often possible to buy produce directly from the farmyard. Alternatively, the farm may deliver daily to the supermarket. A specialist foreign car might, however, need to be imported, in which case the distribution is relatively lengthy and may take time.

The traditional 'push' marketing policy is concerned with manufacturers transferring goods out to wholesalers and retailers who then have the task of selling them to ultimate final customers. The emphasis of a 'push' policy is therefore on getting dealers to accept goods. A 'pull' policy by comparison is one of influencing final consumer attitudes so that a consumer demand is created which dealers are obliged to satisfy. A 'pull' policy usually involves heavy expenditure on advertising, but holds the potential of stimulating a much higher demand. For example, producers of convenience food and alcohol advertise their products nationally rather than relying on supermarkets to promote these products.

4.8.5 Interactive marketing

Prof. John Deighton (1996) first defined interactive marketing as

> the ability to address the customer, remember what the customer says and address the customer again in a way that illustrates that we remember what the customer has told us.

For organisations of any size to 'remember' what the customer has said and then 'communicate' with them is realistically only possible by use of the Internet. Thus IT allows customer information to be collected online and communication made either by e-mail or by 'remembering' when a customer logs on to the company website in future.

Developments in other communication technologies, specifically cable, satellite and digital technologies have also provided a platform for another form of home shopping via the television. Advantages over web-based selling include complete user familiarity with the equipment (the TV) and the ability to extensively demonstrate/advertise the products visually on a dedicated channel.

Telephone technology is not new but ownership is more widespread than ever. Within the UK virtually all businesses, most homes and increasingly all teenagers and adults have a telephone. This provides the potential for contact to be made by telemarketing to stimulate product interest, sell directly or arrange for a visit to be made by a salesperson. There has of late been great emphasis in providing specialist training for telesales personnel including coaching on accent and responses to questions raised by customers. A contemporary trend is also the development of large call centres sometimes based overseas. ('M-marketing' refers to the technique being adopted using mobile telephones.)

This type of selling involves the initiative being taken by the vendor and is unsolicited. As such it may be unwelcome, intrusive even and naturally ethical concerns can surface. Impolite approaches or 'pushy' sales techniques being employed are particularly distasteful.

4.8.6 e-marketing, e-business and e-commerce

General and applied marketing knowledge can be found within the specialised area of e-business, a collective term for all electronically based systems and technologies of doing business (including most significantly the Internet). Here use is made of electronic technologies and systems to facilitate and enable transactions to take place.

Using the Internet as a platform a rapid growth in so-called 'dot.com companies' took place some 15 years or so ago, most taking advance of e-marketing. Although not all of these start-up companies survived more established organisations have since invested in this technology and thinking to enhance their existing marketing efforts.

Berens (2006) explains:

> The dot-com boom was led by start-up companies that had unproven records, but the latest growth is being led by established retailers who understand their customers, have brands that people trust and see the web as a bolt-on

He goes on to cite big names amongst the UK's top 20 Web retailers including Argos, B&Q, Comet, Currys, John Lewis, Marks & Spencer and Next.

With the incredible uptake of use of the Internet a number of benefits present themselves in marketing term (for example, in terms of data collection and providing enhanced value to customers and suppliers). It should, however, be noted that there are potentially a number of drawbacks of Internet trading (e.g. financial security issues, computer disruptions, and a possibility of organisations ceasing trading).

e-business has its roots in B2B transactions that sought to do away with paperwork concerning reorder levels, delivery schedules and invoicing. The obvious advantages of e-business to the customer in a B2C context has helped fuel a rapid growth in this area, including:

- one-stop shopping
- convenience of place
- ability to shop around
- speed and flexibility
- reduced impulse buys
- direct communication over issues of delivery and complaints.

It has become difficult for firms to survive on domestic business alone. To achieve scale economies, firms need to develop new markets and e-marketing has allowed organisations to trade more easily globally and seek out and exploit new markets. This trend is evidenced by the fact that the last 20 years has seen world trade has grown at twice the rate of world GNP.

4.8.7 Internal marketing

With marketing's emphasis on looking outside the organisation and concentrating on customers needs, the workforce itself can get overlooked. To improve the way employees contribute to organisational values, goals and direction of the organisation effective communications and internal marketing has great potential. Internal marketing is the process of training and motivating employees so as to support the organisation's external marketing activities. Through internal marketing an organisation can communicate what delivers value for the business, and so influence behaviour. A further stage might be to recognise and reward individual's achievements against these marketing goals. CIM explain:

> 'The principal role of internal marketing is to ensure everyone within the organisation not only understands why the organisation exists but also its key outputs and metrics, and most importantly, how every person and department contributes to the delivery of the proposition'

The following extracts from an article in Personnel Today explains the importance of internal marketing.

How to…influence employee behaviour through internal marketing

Motivating staff to change their behaviours and thinking to achieve organisational goals.

The best way to do this is through internal marketing, using the same persuasive methods of communication that companies employ to market products and services externally. In effect, this means you must treat your employees as you would your customers, synchronising your internal and external brands in the process.

Internal marketing is distinct from internal communications, as the latter tends to be a one-way, top-down flow of information primarily concerned with ensuring that staff have the relevant information to do their jobs correctly.

Why is it important?

When an organisation wants to implement a new strategy or change programme, for instance, it needs to align employees' attitudes and behaviours to correspond with the vision. The correctly-motivated workforce this leads to is a pre-requisite for any business wishing to gain a competitive advantage through enhanced service levels, which, in turn, strengthens customer loyalty.

For these reasons, internal marketing is likely to feature prominently on the wish list of any CEO. Do it well and you won't fail to be noticed, which will significantly further your career development opportunities. It should also bring a host of other HR and organisational payoffs, including high levels of employee satisfaction, improved retention rates, reduced absenteeism and wider acceptance of any change programme.

Where do I start?

You need to clearly define what you want the exercise to achieve, and then secure the buy-in from the senior management team. If they are not wholly in agreement about the aims, the chances of the exercise succeeding will be limited.

Once the objectives have been decided, the next step is the same as with any external marketing campaign: get to grips with the needs of the marketplace – and that requires market research.

> This needs to extend way beyond conducting simple employee attitude surveys, and is essentially about acquiring an in-depth knowledge of the issues important to staff. Face-to-face interviews are the best way to understand their perspective on matters. What do they think of the way the organisation recruits? What is their view of training? Are they happy with the working conditions? Do they feel committed to the company?
>
> As the aim is to get a qualitative rather than a quantitative sample, you don't need to interview everyone, but the interviews must be thorough.........................
>
> **What mechanics and processes should be included?**
>
> Once the research has been conducted and the data compiled, it needs to be analysed, and a plan of action drawn up. Next, decide on the strategies to employ, which could range from motivational programmes such as 'away days', employee involvement schemes, training and even personnel moves.
>
> You must also put together your package of 'product offerings', which could include flexible working and benefits, as well as the reward and recognition schemes that will support those organisational goals.
>
> Then decide the method and style of delivery of your communication to staff. Remember, it must be viewed as a campaign, so make use of standard marketing methods such as presen-tations, posters, leaflets and even a letter or message from the CEO. It is crucial to communicate in a language that relates to the audience, not the transmitter.
>
> **How can you evaluate whether the programme has been successful?**
>
> It is essential to remember that you are measuring whether the objectives have been met, and not the effectiveness of the communication process. It is here that supporting methodologies such as employee attitude surveys can be most useful in helping to track the programme's development.
>
> *Source*: Personnel Today 8th. April 2003

4.9 The market planning process

4.9.1 Strategic marketing

Developing a marketing strategy is vital to help the organisation manage in a dynamic, volatile and complex environment. Strategically considering marketing issues involves asking a series of basic questions such as:

- Product: What is being 'sold'? What portfolio of products do we offer?
- Place: Where is it sold?
- Price: How much for?
- Promotion: How do we engage our customers?
- What is our capability?

Strategy will not emerge from a simple aggregation of the different elements of 'marketing mix' although these aspects will be key considerations. The strategy itself should:

- be consistent with other organisational business planning processes
- develop key priorities identified in the overall corporate strategy

- cohesively plan and co-ordinate elements in an integrated fashion. It is vital that these factors are blended together to ensure that their product or service satisfies (or exceeds) the benefits demanded whether as consumer or business buyer
- be realistic in terms of capability of the organisation and finance available.

The Chartered Institute of Marketing (2004) explain that

> **!** A marketing plan (strategy) defining objectives, targets and performance measures is ... developed with a financial budget. And when specific goals have been defined, then strategic alternatives to the current position can be discussed, and ways to achieve those alternatives can be chosen. The marketing strategy is then formalised within a specific plan of action, which is constantly revised and updated and the marketing campaign progresses.

Marketers use several analytic frameworks shared by strategists when considering environmental factors. The most common start point is to use a SWOT (strengths, weaknesses, opportunities and threats) analysis usually depicted by a four-cell matrix where SW factors are internal and OT external factors. Internal factors are controllable, but external issues are beyond the control of an organisation (although some limited influence might be exercised). The process of developing a strategy begins with an environmental audit involving:

- A detailed investigation of the market and targeted segments.
- The development of a PESTLE analysis that considers trends influencing the market (see earlier).
- A consideration of the position of the organisation relative to these PESTLE factors including potential realistic ways in which the organisation might influence this environment.
- Discussions centred on developing an appropriate marketing mix to achieve corporate aspirations.

The external environments in which an organisation operates can have a major impact upon its performance either positively or negatively. It is vital that these influences are understood in order that opportunities might be seized and threats compensated for. A PESTLE analysis (see earlier) represents one framework for considering the macro environment and relevant external factors. Results arising from this scanning should clearly indicate marketing implications. Analysis is required of all external factors including:

- *Customers.* Their buying habits, nature, expectations, etc.
- *The market.* What research suggests, segmentation possibilities, the organisation's market position and potential for future development.
- *Competition.* Who they are and the basis upon which they are competing, also their distinctive strengths, weaknesses, track record, etc. Some organisations go to great lengths to discover more about their rivals and their products and services. In this context 'reverse engineering' involves taking apart and analysing a competitors' product *'in order to determine how they are made, costs of production and the way in which future development might proceed'* (CIMA, 2005).

This naturally leads on to future considerations: what could be done and how do we bridge the gap from where we are now? The Chartered Institute of Marketing (2004) note that:

> Marketing focuses on the most fundamental requirements of companies to identify customers, research their needs and preferences, analyse their attitudes to promotion and other factors that influence their purchasing decisions and persuade them to buy products and services from you rather than a wide range of competitors.

All these aspects should be reflected in the marketing strategy. A strategy can ultimately be developed incorporating:

- clear marketing goals and objectives
- targets, measures and performance indicators
- the costing of the plan and the development of a revenue budget
- an identification and costing of any capital requirements
- identification of strategic alternatives
- a detailed action plan-incorporating SMART (specific, measurable, achievable, realistic time bound) targets.

Strategic decisions made about marketing will impact on all other functional areas, for instance:

- *Finance*. Cash flow implications, finance for marketing campaigns, etc.
- *Human resourcing*. Training requirements, specialist recruitment, etc.
- *Operations*. Cost and volume implications of switching production, etc.

The strategy itself should be developed in conjunction with as wide a body of individuals as possible. This will help coordinate marketing with other aspects of the organisation and 'ground' strategies within local realities. Additionally, two very good further reasons exist for such an approach. First, these individuals will need to implement the strategy and will therefore need to be committed to it. Second, the involvement of others leads to a greater depth of shared knowledge and understanding in order to produce a robust strategy.

Marketing research is the investigation of the marketing activities of a company (the entire marketing mix). It looks into how far all these activities are consumer-orientated, and how they might be planned in the future. This therefore includes branding, product mix, pricing, advertising, sales promotion, public relations, packaging and distribution. In this way, the importance of marketing research is to provide information that will enable the correct marketing decisions to be made. One of these key decisions must be the commitment of funds to marketing itself, including research costs, advertising costs, promotions, etc. Marketing research can therefore be used in two contexts; to provide a basis for developing a new strategy and to review the existing strategy.

The processes and techniques used in monitoring, implementing and controlling a marketing plan are arguably as important, if not more important, than the processes involved in formulating the strategy.

Once developed, the strategy should be approved by top management and communicated to staff to ensure effective implementation. This will extend beyond those involved in the marketing function and will include colleagues in other areas such as finance, production and research and development. Marketing is not an island and the strategy will not succeed without the cooperation of others.

Inevitably factors will alter and the action plan should be used for progress monitoring and should be continually reviewed, revised and updated as the marketing campaign progresses. With a greater emphasis being attached to measuring and monitoring performance more sophisticated tools are being developed. This control information is helpful in both coping with volatile environments and also ensuring greater internal accountability.

4.9.2 Product development and the product life cycle

Classically marketing explains products as passing through a cycle of life. Most products are said to have a life cycle, which has distinct stages:

Introduction. An organisation starts to produce and sell a new product. Initially, demand is low. Heavy advertising or other selling costs are needed to make customers aware of the product. High prices can be charged, because the product is new and supply is limited. Only a limited distribution network exists for the product. There is likely to be a single or limited product range to avoid confusing the customer and there will be a need to induce product recognition amongst potential customers.

Growth. Demand for the product builds. Product design improves as producers gain production and marketing experience. Advertising and sales promotion are still important. The distribution network expands. Competition between rival producers intensifies. The most significant feature of this stage is increasing complexity as rivals enter the market and the range of products widens as producers seek to attract customers from each other with novel features. The marketing focus switches to seeking to differentiate the firm's product and brand in the minds of customers. Prices fall, but profits improve because of the higher volume of sales.

> ❗ Some marketers consider that an addition phase (*shakeout*) occurs when sales growth begins to dip and market is saturated by providers. The weakest providers are 'shook' out and exit the business.

Maturity. This is the longest stage in the life cycle of most successful products. This is where purchases settle down into a pattern of repeat or replacement purchasing. Demand has reached its limit. In general, prices fall. A good distribution network has built up, and advertising costs per dollar, euro or pound of sales are low. Further advertising, product design changes, and segmentation can extend the maturity phase of a product's life.

Decline. The product declines into obsolescence as technically superior alternatives replace it. The existence of such alternatives will cause sharp profit reductions among producers of the product. Many firms will have already found alternative industries, while those remaining will be looking for an orderly way to exit the industry. As demand starts to fall, so too do prices (and profits). Eventually the product disappears from the market.

The product life cycle (Figure 4.1) can be used to help determine appropriate strategies for the organisation and help inform decisions over investment in products.

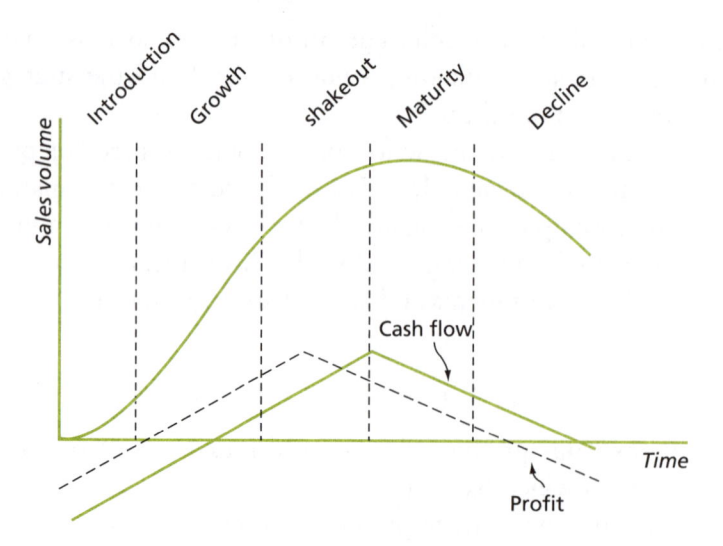

Figure 4.1 The product life cycle

✋ Exercise 4.12

What are the practical problems associated with the model?

✅ Solution

- It is difficult to determine where the product is on the cycle with any accuracy.
- It assumes that all the stages are inevitable yet certain products (e.g. Kellogg's cornflakes) have existed in their present form for many years.
- It considers a product singly and not as part of an overall portfolio.

The marketing mix will change over time as the product goes into different stages of its 'life'. When a product is in its 'growth' stages of life, the marketing mix might emphasise the development of sales outlets and advertising. In its 'mature' phase, there might need to be more concern for product quality. To postpone the eventual decline, it may be necessary to reduce prices and spend more on advertising.

✋ Exercise 4.13

Review the commentary earlier on the four stages of the product life cycle and identify the implications on the variables of price, promotion and place.

4.9.3 Investing in products

A product portfolio is a collection of products or services an organisation provides to its customers. For example, a life assurance firm may offer a number of products such as pensions, endowments, whole life, critical illness and guaranteed income policies. There are three aspects of an organisation's product mix, namely:

1. length, or overall number of individual products offered
2. breadth of product lines (Lancaster and Withey (2006) give an example of a coffee producer having separate lines for ground coffee, instant coffee, and coffee beans)

Table 4.10 BCG product classifications

Cash cow	Characterised by relatively high market share but low market growth. Function: generating cash for use elsewhere.
Problem child	Characterised by relatively low market share but high market growth. For these products to succeed investment is needed to improve market share. If insufficient funds are available choices will need to be made over which to invest in and which to let go.
Star	Characterised by relatively high market share and high market growth. Although investment may be needed to maintain market share it is worthwhile as the market size is growing. Stars will become tomorrow's cash cows.
Dog	Characterised by relatively low market share and low market growth. There may be little justification for continuing to invest in these products.

3 depth, the products in each product line, so for instance within the ground coffee line there might be Columbian rich, Brazilian gold, Mild blend, etc.

An organisation will need to determine how much funding it allocates to each product within its overall portfolio of products. Decisions such as which products to discontinue, promote more, conduct further research into, etc. are all essential considerations. One popular framework for helping understanding is the Boston Consulting Group (BCG) matrix, which plots in a 2 × 2 cell all products according to the growth rate of the market served and the market share held. Products are then classified as being 'stars', 'cash cows', 'a problem child' or a 'dog'. Table 4.10 summarises the possibilities.

Question mark products are in a high growth market which means that it is early in the product life cycle and therefore has the potential to repay present investment over its life cycle. Indeed the high market growth rate means that the firm will already be investing considerable sums in it. The low relative market share, however, means that this business unit is unlikely to survive in the long run because it will have a lower cost competitor. Management must decide between investing considerably more in the product to *build* its market share or shutting it down now before it absorbs any further investment which it will never repay. Investing to build can include: price reductions; additional promotion and securing of distribution channels; acquisition of rivals; product modification.

Star products are competitively strong due to high relative market share, although their current results will be poor due to the need to invest considerable funds into keeping up with the market growth rate. The strategy here is to *hold* market share by investing sufficient to match the commitment of rivals and the requirements of the marketplace.

Cash cows are mature products (with low growth rate) which retain a high relative market share. The mature stage means that their prospects are limited to falling prices and volumes. Therefore investment will be kept under strict review and instead the priority is to maximise the value of free cash flows through a policy of *harvesting* the product. *Harvest* means to minimise additional investment in the product to maximise the case the division is spinning off. This cash can be used to support the question mark products as well as satisfy demands for dividends and interest. Holding may also be used for early-mature stage products where the market may repay the extra investment.

Dogs products are either former cash cows that have lost market share due to management's refusal to invest in them or former question marks which still had a low relative share when the market reaches maturity. Organisations should divest themselves of dogs.

When plotted precisely an organisation's products can be placed against the axes of:

- *Relative market share* calculated as the firm's market share against their largest rival, so a firm with a 20 per cent share of the market which has a rival with a 60 per cent share would have $0.3\times \left(\frac{20}{60} = 0.3\times\right)$, while the rival would calculate their relative share as $\frac{60}{20}\times = 3\times$.
- *Market growth rate*, the annual percentage change in sales volume in the industry as a whole.

This is shown in Figure 4.2.

The principal benefits of the BCG matrix are that it:

- Provides a convenient way for management to visualise a diverse range of businesses or products.
- Ensures that management will pay attention to cash-flow balances within the product portfolio.
- Can be used to analyse the portfolios of rival firms: to identify which products they may decide to devote resources to spot potential areas for attack such as knocking out a crucial cash cow with an identical product.

4.9.4 Pricing strategies

Reference was made earlier to generic competitive strategy and the possibility of an organisation competing on the basis of price. If this is the chosen strategy it is important that excess production costs are squeezed with the overall aim that the organisation will be cost leader within their market. These savings should be passed on to the customer and will be reflected in low prices. Larger, well-established businesses are better able to compete on price. This is generally as a result of two basic concepts:

- *The experience curve.* Reductions in the average unit cost price as a result of learning from past experiences.

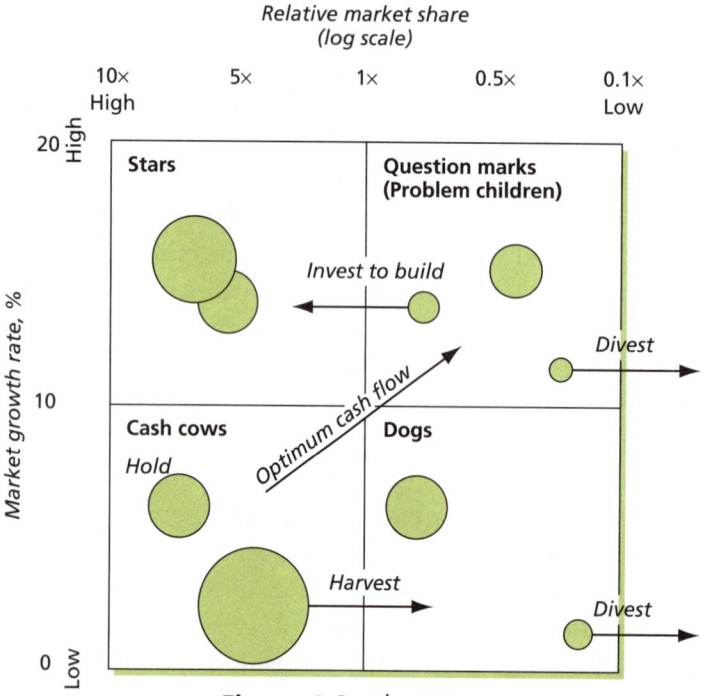

Figure 4.2 The BCG matrix

- *Economies of scale.* Reductions in the average unit cost price as a result of size of operation.

There can after all only be one price leader in a market. It may be more advisable therefore to add value to the product so differentiating it from the competitors offering in some way. Alternatively, part of the market (a segment) might be identified where the competition will find it hard to access. Here the organisation is in a position to price on the basis of 'what the market will bear'.

Pricing can be explained by reference to the product life cycle (see earlier).

Exercise 4.14

For each of the four stages of the product life cycle describe the pricing considerations.

Solution

- *Introduction.* High prices might be charged, because the product is new and supply is limited also initial set up costs need to be recovered.
- *Growth.* Competition between rival producers intensifies so prices will reduce in the hope of penetrating the existing market and either retaining or increasing market share at the expense of competitors.
- *Maturity.* Prices fall mainly in order to beat competitors but the experience curve and scale economies should come into play. Market segments are sought where higher prices can be charged.
- *Decline.* The product declines into obsolescence so it may even be sold off below cost price to clear stocks and exit the market.

Two forms of pricing might also be applied particularly in the introduction stage of the product life cycle, namely:

- *Skim pricing* reflecting high prices but low profit due to high fixed costs.
- *Penetration pricing*, deliberately entering a market to build market share and pricing so as to deny the competitors those opportunities.

There may be several other considerations when fixing price and some of which include:

- The nature of competition. If the competitor is the price leader pricing levels may be determined by *follow the leader* pricing. So, for instance, if the largest oil company cuts the price of fuel, others are likely to follow suit.
- The nature of the market. By way of example, a company may find itself in the fortunate position of being the sole producer of a product due to a monopoly of 'know-how', resources or raw materials, etc.
- Pricing as a result of a short-term promotion. This may lead to *loss leader* pricing on certain items to generate either customer loyalty or more sales of other products. This is particularly popular in pricing consumables in supermarkets.
- Pricing as a competitive weapon. The pricing of product may be set in order to crush competitors rather than achieve returns in revenue.

4.10 Branding

4.10.1 Brand equity

It is impossible to ignore brands. By merely observing what is worn, what is purchased from a supermarket, and the cars that are driven it is apparent that brands are all around us. Brands are however much more than corporate symbols, logos and packaging. Successful brands create special relationships with customers because they rely on intangible attributes that provoke strong emotional responses by individuals. Motorcyclists do not so much ride a large bike such as own a Harley Davidson with all the connotations surrounding that brand which once had the strap line 'ride the dream'. Grandparents by comparison insist on only purchasing one type of cough lozenge; something they have bought all their lives. Whether it is the motorcyclist or the grandparent they are showing brand loyalty. Little wonder then that 'brand loyalty' is a significant source of competitive advantage for organisations with products that have a positive strong brand image. The value of brands exists in the minds of those who use them. CIM identify certain attributes of brands as follows:

- people use brands to make statements about themselves
- goods brands reduce the risk of poor product choice
- brands can be a key asset for a business
- brands are the reason consumers choose one company over another
- although intangible, brands can be of substantial value
- strong brands can positively influence share performance
- brands can command higher prices

4.10.2 Experiential marketing

Experiential marketing (EM) is concerned with brand promotion. EM uses techniques aimed at establishing deeper emotional connection with a market segment (see Table 4.11). Kirkby (2007) explains:

Table 4.11 Examples of experiential marketing

Organisation	Aim	Mechanisms
Strongbow cider	Challenge negative perception of its brand and engage more 18–30 year olds.	'In the know' music events at music festivals with cult DJs; media partnerships with relevant 'hip' music magazines.
Umbro, sports supplier	Demonstrate its love of football.	Organising a touring World Cup photographic exhibition.
Dove, body products	Challenge the stereotypical model of female beauty.	Using 'real' women (not models) in its advertising.

Source: http://www.mycustomer.com/cgi

> ❗ Experiential marketing (EM) is a hybrid of field marketing (FM) shop floor product promotion techniques, e.g. sampling, merchandising and point of sale offers. Only the objective of experiential marketing is not to just sell more products, but to engage a target audience with the 'personality' of the brand through experiencing it..... what EM is not, and has been much mistaken for, is product promotion with entertainment thrown on top. Dressing sampling staff up as drag queens to sell more bleach, as one company did, is amplified product promotion, it is not experiential marketing....

4.11 Summary

This chapter has covered much of the basics of marketing in practice, including the marketing concept, buyer behaviour and the notion of the marketing mix and its associated tools. Throughout understanding has been built of the applicability of marketing to many types of organisation and the particular considerations associated with them.

References and further reading

Anon (2003) How to…influence employee behaviour through internal marketing. *Personnel Today*, 8th April.

Berens, C. (2006) Windows of opportunity. *Financial Management* (UK), November, p.12(5).

Benady, D. (2004) Marketing's age concern. *Marketing Week*, 28 October.

Boddy, D. and Paton, R. (2005) *Management. An Introduction* (3rd edn). Harlow: Financial Times, Prentice Hall.

Bruce, I. (2005) *Charity Marketing: Meeting Need through Customer Focus'* (3rd edn). ICSA.

The Chartered Institute of Marketing (2004) [www.cim.co.uk]

CIMA (2005) *CIMA Official Terminology*. Elsevier.

Deighton, J. A. The Future of Interactive Marketing. *Harvard Business Review* 74, no. 6 (November – December 1996), pp. 151–160.

Entrepeneur.com (2006) *How to Develop and Run a Marketing Campaign.* [http://small-business.aol.com/grow/marketing/article/_a/how-to-develop-and-run-a-marketing/20051213184009990005]

Fine, J. (2005) Hard questions from Google; Asking advertisers: What's the right amount to spend? *Business Week*, 24 October, p. 28.

Gray, R. (2004) Right people, place, time. *Marketing* (UK), 1 August, p. 23.

Holme, R. and Watts, P. (2000) *Corporate social responsibility: making good business sense.* World Business Council for Sustainable Development, 2000: 10

Houston, F. (1986) The marketing concept: What it is and what it is not. *Journal of Marketing*, 5th. April, pp. 81–87.

Johnson, G., Scholes, K. and Whittington, R. (2008) *Exploring Corporate Strategy: Text and Cases* (8th edn). Harlow: Financial Times, Prentice Hall.

Kirkby, J. (2007) *What art thou experiential marketing?* 14th. August [http://www.mycustomer.com/cgi]

Kotler, P. and Armstrong, G. (1994) *Principles of Marketing*. New Jersey, Prentice-Hall.

Kotler, P. and Lane Keller, K. (2006) *Marketing Management* (12th edn). Prentice Hall.

Kotler, P. and Zaltman, G. (1971) Social marketing: an approach to planned social change. *Journal of Marketing*, Vol. 35 No. 3, pp. 3–12.

Lancaster, G. and Withey, F. (2006) *Marketing Fundamentals*. The official CIM Coursebook Oxford: Butterworth-Heinemann.

Levinson, J. L. (1983) *Guerrilla Marketing: Secrets for Making Big Profits from Your Small Business.* Boston: Houghton Mifflin & Co.

MacArthur, K. (2006) Why McD's hasn't cut the fat, *Advertising Age*, 11/6/2006, Vol. 77, No. 45.

Mullins, L. J. (2007) *Management and Organisational Behaviour* (8th edn). Harlow: Financial Times, Prentice Hall.

Porter, M. E. (1980) *Competitive Strategy.* New York: The Free Press.

Proctor, T. (2007) *Public Sector Marketing.* Pearson.

Simms, J. (2007) Biggest Brands. *Marketing*, 22 August, pp. 30–31.

also

National Social Marketing Centre (2008) (www.nsms.org.uk)

Entrepreneur.com

Revision Questions 4

❓ Question 1

In the last few decades, companies have moved increasingly towards the targeting of particular customer segments rather than seeking to sell a single product range to all customers. Explain the advantages that a company might hope to gain by targeting particular segments of the market. **(10 marks)**

❓ Question 2

2.1 Public relations activity can be used within marketing as part of:

    (A) marketing decision support protocols
    (B) a promotional mix
    (C) customer complaints and feedback processes
    (D) segmentation practices. **(2 marks)**

2.2 Charging very low prices in order to generate customer loyalty and increased sales of other items is called:

    (A) market penetration
    (B) loss leader pricing
    (C) product penetration
    (D) skim pricing. **(2 marks)**

2.3 An organisation's credit policy represents a variable within:

    (A) the price marketing mix
    (B) the product marketing mix
    (C) product placement
    (D) the matrix of potential sales and growth. **(2 marks)**

2.4 Explain the concept of physical evidence when applied to the marketing mix. (50 word limit) **(4 marks)**

2.5 Identify the potential benefits of a marketing database and sources from which it might be constructed. (50 word limit) **(4 marks)**

2.6 Explain why a firm might choose not to engage in market segmentation after conducting appropriate research. (50 word limit) **(4 marks)**

2.7 Briefly explain the data and techniques that might be useful in forecasting future market demand for an organisation's products or services. (50 word limit) **(4 marks)**

Question 3

Describe three variables you think would be useful as a basis for segmenting the market for clothing sold by a large retail chain, and two variables for segmenting the market in paint sold to other businesses by a paint manufacturer. Explain your reasons for the choice of all variables. **(10 marks)**

Question 4

Hubbles, a national high-street clothing retailer has recently appointed a new Chief Executive. The company is well established and relatively financially secure. It has a reputation for stability and traditional, quality clothing at an affordable price. Lately, however, it has suffered from intense competition leading to a loss of market share and an erosion of customer loyalty.

Hubbles has all the major business functions provided by 'in house' departments, including finance, human resources, purchasing, strategy and marketing. The Strategy and Marketing department has identified a need for comprehensive review of the company's effectiveness. In response, the new Chief Executive has commissioned a review by management consultants.

Their initial findings include the following:

- Hubbles has never moved from being sales-oriented to being marketing-oriented and this is why it has lost touch with its customers.
- Hubbles now needs to get closer to its customers and operate a more effective marketing mix.
- Additional investment in its purchasing department can add significantly to improving Hubbles' competitive position.

The Chief Executive feels that a presentation of interim findings to senior managers would be helpful at this point. You are a member of the management consultancy team and have been asked to draft a *PowerPoint* slide presentation of some of the key points.

On a single sheet of paper prepare a slide outline and a few notes in response to following sub-questions:

(a) Describe the difference between a company that concentrates on 'selling' its products and one that has adopted a marketing approach. **(5 marks)**
(b) Explain how Hubbles might develop itself into an organisation that is driven by customer needs. **(5 marks)**
(c) Explain what is meant by the 'marketing mix'. **(5 marks)**
(d) Identify examples of ways in which the management in Hubbles could make use of the marketing mix to help regain its competitive position. **(5 marks)**

Question 5

Q's founder first began producing breakfast food from a start-up unit on a small industrial estate. Now Q is the market leader in Europe and Oceania. Once established in Europe, the company made the breakthrough into Oceania thanks to demand from ex-pats and contacts with a family member who happened to be a director of a supermarket chain in Australia. The company's founder is very 'hands on' and has made all the major strategic decisions to date based on intuition.

Q spends heavily on displaying most of their twenty products on television, normally before and after childrens' programmes with high viewing figures. Research conducted 10 years ago shows that children love small gifts contained within packs and the association of certain of the products to cartoon characters. Q also manufactures its most popular lines and packages them as 'own brand' alternatives for some large supermarket chains. These sell more cheaply than Q branded products, are less costly to produce (they contain inexpensive packaging and no gifts) but sales remains low.

Q finds itself at something of a 'cross-roads' as it currently faces increasing competition (from a North American firm), sales levels that seem to have 'peaked' and the prospect of the founder retiring very soon. Management consultants advising Q have identified a need to develop a structured marketing strategic plan for the organisation and for greater involvement of other staff in future strategic decisions. As a further complication Q has recently received some adverse publicity from an international health 'watchdog' body that claims that Q's products contain potentially harmful levels of both sugar and salt.

Requirements

(a) Evaluate Q's situation making specific mention of marketing and ethical issues.

(10 marks)

(b) Explain how Q might develop a marketing strategic plan. **(10 marks)**

Solutions to Revision Questions

✓ Solution 1

Companies have a number of alternatives as to where they will focus their marketing effort. They can adopt an undifferentiated marketing stance in which they make a product offering to the market as a whole. They can alternatively seek to cater for the needs of each individual customer, a bespoke approach, finally they can focus on particular segments of the market. The idea of dividing the market into segments is to identify groups of potential consumers who have similar needs and will respond to a particular marketing mix in broadly similar ways.

The undifferentiated or mass marketing approach is inefficient in many ways because much of the marketing effort is wasted on consumers who have no interest in purchasing the product or service and are unlikely to do so whatever the efforts of the marketing staff.

The alternative of targeting and catering for the different needs of every individual customer is costly and impractical for most organisations. Resources in organisations are limited and the task of dealing with each customer on a one-to-one basis is too costly for most companies to contemplate.

The advantage of market segmentation is that it allows a company to concentrate its resources on meeting the needs of consumers who have been identified by market research as those who are most likely to purchase the product or service. This is, of course, if the product or service is of an appropriate quality and is offered at the right price, in the right place at the right time.

In addition to the advantage of being able to concentrate resources in a way that will bring the greatest return, segmentation has other advantages. These include easier analysis of customers, a better understanding of the competition and more effective market planning.

Segmentation allows a company to gain a better understanding of customer needs, wants and other characteristics because of the sharper focus it allows on the personal, situational and behavioural factors that characterise customers in a particular segment of the market. This detailed knowledge allows marketers to respond quickly to any changes in what the target customers want.

Competitor analysis is also assisted by knowledge of market segmentation because it enables a company to develop an understanding of the nature of the competition they face. By focussing on particular segments, it is much easier for a company to identify its competitors and at which segments it is targeting its products. If the company observes that competition is severe in a particular segment, it may be that this knowledge of market segments will allow the company to focus on a different segment and so avoid head-on and costly competition.

Finally, knowledge of market segments assists with marketing planning. Dividing markets up allows organisations to develop plans that give special attention to the particular needs of customers in different segments. The time scale of such plans can also be facilitated because some segments change more rapidly than others and such changes need to be anticipated in any planning operation. The markets in ladies' fashions and in recorded music are examples of rapidly changing markets and of the need to anticipate and to plan accordingly.

✅ Solution 2

2.1 (B)

2.2 (B)

2.3 (A)

2.4 Marketing mix: a manufacturing firm's 'blend' of price, product, promotion, place.

For service organisations other relevant factors include a lack of 'physical evidence', because:

- Services are intangible
- Potential customers may therefore feel greater risk.

Reassurance is therefore needed. (e.g. testimonials/references from past customers).

2.5

Data	Benefits
One-off market research data already available	Improves problem-solving capacity
Other marketing intelligence	Method of structuring decisions
Internal information on products, trends, markets and competitors, etc.	Integrates all types of knowledge
	Maximises IT potential
	Total system of marketing information to support decisions

2.6
- The market is so insubstantial that the effort is not justified
- Market life cycle in decline therefore little future potential
- Difficulty (and cost) in analysing market
- Homogeneous market making segmentation unnecessary
- Competitors already established in all profitable segments.

2.7
- Buyer survey of intentions
- Sales force forecasts
- Expert opinion/judgement
- Statistical techniques using historical sales data
- Market testing of products
- Assessing total market potential/sales and relative market share
- Estimates based on linked factors (e.g. temperate forecasts and heat consumption)

☑ Solution 3

In the segmentation of consumer markets the availability of information on demographic, socio-economic and geographic location variables have made their usage popular.

Demographic variables include age, gender, family, race, and religion; socio-economic variables include income, occupation, education and social class; geographic location variables include country, region, type of urban area, and type of housing. The use of lifestyle, motives and personality are also increasingly used for segmentation purposes.

There is no single best way of segmenting a market and few if any market segments can be regarded as timeless but experience tells us that a number of variables have been found useful as a basis for segmenting particular markets.

Some of the useful bases for segmenting the market for clothing include the following:

- Differences in the clothing worn by males and females is so evident that it hardly needs to be mentioned. Males and females do, however, wear different styles and items of clothing so it is necessary to design, promote, price and place male and female clothing according to the demands in each market segment.
- A second useful variable is that of age. Common observation tells us that retailers segment the population according to age. So it is common in a retail department store to see not only men's and women's clothing displayed separately but also clothing for children, young teenagers, older teenagers, and young adults to mature adults.
- Another variable that may be used is that of occupation. Professional, managerial and administrative workers tend to wear business suits to the office while other occupational groups tend to wear more casual attire.
- The clothing market can be segmented by other variables related to occupation such as income. High-income earners can afford more exclusive and expensive clothing than middle-income earners who in turn can afford better quality clothing than low-income earners. The above variables represent the more common bases for segmentation.

The segmenting of organisational or industrial markets is less frequently carried out than segmentation in consumer markets but nevertheless, companies find it increasingly useful.

Organisations may segment markets according to personal characteristics of buyers, situational factors such as urgency and size of order, purchasing approach, technologies applied by buying organisations, and demographic aspects like location, industry and size.

An example of segmentation according to personal characteristics of buyers might be a paint manufacturer who segments potential customers into several different groups such as paint wholesalers, do-it-yourself retail outlets, housing developers, contracting decorators, and vehicle manufacturers.

Segmenting according to situational factors such as order size can also be illustrated by the example of the paint manufacturer. The size of container and packaging of the paint will vary according to the user needs of the customer. Contracting decorators, for instance, may need large containers, but will not be particularly concerned about packaging, while do-it-yourself outlets may require containers of various sizes with attractive decoration.

Solution 4

(a)
Slide 1:
Features of sales-orientated organisations:

- Aggressive selling, advertising and sales promotion.
- A concentration on selling not marketing.
- A strong sales department.

Marketing is about:

- Supplying what the customer wants.
- An organisation-wide philosophy.

Notes to Slide 1:
The claim that Hubbles concentrates on 'selling' implies that it is not focussed on customer needs. Instead of finding out what the customer wants, it is trying to sell whatever items it happens to have in stock.

(b)
Slide 2:
Adopting the marketing concept:

- focus on potential customer needs (and how these can be satisfied);
- greatest opportunity 5 meeting needs (gaps) not currently met;
- implies market research, competitor product research;
- possible future benchmarking;
- NOT a change to the Marketing department: a new way of organisational thinking;
- training for all staff;
- management to help by providing the right products and resources.

Notes to Slide 2:
Reorientation means Hubbles to change the way it defines and investigates its markets, prices, products and communication with its customers. The critical people are the front-line staff that customers come into direct contact with. This customer-led focus should permeate every department so that the needs of the customer are kept in view at all times.

(c)
Slide 3:
Components of marketing mix:

- *Product*. Customers' product wants and desired characteristics;
- *Place* (distribution). Desired quantity available at the right place and time;
- *Promotion*. Increasing awareness of products; inform about product features; keep interest;
- *Price*. Is critical and can be used as a competitive tool.

Plus sometimes added for service organisations:

- *People*. Staff decisions, image and actions central to the other marketing mix components.

Notes to Slide 3:
After Hubbles has identified its target market, it will be in a position to develop its marketing mix. Components are decision variables that can be changed and Hubbles must decide how to create and maintain a marketing mix that satisfies consumers' needs.

(d)
Slide 4:

- *Product*. Develop new products, modify/enhance existing ones and eliminate others.
- *Place*. Improve inventory, transport and storage to serve market. Well-sited premises redesigned to reflect brand, and so on.
- *Promotion*. Rebranding, advertising campaigns, using different media to target groups.
- *Price*. Revise pricing structure to convey value, or price below competitors.
- *People*. Training programmes, monitoring systems and on going support can influence buyer behaviour.

Notes to Slide 4:
Must develop a marketing mix that precisely matches the needs of potential customers in the target market. First research the market for data about the age, income, sex and educational level of target market, preferences for product features and attitudes to competitors' products.

✓ Solution 5

(a) CM's situation (marketing including ethical issues)

Major challenges
CM is said to be facing three major challenges:

- increasing competition
- sales levels that seem to have 'peaked'
- the prospect of the retirement of the key decision maker.

Competition: CM is the market leader in breakfast food manufacture in Europe and Oceania but is facing increasing competition (from North America). CM appears to have no presence on the other continents, making it an international rather than global player. Although diets vary across continents it is likely that the North American diet (at least) is similar. This means that potentially other firms are supplying the American market and these competitors could be powerful and have the ability to challenging CM's leadership in its own markets. CM needs to decide how it responds to this threat from international competition. There is no information on the basis upon which CM's competitors' marketing mix varies from their own. If an alternative mix to CM is apparently proving more successful then CM should reexamine their own mix accordingly (See later).

More positively Q should recognise that potential markets on other continents exist and these represent opportunities for development.

Sales: Sales levels seem to have 'peaked'. One interpretation can be drawn from an understanding of the concept of the market life cycle. When the life cycle of a market reaches so called 'maturity' stage demand will have reached its limit. If this is the case, CM should consider new products or new markets before the market life moves into a 'decline' stage. In terms of product range CM has a portfolio of twenty product items, but it unclear how often this range is 'refreshed'. Reference to potential new markets, maybe outside Europe and Oceania has been referred to earlier.

Decision making (and Strategic Marketing approach): CM's founder, as the key decision maker, is retiring soon. He/she is credited with growing CM to its present size from a business 'start-up' operation. He/She is very 'hands on' and has made all the major strategic decisions to date based on intuition. (It is apparent that there is no structured strategic marketing plan). The development into another geographical market typically seems to have resulted through good fortune and market demand rather than a rational decision-making and promotional efforts. (CM made the breakthrough into Oceania thanks to a demand from ex-pats and contacts with a family member who happened to be a director of a supermarket chain in Australia). Organisationally, it is difficult to continue operating in this way, particularly with the retirement of the founder. Although the organisational culture could properly be described as entrepreneurial CM's sheer size may mean that some of the spirit is in any case diminishing.

This can in part be explained by reference to Greiner's organisational growth model (1972). Under this model firms can experience evolutionary growth that eventually leads a situation of revolutionary crisis, when the organisation's ways of doing things become less effective. The implication of this thinking is that change is unavoidable, and ways of overcoming each crisis need to be determined for the organisation to continue growing. Under the model, the first phase of growth is achieved by some creative idea, product or service that enables the organisation to become established in the market place. A crisis occurs when the entrepreneur's informal and personal approach to managing the business simply cannot cope with its increased size. This crisis of leadership appears to have been reached within CM. If the organisation can adopt more formal systems of management (in CM's case strategic marketing), there will be a basis for further growth through 'direction'.

Other issues!

Ethical issues. The adverse publicity from an international health 'watchdog' body that claims that CM's products contain potentially harmful levels of both sugar and salt raises ethical concerns. CM spends 'heavily' on TV advertising and undoubtedly the target audience for CM's promotional effort is children as it advertises before and after childrens' programmes. The inclusion of small gifts contained within packs and the association of certain of the products to cartoon characters and expensive packaging confirms as much. Children influence their parents to purchase the product. The ethical issues are as follows:

IS it 'right' that promotion is based on children placing demands on their parents particularly if their parent cannot afford to buy the product?
The sugar and salt content are apparently important in achieving a taste that children like. Is it ethical to manufacture and sell products that might be unhealthy to vulnerable children?

The adverse publicity may impact upon sales. CM will need to decide how it responds to these claims, for instance:

- Conduct its own research and possibly challenge the watchdog claims.
- Discredit the findings and the body making the claims.
- Modify its product content so there is less salt and sugar present.
- Increase promotion to compensate any fall off in sales as a result of adverse publicity.

Product nature: there is good reason for believing that the associated features and packaging are the most significant product feature, specifically:

Past research confirms that children love small gifts contained within packs and the association of certain of the products to cartoon characters.

Some products are sold as 'own brand' alternatives for some large supermarket chains. Although these sell more cheaply than CM branded products but are less costly to produce as they contain inexpensive packaging and no free gifts. The minimal sales underlining the point that packaging and advertising are crucial.

Marketing mix: CM's current marketing mix has evidently developed over time and seems to be the product of decisions made by the company's founder. CM can properly be described as a 'marketing-orientated' organisation as it has a main focus of the customer (children) and their demands. The mix exhibits in particular product features and packaging, **promotion** through expensive advertising, and (using the fifth P of the marketing) the founder as the key **person**. In terms of **place** sales are through supermarkets and based on two continents. The **price** reflects high promotional costs and expensive packaging.

(b) Developing a marketing strategic plan for CM

An important point, particularly given CM's own position of a lack of formal strategy and the past influence of a single person (the founder), is that a range of people from within the organisation should be involved. Although marketing specialists might lead processes all functional areas should participate in developing the strategy. This is important so that there is ownership, realism and coordination.

In order for CM to develop a Marketing Strategic plan a number of key processes will need to be undertaken. Some of these processes might be undertaken concurrently, and are identified below.

Identify and articulate CM's corporate objectives and the role that marketing can play in achieving them.

Conducting an audit of the external environment

This will involve a detailed investigation of:

- The market for manufactured breakfast food.
- The market segments which CM is interested in (e.g. European childrens' eating habits and preferences).
- The trends influencing the market, typically using a PEST (political, economic, socio-cultural and technological) framework for analysis (Other alternative frameworks might be used including PESTEL which also recognises environmental and legal factors etc.). A consideration of CM's position relative to the most significant factors (including potential realistic ways in which the organisation might influence such factors) should be undertaken.

- The activities, strategic capability and strengths and weakness of competitors.
- Future potential scenarios and tends possibly using industry and other experts.

Conducting an internal analysis

This will clarify what CM wants to achieve over the planning period and its capability including marketing competences, specifically:

- The identification of the factors that contribute towards CM's strengths and weaknesses. These internal factors are controllable and may lead to the development of targets.
- The agreement of corporate aspirations including specific marketing objectives and SMART (specific, measurable achievable realistic and time bound) targets.

Synthesis and discussion

Some of the main factors arising from the above processes might be synthesised into a SWOT (strengths, weaknesses, opportunities and threats) analysis. (SW are internal and OT are external factors).

Discussions should focus on developing an appropriate mix of marketing factors to achieve CM's objectives in the light of earlier analysis; this will include any actions necessary to bridge gaps between expectations and capability. Specifically, the mix will address future actions relating to pricing issues, promotional activity, place, and product features.

Communication and coordination

A strategy can ultimately be developed. It will however need to be carefully coordinated with other functional strategies including Finance, IT and HR.

The strategy should be written, approved by CM's decision-makers and clearly communicated to the workforce. The strategy will include:

- Clear marketing goals and objectives
- Targets, measures and performance indicators
- The costing of the plan and the development of a revenue budget
- An identification and costing of any capital requirements
- Identification of strategic alternatives
- A detailed action plan.

5

Managing Human Capital

Managing Human Capital

5

> **LEARNING OUTCOMES**
>
> This chapter concerns an organisation's most powerful yet unpredictable asset: its human resource (HR). It addresses the functional areas of managing human capital including major developments and associated tools and techniques. By completing this chapter it should help you to:
>
> - Explain how HR theories and activities can contribute to the success of the organisation
> - Explain the importance of ethical behaviour in business generally and for the line manager and their activities
> - Explain the HR activities associated with developing the ability of employees including recruitment, selection, induction, appraisal, training and career planning activities of a project team
> - Discuss the HR activities associated with the motivation of employees
> - Describe the HR activities associated with improving the opportunities for employees to contribute to the firm
> - Discuss the importance of the line manager in the implementation of HR practices
> - Prepare a HR plan appropriate to a team.
>
> This should enable you to explain the relationship of HR to the organisation's operations and discuss the activities associated with the management of human capital.

5.1 Human resource management and organisational success

Organisations at their most basic level are nothing more than collections of people. The policies, procedures and practices associated with people are commonly referred to either 'personnel' or 'human resource' matters. Since organisations came into being it has always been the case that people issues and hence HR theories and activities have been crucial to corporate success.

Human resource management (HRM) emerged as a concept during the 1980s representing a major shift of emphasis in the way in which employees were viewed. Armstrong (2006) defined HRM as 'a strategic approach to the acquisition, motivation, development and management of the organisation's human resources.' Bratton and Gold (2007) offered a more detailed definition of HRM:

> That part of the management process that specialises in the management of people in work organisations. HRM emphasises that employees are critical to achieving sustainable competitive advantage, that human resources practices need to be integrated with the corporate strategy, and that human resource specialists help organisational controllers to meet both efficiency and equity objectives.

HRM forms part of an approach to planning and resource deployment within the context of the external environment. HRM is essentially a strategically driven activity, not only as a major contributor to the strategic process but also a determining part of it. Although prescriptive by nature it is concerned with developing initiatives articulated in various planning documents including business plans. HRM determines general policies for employment relationships. It has long-term perspectives and seeks to coherently integrate all the human aspects of the organisation. It needs to help develop an organisational culture that produces employee commitment and co-operation. Unlike the predecessor concept Personnel, the HRM starting point is not with people, but with the organisation's needs for human resources. Table 5.1 summarises the development of thinking surrounding the management of people.

Early writers such as Frederick W. Taylor (1856–1917) looked at ways of maximising productivity. Taylor's long working experience in industry led him to conclude that:

- workers varied their pace at work to suit the conditions
- managers made little effort to specify what made up a 'reasonable day's work'
- no effort was made to identify the best methods, nor to train the workers in them.

Taylor reasoned that the prime objective of management should be to secure the maximum prosperity for both employer and employee. He established four principles:

1. The development of a true 'science' of work; an assessment of what constituted a fair day's work, as well as a fair day's pay.
2. The scientific selection and progressive development of workers, involving careful recruitment and training to ensure that the worker was capable of achieving output and quality targets.
3. The bringing together of the science of work and the scientifically selected and trained men. The workforce were encouraged to develop to their full potential mentally and physically.
4. The constant and intimate co-operation between management and workers, for instance over the allocation of tasks.

Table 5.1 Eras in managing people

The Industrial Revolution 18th & 19th centuries	Factory owners improved their methods of recruitment, training and other related activities by trial and error.
	Early factories often characterised by the harsh treatment of employees.
	Philanthropic employers contributed to improvements in working life by running 'model factories' and appointing industrial welfare workers to 'look after' their employees.
	1881: University of Pennsylvania launched an undergraduate business education program so saving costs for the local steel company
	1911: Frederick Winslow Taylor argues that there is only one objectively correct way to perform industrial jobs.
First World War	Large numbers of women in factory environments.
	Thousands of women supervisors appointed to observe and regulate conditions of workforce.
	At the end of the war in 1918, the establishment of the industrial welfare officer reflected in the setting up of the 'Welfare Workers' Association.
1918–1939 interwar	Pressure to cut costs and increase efficiency encouraged the use of the ideas of scientific management and, later, the use of human relations techniques to secure the commitment and motivation of workers.
Second World War	Demand for the productivity maximisation led to a strengthening of personnel specialists role.
1945–1980s	Personnel management established as a profession with own institute and examinations.
	Growth and increasing influence of trade unions seeking to improve the pay and working conditions of their members.
	Management of industrial relations and personnel issues dominate.
	1956: General Electric open in-house leadership development 'school' in New York.
	1959: Drucker describes the declining importance of manual labour and describes a new type of "knowledge" worker
The 1980s onwards	HRM became fashionable with more strategic thinking.
	Less conflict with trade unions.
Mid 1990s onwards	The flexible workforce, managing contractors, HR as a strategic advantage.

Taylor believed that workers would be motivated by obtaining the highest possible remuneration so work should be organised in the most efficient way. Perhaps too readily he assumed the view that the individual is wholly rational, calculating both effort required to work and reward. More positively, Taylor recognised that if specialised knowledge and skills were concentrated in the hands of well-trained and able employees, there would be an improvement in productivity. He therefore broke jobs down into separate functions and then gave each function to an individual. Sometimes this meant that as many as eight functional foremen were giving instructions to other workers. Taylor believed that it was only through the effective use of control by specialists that best use would be made of the resources available to increase the size of the incentive surplus to be shared between efficient staff.

With modern trends including the need for flexible working and 'multi-skilling' it would be easy to dismiss Taylorism as outdated. It is still very evident, however in many areas including 'call-centres'. Taylor's thinking has clear implications for a number of areas not least providing a challenge to consider the benefits of:

- work measurement and study
- fair expectations of the individual
- training
- job design
- financial rewards
- operations management as a subject (see Chapter 3).

5.1.1 Human resource management, motivation and opportunity

Gratton (2004), when reviewing what an HR function actually does, suggested that a significant amount of time is spent on 'traditional' activities associated with rewards, job descriptions, appraising and measuring performance and so on. Research indicated, however, that time spent on strategic HR and organisational development issues were more highly valued by chief executives. It is clear that the successful implementation of human resource management theories is integral to the motivation of the workforce and their opportunity to contribute to organisational success. Motivation influences both employee productivity and quality of work. Mullins (2007) defines motivation as 'the driving force within individuals by which they attempt to achieve some goal in order to fulfil some need or expectation'.

The study of motivation involves many complexities and difficulties, not least because it involves behaviours, individuals and internal processes. As a consequence, there are several different theories associated with it.

Exercise 5.1

Motivation is not the only factor influencing employee productivity and quality of work. What are some of the other factors you would expect to be important?

Solution

Other organisational factors, such as the availability of technology, raw materials and financial resources will also have an important effect on productivity and quality.

Much of a manager's functioning concerns performance management. As such a manager operating to an ethical code will attempt to improve performance in a way that is both legitimate and fair. Attempts to improve performance should start by addressing the question of whether there is a problem of motivation. The simplest way of viewing motivation is in terms of how much effort an individual puts into a particular course of action. The outcome of the course of action, however, depends on other attributes of the individual besides effort including ability, skills and support.

Exercise 5.2

Reflect and make notes on a manager's ability to influence the variables of effort, ability, skills and rewards. Which in your opinion are easiest to influence positively?

Mullins (2007) identified certain broad classifications that could be applied to understanding motivation, namely:

- Economic rewards such as pay, security, perks of the job, etc.
- Intrinsic satisfaction, derived from the nature of work, interest in the job, self-development, etc.
- Social relationships, such as friendships, being part of a team, etc.

In order to understand the theories of HRM and how they have developed and altered over time it is necessary to briefly consider some key theories of motivation. These are very briefly outlined here.

Scientific. Early motivation theories emerged from Taylor's scientific approach and the 'managers' job involved effective job design and workers were offered wage incentives for productivity.

Human relations. Elton Mayo's research, over a 5-year period at the Hawthorne Works of the Western Electric Company, Chicago indicated that work satisfaction depends to a large extent upon social relationships. These are both informal between workers in a group and between workers and their bosses. The effects of the group proved more powerful than altered working conditions, new payment systems, rest breaks, varying the length of the working day, and offering food and refreshments. Most recently in many manufacturing organisations there has been a move towards team working and groups.

Human resources. Douglas McGregor suggested that managers make assumptions about what employees are 'like', what their needs are and what motivates them. These beliefs impact on their methods of managing certain individuals and groups. Managers tend to see workers in terms of two theories, X and Y. Under theory X work is inherently distasteful, and individuals prefer to be directed, wish to avoid responsibility and want security above all. Under theory Y people want to contribute to meaningful goals they have helped to establish. The person learns under the right conditions not only to accept, but to seek responsibility. Theory X implies that the manager must control people's work tightly, supervise them closely and give them simple, repetitive tasks to do. The key 'motivators' are economic rewards and punishments. Theory Y, on the other hand, suggests that the manager should seek to create a participative environment in which each person can contribute to the limits of his or her ability, and to encourage self-direction. The limitations of an uncritical application of a Theory X approach to management are easily apparent:

- some workers are disinterested in economic rewards and unafraid of punishments
- individuals may resent close supervision and this may cause conflict
- the danger of a 'self-fulfilling prophecy' arises if individuals are treated in a Theory X manner.

It is worthwhile considering the application of a Theory Y approach that attempts to provide greater self-direction and satisfy individual needs at work.

Content theories. Content theories of motivation attempt to describe and categorise the needs that influence behaviour. They assume that behaviour is caused by, and is directed towards, the satisfaction of these needs. Psychologists have suggested many needs, and there are several different theories including Abraham Maslow's hierarchy of needs and Frederick Herzberg's dual factor theory.

- Maslow's theory is founded on the basis that an individual is 'a perpetually wanting animal' and only relatively unsatisfied needs are capable of motivating behaviour. Five levels of needs can be arranged in a hierarchy of potency. This means that at any one time, the lowest level of relatively unsatisfied need will be the one that motivates current behaviour, and the less it is satisfied the more it will motivate. The individual will act primarily in order to satisfy that need, then move on to the next level and so on. The hierarchy of needs is as follows:

Level of need	Category of need
Highest	Self-actualisation
	Esteem
	Belongingness
	Safety and security
Lowest	Physiological

Taylor's thinking on motivation is economic by nature, and this of course fits with the lower levels of Maslow's theory.

- Herzberg's motivation-hygiene (dual factor) theory is based on the idea that the opposite of job satisfaction is a lack of job satisfaction, not job dissatisfaction. Similarly, the opposite of job dissatisfaction is an absence of dissatisfaction. It is not simply that satisfaction and dissatisfaction are different but, in Herzberg's view, that they are affected and caused by different factors. Factors associated with job satisfaction are called 'motivators', factors that cause dissatisfaction are called 'hygiene factors'. Herzberg suggested that the main motivator and hygiene factors can be categorised as follows:

Motivators	Hygiene factors
Recognition	Status
Achievement	Pay
Possibility of growth	Interpersonal relations
Advancement	Supervision
Responsibility	Company policy and administration
Work itself	Job security
Personal life	Working conditions

Herzberg's theory and, particularly, its job-enrichment applications, has been very influential and popular across a wide range of jobs, organisations and countries.

Process theories. The most influential type of process theory is probably expectancy theory. In its simplest form, this approach suggests that when faced with a choice between alternative courses of action an individual bases his or her selection on the following two factors:

1. the value placed on achieving the outcome of each alternative (referred to as 'valence')
2. the likelihood of being able to achieve each outcome ('expectancy').

Choice is then based on a multiplicative relationship between valence and expectancy. If either factor is nil there will be no motivation, otherwise the individual will choose the alternative that results in the best outcome. All expectancy theories assume a high degree of rationality in individual choice decisions. They also suggest that managers ought to take the following steps to improve employee motivation by:

- determining what each individual values
- identifying the type of behaviour desired

- ensuring that the desired levels of performance are thought to be attainable
- finding ways of linking outcomes valued by individuals with desired behaviours
- ensuring that improvements in performance result in changes in valued rewards that are large enough to motivate individuals
- making sure that reward systems are seen to be fair and equitable.

Combined theories. Edgar Schein's contribution to motivation concentrates on the behaviours of people not as individuals but as social groups. In his work on culture, Schein (2004) showed how behaviour altered to suit varying circumstances in organisations. Four useful categories of worker (referred to in a sexist manner as 'man') are generally applied in this area:

Category	Basis	HR implication
Rational economic man	Derives from the theories of Adam Smith: the pursuit of self-interest and the maximisation of gain are the prime motivators of people.	People can be classified according to two extremes: the untrustworthy (money motivated and calculating) and the trustworthy (more broadly motivated, moral elite who must organise and manage others).
Social man	Derives from Elton Mayo and the Hawthorne study, 'socialisation' at work motivated people.	Workforce morale levers superior performance. Managers should pay attention to people's needs and move from controlling to coordinating and facilitating.
Self-actualising man	Based on Maslow's hierarchy of need, self-fulfilment is the driving force behind individuals, not money.	Such individuals need challenge in tasks at work, and to be given responsibility and a sense of pride in what they do.
Complex man	Motivation is based on the expectations that the employee and the organisation have of each other, and the extent to which these are mutually fulfilled.	The maintenance of the 'psychological contract' is crucial.

5.1.2 The psychological contract and retention

Reasonable expectations a new employee might have of an employer is that he or she will be treated 'properly' in terms of (for instance) job security, career progression and a work/life balance. Such an employee would expect to fulfill a number of reasonable requirements in return. This thinking forms the basis of the psychological contract. The psychological contract is important in a number of ways due to its impact on HR issues such as motivation (and therefore productivity) and retention. Guest and Conway (2002) define it as:

> … the perceptions of the two parties, employee and employer, of what their mutual obligations are towards each other

Exercise 5.3

Identify a number of promises and obligations that are likely to feature in a psychological contract.

Table 5.2 Mutual commitments employers under a psychological contract

Employees promise to	Employers promise to provide
Work hard	Pay commensurate with performance
Uphold company reputation	Opportunities for training and development
Maintain high levels of attendance and punctuality	Opportunities for promotion
Show loyalty to the organisation	Recognition for innovation or new idea
Work extra hours when required	Feedback on performance
Develop new skills and update old ones	Interesting tasks
Be flexible, for example, by taking on a colleague's work	An attractive benefits package
Be courteous to clients and colleagues	Respectful treatment
Be honest	Reasonable job security
Come up with new ideas	A pleasant and safe working environment

Source: CIPD (2008)

Solution

CIPD (2008) offer a number of examples of mutual promises and obligations (see Table 5.2).

Even though the contract has little standing in law it effectively tells employees what 'bargain they have struck': what they are expected to do and what they can expect from their employer in return. The Chartered Institute of Personnel and Development (2008) explain:

These obligations will often be informal and imprecise: they may be inferred from actions or from what has happened in the past, as well as from statements made by the employer, for example during the recruitment process or in performance appraisals. Some obligations may be seen as 'promises' and others as 'expectations'. The important thing is that they are believed by the employee to be part of the relationship with the employer.

If employees believe that management have broken the contact by failing to deliver on their promises a negative impact can lead to difficulties of job dissatisfaction and individual commitment. At the extreme it can force an employee to leave. Quite apart from the expense of recruiting and selecting a replacement and the disruption in the workplace this can lead to an organisation damaging its external reputation. In an environment where there are 'talent' wars with employers seeking to brand themselves positively this can be very harmful.

5.1.3 Employees and the corporate dimension

An HR strategy can only make sense when related to business objectives. The demand for human resource comes from the organisation's need to continue to supply goods or services to its customers. It is also true that human resources themselves can have a vital influence on organisational objectives. Plans for training, promotion and productivity all indicate the importance of obtaining the right type of staff as well as the right numbers. However, larger or more complex organisations need a more strategic approach.

One model that clearly demonstrated the relationship between HRM activities and strategy was proposed by David Guest (1997) and comprised six components:

1. HRM strategy
2. HRM practices
3. a set of HRM outcomes
4. behavioural outcomes

HRM stategy	HRM practices	HRM outcomes	Behavioural outcomes	performance outcomes	Financial outcomes
Differentitaion (innovation)	Selection	Commitment	Effort/ motivation	High productivity, Quality, innovation	Profits
Focus (quality)	Appraisal		Co-operation		
	Rewards	Quality	Involvement	Low: Absence,	Return on investment
Cost (cost reduction)	Job design			Lobour, Turnover,	
	Involvement	Flexibility	Organisational citizenship	Conflict, Customer complaints	
	Status and security				

Figure 5.1 The Guest model of HRM

Source: Guest (1997). Reprinted by permission of Taylor and Francis UK.

5. a number of performance outcomes
6. financial outcomes.

The relationship can be depicted in the form figure similar to that in Figure 5.1.

The central idea of the model is that HRM practices should be designed to lead to a set of positive outcomes including high staff commitment and quality, and highly flexible employees. The main features are:

- a goal of binding employees to the organisation and obtaining behavioural outcomes of increased effort, co-operation, involvement and organisational citizenship.
- high-quality employees, involving workplace learning and the need for a capable, qualified and skilful workforce to produce high-quality services and products.
- flexibility concerned with ensuring that workers are receptive to innovation and change and operation.

The right-hand side of the model focusses on the link between HRM and performance. According to the model, only when all three HRM outcomes (commitment, quality and flexibility) are achieved, can behaviour change and superior performance outcomes be expected. These HRM goals are a 'package' and each is necessary to ensure superior performance and financial outcomes depicted on the right-hand side of the model. Guest (1997) argued that:

only when a coherent strategy, directed towards these four policy goals, fully integrated into business strategy and fully sponsored by line management at all levels is applied, will the high productivity and related outcomes sought by industry be achieved.

5.2 Ethical behaviour

Reference has been made to the psychological contact based on an employee/employer relationship of mutual reasonable expectation. Fairness and reasonable expectation can embrace many aspects of people management including recruitment, dismissal and redundancy. Compliance with the law, local agreements and moral considerations all relate to ethical management approaches. Arising from this the term 'ethics' refers to the code of behaviour considered correct by a particular group, profession or individual. Managers of organisations face many situations that require ethical judgements, and the question of what criteria these judgements should be based on is one that requires careful attention. The importance of ethical behaviour in business generally and personal business ethics for line managers as part of their activities are explained in this section.

'Ethics' is often used interchangeably with the term 'morals' however, there is an important difference between them. Morals resolve problems with reference to the individual's personal belief system about right or wrong, and so are linked to personal conscience, and religious or other convictions. Just because an individual believes a course of action to be morally wrong does not mean that it is ethically wrong. Following one's own conscience at the expense of professional standards, while being the right thing to do personally, may amount to a breach of professional ethics. For example, a management accountant may be aware of confidential figures relating to the performance of an area under threat of redundancy. He or she may also aware of the amount of money being spent on management performance bonuses. Morally, that accountant may think it is reprehensible that the organisation is making people redundant while their managers receive bonuses. A person might feel that it is their moral duty to make this known. However, that would certainly be a breach of confidentiality, which would be breach of professional ethics (as well as breach of the terms of employment).

In practice it is relatively unusual for there to be a conflict between moral judgement and professional ethical duty. More often, however the situations that give rise to ethical difficulties are ones that may be morally ambiguous. Ethics could be stated as answering the question, *'what can I do for the best?'* and contains three key elements:

1. ethics are about *individual* professional responsibility to act
2. ethics are about practical courses of action in the real world
3. ethics often involve making choices between courses of action.

Ethical reasoning unlike most professional practices, is not something that can be learned through practice, significant ethical problems come up rarely and are rarely easy to deal with. However, solving ethical problems like being in a maze, the first problem is to maintain a sense of direction. Ethics involve doing things for the best, and a person does need to have some motivation to do whatever the best is.

Accounting practice allows flexibility in the manner of preparation and presentation of accounting information. Human nature allows for the selective emphasis or de-emphasis of aspects. There will clearly be temptations to present a particular bias according to the circumstances which present themselves. The management accountant must not allow these aspects to affect their professional judgement. The exercise of good judgement is a fundamental attribute of a competent accountant.

In order to help the management accountant in his or her day-to-day role, CIMA has followed the approach of many professions in preparing a Code of Ethics, which seeks to help management accountants identify common areas where ethical pressures may exist; the sort of pressures which might compromise independent and sound decision-making. The Code is there to help the accountant analyse those situations and provide a recommended course of action for their resolution.

The ability to identify, explain and resolve or address ethical problems is regarded as being a core competence that the management accounting student needs to have a firm grasp of.

The CIMA Code of Ethics for Professional Accountants. In June 2005, the International Federation of Accountants published their Code of Ethics for Professional Accountants meant to be *high-quality ethical standards and other pronouncements for professional accountants around the world.* This reflected what has been seen as a growing crisis of confidence in accounting ethics internationally, following financial scandals with global implications. Then in 2006, the CIMA 'Code of Ethics for Professional Accountants' was launched. The CIMA Code reflects the standards and CIMA expects of its members and students and is aligned with global standards across the profession.

CIMA's Code states the fundamental values that accountants should work by, and a framework by which they can put these into practice in challenging practical situations, where there may be more than one course of action which may have undesirable consequences. The CIMA code aims to:

- Identify the nature of the personal responsibility that the management accountant takes on as part of the price for getting a reasonable salary and status.
- Provide guidance on how to identify the practical situations where particular care might need to be taken because of the ethical pitfalls involved.
- Provide general guidance on how to address those difficult questions.

CIMA's Code acts as a basis for any complaints or cases under CIMA's disciplinary procedures. The Code itself is split into three parts as reflected in Table 5.3.

Cohen (2006) explains:

Rather than stipulating a set of rules, it (the code) establishes a framework of fundamental principles, describes potential threats to compliance and identifies possible safeguards to help mitigate these threats. The code requires accountants to analyse situations in order to assess threats to the principles and then apply appropriate safeguards to remove or reduce the threats. Many people consider this approach to be more comprehensive than that of a system based on rules, because, although rules can sometimes be circumvented, principles are applicable across a wider range of circumstances.

The Code itself provides examples of both threats and safeguards to clarify what CIMA sees as fundamental principles (namely integrity, objectivity, professional competence and due care, confidentiality and professional behaviour). Part A of the Code defines and explains these principles and gives guidance on how to resolve an ethical conflict.

Table 5.3 The CIMA Code of Ethics for Professional Accountants

Part	Content
A – General Applications of the Code	This covers an introduction and the fundamental principles of integrity, objectivity, professional competence and due care, confidentiality and professional behaviour.
B – Professional Accountants in Public Practice	This covers particular issues identified as being of relevance to accountants in public practice such as professional appointment, conflicts of interest, second opinions, fees and other types of remuneration, marketing professional services, gifts and hospitality, custody of client assets, objectivity in all services and independence in assurance engagements.
C – Professional Accountants in Business	This covers issues such as potential conflicts, preparation and reporting of information, acting with sufficient expertise, financial interests and inducements.

5.3 Developing the human resource

One model devised by Devanna et al. (1984) emphasises the interrelatedness and the coherence of HRM activities. The HRM cycle is seen as four key constituent components: selection, appraisal, rewards and significantly development (Figure 5.2).

These four human resource activities aim to increase organisational performance. The model emphasised the coherence of internal HRM policies and the importance of matching internal HRM policies and practices to the organisation's external business strategy.

It is important to note that the overall performance of the organisation depends on efficient and effective operation of each of the four components and the co-ordination of each particularly in the context of developing the human resource:

- The selection process is important to ensure that the organisation obtains people with the right skills and the potential to **develop** further.
- Appraisal is a pivotal process enabling managers to set targets for future performance in line with an organisation's strategic objectives. It also enables managers to assess the gap between the competences already possessed by staff and the skills and knowledge that the staff will require to **develop**.
- Training and development is essential to ensure that staff can compete with the best in the industry in terms of their ability to develop key competences. It is in this sense that their skills are a key source of competitive advantage.
- The reward system has to be such as to motivate people and to ensure that those key employees do not leave but instead continue to **develop** and contribute.

An individual's relationship with an organisation can be viewed as a series of staged processes that extend from the arrangements made by the organisation for the post to be filled through to that individual completing their engagement with the organisation and leaving (see Table 5.4).

This section deals with certain of these processes and gives some background on the associated techniques.

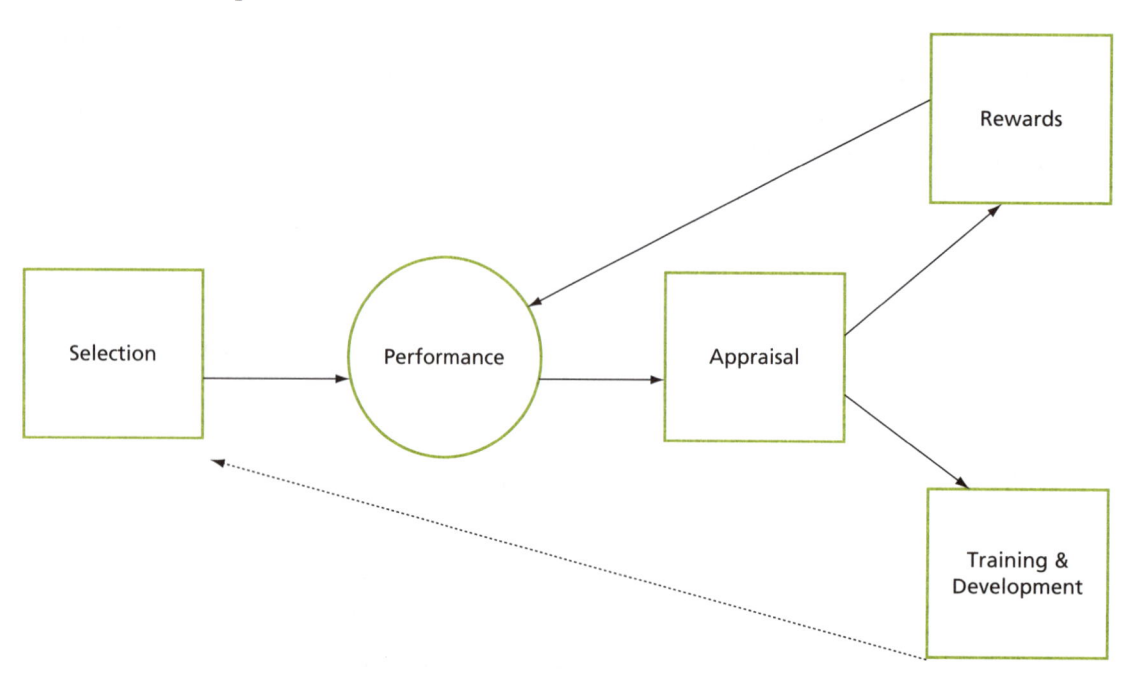

Figure 5.2 The human resource cycle. Reproduced from Devanna et al. (1984); © 1984 John Wiley & Sons, Inc. This material is used by permission of John Wiley & Sons, Inc.

5.3.1 Recruitment

When a decision is made for the first time that a particular post should be created, some form of job analysis should take place. *Job analysis* is also useful when an organisation wishes to assess whether or not a post that is due to fall vacant should be filled. The *job description* defines the overall purpose of the job and the main tasks to be carried out within the role.

A robust job description is essential to successful recruitment and selection since it is the foundation upon which other processes are based. The job description should be considered as a quasi-legal document, since once issued to an employee, it may be viewed as contractual (see Table 5.5).

It is also useful to set out the terms and conditions of employment such as salary, normal working hours and holiday entitlement, etc. separately in a letter when making a formal job offer. *The person specification* defines the personal characteristics, qualifications, and the experience required by the jobholder in order to do the job well. Any other special demands or requirements such as physical aspects and unusual working hours should be included. The information relating to qualifications and experience demanded by the job can only be derived following a thorough job analysis that identifies the knowledge, skills and other behaviours required. The list of personal characteristics needs to be as precise as possible so that the assessment process can identify what a candidate knows and can do. A danger in overstating the qualifications and experience demanded by the job is that it

Table 5.4 The human resource cycle

Activity	Description
Job analysis	Analysing and defining jobs
Job description	Purpose and the main tasks of the job
Person specification	Personal characteristics, experience qualifications, etc. of post holder
Recruitment	Attracting a pool of suitable applicants
Selection	Making a choice
Induction	Making the settling-in period easier
(Ongoing processes)	Appraisal, training, development, career planning
Termination	Promotion, resignation, retirement, redundancy

Source: Author

Table 5.5 Main points to be covered in the job description

- The location of the job within the organisation structure (division, department and section).
- Title of the job, and the job code if available.
- Job title of the person to whom the jobholder is responsible.
- Job title(s) of the person(s) responsible to the jobholder, and the number of staff directly supervised.
- Brief description of the overall purpose of the role (listed chronologically or in order of importance, preferably using action verbs).
- Details of any technical procedures, tools, machinery or equipment used by the jobholder.
- Any special requirements to liaise or deal with contacts of high significance inside and outside the organisation.
- Physical location of the job and the amount of travelling required. Special circumstances (if any) attached to the job, such as shift, night work, on-call, degree of overtime commitment, weekend working, physically demanding activities, etc.
- Responsibility for budgets, etc.

Table 5.6 Example Seven-Point Plan for a shift process operator

Essential	
Physical make-up	Good health record (from references)
	Acceptable bearing and speech
	Smart appearance
Attainment	GCSE English language and Maths grade C or equivalent, e.g. GNVQ
General intelligence	Average
Special aptitude	Manual dexterity and reasonable facility with figures, experience of extended shift work
Interest	Mechanical – cars, model airplanes, etc.
Disposition	Calm, self-reliant
Circumstance	Living within ten miles
	Own transport (no public transport operators at shift change times)

could lead to appointing a new employee who quickly becomes dissatisfied with the lack of challenge and subsequently leaves.

When the job requirements have been agreed with the line manager, person requirements should be analysed using a suitable structure. The most straightforward is the Alec Rodgers Seven-Point Plan which can provide a framework for the selection process (see Table 5.6).

Recruitment is a set of activities designed to attract a qualified pool of applicants to an organisation. Typically, there are three steps in the recruitment process:

1. advertisement of a job vacancy
2. preliminary contact with potential job candidates
3. initial screening to create a pool of suitable applicants.

Recruitment need not involve advertising (see Table 5.7), but if it does it must be effective. The appropriate media needs to be selected depending on the target audience and the speed with which the position needs to be filled. Professional journals, for instance, may be more precise in targeting the audience but are expensive, have long intervals between issues, a long lead time and a subsequent slow response rate.

5.3.2 Selection

Once a process of recruitment has taken place, selection follows with typical steps including:

- completion of a formal application form (and/or the curriculum vitae)
- interviewing
- testing
- reference checks
- medical examination
- final analysis and decision to hire or not to hire
- official job 'offer' letter.

Any techniques used in selection should be:

- *Reliable*: give consistent results.
- *Valid*: accurately predict performance.

Table 5.7 Recruitment mechanisms and media

Most popular	
Press	Regional: for local markets, evening papers
	Specialist: trade journals or quality press
Employment agencies	Government operated. Employment agencies in the UK include Government-funded initiatives such as Jobcentres and Jobclubs, which aim to help the unemployed get back to work
	Private sector agencies often deal with temporary support staff such as secretaries, or specialist staff such as computer programmers
Recruitment consultants	Private sector agencies, Executive Search consultants
Web recruitment	A growing area
Other	
Careers conventions	Exhibitions, fairs and conferences – to target highly selective groups
University Milk Rounds	For graduate recruitment
Radio	Often used locally, particularly for opening new stores or for temporary jobs, as it has an immediate effect
Cinema	Still used for local jobs. Often advertises agencies rather than vacancies
Posters	A low-level method that does not target applicants in a helpful way (used by small retailers, etc.)
TV	Unusual unless local or large numbers needed as it is expensive
Locally maintained registers	There is some cost associated with maintaining these records and drop out rate of candidates tends to be high. Registers can be compiled from the data of previously unsuccessful candidates and those who unsolicited have forwarded their CVs to the organisation

- *Fair*: select employees in a non-discriminatory way, particularly in terms of race, age and gender. This may be to fulfil legal requirements and the ethical frameworks under which the organisation operates.
- *Cost-effective*: the costs of devising and operating the selection methods must be justified in terms of the benefits of selecting good applicants for the particular jobs in question.

Exercise 5.4

What are the likely outcomes of a faulty selection process?

Solution

- rejecting applicants who would have been suitable
- employing people who turn out to be unsuitable.

This can lead to a loss of morale, operating efficiency and involve additional costs and missed opportunities.

Interviews. Once a shortlist has been drawn up, the most common way of selecting a candidate is by interview or series of interviews. Very few selection decisions are made without an interview, even for internal promotions where the candidates are well known. Repeated research shows that the interview used in isolation is unreliable as a selector, however when it is used along with other methods greater reliability is achieved. It is important therefore to consider all methods of selecting staff and to use those that seem appropriate in each circumstance. Interviewers should determine before the interview the criteria against which

Table 5.8 Types of job interview

The individual or 'one to one'	The most familiar method involving face-to-face discussion. It provides the best opportunity for the establishment of a rapport between the interviewer and the candidate. If only one interviewer is used, there is more scope for a biased or superficial decision to emerge. Highly unreliable when used as the only selection method.
Tandem interviews	Involves two interviewers per candidate. Rapport may be reduced but so is the possibility of bias. Typical interviewers would be an HR officer and the relevant line manager.
Panel interviews	Consists of a number of people who interview the candidate together. The interview is conducted on a very formal basis but it does enable a number of different people to have a look at applicants and compare notes in 'real time'. The disadvantage is that a single member of the panel could dominate proceedings. Confident, articulate candidates may be more comfortable with this approach.
Sequential interviews	Involves the candidate being passed from one interviewer to another until several one-to-one interviews have taken place. The advantage here is that several people may see the candidate but the disadvantage is that interviewers may vary in their opinions when results are collated.

they are judging applicants and then after interview assess how each applicant 'measured up'. Some believe that the main value of an interview is to provide a two-way dialogue in exploring the motivation and enthusiasm of a candidate, and the potential 'fit' with the nature and culture of the organisation. There are several types of interview as reflected in Table 5.8.

Tests. The main types of test that can be used as part of a selection process as follows:

- *Cognitive tests* which relate to thinking processes and include tests of intelligence, ability, aptitude, communication, numerical skills, etc. Usually *intelligence tests* are described to candidates as 'aptitude' or 'skills' tests and comprise mathematical or number skills, communication or verbal skills and a general logic or problem-solving testing. Originally they were work-related, such as typing tests, but gradually more abstract forms were developed for aptitudes seen to be important for some jobs. Manual dexterity, mechanical, numerical ability and spatial testing are included in this category.
- *Personality tests* which involve assessing non-cognitive and non-intellectual characteristics of an individual, usually the emotional make-up, reflected in the style of behaviour. Beaumont (1993) noted that 'there is probably no subject more controversial in occupational psychology than the merits and demerits of personality assessment'. Results from personality tests have to be interpreted carefully alongside the applicant's other known attributes. Many categories of personality tests exist, including questionnaires, which have doubtful validity if candidates attempt to predict likely required answers. Such techniques tend to have low reliability and less predictive validity. The most-well known personality test is the Cattell 16 PF (Personality Factors) which provides 16 basic dimensions, such as extrovert/introvert, tough-minded/tender-minded, along which individuals score from 0 to 10. These standard-ten or 'sten' scores can be aggregated to produce higher-level factors such as leadership or toughness. This test has norms against which candidates can be compared, and also has a 'motivational distortion' score, which can be used to assess how far the candidate has tried to manipulate their responses. There are several books interpreting the scores of such tests and computer software that can produce written narratives explaining the results.

Table 5.9 Psychological Societies

British Psychological Society
'The Society is a learned and professional body controlled by our Royal Charter. This means that our primary duty is to preserve and nurture the discipline on behalf of the nation. Our main objective is to advance and diffuse knowledge of psychology. This combines with our charitable status which says that as an organisation we are not permitted to do anything outside of the objectives as specified in the Charter.'
(*Source*: http://www.bps.org.uk)

American Psychological Society
'The American Psychological Society's mission is to promote, protect, and advance the interests of scientifically-oriented psychology in research, (and) application' (*Source*: www.psychologicalscience.org/)

- *Psychometric testing* is sometimes also undertaken in this context. The term 'psychometric' derives from 'psyche' meaning the mind and 'metric' meaning measuring so psychometric applies to both personality and cognitive testing. The quality of tests used ranges from good to of dubious quality. Others are expensive to administer and score, often requiring the involvement of the commercial consultants. Organisations intending to use such tests should first seek guidance from the British Psychological Society, the American Psychological Society (Table 5.9) or other reputable agencies in other countries. In psychological testing, ethical considerations should be applied to critical aspects of the science. Since administration, scoring and interpretation of tests is a skilled operation only qualified people are entitled to use them. Credible Psychological Societies require proper training of test administrators and interpreters and there is a strong recommendation to give the candidates feedback on their results.

In the following extracts from an article by Bryan Appleyard the growth and usefulness of psychometric testing is reviewed:

> ❗ Welcome to the weird world of psychometrics. If you want to work for a big company there's at least a 70% chance that before being given a job you will be subjected to a personality test by one of the big four – MBTI (Myers-Briggs Type Indicator), 16PF (16 personality factors), OPQ (occupational personality questionnaire) or Hogan – and an ability exam measuring verbal reasoning and numeracy. These are basically IQ tests by another name.
>
> ....
>
> according to the Association of Graduate Recruiters, it's because nobody trusts university degrees any more. It has just issued a report saying degree standards are inconsistent and, as a result, companies are turning to psychometrics. But Ceri Roderick at occupation psychologists Pearn Kandola adds two other reasons. 'Companies want to know things like the motivational characteristics of recruits and the technology is now available to do these things.' There's also a fourth reason: the need to compete for quality recruits. 'There's a war for talent,' says Professor David Bartram of the British Psychological Society (BPS), 'companies are fighting to get the best people.'
>
> All of which means there is now a rapid proliferation of psychometrics consultancies, most of them offering candidates the chance to do all the tests online. . . .

> Sceptics think the whole enterprise is misguided. In America a book – The Cult of Personality by Annie Murphy Paul – has cast doubt on the intellectual credibility of psychometrics......................
>
> In support of Paul's book the author Malcolm Gladwell questions the very idea of measuring personality: 'We have a personality in the sense that we have a consistent pattern of behaviour. But that pattern is complex and that personality is contingent: it represents an interaction between our internal disposition and tendencies and the situations that we find ourselves in.'. . .
>
> But are Gladwell and Paul right to question the whole theory on which they are based? The history of psychometrics marches hand in hand with the history of IQ testing. Alfred Binet, the French psychologist, produced the first modern IQ test in 1905 and Walter Dill Scott subjected 15 engineering graduates to the first psychometric test in 1915. Both ideas were inspired by the conviction that there could be no reason why the human mind should be impervious to scientific investigation. . . .
>
> Psychometrics works, but only if the tests are properly applied, rigorously interpreted and accompanied by traditional interviews. This means that they do not necessarily speed up the recruitment process. They might, however, help weed out unsuitables in advance, a huge benefit at a time when all companies are swamped with applicants for attractive jobs.
>
> *Source*: Appleyard, B. (2007) Want a job? Let's play mind games. *Sunday Times*, 22 July.

Assessment centre. An assessment centre does not necessarily mean a physical centre but is a particular approach and philosophy. An assessment centre involves the assessment of a group of individuals by a team of assessors using a comprehensive and interrelated series of techniques. It is important to ensure that jobs have been analysed and the results classified to provide a list of criteria or competencies around which the assessment centre should be designed. These assessment instruments such as 'in-tray' exercises, negotiations or presentations, can be designed by the organisation or bought off the shelf, but it is important to ensure that there are a sufficient number of the right type of activities to measure all relevant criteria. It may be helpful to combine interviews with other selection techniques such as some of the tests described earlier, group exercises and simulations. A typical assessment centre will involve applicants attending for one or two days and being subjected to a range of selection techniques. Trained assessors observe candidates and at the end pool their judgements of the applicants based on their performance on the range of selection devices so that an overall assessment of each individual's suitability will then be reached. Although assessment centres can be very accurate methods of selection, they are expensive to design and administer and can only be justified for certain types of jobs.

Where reliable past data is available on performance (e.g. in sales) assessments are really not necessary, nor for jobs where significant factors are already known. Managerial jobs or those where the field of applicants are unfamiliar with the new setting (such as university graduates, or line managers applying for consultancy) often require the assessment centre approach.

Group selection methods are relevant if the emphasis on selection is placed less on technical ability and more on social skills, influencing, communication, intellectual ability,

Table 5.10 An example of an assessment centre

A leaderless group exercise. Candidates are given a group task to undertake in a given time, for example in the form of a business game. Observers judge performance under pressure and look for leadership and team working abilities

A report-writing exercise. Participants under time pressure, write a report on some aspect of business. Here time management, written communication skills and understanding can be assessed

An in-tray exercise. This consists of issues that a manager might find on a day performing the job for real. Ability to work under pressure, delegate, analyse and problem solve might be tested by this method

Other tests

Formal interview

attitudes and personality. Beaumont (1993) reported a further dimension to the selection decision as follows:

> …(it has become) less about matching an individual employee to the fixed requirements of an individual job at a single point in time (and) as a consequence, immediate skills and employment background … and more about willingness to learn, adaptability, and willingness/ability to work as part of a team. These changes are concomitant with moves away from Tayloristic work organization which involved a hierarchy of narrowly designed and highly specialised job tasks to each of which was attached the rate for the job and moves towards a reduction in the number of individual job classifications, team working … and the integration of all responsibility for quality control.

Group selection is often included as part of an assessment centre (Table 5.10).

Research suggests generally positive findings about group selection methods and high validity correlations have been achieved between assessments and subsequent job performance achieved.

Post selection issues. Once a candidate is selected a medical examination and a request for references takes place. A physical check up by a medically qualified person or the completion of a health check questionnaire may be required. The purpose of a reference is to obtain in confidence factual information about a prospective employee and opinions about his/her character and suitability for a job. Employer references are viewed as essential but are notoriously unreliable. References might be sought after job interviews but before a job offer or before the selection process commences as part of the process of short listing a suitable group of candidates.

5.3.3 Induction

Induction involves all arrangements meant to familiarise a new employee with the organisation, including safety rules, general conditions of employment, the work of the section/department, etc. (see Table 5.11)

Table 5.11 Indicative elements in the induction package

Terms of employment, such as information about hours of work, shift arrangements, timekeeping and clocking-on and -off systems

Housekeeping and security issues, such as catering facilities, energy conservation and speed limits on site

Health and safety regulations, such as safety procedures, protective clothing and hazards of office equipment

Remuneration and benefits, holiday and sick pay, profit sharing, expenses claims, welfare

Organisational rules and policies, such as disciplinary and grievance procedures, trade union membership, works rules, time off for statutory or trade union duties, equal opportunities

Employee development opportunities, sports and social amenities

Information about the company and the industry, such as a mission statement, history, product markets, organisation structure and communications

Job performance issues, such as standards, appraisal and role within the department

Table 5.12 Induction perspectives

Administrative. The main issues appear to be what topics to include and when to deal with them so as to prevent information overload. HR specialist is seen as particularly relevant in maintaining quality standards during the induction process, as well as in delivering some parts of the programme (such as information about welfare, wage and salary administration, grievance and disciplinary procedures, etc.) Induction should be systematic enough to ensure that essentials are covered.

Welfare. During the 'period of after-care' when people start employment with an organisation, the manager must try to settle the new person in quickly, as an act of benevolent paternalism. For those lacking in confidence (e.g. school leavers, women returners, etc.) it is particularly appropriate.

Strategic. Employers make use of various techniques to 'educate' employees about the organisation's ethos, aiming to integrate them culturally.

Many definitions also mention the importance of helping employees 'settle into their new jobs', welcoming them and arranging for them to get to know others. A formal induction programme need not be expensive, and the benefits far outweigh the costs of recruiting more staff if new staff fail to settle and leave. Induction can be viewed from a number of perspectives summarised in Table 5.12.

5.3.4 Appraisals

Appraisal of performance is a vital part of the HR cycle. Most appraisal systems should provide the individual with necessary feedback on their performance and focus on future activities. Most schemes rely on an annual meeting between the employee (appraisee) and his or her appraiser. The purpose of appraising may be seen as:

- aiding technical, professional and management development
- allowing a systematic follow-up of the results of staff development activities
- a source of motivation
- enabling the achievement of rewards (such as promotion)
- (possibly) feeding into a wider reward system
- increasing performance
- helping achieve important organisational and individual objectives.

Exercise 5.5

What other potential benefits of appraisal are there?

Solution

- a mechanism to set objectives for the next period
- identifying good prospects for promotion or transfer
- developing psychological dependence on the manager
- fostering an open atmosphere
- developing relationships
- enhancing corporate cultural norms.

Many of the pitfalls associated with the selection interviews also apply in appraisal, including:

- a lack of preparation on either side
- an appraiser talking more than the appraisee and asking leading questions to which the answer is obvious and important aspects may be left unexplored
- appraisers being just as nervous as the appraisees
- little or no appraiser training.

Appraisers can improve the quality of interviews considerably if they keep in mind the overall objective, which is to get an accurate ideas of performance and improvement needs. The first task is to try to overcome the rather unnatural circumstances of the formal interview and to encourage the applicant to relax and speak freely. To do this the interviewer must keep the conversation flowing, while speaking no more than is necessary. By careful questioning the interviewer should bring out how well (or badly) the employee has matched the requirements of the job. The interviewer should always retain control of the situation.

Exercise 5.6

What factors should be present in an effective appraisal system?

Solution

- Careful planning which ensures the purpose and objectives of the system are widely understood.
- Skill in carrying out the appraisal interview.
- Selecting the most appropriate method of appraisal.
- Setting challenging targets which the appraisee can influence.
- Adopting a participative system that enables those being appraised to have a meaningful input to the system.

Table 5.13 indicates some of the detailed considerations that an appraiser should take into account.

Table 5.13 Detailed considerations that an appraiser

- Be properly organised and allow enough time
- Make sure there will be no interruptions (divert telephone calls, etc.)
- Discuss issues of principle beforehand with senior manager and/or HR expert
- Identify possible reasons for unusual performance, particularly if it is possibly 'below par'? (Problem recruitment, inadequate training or experience, qualifications, etc.?) Check beforehand the policy to address poor performance
- Plan questions to be asked (they should be designed to probe performance and the training or development needs arising)
- Identify mechanisms to address individual training needs (e.g. refer to corporate training programme)
- Identify potential rewards for high performance (promotion policy, levels of salary increase, opportunity available for job moves)
- Identify opportunities for sideways development moves or job enrichment
- Anticipate the information needed to meet likely questions from the appraisee

Overell's (2003) research into employee appraisals identifies that most large companies use such a system. This practice does, however, vary according to the industry (for instance in financial services, 80% of employees are exposed to them compared with 50% in retail). Private sector appraisals are conducted mainly to identify training needs, with evaluating performance secondary. Surprisingly perhaps only 15% of companies use appraisals to determine pay.

Overell also reports that disturbingly it was once found that in the UK's Civil Service that the appraisal system was felt to discriminate against ethnic minority and disabled workers. (As a safeguard management have since set up an independent assessor system, allowing staff a right of appeal.)

The question of who should appraise and when depends on determining the goal of appraisal and who is best placed to evaluate the employee's performance or needs against these. Managers often save up bad news rather than 'disciplining' staff at the time so that they will have 'ammunition' if necessary at the annual appraisal. Moves to more frequent appraisals run against the problem of time. Nevertheless, some managers do have weekly team briefings or individual discussions with staff as part of their ongoing managerial role that can be specifically aimed at assessing progress towards objectives.

Setting objectives as part of a performance appraisal (Table 5.14) involves agreement on SMART objectives (specific and challenging, measurable, but achievable, relevant and realistic and time-bound). A system of 'management by objectives' (MBO) is helpful if the employees are participants in their own objective setting. Otley's (1987) research into managers in the budget-setting process indicated that performance collapses if objectives have been set inappropriately. This means that appraisal of performance is potentially a very damaging activity for managers who treat it lightly or for organisations who do not consider the implications. This is particularly true of systems that apply pay to performance (PRP) based on appraisal interviews. These systems are treated with great suspicion by trade unions wary of unfair application and treatment.

A number of types of appraisal exist:

Self-appraisal. This often takes place in preparation for a supervisor/appraisee meeting. This can save managerial time but the value may be questionable (if the appraisee is too self-critical or too selective and critical incidents have been omitted).

Supervisor/appraisee. Normally the person who allocates work and establishes priorities and standards appraises. In some cases where there are many workers this may not be possible.

Table 5.14 Guidelines for setting performance standards

Clearly identify the individual's main result areas (e.g. finance, communication, staff development, supervision)

Select the vital key tasks from the result areas which, when performed well, ensure that the required objectives are being achieved

Set standards of performance against each of the key tasks which, when met, are acceptable to all concerned. Use information from past experience, present conditions and any foreseeable future changes. Standards must be valid in terms of result in the job

Ensure that standards are realistic and not too easy but present a challenge that is within the jobholders' capability

Strive for a clear definition at all times; standards that can be defined clearly minimise doubt and ambiguity

180 degree. Often managers, especially those in project teams or matrix organisations and professional bureaucracies, do not 'know' the appraisee sufficiently well. To some extent collecting anonymous or named views of colleagues can solve this. This can also be performed in the open groups session with the emphasis on first how the group performed and then the individuals' contribution (or the lack of it).

360 degree. This is where the appraisee prepares feedback on the appraiser as well as getting 180-degree feedback from colleagues. Problems include potential conflicts, power, influence issues, time and bureaucracy.

5.3.5 Development and training

HRM's emphasis on employee commitment and flexibility implies the importance of investing in employee development and training. (This is consistent with the notion of viewing human resources as an asset rather than as a cost.)

Learning is a complex process that underpins development, education and training. One perspective on learning first developed by David Kolb (1984) when he captured a four stage cycle of concrete experience-reflection-theorising-active experimenting. Effective learning involves completing this cycle. Formal lectures for example have little real effect on learning if they are simply concerned with imparting knowledge which students may not reflect on and modify their behaviour accordingly. The matter is complicated by the fact that individuals have different preferred learning styles with, for example, some favouring analytical reflection, while others may strongly prefer active, practical problem solving, etc. Nevertheless, the following general principles can guide the design of effective learning programmes:

- Participants should have both the ability to learn the required skills/knowledge and the motivation to learn.
- It usually helps to provide an overview of the tasks to be learned before dealing with particular, specific aspects.
- The availability of timely, accurate feedback greatly enhances the effectiveness of most forms of training.
- There should be positive rewards or reinforcements when activities are carried out correctly. These rewards may be internal (e.g. a feeling of accomplishment) and/or external (e.g. the issue of a certificate, a compliment from the trainer, etc.).
- Active involvement is usually associated with more effective learning rather than simply listening or reading.
- Most training will involve a learning curve which may be initially very flat as the learner struggles to acquire basic competence or in other cases quite steep when the skills required for modest competence are learned more quickly, but all learning will involve periods when there seems to be no improvement in performance (a learning plateau).
- Training should be as much like the job as possible to minimise problems of conceptualising theory to the workplace.

Management development is sometimes thought of as an activity that only takes place in certain special situations, such as a short course or studying for an MBA, but in fact it can and does take place in a much wider variety of contexts. This point can be understood most clearly if the process is seen as one of self-development which is based on the premise that 'any effective system for management development must increase the managers' capacity and willingness to take control over and responsibility for events, and particularly for their own learning' (Pedler et al., 2006). This highlights the possibilities for learning and management development sometimes being accidental (unconscious) as well as planned (conscious), and that it may take place on-the-job as well as outside the normal place of work.

The importance of self-development is reinforced by the emphasis many professional bodies (including CIMA) are placing on continuous professional development (CPD), which recognises that being admitted to a professional body does not guarantee proficiency forever. Individual members of the profession must take responsibility for their own post-qualification continuing development and updating. In this way individuals can ensure they remain up to date in a rapidly changing world and can facilitate career planning.

Education can be seen as a more generic kind of development. In management terms this often applies specifically to accredited training and development leading to a certificated course often through use of a local university. By utilising local case study material and data assignments help focus learning on the candidate's own organisation.

The benefit of an accredited course is that the learning is focussed and progressive, and leads to a definitive end-stage.

Either training or development or both can be accredited by internal or external sources to produce vocational or generic managerial qualifications, though some of this more general process may be termed education as it is not so goal-specific as either training or development.

Some occupational groups, such as lawyers and accountants, have a tradition of education and training controlled by professional bodies and this enables them to take advantage of external labour markets (often national and international rather than just local). Managers as a group, however, have not succeeded in establishing themselves as a recognised profession, in large part because of the sheer diversity of managerial roles and responsibilities.

Training can be seen as a formal, often short-term process where the organisation attempts to increase an individual's ability to better perform a particular set of tasks. It can take place off or on the job, or be a combination of both. Much management training is 'ad hoc' based on a specific training need identified through appraisal. Many organisations are moving to preferred suppliers for training in order to control cost and outcomes more closely. In this way the value adding effect of training is increased.

'On-the-job' training from others can be effective if the existing employees have time to devote to the process, and are themselves competent and know how to impart the necessary skills. Unfortunately these conditions are often not satisfied in practice therefore, other methods such as simulations, class or laboratory-based training or off-site training may be more effective.

One development in the UK is competence-based training linked to a system of NVQs. The essence of competence-based training is that it assesses the ability of the trainee to carry out specified activities to predetermined standards rather than concentrating directly on an individual's knowledge and understanding. This development can be seen as a consequence of the collapse of the traditional apprenticeship system and the uncoordinated proliferation of vocational qualifications. NVQs operate at five level from basic training to professional level and provide the basis for national training targets specifying the proportion of young people and employees who will have obtained these NVQs by specified dates.

Whatever form of training or development is used it ought to be part of a systematic overall training system involving:

- determining training needs
- identifying training objectives
- development of criteria against which to assess performance

- developing methods to determine current levels of proficiency among potential trainees to enable the right people to be selected for training
- making arrangements for the location, type and duration of the training
- devising methods for carrying out the training and encouraging effective learning
- monitoring the effectiveness of the training and comparing outcomes against criteria.

Most learn best when they genuinely are motivated to do so. Any training is most likely to be effective therefore if the individual is involved in agreeing his or her training plan and in choosing the method or means by which the training is to be provided. There are potentially many training methods that an organisation may wish to develop and these are listed in the (Table 5.15).

Table 5.15 Training methods that an organisation may wish to develop

Action learning: learning by doing, for example, participation of person with others in project work or group assignment, or by secondment to another section/department

Briefing group: short exposition by manager to a workgroup, followed by questions and answers, and discussion

Business games: board games or computer-assisted evolving case studies in which managers assume roles in a fictional business and see the consequences of their decisions in a given situation

Case studies: write-up of a real management situation, with questions for analysis

Coaching: a manager maximises training opportunities in the course of everyday work with their staff

Computer-assisted learning (CAL) or computer-based training (CBT): essentially programmed learning via interaction with a computer

Delegation: manager actively delegates parts of their own job to subordinates and coaches them in its execution

Demonstrations and guided practice: supervisor (trainer) shows employee (trainee) how to (e.g. operate machine); then trainee attempts it with guidance. Films, DVDs and/or video can also be used to demonstrate off the job

Discovery or experiential learning: essentially learning by doing it for yourself, but within some structured logical sequence

Distance learning: learning at a distance with interactive texts and exercises

Job or work rotation: involves the employee moving to a new job or new area of work for short periods to widen experience

Lectures: delivery of a prepared exposition

On-the-job training: training while the job is actually being carried out in the normal work situation

Programmed learning: book/machine that paces reader and checks knowledge through periodic questioning

Role play or behaviour role modelling: person puts him/herself in 'someone else's shoes' for purposes of practical exercise, usually to develop inter-personal skills, and receives feedback on behaviour (often via closed circuit television/video)

Rote learning: by oral repetition (could be useful in some instances for non-English speakers or young trainees)

Seminar or workshop: a meeting of several employees in which all attempt to improve their knowledge in a specific area by sharing information and practice (Seminars usually have an 'expert' to lead)

'Sitting next to Nellie': learning by copying someone doing the same job

Simulations: attempt to reproduce the conditions of work (e.g. flight 'simulators' for pilots, war games for the armed services or desk-top in-tray exercises for executives)

Special projects or assignments: manager/supervisor asks subordinate to research, report and make recommendations on specific topic (or as part of a group project)

Structured work experience: a specific programme of work activities (drawn from the job description), structured in priority order and to be experienced within set time limits

Trainee logbooks: books/diaries in which a record is kept of a trainee's work programme, performance and progress

Training manuals: written collection of instructions (e.g. how to operate a machine)

Training delivery can be provided either in-house, through use of external trainers or by means of open learning, each method having its own advantages and disadvantages. In-house training could also include the 'buying in' of an external trainer specifically to meet the organisation's own needs either on or off site.

Exercise 5.7

Identify the advantages and disadvantages of in-house training.

Solution

Advantages	Disadvantages
Course content and timing can be tailor-made to the organisation's needs	Participants are not exposed to outside influences
An organisation's specific technical equipment, procedures and/or work methods can be used	Participants may be called away at short notice to deal with work problems
Cost effective (provided there are sufficient delegates with the same training needs, and the necessary resources, expertise of trainers to meet these)	Participants more likely to withdraw at short notice than for an external course with non-returnable fees
Easily monitored	Inhibits open discussion if immediate colleagues or bosses are present
Can involve expert sessions from senior managers or technical staff	
Can generate a team spirit and develop culture	
Can be linked to specific outcomes that are then monitored by participants	
Can be enhanced by incorporating work-based projects	

External provision can include all the courses available at local colleges or universities or through specialist training companies. Although courses are unlikely to be wholly specific to an organisation's own needs it does overcome many of the difficulties associated with in-house provision. In particular, participants can mix and share problems and experiences with like-minded people from other organisations. The greatest disadvantage is that such training is usually provided to all-comers, on an unselective basis, across different types of industry and every level of ability. It will inevitably be difficult, therefore, to make it immediately relevant to the in-company situation and to the particular needs of selected staff.

Open learning has two meanings. One interpretation is learning for which no rigid entry qualifications are required. Increasingly it is used to mean learning that enables people to learn at the time, place and pace which meets their needs and their requirements. It can take the form of a whole range of updating and training facilities that can be used in the workplace, at home or in some combination of the two. Employees can be offered a range of study packs or courses, in print, video, audio and/or computer-based programmes, selected according to the individual's training needs. Open learning can be fitted around workplace operations and does not involve any absence from the site. Open learning can complement an existing training provision and assist greatly in your training role. With the increasing growth in numbers of DVDs, and personal computers, both at the workplace and at home, open learning is becoming increasingly available to everyone. However, developing good open learning material is expensive. Usually it will only be financially viable if the same material is appropriate to large numbers of people.

Information technology and particularly the Internet and Intranet systems have provided new opportunities for training and development at relatively low cost (Prithcard, 2003), for example:

- UK DIY products retailer B&Q (with 20,000 staff) uses computer-based training with locally run DVD-ROMS. B&Q also uses networked management tools to keep track of training progress.
- Car producer Ford uses e-learning powered by an intelligent search and retrieval system (Ford Learning Network). This allows all its 335,000 employees worldwide to access training material in a wide range of subjects from engineering to finance. It also contains a search facility to assist with work-related problems.

Finally, managerial control needs to be exercised over training just as for any other activity. A professional service from those who provide it should be insisted upon. There are five dimensions to this control:

- drawing up training plans
- checking that training takes place according to these plans
- checking on the quality of training and success in achieving the stated objectives
- managing the tasks of the learner back in the work situation so that the effects of training are reinforced
- checking that the results of training justify the resources allocated to it.

Regrettably much training is not subject to systematic planning, and careful evaluation is the exception rather than the norm. It is generally recognised that there are four levels at which training can be evaluated (Kirkpatrick, 1998):

1. Reaction – evaluates how well the trainees liked the training.
2. Learning – measures the extent to which trainees have learned the principles, facts and theories covered in the training.
3. Behaviour – concerned with the extent to which behaviour changes as a result of the training.
4. Results – considers what benefits (e.g. better quality, reduced costs, etc.) result directly from the training.

These levels will not necessarily be independent of each other, but each dimension represents a rigorous evaluation. When designing methods of evaluation the most common approach is simply to measure outcomes at one or more levels after the training. The limitation of this design is that it makes it difficult to know whether the outcomes being measured are a result of the training or not. This can be overcome to an extent by measuring outcomes before and after the training: a pre/post measure evaluation.

Some organisations devise well thought out mechanisms to aid development and career advancement such as formal mentoring. A mentor is (according to Daft, 2000) 'a higher ranking senior organisational member who is committed to providing upward mobility and support to a protégé's professional career'. Mentors under such arrangements can act in a number of roles, including coach, counsellor, sounding board and facilitator.

> Note: In some organisations the learning benefiting from, mentoring is referred to as a mentee, in others a protégé.

Both training and development might also be seen as part of the reward system, possibly in a short-term way (e.g. the exotic location of a training course) or longer term as developmental assignments (especially overseas).

Exercise 5.8

Outline the steps you would follow to devise an appropriate management development programme for a group of qualified accountants. What activities other than formal training courses might be appropriate for such a management development programme?

Solution

A systematic review of the management development programme appropriate to a group of qualified accountants would involve:

- determining their management development needs
- identification of the organisation's management development objectives
- developing criteria against which to assess performance
- finding ways of selecting the appropriate people for the training programme
- identifying methods of management development to encourage learning
- making arrangements about location, type and duration of training
- devising ways of monitoring effectiveness.

Other than formal training courses the programme could include an emphasis on self-development so that the accountants pay systematic attention to learning opportunities on and off the job.

5.3.6 Career planning

Career planning has traditionally been viewed as an organisation-driven activity that enables human resource managers to concentrate on jobs and building career paths so providing for logical progression of people between jobs. These career paths, particularly for people such as management accountants, have tended to be mainly within one specialised function and represent ladders on which individuals could progress within their functional specialism. Organisational career planning suffered severe setbacks from the layoffs during the recession of the late 1980s and early 1990s. In addition these core concepts have increasingly been challenged due to a number of other developments including:

- Non-traditional organisational structures emerging. These flatter organisation structures have removed some career paths entirely and reduced opportunities in other areas. Additionally these structures imply a need for multi-skilling and teamwork at the expense of promotion 'ladders' found within traditional hierarchies. Increasingly workers are seeking to be 'multi-skilled' often developing a good understanding of more than one function rather than specialists.
- The development of general management skills and the concept of cross-functional career paths long been accepted as the norm in Japanese firms.
- Increasingly, career development has become led by the individuals themselves. An individual philosophy of building a portfolio of experience qualification and networks

arose in order to develop a career outside a single organisational structure. This individual career planning focuses on individuals' goals and skills. It considers ways in which each individual might expand his or her capabilities and enhance career opportunities both within and outside a particular organisation. (Within the UK the Association of Graduate Recruiters recently warned that career paths no longer exist: only crazy paving that the individual lays himself or herself!)

Given this background, it is unsurprising that succession planning as an alternative to external recruitment may be seen as of decreasing HR significance. Problems have in any case always been associated with succession planning, including:

- *Retention*. Unlike other assets that have received investment, employees who are well trained especially those who are over-trained in anticipation of future developmental moves and are highly marketable.
- *Individual failure*. A failed assignment damages the individual, the company and the working relationships. 'Failure' may be attributable to one of a number of HR defects including poor control or managerial judgement, the over-promotion of individuals, and defective appraisal monitoring systems.
- *Timing*. One person failing to move because of personal circumstances can hold up the development of others unless some other kind of arrangement can be made. Slow promotion or development can lead to frustration and (for instance) graduate staff leaving shortly after becoming useful to the organisation. As the process depends on political expediency, many talented staff find that their present manager is reluctant to release them.
- *Size of organisation*. For a multi-national organisation, extensive relocation can be financially costly and for the family potentially distressing, demotivating and stressful. For many in small organisations a feeling of 'waiting for dead people's shoes' (as the old expression has it) may exist.
- *Overseas postings*. The issues of combining multi-cultural groups and three types of employee (the parent country nationals (expat), the home country national and the third country national) may prove problematic. Planning the correct combination of these staff is virtually impossible because of competing priorities and so many firms merely rely on the ability of all employees to 'mutually adjust' to each other and the new situation.

Exercise 5.9

List the advantages and disadvantages of:

(a) recruiting leaders from outside the organisation
(b) developing leaders from within.

Now read the article that follows. The extract argues strongly for developing leaders from within and identifies a number of things that an organisation might do. (Note that the use role-play and psychometric testing is normally associated with an assessment centre used in selection, and 360 degree feedback with performance appraisal. Here the techniques are suggested within the context of career development.)

> In the war for talent, identifying and nurturing the bright young things under your nose is not just a strategic manoeuvre, it's your lifeblood.
>
> Fail in this and your most promising people will achieve their potential elsewhere, leaving you with a vacuum at the top of your organisation...............
>
> Line managers are the best-placed people to spot talent, says Lucy McGee, a director of HR consultancy DDI. 'Historically, HR has tried to own the process, but the guys at the edge of the pitch are the best placed to identify tomorrow's stars.'
> ......
>
> Look to the future. 'Don't assess high potentials for what you need now or what has worked in the past – think about the business's future needs', says Yapp. IBM used to make computers, now it's all about services.
>
> Evaluate your assets. Once you've conducted your trawl, establish just how good the chosen few really are. Role-playing, psychometric tests and 360-degree appraisals are often used.
> ......
>
> Fast forward. The next job is to create an accelerated development plan that brings them up to speed in the required areas. They'll need extensive support.
>
> Keep it open. If the process is secretive, people will think it's unfair.
>
> *Source:* Extracted from Brainfood: Crash course in . . . developing future leaders, *Management Today*, September 1, 2005 p. 24 Haymarket Business Publications Ltd.

5.3.7 Employment practices

Dismissal is termination of a worker's employment with or without notice by the employer. Dismissal without notice is usually wrongful because it breaches the contract of employment. For a dismissal to be fair, the employer must show that the reason for it is of a type acceptable under statute. In the UK a fuller consideration involves whether the employer also acted reasonably in the circumstances. Factors considered reasonable include both the interest of business efficiency and the likely effects of possible courses of action on someone's behaviour. It is important to follow agreed procedures wherever they exist, and to treat people consistently and fairly. To defend itself against claims of unfair dismissal, an organisation also needs to have kept a written record of all of the stages in any disciplinary procedure.

If an individual's employment contract is terminated it must be done in a way which follows the correct procedures otherwise the employee may be able to claim compensation for unfair or wrongful dismissal. 'Constructive dismissal' involves an employee resigning because the employer has made matters so difficult for them which equates with having in effect terminated their contract of employment.

When analysing whether dismissal is fair or a breach of contract, a number of issues are relevant, including:

- *Conduct.* A well-documented and fair disciplinary procedure is the best way of handling conduct problems. Large organisations especially need to demonstrate why they did not transfer the employee or counsel them.
- *Capability.* Normally an employer would have to demonstrate what standards there were, how the employee failed to meet them, detail the informal/formal warnings and any remedial action it tried to take, for example, extra training, or transfer. It is difficult to show that loss of efficiency has had an effect on the business.

- *Breach of statutory duty.* Continuing the employment might place the employer in breach of a statutory duty, e.g. under health and safety legislation. In such cases, there may be a valid ground for dismissal.
- *Some other substantial reason.* Possibilities include dishonesty, refusal to transfer elsewhere within the organisation, etc.
- *Redundancy.* A dismissal on the grounds of redundancy may be justified on any of the following grounds: cessation of business; cessation of business in the place where the employee was employed; cessation of the type of work for which he or she was employed.

Before any employee is declared redundant, 'good' employers will have considered and discussed all possible alternatives with the relevant trade unions or staff representatives such as:

- reducing overtime (with excess work passed instead to other under-utilised employees)
- limiting future recruitment for vacancies that arise
- retraining (for new roles)
- transfers (to jobs in other departments)
- job-sharing (between two or more people)
- a shorter working week
- more effective HR planning in the future.

If despite these measures redundancies are still inevitable, then an organisation may decide to:

- offer early retirement to eligible employees (provided that the rules of the occupational pension scheme allow it)
- target part-time and temporary employees first
- ask for volunteers by offering attractive terms (voluntary redundancy). This option may attract older workers, since cash incentives tend to be linked to length of past service.

An employee's post can be made redundant if the employer ceases to need it. This should however be viewed as a last resort.

A claim of 'unfair dismissal' due to redundancy may be justified if:

- other employees in similar circumstances within the organisation were not dismissed (i.e. the selection for redundancy was unfair), or
- an inadmissible reason for redundancy was used, (e.g. such as the person was chosen because he or she was member of a trade union or took part in legitimate trade union activities), or
- the organisation did not follow an agreed procedure or an agreement justified by 'custom and practice'.

In the UK, legislation demands that redundancies are fair and consultation must take place. Once employees and the relevant trade unions have been consulted, managers may also wish to contact the local newspaper, as an informed controlled press release is better than stories based on speculation which could be damaging to the organisation's reputation and image. The best method to inform any employee of redundancy is to tell them personally. Since any person who is to receive a redundancy payment must be given a statement in writing detailing the full amount to be paid and how it was calculated. Employees eligible for redundancy pay are entitled in some countries to reasonable time off work, with pay, to look for other work. Management may also like to invite local employment agency advisers to come to the premises, and a good counselling service support individuals should be provided wherever possible. By helping redundant employees both to explore the range of options open to them and their own response real benefits have resulted. A study once carried out by the UK Government's Manpower Service Commission showed that unemployed executives were more likely to find jobs if they received counselling than if they had only 'technical' help (e.g. preparing a curricula vitae, interview, techniques, etc.).

Employees whose jobs become redundant are entitled in most countries to some compensation (redundancy payments) based on their length of service. These 'golden handshakes' do not give most redundant people the financial means to survive for very long without working. The payments go a little way towards providing compensation for the real (and sometimes long-term) social, psychological and economic effects of the experience.

For the individual redundancy is normally met by frustration and anger, followed by diminished self-esteem. If another job cannot be found, long-term unemployment can damage both physical and mental health, as well as carrying obvious financial penalties.

Redundancy is likely to be unpleasant not only for the individual and for the organisation. The manager may have a role to play in maintaining the morale and performance of those employees remaining, as well as dealing with potentially the damaged external image.

One consequence of redundancy may be a loss of some of the valued and most experienced employees. Management should act as honestly and as sympathetically as it can throughout (it will have to work with the survivors who have seen their work colleagues lose their jobs). It is as important for a manager handling redundancies, just as in handling discipline, to be seen to be fair in the treatment of individuals and adhere to recognised procedures.

For the individual a threat of redundancy and job insecurity can potentially manifest itself in stress, lost productivity, conflict and a lowering of loyalty to the organisation. It may also lead to individuals rethinking their career development opportunities and aspirations (see later).

5.4 Motivation and incentives

Gratton (2004) addresses both motivation and incentives by synthesising recent research into the area. She concludes that financial gain is overestimated as a staff motivator, but that money is still important:

- not because of what it can purchase, but the status it signifies in comparison with others
- there is little evidence that higher rewards or bonuses have an effect on subsequent performance
- the process of allocation can be as important as what is actually allocated, people prefer procedures that involve them.

> **❗ Note: Motivation – a case in point**
>
> A summer heat wave was met with an innovative response by the management of Volkswagen (VW) Group UK. The 500 plus staff were invited to cool down, both morning and afternoon, with ice cream, watermelon and anything else restaurant staff could come up with. This contrasts with a tale of a large financial institution who had a rule that employees could only remove their jackets if temperatures soared

> above 80 degrees (F) for 3 days or more. By the time the memo granting permission had got to staff, temperatures had usually gone back down. Volkswagen looked at what staff needed and someone was able to make the decision right away. Undeniably an inexpensive treat, it was well received by staff because it showed they were valued as people. The Head of HR explained: *we're just the organisation in the middle, so all our value added has to be through our people. This means they have to be as motivated as possible.* People may be still driven by cash rewards, but these are recognised by VW as not enough. In addition to being a good payer, VW also boasts a good pension scheme and exceptional maternity benefits.
>
> *Source*: Carrington (2004)

5.4.1 Designing reward systems

Armstrong and Murlis (2007) suggest that reward systems consist of two elements:

1. pay ranges, with a method for moving through (progression) or up (promotion)
2. the benefits package (pensions, sick pay, medical and other insurance, car schemes, etc.).

Typically, larger organisations have grade structures that put jobs into grades based on the job value to the organisation. (Small organisations may only pay spot rates for the job based on market prices.)

Exercise 5.10

What are the managerial aims of a reward system?

Solution

- recruitment (from the marketplace)
- retention (keeping up within the market)
- provide a fair and consistent basis for motivating employees
- provide a fair and consistent basis for rewarding employees (paying for performance)
- recognise the various factors apart from performance such as job/role size, contribution, skill and competence
- reward performance by progression or promotion via developmental pathways and career ladders
- control payroll costs.

The design of reward systems should be appropriate to the characteristics and needs of the organisation (e.g. size, stability of the environment, competitors' policies, local pay rates, and internal culture). It might include one of a number of factors both financial and non financial.

'Differentials' in levels of pay can be methodically defined through job evaluation. There is often a need for different career structures according to the level or category of employees. A number of organisations have two levels: one for 'white collar' staff and one for manual workers, some have three: one for the managers, one for the professional staff and

Table 5.16 Types of organisational remuneration structures

Type	Description
Graded pay	A sequence of job grades against which a payment range is attached.
Broad-banded	The range of pay in a band is significantly higher than in a conventional graded structure. The structure usually covers the whole workforce from the shop floor to senior management.
Individual job ranges	Used where the content and size of jobs is widely different throughout the organisation. This approach avoids jobs being either underpaid and or overpaid.
Job family structures	Consists of jobs in a function or discipline such as financial specialists. Jobs will be related in terms of the fundamental activities carried out and the basic skills required, but will be differentiated by the level of responsibility, skill or competence involved.
Spot rates	Allocation of a specific rate for the job.
Pay spines	Consists of a series of incremental points extending from the lowest to the highest paid jobs covered by the structure. Pay scales or ranges for different job grades may then be superimposed on the pay spine. This method is favoured particular within the UK for most NHS and central and local government employees.
Integrated pay structures	Cover groups of employees who have traditionally been paid under separate arrangements. There may be one grading system which includes all employees.

one for the junior staff and manual workers. In many cases, top management or directors may be left out of the main structure with their remuneration being agreed individually.

External comparisons made through market rate surveys and decisions on external relativities tend to follow the organisation's policy on how its pay levels should relate to the market rate.

Numerous types of organisational pay structures exist, the most common are identified in Table 5.16.

Profit-related pay schemes attempt to produce a sense of shared ownership and commitment. They are not as popular as they once were, for a number of reasons including:

- the ability of the firm to 'massage' year end profits
- the tax implications of share purchase and share option schemes, etc.
- the problem of 'free-riders' benefiting from the scheme
- the restricted use of the scheme to only a few groups (e.g. directors and senior managers) in some companies leading to resentment by other groups.

> An example of profit sharing:
> In May 2005, Royal Mail announced a record of £537 million profit on its operations with quality of service to customers hitting the highest levels in a decade. As a reward for this turnaround postal workers received a 'Share in Success' payment of £1,074 amounting to £218 million of the company's profit. This represented one of the biggest profit shares with employees in UK corporate history.

'Piece rates': in the early days of industrial mechanisation, the Taylorist philosophy of paying employers on the basis of output alone was straightforward as output was clear and easily measurable. Payment was referred to as *'piece rates'* because employees were remunerated based on the number of manufactured pieces they completed.

The modern organisation has, however, changed considerably and individual labour inputs are less likely to be traced as direct outputs. Group and *team bonuses* have been pioneered in some new manufacturing plants and car dealerships in order to recognise staff co-operating to achieve shared outputs. However new challenges such as rewards shared by free riders (those who shirk work and unfairly rely on others in the team) have caused ill feeling and have been counterproductive.

Where direct output data can easily be measured and attributed mainly to one individual (e.g. in sales), management have continued to operate individual, quantitative, performance-based rewards ignoring factors that might have contributed to outputs such as managerial support and advertising outputs.

Performance-related pay (PRP). Appraisal based performance-related pay is a method of payment where an individual receives increases in pay based wholly or partly on the regular and systematic assessment of job performance.

It is argued that performance-related pay, in the right context, can be of potential benefit to both employers and employees. It can, for example, help employers improve the efficiency and effectiveness of their workforce by emphasising the need for high standards of job performance. It is further argued that it can offer the flexibility to help motivate and retain valuable employees by targeting higher pay at better performers. Employees in turn may welcome a system that rewards extra effort by extra pay.

The introduction or revision of PRP is often linked with other organisational and HR changes including:

- greater decentralisation of the responsibility for pay determination
- the introduction or extension of appraisal schemes
- moves towards harmonised terms and conditions of all the workforce
- the greater use of flexible working arrangements, for example in skills acquisition.

The way in which payment systems are modified to take account of pay for individual performance include:

- replacing part or, occasionally, all of general pay increases with PRP awards
- strengthening the link between pay and performance by introducing additional payments above the scale maximum to recognise high performance
- introducing PRP in place of incremental pay increases which is based on length of service, age or qualifications.

PRP should be based on the foundation of a sound payment system and accepted salary levels. It should not be introduced if what is really required is a general increase in wage rates. PRP is not an effective substitute for adequate basic rates of pay.

Exercise 5.11

What are the benefits of PRP?

Solution

As organisations seek to compete more effectively to meet customer requirements they are increasingly examining methods of improving workforce flexibility and engendering a culture of high performance. By linking rewards more closely to performance in a way that is properly measured against appropriate criteria, employees may be encouraged to increase productivity. Resources can be better targeted to recognise effort and achievement, and to reward and retain more effective employees. Properly introduced, PRP can be used as a mechanism for promoting greater employee involvement and commitment to an organisation. Improved quality and customer service can be additional benefits.

There are in practice undeniable difficulties with PRP, whether because of poor design, inappropriate introduction, the use of subjective measures or secret awards. Under these conditions PRP may not only fail to motivate but may cause dissatisfaction if:

- employees are not aware of the levels of performance they need to attain
- PRP awards are not applied consistently across the eligible participants
- financial constraints by the use of budgets or 'quotas' restrict the amount of awards
- there is subjectivity in assessment
- there is divisiveness in operation.

Kent County Council has introduced performance-related pay for its 25,000 staff. The following extract explains something of the detail:

> ....all council employees, other than teaching staff, received an appraisal rating of between 1 and 5, based on their total contribution.
>
> Each point awarded pushes the employee half a point further up their pay scale. So a worker receiving a 'good' rating of 3 is raised one point further up the pay scale, while an 'excellent' 4 would raise them 1.5 and 'exceptional' 5 puts them up 2 points.
>
> The 'total contribution' of staff is measured against four criteria: meeting objectives, their behaviour, personal development and any other responsibilities they take on beyond their job description that add value.
>
> 'What we are trying to do is distinguish between individuals and their performance levels throughout the council, which wasn't the case before,' said Miller (Reward Manager Colin Miller). 'While we expect most (rated as "good") to make steady progress, the system allows us to reward those who are performing exceptionally well.'
>
> There should be few surprises at the bottom end since those rated at less than 3 should have their performance addressed in the normal course of the year, he added.
>
> Miller has also introduced an initiative whereby managers can pay £500 one-off bonuses to high-performing staff, providing the chief officer gives approval. 'That met with some resistance, along the lines that the money would be better off given to services,' said Miller. 'But if we are rewarding top performance and, as a consequence, top performance is more likely to happen in future, then that's money well spent.'
>
> *Source*: Brockett, J. (2007) Kent council reviews reward system. *People Management*, 26 July.

Non-financial rewards. Findings from one retention initiatives report claims that employees are more likely to look for a new job when their needs for career advancement or training are not being met, or when their relationship with their manager is poor (Anon, 2005). The report concludes that employers looking for ways to hold on to workers should consider training managers and implement more flexibility in pay and conditions.

The past few years have seen organisations put a name to the whole range of benefits they have offered for a while, cash and non-cash, and for the first time publicise the fact more fully. '*Total reward packages*' originated in the US and represents a bundling together of all cash and non-cash motivators an organisation has to offer.

The concept recognises that money is not the only motivator and that employees, prospective employees and other stakeholders might find the organisation more attractive because of its total reward package. The package might include non-cash benefits, such as flexible working, flexible hours, training, career progression and a pursuit of green policies but must not be seen as a way of keeping pay rates down.

Carrington (2004) explains that a range of factors have driven the initiative including 'talent wars' amongst recruiters for staff with scarce skills and a way of developing organisational vision and culture. Carrington believes the total rewards approach has the advantage of:

- making positive statements to stakeholders about the organisation and its culture
- helping employer branding so that retention and recruitment is enhanced
- eroding the 'us and them' attitude in the workforce.

The following short extract is from an article that explores approaches to rewarding and motivating employees at a time when it seems more difficult than ever. In purely financial terms the factors cited are low cost, but in outcome terms they are apparently high-impact:

> Andrew Sellers, corporate business manager at John Lewis Direct, agrees that companies are using incentives in a broader way. 'In the call centre environment, where call-handlers are employed at roughly the same salary across the industry, it's the small things that make a difference to the workforce.'
>
> Vodafone used John Lewis Direct to send a bottle of champagne to a team that had achieved a project ahead of time and on budget. Such a discretionary approach allows employers to target incentives more widely to reward attendance, productivity, customer service and good ideas.
>
> The key to reward and recognition in this environment is to make awards as instant as possible. This spontaneity is hampered when rewards have to be ratified and paperwork completed, risking resentment rather than goodwill.
>
> John Lewis relaunched its vouchers last year with an online redemption element. The innovation addresses two issues, says Sellers. 'We want to grow our online business and when people are in front of a screen all day, the PC is their interface with the world, so they can spend their reward there and then.'
>
> Successful schemes are not prescriptive, so despite a sometimes dull reputation, vouchers are the most popular choice of reward after cash.
>
> 'The problem with cash is that no one ever remembers what they did with it, so its motivation effect is lost', says Sellers. 'With vouchers, people will treat themselves and tell their colleagues about it.'
>
> *Source*: Extracted from Incentives: The rewards of work by Stuart Derrick, *Marketing*, 13 July 2005 p. 37, Haymarket Business Publications Ltd.

Table 5.17 Popularity of incentives

Growing	Static	Declining
Schemes such as home PCs, bicycles and childcare vouchers. (all are tax-efficient)	Concierge services, (e.g. shopping and dry-cleaning) These are mainly confined to large City firms.	Final-salary pension schemes
More flexible pension schemes that offer choice	Store cards/vouchers Gym membership Health insurance Optional extras such as dental insurance and pet cover	Golden parachutes Bonuses Share schemes, (stock prices, which are easily affected by external events, do not accurately reflect the performance of an individual or team)

Source: Prickett (2006)

Sherman's (2005) research into female business owners concludes that they may not offer more perks to the workplace than men, but the perks they offer employees 'often have a decidedly feminine touch'. She cites Hillary Kelbick, president of a medium-sized New York marketing and consulting firm. Flexible working and telecommuting is commonplace, additionally staff are allowed to bring their young children to work when day care is difficult. Kelbick also funds staff to purchase new outfits for important client meetings. The reasoning is faultless: perks' such as these enabled the company to compete with larger, more established companies in hiring and keeping the 'right' people.

Prickett (2006) explores the fact that firms are realising that flexible benefits are a practical and affordable way to reward their staff, and in so doing identifies what incentives she feels are growing in importance and those that are not are summarised in Table 5.17.

5.5 Improving the opportunities for employees contribution

This section considers practices aimed at creating opportunities for employees to contribute to the organisation whether through job design, communications, involvement procedures or engaging in formal negotiating and bargaining.

A relatively recent concept of organisational citizenship behaviour (OCB) has grown up to describe the efforts of those who voluntarily undertake innovative, spontaneous tasks that go beyond their normal job role. Organ (1988) describes such behaviour as

…discretionary, not directly or explicitly recognized by the formal rewards system and that in aggregate promote effective functioning of an organization.

Clearly such behaviour is most apparent in organisations that have positive inclusive cultures that value team work and adopt supportive management approaches. The approach adopted by a particular manager can in many situations have a significant effect on efficiency, effectiveness and motivation. The potential impact of work groups on individual motivation has long been recognised and was famously illustrated by the Hawthorne Studies. Elton Mayo's research over a 5-year period at the Hawthorne Works of the Western Electric Company in Chicago indicated that work satisfaction depends to a large extent upon the social relationships. These

Figure 5.3 Job characteristics model

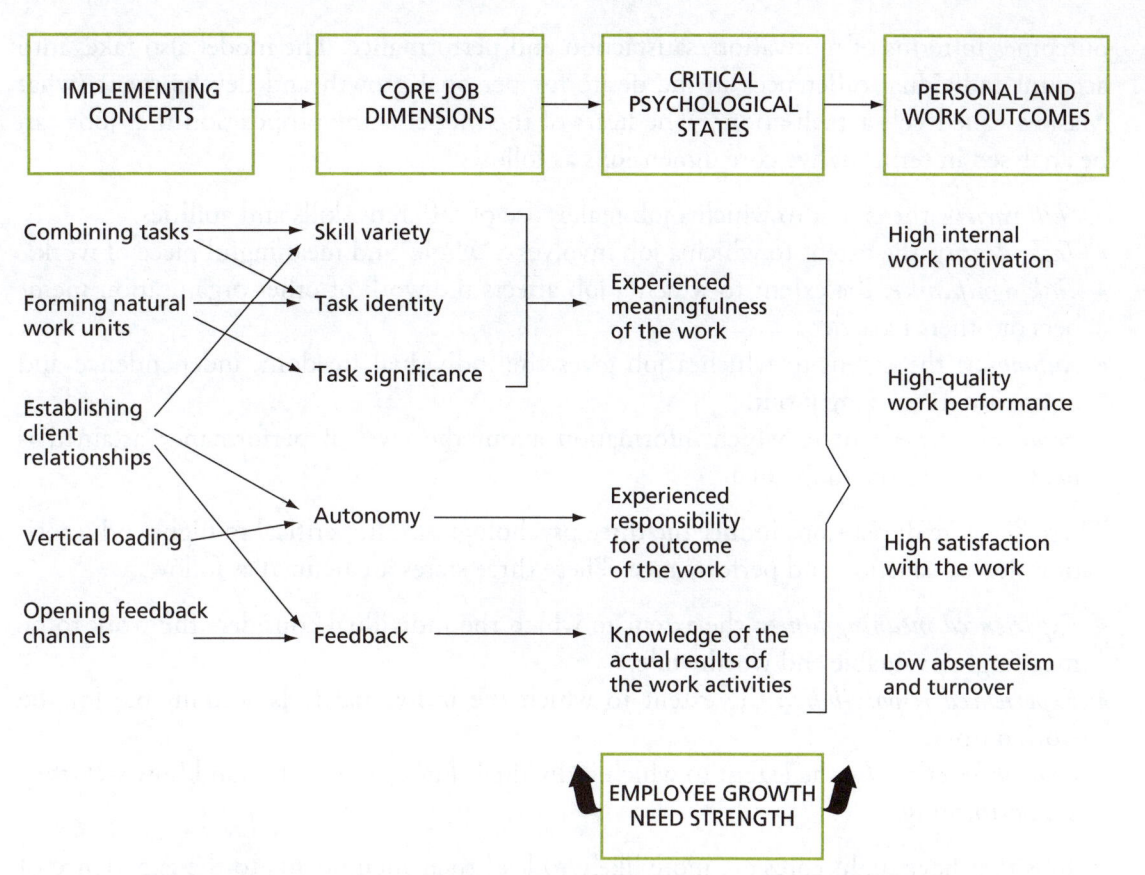

From J. R. Hackman, G. Oldham, R. Janson and K. Purdy, 1975; © 1975 by the Regents of the University of California. Reprinted from the *California Management Review*, 1975, vol. 17, no. 4, p. 62, Reprinted with permission.

are both informal between workers in a group and between workers and their bosses. The effects of the group proved more powerful than altered working conditions, new payment systems, rest breaks, varying the length of the working day, and offering food and refreshments.

This thinking naturally goes to the heart of *job design* and the methods by which team working is encouraged. Traditionally, jobs have been designed on the basis of the scientific management approach with a high degree of specialisation and strict controls. This is highly effective for bringing about conformity in many situations, but is hardly conducive to commitment. A number of other approaches to job design attempt to build more interest, variety, challenge and collaborative working into jobs.

Self-directed work teams have emerged from group technology developed by motor manufacturer Volvo. The initiative arose as a result of recruitment and retention problems for production line jobs which involved repetitive working procedures. Under cellular manufacturing methods, teams form a cell that jointly make a substantial proportion of the finished product rather than singly assemble one component of it. Cellular production often forms part of programmes of quality improvement. Indeed 'Total Quality Management', which seeks to move the emphasis away from detecting faults to preventing them, stresses employee involvement and team working as important ways of achieving this.

Job redesign can therefore be used to help develop individuals and groups within the workplace.

The job characteristics model (as shown in Figure 5.3) sets out the links between characteristics of jobs, the individual's experience of those characteristics, and the resultant outcomes in terms of motivation, satisfaction and performance. The model also takes into account individual differences in the desire for personal growth and development (what Maslow called 'self-actualisation'). The heart of the model is the proposition that jobs can be analysed in terms of five core dimensions as follows:

- *Skill variety*: the extent to which a job makes use of different skills and abilities.
- *Task identity*: the extent to which a job involves a 'whole' and meaningful piece of work.
- *Task significance*: the extent to which a job affects the work of other organisation members or others in society.
- *Autonomy*: the extent to which a job gives the individual freedom, independence and discretion in carrying it out.
- *Feedback*: the extent to which information about the level of performance attained is related back to the individual.

These five core dimensions induce the three psychological states critical to high work motivation, job satisfaction and performance. These three states are defined as follows:

- *Experienced meaningfulness*: the extent to which the individual considers the work to be meaningful, valuable and worthwhile.
- *Experienced responsibility*: the extent to which the individual feels accountable for the work output.
- *Knowledge of results*: the extent to which individuals know and understand how well they are performing.

Jobs that have high scores are more likely to lead their incumbents to the experience of these critical psychological states than jobs that have low scores.

In order to improve employees contributions the following approaches might legitimately be considered:

- *Job enlargement*: horizontally expanding a job role with tasks at a similar level of difficulty.
- *Job rotation:* arranging for individuals to swop roles periodically in order that they do not become stale and so that new approaches are tried out.
- *Job enrichment:* adding to a post tasks that might normally be carried out by someone on a superior grade so as to increase employee control, responsibility or experience .

5.6 Line managers and human resource practices

Organisational HR practices inevitably vary dependent upon the individual size and culture of the organisation and availability of specialist HR or personnel managers to support management in carrying out their duties. The need to respond to a fast moving environment has led to organisations moving from traditional hierarchies to adopting more flexible organisational structures including fluid matrix or project-based firms. Alongside these virtual or networked firms have grown up. Inevitably these non-traditional structures have presented new HR challenges and required managers to adapt traditional approaches to these local contexts. Clearly HR thinking and practice needs to evolve in responses to these challenges of flexibility and environmental uncertainty, specifically in the areas of:

- planning horizons
- staff appraisal where there may be no formal supervisor/subordinate reporting relations

- remuneration strategies where outputs are not easily attributable to individuals alone
- the structure of the workforce and the use of consultants and contractors
- development, promotion and succession planning.

Exercise 5.12

What are the main organisational disadvantages of employment flexibility?

Solution

- Potentially reduced commitment and/or quality
- Potential loss of stability
- Problems with continuity and team working
- Training expenditure. Flexibility implies a necessity to significantly increase expenditure on training and yet temporary working implies minimal training commitment
- Conflict with the workforce and trade union opposition
- Resistance, especially from crafts people who are unlikely to willingly give up time-honoured job definitions
- A redefinition of the role and focus of managers

Charles Handy's (1999) concept of the shamrock organisation depicts an organisation with 'core' and 'periphery' workers as well as a contractual fringe. (Core employees possess key and scarce skills and enjoy relatively high status positions with good prospects of security and promotion. Periphery workers on temporary or part-time contracts act as a buffer against changes in demand.) The use of these distinctions may be challenged as some industries rely almost exclusively on 'periphery' workers and these groups become more central rather than peripheral. In addition, groups of employees who might be classified as 'core' do not necessarily enjoy the status that is suggested by the framework (e.g. skilled manual workers). Nevertheless, these concepts provide a background against which consideration can be given to the different forms of flexibility, namely task, numerical and financial (Atkinson, 1984).

- *Task or functional flexibility*. There is evidence that traditional demarcations between jobs are being eroded and employees are being required to undertake a wider range of tasks. In white-collar employment functional flexibility has been facilitated by IT developments that cut across previous job classifications. There is also considerable evidence of organisations significantly reducing the number of job grades and this, of course, implies that individuals are undertaking a broader range of tasks. The integration of tasks can be viewed both horizontally, involving employees undertaking a broader range of tasks at the same level as their original task(s), and vertically, involving undertaking tasks that were previously carried out by employees at higher or lower levels.
- *Numerical flexibility*. Temporary, part-time, short-term contract working and sub-contracting have been in the ascendant in recent years and have been adopted by organisations as a means of responding to demand fluctuations. The evidence of increasing sub-contracting is relatively widespread but the trends in temporary working are more ambivalent. Numerical flexibility can be achieved by using both contractors and agency staff. There is some research evidence of a general trend in some sectors towards greater use of agency staff mostly in ancillary services such as maintenance, cleaning, transport, catering, computer services and security.

- *Financial flexibility*. The growth of individualised and variable systems of reward has been noticeable and performance related pay schemes are now widely in use. Fees for service payments are used for increasing numbers of self-employed sub-contractors.

5.7 HR planning

There are a number of compelling reasons why organisations should plan their human resourcing, including:

- a need to establish cost and develop budgeting, especially in new projects to control costs and numbers employed
- to rationally plan recruitment
- to provide a smoother means of coping with redeployment, redundancies and retirements
- to provide structured education, development and training needed by a future workforce
- to allow a degree of succession planning
- to adapt more quickly to ever changing circumstances.

Before beginning a human resource planning exercise a considerable amount of data, both internal and external, must be collected and analysed (Table 5.18).

Forecasts of people requirement are based on predictions. Most organisations estimate the demand in the light of:

- future output/volumes/sales/product projections
- future methods of production and IT usage
- likely external influences such as competitor action, trade unions, government and other pressures
- changes in corporate strategy
- organisation of work

Table 5.18 Human resource planning: some data requirement

Internal
Employee analysis: numbers, gender, qualification, trade and job, skills, experience, etc.
Categories of staff
Staff suitable for promotion or redeployment
Overtime levels and trends
Labour turnover analysis and reasons
Absence level by category and trends
Productivity ratios and trends
Comparison with national/regional/industry trends

External
Regional employment trends and unemployment levels
Demographic projections
Skill levels and shortages
Education levels and proposals
Transport and planning proposals
Labour mobility
Migration and immigration trends
Growth of competing firms in the area

Source: Author

- productivity trends
- employee (industrial) relations atmosphere.

An analysis of labour supply needs to commence with a positional assessment of the organisation's current employees. Staff retention, turnover, wastages, leaves of absence raises a number of issues such as:

- historic rates and those expected in similar businesses
- the rate at which staff are leaving and their reasons for leaving
- numbers retiring and likely future projections based on age profiles.

If a significant cause of turnover is due to a lack of promotion opportunities, inadequate training, low morale or poor management, then these problems need to be addressed within the strategy. To this end the use of 'exit interviews' conducted by those independent of line management are helpful in identifying problems. Consideration should also be given to the organisation's ability to continue to attract suitable recruits into its various operations. Again if there are difficulties these should be addressed through the HR plan.

Having considered the existing supply of labour, an organisation will need to project a view of what the workforce will need to be like in the future in order to fulfil its strategic plans. The difference between the two projections of supply and demand can be made ('gap analysis') and plans developed accordingly. This might involve, for example, retraining, part time workers, use of consultants overtime, computerisation recruitment, redundancy policy, etc.

Since employees are probably the most unpredictable organisational resource, the best plans will be those that allow the greatest flexibility. Most HR plans are developed on a rolling 3-year basis, which means that forecasts for next year and the succeeding years in the cycle are updated every year in the light of this year's experience. Detailed plans for securing sufficient and suitable employees for current needs are made for a 1-year period, in line with current budgets. Less detailed plans are made for the 3-year period, prepared in line with the organisation's corporate strategy.

Mullins (2007) captures all elements involved in planning (Figure 5.4) and articulates the HR plan and consequent action programmes as a means of reconciling supply and demand.

HR planning links to other business plans by implementing the resource element so that necessary numbers and quality of staff are available at the right time to implement the business's other plans.

Exercise 5.13

Manchester United is fast becoming more a global brand than a football club. Its financial performance reflects fast growth and profitability. Their impressive financial credentials made them until recently the world's largest club (generating well over £100 million revenue per annum 'before a ball is kicked'). Players enjoy huge salaries and the club is better placed than most to pay the top dollar in terms of transfer fees and wage demands. This means they could recruit the best footballers from anywhere in the world. Yet the club continues to spend heavily on their youth policy. Why should this be the case?

Solution

It partially insulates the club from the transfer market and also importantly brings loyalty and commitment to the playing staff. The first team itself represents a combination of

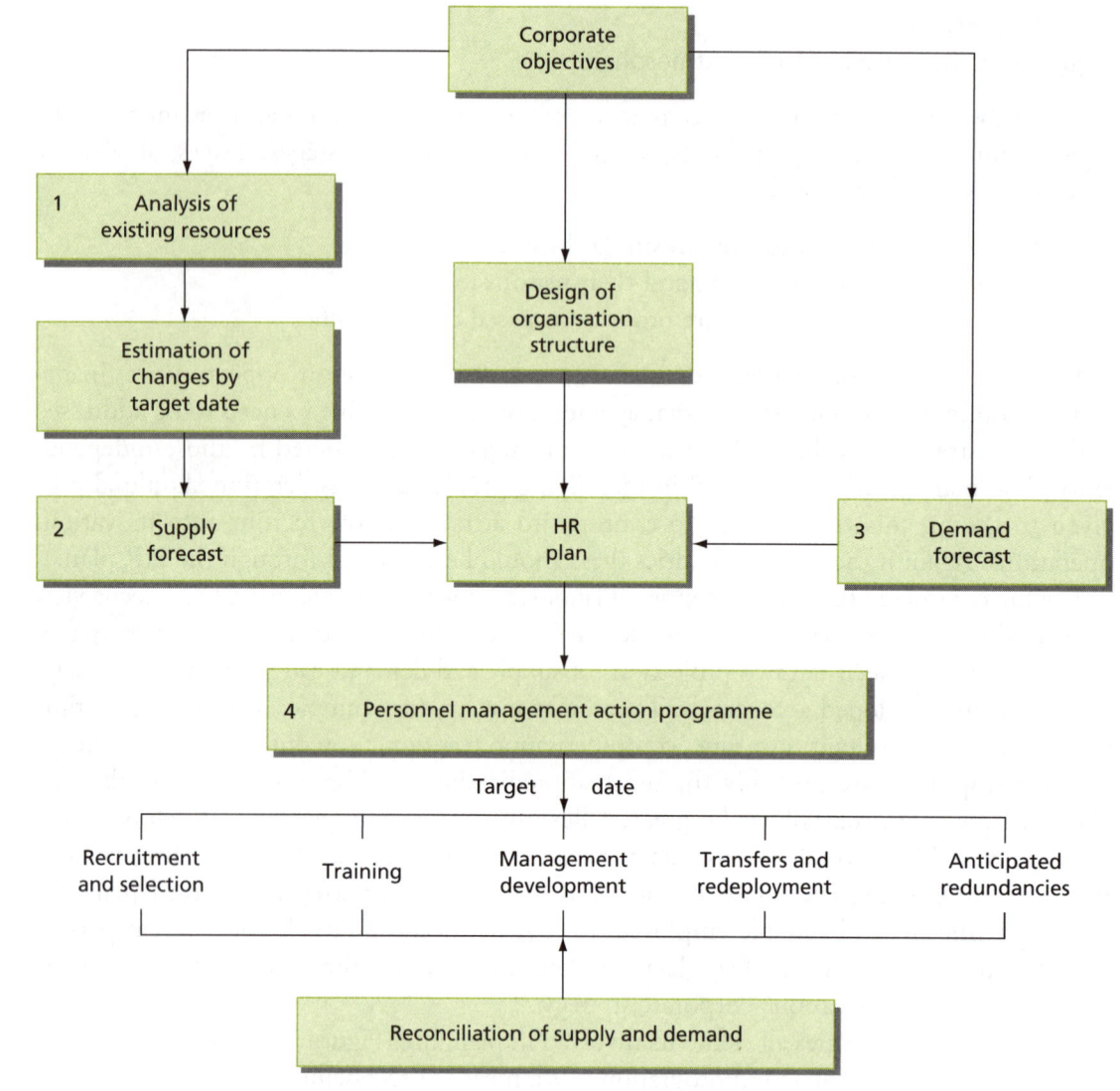

```
                        ┌─────────────┐
                        │  Corporate  │
                        │ objectives  │
                        └─────────────┘
                              │
      ┌───────────────────────┼───────────────────────┐
      ▼                       ▼                       │
┌─────────────┐        ┌─────────────┐                │
│1 Analysis of│        │  Design of  │                │
│  existing   │        │organisation │                │
│  resources  │        │  structure  │                │
└─────────────┘        └─────────────┘                │
      │                       │                       │
      ▼                       │                       │
┌─────────────┐               │                       │
│Estimation of│               │                       │
│  changes by │               │                       │
│ target date │               │                       │
└─────────────┘               │                       │
      │                       ▼                       ▼
┌─────────────┐        ┌─────────────┐        ┌─────────────┐
│2  Supply    │───────▶│     HR      │◀───────│3  Demand    │
│  forecast   │        │    plan     │        │  forecast   │
└─────────────┘        └─────────────┘        └─────────────┘
```

Figure 5.4 Main stages in human resources planning

Source: Mullins (2005) © Laurie J Mullins 2002. Reprinted with permission of Pearson.

expensive buys and players who have progressed through thanks to the club's youth policy. The average age of the talented professional playing staff is a youthful 25 years old. The youngsters continue to benefit from the best training facilities money can buy at the purpose built multi-million pound Trafford Training Centre, Carrington set in 70 acres (Perry, 2005).

HR planning is a corporate activity across all divisional and departmental boundaries of an organisation link to behavioural aspects and implementation. It is not the preserve of any one group of specialist managers (e.g. Personnel), even though such specialists may well play a key co-coordinating role in the implementation and review.

Exercise 5.14

How can an organisation plan rationally in an unstable environment?

✓ Solution

- by staying flexible
- by taking greater account of external factors
- by more sophisticated monitoring and control mechanisms
- by planning in shorter time frames.

Problems in achieving plans might to a degree be predictable and in the past have also traditionally centred on:

- retention especially when employees are well trained or have specialist skills
- slow promotion leading to staff turnover
- difficulties associated with putting succession planning into practice
- unexpected vacancies arising in very senior positions or in vital skills areas.

5.8 Summary

Human Resourcing is a detailed and complex subject worthy of study in some depth. Inevitably there is a limitation in coverage within the confines of a single chapter in a Learning System, however, many aspects have been considered here. An understanding of HRM has been established and the determinants, content and implementation issues of an HR plan has been discussed in the context of motivation theory. Specifically managerial and contextual considerations relating to recruitment selection channels, induction, appraisals, development and training in particular have been highlighted.

References and further reading

Anon (2005) *Brainfood: Crash course in . . . developing future leaders*, Management Today, September 1, p. 24 Haymarket Business Publications Ltd.

Appleyard, B. (2007) Want a job? Let's play mind games. *Sunday Times*, 22 July, p. 9.

Armstrong, M. (2006) *A Handbook of Personnel Management Practice* (10th edn). London: Kogan Page.

Armstrong, M. and Mulis, H. (2007) *Reward Management: A Handbook of remuneration strategy and practice*. London: Kogan Page.

Atkinson, J. (1984) Manpower strategies for flexible organisations. *Personnel Management*, August.

Beaumont, P. B. (1993) *Human Resource Management: Key Concepts and Skills*. London: Sage.

Bratton, J. and Gold, J. (2007) *Human Resource Management, Theory and Practice* (4th edn). Basingstoke: Macmillan Business.

Brockett, J. (2007) Kent council reviews reward system. *People Management*, 26 July, Vol. 13, No. 15, p. 16.

Carrington, L. (2004) Just desserts. *People Management*, 29 January, Vol. 10, No. 2, p. 38.

CIMA (2006) *Code of Ethics for Professional Accountants*. www.cimaglobal.co.uk
CIPD (2008) *The Psychological Contract: Factsheet*. www.cipd.co.uk

Cohen, D. (2006) Professional standards: CIMA's new code of ethics, which is now in force, is based on principles rather than rules. *Financial Management*, February.

Derrick, S. (2005) Incentives: The rewards of work. *Marketing*, 13 July, p. 37, Haymarket Business Publications Ltd.

Devanna, M. A., Fombrun, C. J. and Tichy, N. M. (1984) A framework for strategic human resource management, in Fombrun, C. J. et al. (eds), *Strategic Human Resource Management*, Chichester: John Wiley.

Gratton, L. (2004) More than money. *People Management*, 29 January, Vol. 10, No. 2, p. 23.

Guest, D. (1997) Human resource management and performance: a review and research agenda. *The International Journal of Human Resource Management*, Vol. 8, No. 3, pp. 263–276.

Guest, D. E. and Conway, N. (2002), Communicating the psychological contract: an employer perspective, *Human Resource Management Journal*, Vol. 12 No.2, pp.22–38.

Guest, D. E. and Conway, N. (2002) *Pressure at Work and the Psychological Contract*. London: CIPD.

Handy, C. (1999) *Inside Organisations: 21 Ideas for Managers* (2nd edn). Harmondsworth: Penguin.

Kirkpatrick, D. L. (1998) *Evaluating Training Programs: The Four Levels*. New York: Pfeiffer Wiley.

Kolb, D. A. (1984) *Experiential Learning: Experience as the Source of Learning and Development*. London; Englewood Cliffs [NJ]: Prentice-Hall.

Mullins, L. J. (2007) *Management and Organisational Behaviour* (8th edn). Harlow: Financial Times Prentice Hall.

Organ, L. (1988) *OCB: The Good Soldier Syndrome*. Lexington, MA: Lexington.

Otley, D. T. (1987) *Accounting Control and Organisational Behaviour*. London: Heinemann in association with CIMA.

Overell, S. (2003) Employee appraisals. *Financial Times*, 6 March, p. 13.

Pedler, M., Burgoyne, J. and Boydell, T. (2006) *A Manager's Guide to Self-Development* (5th edn). London: McGraw-Hill.

Perry, B. (2005) Manchester United, Brand of Hope and Glory, in Johnson, G. and Scholes, K. (eds), *Exploring Corporate Strategy – Text and Cases* (7th edn). Pearson Education Limited.

Prickett, R. (2006) Pliable and viable. *Financial Management*, April, Vol. 19, No. 4.

Prithcard, S. (2003) DIY programme suits DIY staff. *The Financial Times*, 2 April, p. 3. www.jobs.ac.uk

Schein, E. H. (2004) *Organisational Culture and Leadership* (3rd edn). San Francisco: Jossey-Bass.

Sherman, A. P. (2005) Central perks: women use unique benefits to show employee appreciation. *Entrepreneur*, September, Vol. 33, No. 9(1), p. 34.

Also

The Chartered Institute of Personnel and Development (2008) www.cipd.co.uk

Revision Questions 5

Question 1

1.1 Attempts to add new, stimulating dimensions to a person's job is called:

    (A) multi-skilling
    (B) job enrichment
    (C) HR development
    (D) career scoping. **(2 marks)**

1.2 'Spot rates' normally refer to a specific pay rate determined by reference to:

    (A) the market place
    (B) incremental progression
    (C) a negotiated point on a pay spine
    (D) experience and qualifications of a newly recruited person. **(2 marks)**

1.3 Roger's seven-point plan refers to:

    (A) quality targets for world class operations
    (B) implementation guidelines for introducing new hardware
    (C) the likely headings to be found as part of a person specification
    (D) lean production processes. **(2 marks)**

1.4 Identify the potential solutions that an organisation in its HR planning might use to match the future demand for and projected 'supply' of human resources. (50 word limit) **(4 marks)**

1.5 Identify the advantages and disadvantages of a policy of succession planning for a large organisation. (50 word limit) **(4 marks)**

1.6 Identify the advantages and disadvantages of a decentralised Human Resource provision for an organisation that has many business units and sites. (50 word limit) **(4 marks)**

1.7 Describe the important documents and information an interviewer should have access to when conducting a job selection interview. (50 word limit) **(4 marks)**

Question 2

2.1 Charles Handy's vision of a 'shamrock' organisation suggests a workforce that comprises of three different types of worker, namely:

    (A) strategic, operational and support
    (B) qualified, trainee and unskilled

(C) 'white collar', 'blue collar' and e-worker
(D) core, contractual fringe and flexible labour.

2.2 The set of activities designed to attract a suitable pool of candidates to an organisation is called:

(A) job analysis
(B) recruitment
(C) selection
(D) induction.

2.3 Three hundred and sixty (360) degree feedback is normally associated with:

(A) exit interviews
(B) quality circle activity
(C) appraisal processes
(D) reflection as part of a cycle of learning.

Question 3

A year ago, the owner-manager of a taxi service also moved into a new business area of fitting tyres. This came about as a result of the experience of using unbranded tyres on the fleet of ten taxis. Based on several years of use, the owner-manager found that the unbranded tyres lasted almost as long as the branded tyres, but had the advantage of being obtainable at half the price. The set-up costs of the tyre-fitting business were relatively modest and the owner-manager initially fitted the tyres himself. Demand picked up quickly, however, and he was forced to employ an experienced fitter. A few months later, demand accelerated again and he has just advertised for another fitter but, unfortunately, without success.

The tyre-fitting business has produced additional challenges and the owner-manager is finding it increasingly difficult to manage both the taxi service and the new business where he seems to be spending more and more of his time. He already employs one receptionist/taxi controller, but has realised that he now needs another.

As if this were not enough, he is in the middle of extending his operations still further. Customers who buy tyres frequently request that he check the wheel alignment on their car following the fitting of new tyres. He has started to provide this service, but when done manually it is a slow process, so he has invested heavily in a new piece of electronic equipment. This new technology will speed the alignment operation considerably, but neither he nor his tyre-fitter can operate the equipment. The owner feels that tyre fitters should be able to operate the equipment, and an additional member of staff is not required just to operate the equipment.

To add to all these problems, two of his taxi drivers have resigned unexpectedly. Past patterns suggest that of the ten drivers, normally one or two leave each year, generally in the summer months, though now it is winter.

Given all these staffing difficulties, the owner-manager has made use of a relative who happens to have some HR expertise. She has advised the owner-manager on recruitment and selection, training and development. The relative also suggests that the business needs a well thought out human resource plan.

Requirements

(a) Prepare an outline of human resource plan for the business and explain each aspect of your plan. **(12 marks)**

(b) Discuss the important human resource activities to which attention should be paid in order to obtain the maximum contribution from the workforce.

> *Important: For requirement (b), exclude those areas upon which the relative has already provided advice to the owner-manager (recruitment and selection, training and development).*

(8 marks)
(Total = 20 marks)

Question 4

ZnZ is a large government-funded body that employs several hundred staff performing a wide variety of roles. ZnZ is proud of its commitment to people development and is well known for providing equal opportunities for all its employees. The organisation invests heavily in training and development and employs a number of trainees who are studying for their professional examinations.

ZnZ's human resource plan is currently being reviewed. As part of this process two significant recommendations have emerged from groups and committees considering future human resource issues.

Recommendation 1
(From the HR planning group).

The group has recommended that a more systematic approach to the training and development of qualified staff should be adopted.

Recommendation 2
(From the Diversity Committee)

The Committee has recommended that every person who is part of a minority or disadvantaged group should have an individual career coach. Under such a scheme individuals from these groups would be paired with an experienced colleague on a higher grade who would act as their personal individual career coach. The committee has issued the following guidelines:

- The scheme will not be associated with the appraisal process.
- Coaches should be approachable, suitably experienced and appropriately trained.
- Coaches will not be the individual's own line manager.
- Regular meetings should take place between the two individuals where individuals should be able to confidentially discuss any concerns and areas for self-development. Inevitably individuals will wish to discuss career-related issues and they should receive appropriate advice from their career coach.

You work for the Director of Human Resourcing who is very sympathetic to the recommendation of the Diversity Committee in particular. (So much so that she feels that the scheme should include all trainees and those middle managers that have been identified as having promotion potential.) She has asked you to investigate both recommendations and brief the management team appropriately.

Requirements

(a) Explain how a more systematic approach to the training and development of qualified staff might be adopted. **(10 marks)**

(b) Evaluate the positive role the individual career coach scheme could play within ZnZ. (You may wish to consider culture, HR initiatives, key groups and cost effectiveness issues.) **(10 marks)**

(c) Discuss the likely difficulties of setting up and operating the individual career coach scheme. **(10 marks)**

(Total = 30 marks)

Solutions to Revision Questions

✅ Solution 1

1.1 (B)
1.2 (A)
1.3 (C)
1.4 HR planning: Satisfying projected demand by adjusting projected 'supply'

Increasing	Reducing
Retraining/re-skilling/multiskilling for potential 'gaps'	Early retirements
Development for internal promotions (succession planning)	Redundancy
Overtime	Short-time working
Increased use of IT	Job-sharing
Outsourcing	
Recruitment and selection (new employees)	
Internal transfers/ redeployment to balance requirements	

1.5

Advantages
- career structures, rewards visible
- positive motivation
- reinforces existing culture
- rational approach.

Disadvantages
- lack of exposure to other influences
- ignores possible better candidate from outside
- trend for movement between companies strong
- vacancies may arise at inconvenient times
- expensive
- needs managing
- only possible within a very large organisation
- outdated concept?

1.6

Advantages
- empowerment/delegation strengthened
- in touch with detailed issues
- greater local knowledge
- visible.

Disadvantages
- lack of central control
- lack of specialist knowledge
- may lead to 'maverick' actions/policies
- HR function may be diluted
- uneven provision within organisation.

1.7

Organisational	Individual candidates
• Job description	• Completed application
• Person specification	• CV
• Structure and other detail	• References
• Standard assessment form	• Letter of application
• Pay scales	
• Policies	
• Terms and conditions of service	

✓ Solution 2

2.1 (D)
2.2 (B)
2.3 (C)

✓ Solution 3

(a) *Draft Human Resource Plan*
The human resource plan should include:

Strategic review
- Maintain taxi service at current level
- Continue expansion of tyre fitting service by continuing to offer unbranded low price tyres and develop electronic wheel alignment service as an additional optional service.

Audit of Existing HR Staff
- Owner-manager   1
- Taxi driver   8
- Reception/Taxi Co-ordinator   1
- Tyre Fitter   1

Demand for additional staff due to change in strategy and labour turnover

- Replacement of taxi driver　　　　　　　　　2 (possibly 2 more in the summer)
- Appointment of co-ordinator　　　　　　　　1
- Appointment of tyre fitter　　　　　　　　　　1

Action plans to reconcile gap between demand and supply

- Recruitment and selection of two taxi drivers
- Recruitment and selection of a tyre fitter or of a person capable of training to be a tyre fitter
- Training of taxi drivers
- Training of tyre fitters in use of electronic wheel alignment equipment
- Justification of each aspect of the human resource plan.

It is necessary to review the strategy of the organisation because changes in strategic direction usually have implications for human resources. In this case, we have an emergent strategy that is proving very successful in that it is resulting in the rapid expansion of a tyre fitting business. The expansion not only is affecting the tyre fitting side of the operation, but is also impacting on the human resources of the organisation as a whole. The owner-manager can no longer cope with the demands on his time as a manager/operator and so it is necessary for the company to employ additional staff to cope with the co-ordination of the taxi service and reception work.

The audit of the existing staff is necessary to provide a kind of stock-take of what the organisation already has in terms of human resources. In this case, the numbers are small and we can work out mentally what the current human resource situation is.

The demand for additional staff is once again easy to estimate for the company because small numbers are involved and requirements are for a limited range of skills. The principle involved, however, is just the same as if we were looking at the additional demand for workers of many different skills working in a very large and complex organisation. We need to know about any extra numbers demanded because of a change in strategy, or some other reason for extra demand or alternatively for a contraction in demand. It is also necessary to take into account numbers lost through labour turnover during the planning period, so that extra employees with the required skills can be recruited to compensate.

When we have the figures of existing employees, we can use these as a basis to calculate the gap between what we have and what we need by estimating what the expansion is, caused by the change in strategy, entails. This figure plus an adjustment for labour turnover will provide us with the number of employees we need to recruit.

The activities to reconcile demand with supply follow simply from our calculation. It may, as in this case, be difficult to recruit people with specific skills we want and so it may be necessary to recruit unskilled people and provide them with the necessary training (e.g. the use of wheel alignment equipment).

(b) In addition to training and development, and recruitment and selection, the company will need to ensure that other aspects of human resource management are carried out so that the performance of the workforce is maximised.

Two of the most important human resource activities that are necessary in order to ensure good performance of employees are:

1 first, a system of performance appraisal, so that each worker's performance can be evaluated

2 second, a system of rewards and benefits that will both compensate workers fairly and motivate them to perform to an appropriate standard.

Performance appraisal is a systematic process of evaluating each employee's contribution, his or her strengths and weaknesses and ways of determining how to improve performance. Such an evaluation may provide the basis for the allocation of merit payments that can be used to motivate workers. The information gained can also be used to move staff either between jobs by way of promotion or even out of the company because of underperformance. It can also be used as a means of identifying training and development needs and it provides an opportunity to provide feedback to employees on their past and present performance and to set targets for future performance.

The reward system is also important; first to compensate workers for their efforts. This is the function of base payments. The company might also make use of incentive payments of various kinds in order to motivate employees to work harder. Taxi drivers, for example, might be rewarded on the basis of their overall takings per week, tyre fitters on the number of extra services they sell, such as number of customers who are persuaded to have wheel alignments carried out.

There are, of course, other important human resource activities that need to be covered such as health and safety provision, which is very important when working with heavy equipment.

✓ Solution 4

(a) Explain how a more systematic approach to the training and development of qualified staff might be adopted.

Establish responsibility for the process
In order that a systematic approach is adopted, then a process should be developed and led by Human Resourcing. They should be accountable to ZNZ executive for the successful delivery of training and development for this group. It is likely that ZNZ is organised into departments or divisions and these should be involved throughout.

A more systematic approach to the training and development of qualified staff might involve the following stages (or similar).

Establishing a base line
From what information is available the following is known (or can reasonably be guessed at):

- ZNZ invests heavily in training and development and employs a number of trainees who are studying for their professional examinations. Dependent upon staff turnover rates and retention of this group of employees, it is reasonable to assume that qualified staff might represent a substantial number.
- ZNZ employs several hundred staff performing a wide variety of roles, implying that there are a number of professional groups to be catered for.
- The HR planning group has not indicated that the resource directed to the training and development of qualified staff is too little, more that it could be more systematically applied. It may be that different professional groups are being dealt with in different ways.

As part of establishing the present position, Human Resourcing should identify the numbers of staff involved, the professional groupings they belong to and the level of training and development they have received to date.

Training and development: Professional requirement

Most professional bodies (including CIMA) require their members to engage in continuing professional development (CPD) in order that the currency of their members skills and knowledge is maintained. This requirement should be readily available for each group involved by reference to the professional bodies/the departments concerned.

Training and development: Organisational requirement

Functional plans (such as the HR plan) should be consistent with and support the overall corporate plan or strategy. An assessment should be made of the knowledge, skills and competencies required of the workforce in order to deliver ZNZ's strategy successfully. This will undoubtedly imply management and other business skills that qualified staff will require.

Training and development: Personal requirement

A training needs analysis (or similar) could be conducted whereby the existing skills and competences of an individual is mapped against the organisational and professional needs and an individual training plan developed. Similarly, training needs identified as part of the appraisal processes might usefully be collated. The outcome of this process could then be discussed and agreed with departments.

Establish options for training and development provision

The next stage is to identify the most appropriate means of filling the training and development gaps identified. Attention should be given to the following main considerations:

- Methods of feasible delivery methods (such as classroom delivery, distance learning, on the job training, technology supported learning, etc. or some blended combination).
- In house provision or external provision. ZNZ may already have in-place trainers who are part of the payroll and/or specialist providers and consultants who have successfully worked on their behalf in the past.
- Onsite or offsite provision. There are advantages and disadvantages of each and it may be that a mixed approach rather than either/or might be adopted. Provision onsite would require adequate training facilities to be available to ZNZ.
- Availability of externally provided support and courses. Rather than a bespoke provision it may be sufficient to meet some individuals needs by sending them to other commercial providers or educational or professional establishments.

It would be a good idea to liaise with departments and professional staff when making decisions over the options available.

Costing of options and agreement of a budget

The financial cost should be equated as should other resource commitments including the number of days release required from work. These should be presented to ZNZ's management and approved as appropriate.

Feedback and means of measuring effectiveness of training and development provision.

This should include the establishment of criteria for provision and the establishment of measures and performance indicators. With this information monitoring can take place, and improvements brought about.

It is also important that regular structured feedback should be received from qualified staff both as individuals and as small focus groups.

(b) Evaluate the positive role the individual career coach scheme could play within ZnZ. (You may wish to consider culture, HR initiatives, key groups and cost effectiveness issues.)

The proposed scheme, if properly introduced and operated should be capable performing a positive role within the organisation at a number of levels. Specifically, it should help to:

Strengthen the existing culture

ZnZ is likely to have a distinctive culture that could be further strengthened by the proposals. The organisation may be diverse in its operations but it is distinctive due to the fact that it is a public sector body and it has (an apparently) caring, people-orientated culture. The scheme should fulfil the role of reinforcing the organisation's commitment to people development and confirm in deed as well as word. The fact that it is a genuine equal opportunity employer is evidenced by its attention to diversity, and support for minority and disadvantaged groups through effective career coaching.

The scheme may strengthen organisational communication, positively contribute to knowledge sharing and erode departmentalism (a commitment to ones department rather than the organisation more widely) particularly if participants and coaches are from different working areas. (There is no suggestion of departmentalism from the scenario but this often the case in large diverse organisations).

The scheme might be viewed as an example of best practice and a demonstration of a considerate attitude by the organisation, so reinforcing the overall culture.

Support HR initiatives

Career coaching can assist current HR initiatives and strategies in the following ways:

- By enhance a total employment package by offered to existing and potential employees. This should make both recruitment and retention less problematic. Dedicated individual support through career coaching might be viewed as an additional valued part of the employment package and an incentive for those groups who may feel alienation (the disadvantaged, the minorirty groups, those studying and under pressure middle managers).
- By offering new training and challenges for career coaches who are involved in the process. This might lead to greater personal development, motivation and job enrichment.
- The scheme will certainly increase the effectiveness of ZnZ's heavy investment in training and development, particularly for trainees.
- The scheme might be viewed by the organisation as a way of maintaining harmonious relationships in the workplace so avoiding damaging and confrontational industrial relation tensions.

ZnZ's future human resource plan is currently being reviewed and career coaching should enhance future provision.

Support key groups

The Diversity Committee has recommended that the scheme should be introduced for minority and disadvantaged groups and the Director of Human Resourcing has expanded the suggestion to include all trainees and those middle managers that have been identified as having promotion potential. All these are key groups within the organisation who should now feel better supported by the proposal.

In particular vulnerable groups will feel more valued and less marginalised. The scheme should help avoid organisational discrimination (which is undesirable and possibly illegal). It should also avoid the isolation of disadvantaged groups. Trainees studying for their professional examinations should feel encouraged knowing that 'help is at hand'. Middle managers that have been identified as having promotion potential are a group who require nurturing as part of career development plan. It would be counterproductive if this group were to feel isolated or disaffected and leave. Mentoring should help them.

Organisational behaviour is shaped by the so-called 'psychological contract' (an unwritten series of mutual expectations of rights, privileges, duties and obligations). It involves a process of giving and receiving by both the organisation and the individual.

For instance the individual might expect of the organisation a decent, clean working environment, respect of the individual and recognition of contribution and achievement, etc. In return the organisation might expect of the individual a respect of authority, fellow workers, customers and suppliers, and a degree of loyalty, etc. The mentoring scheme might be viewed by the individual as a way of valuing the individual and seeking ways of overcoming difficulties that make work difficult or unpleasant. As such it should strengthen the psychological contract.

The cost advantages of the scheme

The scheme might be seen as cost effective in that it will:

- increase the effectiveness of expenditure on professional training (hopefully fewer trainees will fail their professional examinations)
- potentially increase job satisfaction, motivation and feelings of commitment which will be reflected in better job performance and hence greater productivity levels
- support minority, disadvantaged groups, trainees and some middle managers which will hopefully lead to less staff turnover negating the need to undertake expensive recruitment of replacement staff.

(c) Discuss the likely difficulties of setting up and operating the individual career coach scheme.

Recognising and overcoming negative attitudes

- Undeniably there are potential benefits associated with the proposals (see Part (a)).
- There may be individuals and groups however who do not share the same enthusiasm shown by the Diversity Committee and the Director of Human Resourcing. Indeed rather than displaying apathy for some there may be hostility to the scheme.

Some may be cynical about the schemes motives, others may believe that it is an example of tokenism and more should be done for these groups.

For the uncommitted, the potential benefits of the scheme will need to be communicated and the proposals positively 'sold'. There will be need to respond to negative attitudes and real concerns with practical solutions that can be incorporated into the schemes design.

Accommodating excluded groups

The scheme could be attacked for being elitist and selective. Currently the scheme is to extend to:

- minority groups (however defined)
- disadvantaged groups (however defined)
- all trainees
- middle managers that have been identified as having promotion potential.

For those groups who are not offered the same facility there may be some resentment and loss of motivation. The following groups will not be (apparently) eligible:

- newly qualified professionals
- first-line managers
- senior managers
- middle managers who have been identified as having no promotion potential.

For the latter group this may be very demotivating, particularly if the group are identified for the first time. They may also feel stigmatised if they see their contemporaries benefiting from career coaching.

HR will need to consider either the potential benefits of expanding the scheme still more widely or considering how they might best support those groups excluded by the scheme.

Overcoming line manager/mentor tensions

Line managers of participants may feel that the process could undermine their authority or position. Clear guidelines as to the extent of their duties will need to be issued to coaches to overcome this potential difficulty.

Setting up the scheme

There will be a number of practical difficulties associated with the proposal initially involving setting up the scheme and then operating and maintaining it. The scheme will require careful investigation of best practice elsewhere, planning and communication and well as engaging a wide number of stakeholders in establishing the scheme.

Appropriate training for mentors will need to be organised, which has cost and scheduling implications.

Running the scheme

Once operational, certain participants may be too demanding of their coaches in terms of (possibly unreasonable) expectation, demands and time. Ways of overcoming these difficulties will need to be devised.

The scheme will not be cost neutral, as coaches will all be experienced and 'on a higher grade'. Their time therefore will involve an opportunity cost (as there is a need for regular meetings). For the coach this might translate into making their working lives more stressful and lead them to being less effective in their day-to-day working. This issue will need to be considered by the HR.

Other practical issues may arise from the operation of the scheme including:

- The position of trainees. Should they also be allowed to continue being coached once they have passed their examinations?
- Coaches who leave the organisation or who do not fulfil their obligations correctly.

Reviewing the scheme
There will be a need to review the effectiveness of the scheme after it has operated for a while. It would be helpful therefore to establish appropriate criteria and performance indicators before the scheme commences and these can be used as measures of effectiveness as part of such a review. Such indicators of performance may be difficult to arrive at and agree upon.

6

Preparing for the Examination

Preparing for the Examination 6

> This section is intended for use when you are ready to start revising for your examination. It contains:
>
> ▸ a summary of useful revision techniques;
>
> ▸ details of the format of the examination;
>
> ▸ a bank of examination-standard revision questions and solutions;
>
> ▸ past examination papers only to be attempted when you consider yourself to be ready for the examination. (Try to emulate examination conditions when attempting this work.)

Revision technique

Planning

The first thing to say about revision is that it is an addition to your initial studies, not a substitute for them. In other words, do not coast along early in your course in the hope of catching up during the revision phase. On the contrary, you should be studying and revising concurrently from the outset. At the end of each week, and at the end of each month, get into the habit of summarising the material you have covered to refresh your memory of it.

As with your initial studies, planning is important to maximise the value of your revision work. You need to balance the demands for study, professional work, family life and other commitments. To make this work, you will need to think carefully about how to make best use of your time.

Begin as before by comparing the estimated hours you will need to devote to revision with the hours available to you in the weeks leading up to the examination. Prepare a written schedule setting out the areas you intend to cover during particular weeks, and break that down further into topics for each day's revision. To help focus on the key areas try to establish:

- which areas you are weakest on, so that you can concentrate on the topics where effort is particularly needed;
- which areas are especially significant for the examination.

Do not forget the need for relaxation, and for family commitments. Sustained intellectual effort is only possible for limited periods, and must be broken up at intervals by lighter activities. Do not continue your revision timetable right up to the moment when you enter the exam hall: you should aim to stop work a day or even 2 days before the exam. Beyond this point the most you should attempt is an occasional brief look at your notes to refresh your memory.

Getting down to work

By the time you begin your revision you should already have settled into a fixed work pattern: a regular time of day for doing the work, a particular location where you sit, particular equipment that you assemble before you begin and so on. If this is not already a matter of routine for you, think carefully about it now in the last vital weeks before the exam.

You should have notes summarising the main points of each topic you have covered. Begin each session by reading through the relevant notes and trying to commit the important points to memory.

Usually this will be just your starting point. Unless the area is one where you already feel very confident, you will need to track back from your notes to the relevant chapter(s) in the Study System. This will refresh your memory on points not covered by your notes and fill in the detail that inevitably gets lost in the process of summarisation.

When you think you have understood and memorised the main principles and techniques, attempt an exam-standard question. At this stage of your studies you should normally be expecting to complete such questions in something close to the actual time allocation allowed in the exam. After completing your effort, check the solution provided and add to your notes any extra points it reveals.

Tips for the final revision phase

As the exam approaches closer, consider the following list of techniques and make use of those that work for you:

- Summarise your notes into a more concise form, perhaps on index cards that you can carry with you for revision on the way into work (alternatively consider buying revision cards).
- Go through your notes with a highlighter pen, marking key concepts and definitions.
- Summarise the main points in a key area by producing a wordlist, mind map or other mnemonic device.
- On areas that you find difficult, rework questions that you have already attempted, and compare your answers in detail with those provided in the Study System.
- Rework questions you attempted earlier in your studies with a view to producing more 'polished' answers (better layout and presentation earn marks in the exam) and to completing them within the time limits.
- Stay alert for practical examples, incidents, situations and events that illustrate the material you are studying. If you can refer in the exam to real-life topical illustrations, you will impress the examiner and earn extra marks.
- Now revisit the chapter end questions that you have not yet attempted. Time your-self and attempt each question in turn. Commit your answers to paper and then compare them with the Examiners Answers (also at the chapter ends). Note the main differences.

Format of the examination

This is a 3-hour paper with three compulsory sections. The format of this exam paper will be:

- Section A – 20% Mainly objective test questions
- Section B – 30% Short answer questions (6 sub-questions at 5 marks each) based on a brief scenario
- Section C – 50% One of two scenario based questions.

Section A: compulsory objective test questions

Section A will comprise a variety of objective test sub-questions, valued at 2 marks and 4 marks each.

For the sub-questions worth 2 marks a conventional 'multiple choice' format is likely. The basis upon which these sub-questions are set is that only ONE option represents a correct answer. An example 'multiple choice' sub-question would be:

> **1.1** Activities aimed at attracting a number of suitable candidates interested in joining an organisation are called
>
> (A) human relationship marketing.
> (B) recruitment.
> (C) selection.
> (D) human capital harvesting.
>
> **(2 marks)**

For sub-questions worth 4 marks answers should be in note form. The nature of the question will vary but may be along the lines of:

Explain the relationship between a (Just-in-Time) JIT system and cash flow management.

> **!** Responses for each sub-question are expected to conform to the word limit indicated (in this case 50 words).

An example of an alternative style of 4 marks question is as follows:

When identifying the requirements of a new system both 'functional' (or logical) and 'physical' aspects should be taken into account. From the listing below indicate those that are functional and those that are physical requirements.

- Work and data flow
- Peripherals
- Volumes, frequencies, etc.
- File size
- Output formats
- Control and backup features
- Screen layouts
- Volumes, frequencies, etc.
- Data storage facilities (e.g. database)

Section B: compulsory short answer questions

Section B comprises six compulsory short answer sub-questions, each worth 5 marks (in total 30 marks). A short scenario may be given, to which some or all questions relate. As with the 4 mark questions referred to earlier you will be encouraged to answer in a concise fashion. These answers will *not* take the form of either a flowing narrative or a business report, and should be no more than one page in length for each sub-question. This limit was imposed for two reasons:

1. to simulate a real-life scenario in which accuracy, brevity and clarity is called for;
2. to prevent candidates from spending a disproportionate amount of time on 5% of the marks available.

> ❗ Responses for each sub-question are expected to conform to the word limit indicated (in this case one page).

Section C: a choice of question

You will be required to answer all questions, worth in total 50 marks. Short scenarios are highly likely to feature and there may be one or two questions.

Examination-standard revision questions and solutions

The bank of examination-standard revision questions and solutions is structured, as follows:

- Section A style questions
- Section A style solutions
- Section B style questions
- Section B style solutions
- Section C style questions
- Section C style solutions.

To strengthen your understanding of the subject matter it is strongly recommended that you refer to the appropriate chapter when reviewing your written answers of these.

Table 6.1 indicates syllabus coverage of the questions that follow:

Table 6.1

2 Marks	Information systems	Marketing	Human capital	Operations management	Global environment
A1	3				
A2				✓	
A3				✓	
A4				✓	
A5			✓		
A6				✓	
A7	3				
A8			✓		
A9				✓	
A10			✓		
A11			✓		
A12				✓	
A13				✓	
A14					✓
A15				✓	
A16		✓			
A17		✓			
A18			✓		
A19			✓		
A20	✓				
A21		✓			
A22	✓				
A23			✓		
A24		✓			
A25	✓				
A26	✓				
A27				✓	
A28		✓			
A29		✓			
A30			✓		

4 Marks	Information systems	Marketing	Human capital	Operations management	Global environment
A100	✓				
A101	✓				
A102	✓				
A103	✓				
A104				✓	
A105	✓				
A106			✓		
A107		✓			
A108				✓	
A109	✓				
A110				✓	
A111				✓	
A112				✓	
A113		✓			
A114			✓		
A115					✓

5 Marks	Information systems	Marketing	Human capital	Operations management	Global environment
B1(a)		✓			
B1(b)			✓		
B1(c)		✓			
B1(d)	✓	✓			
B1(e)		✓			
B1(f)		✓	✓		
B2(a)				✓	
B2(b)		✓		✓	
B2(c)				✓	
B2(d)				✓	
B2(e)	✓				
B2(f)	✓	✓			
B3(a)	✓				
B3(b)	✓				
B3(c)	✓				
B3(d)	✓				
B3(e)			✓		
B3(f)	✓				
B4(a)					✓
B4(b)					✓
B4(c)					✓
B4(d)			✓		

Marks vary in weighting	Information systems	Marketing	Human capital	Operations management	Global environment
C1(a)			✓		
C1(b)			✓		
C1(c)		✓			
C2(a)		✓			
C2(b)		✓			
C2(c)		✓			
C3(a)			✓		
C3(b)			✓		
C3(c)			✓	✓	
C4(a)					3
C4(b)					3
C4(c)					3
C5(a)					3
C6(a)			✓		
C6(b)			✓		
C6(c)			✓		
C7(a)				✓	
C7(b)				✓	
C7(c)				✓	
C8(a)	✓				
C8(b)	✓				

A Style Revision Questions

6

A1 'Corrective' refers to a type of systems maintenance performed to:

(A) remedy software defects
(B) allow executive level unstructured decision-making
(C) adjust applications to user preferences
(D) prevent future operation delays.

A2 Core features of world-class manufacturing involve:

(A) competitor benchmarking and an investment in training and development
(B) an investment in IT and technical skills
(C) global sourcing networks and an awareness of competitor strategies
(D) a strong customer focus and flexibility to meet customer requirements.

A3 An ABC system refers to:

(A) a Japanese style problem-solving device that is particularly helpful in inventory management
(B) an inventory management method that concentrates effort on the most important items
(C) accuracy, brevity and clarity in the quality of system reporting
(D) a mainframe solution to managing inventory.

A4 Corrective work, the cost of scrap and materials lost are:

(A) examples of internal failure costs
(B) examples of external failure costs
(C) examples of appraisal costs
(D) examples of preventative costs.

A5 An assessment centre:

(A) helps selection by assessing job candidates by using a comprehensive and inter-related series of techniques
(B) is the training headquarters where job interviews take place
(C) is a desk-based process of reviewing job application forms for suitability
(D) is a place where job applicants are subjected to psychological testing.

A6 Training workers in methods of statistical process control and work analysis:

(A) overcomes a crisis of control in an organisation's life cycle
(B) is part of a succession planning approach to Human Resources

(C) is part of a quality management approach
(D) is part of a scientific management approach.

A7 When an organisation securely shares part of its private network with customers or other outside parties it is said to operate

(A) an Internet
(B) an Intranet
(C) an Extranet
(D) a joint venture.

A8 The so-called 'psychological contract' is a notion that is based on:

(A) segmenting then accessing a market
(B) the buyer–supplier relationship
(C) a distinctive style of testing used in selection procedures
(D) the expectations the organisation and employee have of one another.

A9 Economies of scope refers to:

(A) the economic viability of making alterations to systems
(B) an organisation becoming economically viable through a process of 'rightsizing'
(C) mass production assembly lines achieving economies through volume of output
(D) economically producing small batches of a variety of products with the same machines.

A10 According to Douglas McGregor:

(A) 'Theory X' people dislike work, need direction and avoid responsibility
(B) 'Theory Y' people dislike work, need direction and avoid responsibility
(C) self-actualising people dislike work, need direction and avoid responsibility
(D) hygiene factors determine whether people like work, need direction or take responsibility.

A11 The purpose of a person specification is to provide details of:

(A) organisational size and diversity of activity
(B) the types of responsibilities and duties to be undertaken by the post holder
(C) personal characteristics, experience and qualifications expected of a candidate
(D) individual terms of engagement and period of contract.

A12 Reck and Long's strategic positioning tool identifies an organisation's:

(A) purchasing approach
(B) sales approach
(C) manufacturing approach
(D) warehousing approach.

A13 Inbound logistics is:

(A) a secondary activity that refers to price negotiation of incoming raw materials
(B) a secondary activity that refers to receipt, storage and inward distribution of raw materials
(C) a primary activity that refers to inbound enquiries and customer complaints
(D) a primary activity that refers to receipt, storage and inward distribution of raw materials.

A14 The relocation of a business process by a company from one country to another is known as:

(A) joint ventures
(B) outsourcing
(C) outshoring
(D) offshoring.

A15 Supply chain partnerships grow out of:

(A) quality accreditation
(B) recognising the supply chain and linkages in a value system
(C) an expansion of trade
(D) adopting a marketing philosophy.

A16 M-marketing refers to marketing practices using:

(A) mobile telephone technology
(B) manipulation and image projection
(C) market forecasting of current and future product demand
(D) marketing decision support systems.

A17 Undifferentiated market positioning involves the targeting of:

(A) a single market segment with a single marketing mix
(B) a single market segment ignoring the concept of the marketing mix
(C) an entire market with a different marketing mix for each segment
(D) an entire market with a single marketing mix.

A18 The processes of job analysis and individual performance appraisal are related in the sense that:

(A) they are different terms for the same process
(B) performance appraisal is based on job analysis
(C) both form part of the selection process
(D) job analysis is based on performance appraisal.

A19 Content theories of motivation tend to focus mainly on:

(A) the needs of the group
(B) feelings of complacency or dissatisfaction
(C) the needs of individuals
(D) the use of 'carrots' and 'sticks' as devices.

A20 The Internet is an example of:

(A) electronic data interchange
(B) distributed processing
(C) a local area network
(D) a wide area network.

A21 'Market shakeout' involves the weakest producers exiting a particular market and occurs in a period between:

(A) market growth and eventual decline
(B) introduction and market growth

(C) market growth and market maturity
(D) market maturity and decline.

A22 Computer to computer transmission of structured data in standard business documents is referred to as:

(A) technology interface
(B) process compatibility
(C) electronic data interchange
(D) social networking.

A23 F. W. Taylor's thinking on motivation in the workplace involved a belief that:

(A) social groups and individuals as part of a culture should be key considerations
(B) reward for effort and workplace efficiency should be key considerations
(C) managers had two different sets of assumptions about their subordinates
(D) 'motivators' and 'hygiene factors' should be key considerations.

A24 The choice to buy a fast-moving consumer good (FMCGs) is normally:

(A) a personal choice involving relatively low financial outlays
(B) a personal choice involving relatively high financial outlays
(C) a choice made on behalf of an organisation involving moderate outlays
(D) a personal choice influenced by new features, fashions and old product wear-out.

A25 A duplication of data held by an organisation is called:

(A) disaster recovery planning
(B) data redundancy
(C) data integrity
(D) data archiving.

A26 A main aim of electronic data interchange (EDI) is:
(A) to improve communication exchanges within an organisation
(B) to replace conventional documentation with structured electronically transmitted data
(C) to allow employees to work at home
(D) to create a shared data resource within an organisation.

A27 International standard ISO 14001 'Environmental Management Systems' encourages processes for controlling and improving an organisation's:

(A) performance on 'green' issues
(B) performance on quality issues as they relate to the competitive environment
(C) performance on scanning an industry environment
(D) performance on its internal investment in people.

A28 Direct mailing, branding awareness exercises and public relations campaigns are all examples of:

(A) market process
(B) product placement

(C) promotion

(D) marketing research.

A29 The product life cycle is depicted on a chart or diagram as a line against the variables of:

(A) cash flow and market share
(B) finance, customers, internal processes, and learning
(C) sales volume and time
(D) relative market share and market growth rate.

A30 360 degree feedback is part of a system that encourages:

(A) organisational appraisal based on feedback from customers and suppliers
(B) organisational appraisal based on relative industry and competitor performance
(C) personal appraisal based on feedback from peers, subordinates, bosses and even external parties
(D) personal appraisal based on feedback from your boss and your self-appraisal documentation.

Answer the following sub-questions using no more than 50 words per sub-question:

A100 Describe the main advantages of an organisation developing and using an 'extranet'. **(4 marks)**

A101 Explain the relationship between open systems and adaptive maintenance. **(4 marks)**

A102 Parallel running and pilot schemes are methods of systems changeover. Explain the reasons why an organisation might instead choose a direct approach to a system changeover. **(4 marks)**

A103 Explain the reasons why a department of an organisation might be continuing to use manual records rather than using a new, recently installed and fully operational computer system. **(4 marks)**

A104 Describe the ways in which Total Productive Maintenance might contribute towards a manufacturing organisation's quality programme. **(4 marks)**

A105 Explain the relationship between 'data independence' and a database approach to flexible data management. **(4 marks)**

A106 Explain how reliability (the same result for a repeated event) might be improved in selection interviews. **(4 marks)**

A107 Compare and contrast product-orientated organisations and production orientated organisations. **(4 marks)**

A108 Distinguish quality assurance (QA) systems from quality control systems. **(4 marks)**

A109 Briefly explain the main factors management should take into account when choosing computer hardware. **(4 marks)**

A110 Describe the relationship between operations management and (using Mintzberg's terminology) the organisational technostructure. **(4 marks)**

A111 Explain how continuous inventory systems might work against an organisation's JIT philosophy. **(4 marks)**

A112 Identify (with examples) types of external failure costs, and explain the significance for an organisation with a reputation for quality. **(4 marks)**

A113 Distinguish between push and pull marketing policies and their impact on the promotion of goods. **(4 marks)**

A114 Explain the main stages involved in developing human resource plans and programmes following the production of a corporate plan. **(4 marks)**

A115 Identify four benefits of corporate governance. **(4 marks)**

Solutions to A Style Revision Questions 6

A1 (A)
A2 (D)
A3 (B)
A4 (A)
A5 (A)
A6 (C)
A7 (C)
A8 (D)
A9 (D)
A10 (A)
A11 (C)
A12 (A)
A13 (D)
A14 (D)
A15 (B)
A16 (A)
A17 (D)
A18 (B)
A19 (B)
A20 (D)
A21 (A)
A22 (C)
A23 (B)
A24 (A)
A25 (B)
A26 (B)
A27 (A)
A28 (C)
A29 (D)
A30 (C)

A100 Extranet: an extended Intranet that links business partners.
Advantages:

- fosters collaboration and information sharing
- adds speed and cohesion
- facility to link and maximise dispersed networks
- enhanced inter-organisational communication
- allows electronic data interchange and e-procurement

- communication strengthens relationships with customers, suppliers, and trade organisations.

A101 An open system interacts with its external environment. This thinking is consistent with adaptive maintenance. Adaptive maintenance is a mid- to long-term process that adjusts Information Systems (IS) applications to reflect changing business operations and environments. In this way it accounts for opportunities or threats.

A102 At a predetermined time old system ceases entirely and new one starts. Why use?

- complete confidence in system
- symbolic act to encourage commitment
- part of unfreezing change process
- reduced system usage: lower risk of disruption at chosen time.

A103

- group resistance to change
- cultural resistance
- lack of confidence in new system
- complexity of new system
- efficiency of manual system
- individuals lack confidence to cope
- individuals jobs feel threatened
- ineffective management, control, communication, training, lack of support, and so on.

A104 Total productive maintenance plans and implements the systematic maintenance of all equipment. This increases productivity and prevents unplanned breakdowns.

- Helps consistent production
- Reduces scrap and rework so lowering cost of quality
- Improves accuracy of forecasting requirements
- Staff morale improved as quality increases.

A105 A database approach involves collecting integrated common data that is then shared throughout the organisation. Data independence is an essential feature of a database approach. It means that data exists independently of the programs that use it. The flexibility this gives includes:

- data or programs can be amended without changing the other
- multiple users, using different programs can access the same data at the same time
- data being wholly shared represents an expanded collective resource allowing a greater potential for flexible and enhanced usage.

A106 Reliability = repeatability of outcome

- Structured pre-determined interview format (equal time allocations, identical questions, identical ordering of sequence)
- Standard paperwork (application forms, scoring grids, person specs)
- Avoid first impressions/gut reactions
- Put candidates at ease, ensure conducive environment.

A107

	Product orientated	**Production orientated**
Main focus	Product features	Production efficiency
Quality	May be high	May be low
Cost	May be high	Low
Sales	Not sufficiently considered	Low quality may lead to lower sales

Neither organisation:

- has researched market demand
- is in touch with the customer and their requirements.

Both risk products not selling sufficiently.

Note that an alternative valid interpretation of the organisations could be as follows:

Production-orientated companies have a production department budget (excluding purchasing) representing the largest percentage of company turnover whereas a product-orientated company is one where the design department budget represents the largest proportion of turnover. Examples of the former include a subcontract painter or Rolls Royce, and examples of the latter include an Architects practice or Amstrad with their e-phones.

A108 Both have a different philosophy on quality:

- Quality control (QC) systems attempt to *control* quality, whereas
- QA systems attempt to *create* quality.

QC involves managing each stage of production to minimise errors, (a third party, negative intervention process). QC inspects afterwards.

QA check quality in a positive way encouraging worker ownership for quality. QA prevents beforehand.

A109 Main factors when choosing computer hardware include:

- *Suitability*. Cost, User requirements
- *Acceptability*. Manufacturers reputation, Computer specification, Built in features (e.g. security)
- *Feasibility*. Compatibility with existing systems, Computers used elsewhere within the organisation's industry and so on.

A110 The relationship between operations management and the organisational techno-structure.

Operations management:

- Developing outputs (products/services) by transforming inputs (stock, human) through operations (manufacturing, assembly, etc).

Technostructure:

- Expert advice, training, research, standardising processes, outputs and skills.
- Involves work-study, HR managers and so on.

Relationship: OM 5 operating core and finances a technostructure that helps make operations effective.

Note to readers: In larger organisations, some parts of the technostructure may devote themselves to operations management issues alone.

A111 Continuous inventory systems working against a JIT philosophy.

Continuous inventory:

- Monitoring to keep above a predetermined level
- Fixed amount ordered
- Zero demand = buffer stocks ('just in case'); inconsistent with JIT.

JIT philosophy (eliminate all waste; right part at the right place at the right time) better supported with JIT inventory approach.

A112 The type and significance of external failure costs for an organisation with a reputation for quality.

External failure = costs of sub-standard goods sold, for example:

- 'Free' replacement
- Redesign/rework costs, wastage and so on
- Warranty claims
- Product liability and damages.

Significance = Goods with customer, meaning:

- Damaged reputation/staff morale?
- Loss of repeat sales/future custom?
- Reduced customer confidence?
- Bad PR (complaints).

A113 Push and pull marketing policies and their impact on the promotion of goods. Firms may have:

- Suppliers (downstream)
- Supply others (upstream).

in a value chain that links to ultimate consumer.

	Push	**Pull**
Aim	'push' to wholesalers/retailers who sell to customers.	Influence final consumers' attitudes through, for example, advertising. Consumer demand 'pulls' through.
Promotion to consumer	Final firm in value chain.	Shared by manufacturer.

A114 Main stages in developing HR plans and programmes following production of a corporate plan.

Stages:
1 A supply forecast:
- Analysis of existing resources
- Projection of likely changes over period (natural wastage, turnover etc.).
2 Identify demand implied by corporate plan.

3 Articulate both forecasts in HR plan.
4 Develop programmes with target dates to reconcile supply and demand. (Address recruitment, selection, training, management development, transfers, redeployment, redundancies, etc.)

Note: This explanation is based on Mullins (2005). It is not the only way of understanding the stages. Other thinkers may express a need for internal and external data collection and analysis using models such as PESTLE, and so on. Valid alternative approaches to that suggested by Mullins will also receive credit.

A115

Reduces risk
Improves access to capital markets
Demonstrates transparency
Demonstrates social accountability

(Other benefits that could be mentioned include: stimulates performance; improves leadership; enhances marketability of goods and services.)

NOTE: IT IS IMPORTANT TO CONTAIN YOUR RESPONSES TO THE GIVEN WORD LIMIT

B Style Revision Questions 6

(Note that all the sub-questions are valued at 5 marks each. Responses for each sub-question should be contained to one page).

B1 Vertigo is an innovative company run on the principles of its entrepreneurial owner. The company operates a package distribution service, a train service, and sells holidays, bridal outfits, clothing, mobile telephones, and soft drinks. Its approach of challenging the norm and 'giving customers quality products and services at affordable prices and doing it all with sense of fun' is well known. Vertigo spends little on advertising but has great brand awareness thanks to the 'visibility' of its inspirational owner.

Vertigo has just announced the launch of 'V-cosmetics' to exploit a gap in the market. The cosmetic range will be competitively priced against high street brands and have the distinctive Vertigo logo.

You work for a market analyst who is about to appear on a radio discussion of Vertigo's business interests. You have been asked to provide a clear, short briefing on the thinking behind 'V-cosmetics'. Your research of the 'V-cosmetics' identifies innovative marketing proposals. V-cosmetics will not be on sale in shops, instead it will use two approaches to promotion and selling, namely:

The use of 'cosmetic associates'. Individuals may apply to become an associate and if accepted are required to buy a basic stock of every V-cosmetic product. The associate will then use these products as samples and 'testers'. After initial training associates organise parties in the homes of friends, and their friends where they take orders for products at a listed price. Associates receive commission based on sales. The Internet and mobile telephone technology will also be heavily used to offer V-cosmetics to the public.

Requirements

Prepare brief notes containing bullet points and no more than two to three sentences for each of the key points identified below. Use a separate page of your answer book for each key point (meaning that your notes are contained on no more than six pages in total).

(a) Explain how the proposed approach can be understood within the context of the marketing mix.
(b) Outline the human resource implications of using cosmetic associates.
(c) Explain the concept of direct marketing.
(d) Explain the advantages of the Internet as a marketing channel.
(e) Identify how Vertigo might use Internet and mobile telephone technology as part of their marketing approach.
(f) Identify the main ethical issues associated with the proposal.

B2 You are a researcher employed by a topical business television show 'Round the table'. Next week's discussion is about managing supply to achieve quality and customer satisfaction. Invited guests will be a leading academic, public and private sector senior managers and the chief executive of a car producer.

You have been asked to produce an outline briefing that will give some background information to the show's presenter.

Your research shows that the automobile industry is highly competitive and globally suffers from 'overcapacity'. In certain countries, however, there is unfulfilled demand for specialist makes and models, implying some under capacity 'hot spots'. You understand that for any organisation whether producing goods or services, effective capacity management is vital. It ensures that customers' needs are more fully met, and that there are fewer unfulfilled delivery date promises. There are several ways of dealing with variations in demand and matching production capacity including:

- Concentrating on inventory levels ('Level capacity' strategy)
- Concentrating on demand ('Demand' strategy)
- Adjusting levels of activity ('Chase' strategy).

As part of your investigation you note that distinctive issues exist for service organisations (such as those found in the public sector).

Requirements

As the shows researcher you are required to produce outline notes to support the show's presenter.

These notes should have particular regard to quality, capacity and other organisational issues:

(a) Discuss why a level capacity strategy might be difficult for a firm wishing to adopt a JIT philosophy.
(b) Discuss the impact of demand strategies on an organisation's marketing practice.
(c) Discuss the relationship between chase strategies and the flexible organisation.
(d) When considering capacity management identify the ways that service organisations differ from manufacturing organisations.

These notes should:

(e) Identify and describe the types of software applications a manufacturing firm might introduce to improve its supply operations.
(f) Describe the types of computerised assistance that could be used by those involved in selling cars and wanting to improve demand.

B3 S&C is a medium-sized firm that is experiencing rapid growth thanks to increased turnover. It has been able to develop a range of new consultancy and specialist business advisory services that it offers to its growing customer base. To cope with these developments several company-wide initiatives have been launched over the past 2 years.

The existing financial systems are struggling to cope with these developments. The replacement of the existing software is due to go ahead within the next 6 months. The new system was justified partly because it could reduce costs (although precise details have not been given). Although the application software does not fit existing business processes exactly it has the clear advantage of giving S&C access to an industry best practice system and is identical to that used by all its main competitors and some of its clients. A three-person project steering group has recommended that a phased approach to introduction will be used and has undertaken most of the project planning. A programme of events for implementing the system has been agreed but is not yet fully operational. This group has not met for a while because the designated project manager has been absent from work with illness.

You are Head of S&C's Central Support Unit. You also serve on the project steering group.

A partners meeting is due to take place soon. The firm's senior partner has asked you to prepare a PowerPoint presentation to other partners on implementation issues. You understand that partners are conscious that system implementation represents a form of further organisational change and are asking questions about the approach that will be taken to the introduction of the new system; likely changes to practices; critical areas for success, system testing, support after implementation and system effectiveness, and so on.

Requirements

You are required to produce *outline notes* that will support your eventual PowerPoint presentation. These notes should:

(a) Explain why a phased approach to introducing the system is, in this case, particularly more suitable than a more direct 'big bang' approach.
(b) Describe the options to overcome the fact that the software does not fit existing business processes exactly.
(c) Discuss the ways in which particular individuals and groups within S&C are important for implementation to succeed.
(d) Explain the aims of a post-implementation review.
(e) Describe the training that should be given in terms of topics, methods and targeted groups within S&C.
(f) Explain how users might be involved in testing the system during the implementation phase.

B4 M is Chairman and Managing Director of the company OK1 which he started 15 years ago. The company has been very successful and, through a series of acquisitions, has diversified its operations and employs 3,500 people. M is a major force in the company. His management style is very autocratic and he is unwilling to involve others in decisions about the future strategic direction of the company. Recently, M announced to the Board that he is intending that OK1 becomes listed on the stock exchange.

Some of OK1's main competitors include explicit reference to their commitment to act in a socially responsible manner in their mission statements, so informing their strategies and policies. This is not the case for OK1. Indeed, M sees social responsibility as conflicting with the main interest of the company which is that of creating maximum wealth.

The Finance Director of the company has become increasingly concerned about the decisions being made by M and the fact that he has put pressure on her to participate in some questionable accounting practices. She has had to cover up M's substantial remuneration package, which M has awarded to himself. She is also aware that M has accepted bribes from foreign suppliers and of insider dealing relating to a number of the acquisitions. There is a lack of appropriate control systems and accountability in the company.

The Finance Director has discussed her concerns with other members of the Board, including the Marketing Director, Production Director and HR Director. However, they seem willing to overlook the wrongdoings of M and never challenge the decisions made by him. The opportunity to do so is limited since the Board meets on an irregular and infrequent basis.

At the last Board meeting M set out his plans to close the majority of existing factories and move operations to L country where he has been in secret negotiations with representatives of the government. The main objective is to benefit from low cost labour, since the country has very little employment legislation to protect workers and has a poor human rights record. It is not clear how many jobs will be lost or how many new jobs will be created. The HR Director is aware of the need to develop human resource plans in the light of M's plans.

Requirements
(a) Explain the concept of corporate governance.
(b) Explain the corporate governance issues facing OK1 particularly if it became listed on the stock exchange.
(c) Explain ways in which a socially responsible business might operate.
(d) Explain the main stages involved in developing human resource plans and programmes following the announcement of M to close the majority of existing factories and move operations.

Solutions to B Style Revision Questions 6

B1(a) **The marketing mix**

The marketing mix involves four marketing tools, Product, Price, Promotion and Place, that are 'mixed/blended' in terms of effort, emphasis and integration. Here is V cosmetics' mix:

- *Product.* Good quality and branded products. Likely to be attractive due to brand strength.
- *Price.* Competitive but not cheap (affordable). Price seems inflexible (list price). Are Internet sales also placed at list price? Savings that V made on advertising, shops and expensive distribution networks can be passed on to customers. Also reward associates and invest in IT. Likely to be profitable given saving potential over rivals.
- *Promotion.* Little advertising, focussing instead on Public Relations. Given success in other ventures, this should work with cosmetics. The strength of brand name is significant.
- *Place.* That is getting the right products into the right places at the right time. Approach is through one-level marketing (cosmetic associate) and interactive marketing. Assumes expertise of associates and user acceptance of Internet. As philosophy is based on sense of fun, it may work. Need efficient distribution once order is placed; link to V's distribution services?

Maybe a fifth P is relevant, that is People (see answer to B1 (b)).
Key point: the mix must satisfy customer needs.

B1(b) **Human resource (HR) implications of cosmetic associates**

The reputation of V is important and must be maintained through effective HR.

- Selection Criteria: Attitude; applicants should (a) display a sense of fun and (b) reflect the image of the company. Trustworthiness important; need for interview and references.
- Training of cosmetic associates in sales techniques and how to arrange parties. Also those servicing the Internet and text queries.
- Remuneration package needs to be right to attract and retain associates. Commission on sales must be sufficient incentive. Appropriate remuneration package for Internet sales needs to be devised.
- Supervision, monitoring and control: A system is needed (maybe customer questionnaires, area supervisors, etc.)

B1(c) **Direct marketing**
- A business, possibly manufacturer, deals directly with end customer, possibly using the Internet.
- A 'zero level channel', that is, direct between supplier and end customer.
- Shortens supply chain so takes costs out of value system.
- Examples include the web-based company Amazon.com and the direct booking of air travel on line.
- Direct marketing mix implications for place and promotion. 'Place' is not physical, it is cyberspace. Promotion is possible in electronic form through targeting Web users.

B1(d) **Advantages of the Internet**
- Speed of communication.
- Flexibility of use: promote, answer queries, sell, display products.
- Convenience for user: in own home and can be accessed any time.
- Attractive use of time for user: can compare and contrast prices and so on with rivals 'on line'.
- Potential for lower prices as costs are lower than physical stores with capital and running costs.
- Potential for companies to develop databases of customers, those making enquiries for further sales promotions.

B1(e) **Internet and mobile telephone: use as part of V's marketing Internet**
- Fits sense of fun – not a physical event (browsing, enquiries and purchasing on line):
- Relies on user acceptance of credit cards; this is likely given other V businesses.
- Expectations that prices are cheaper than high street; fits affordable prices philosophy.
- Orders on line (needs efficient distribution once the order is placed, maybe linking to V's distribution services).
- Promotion using, for example, Web banners, affiliation websites, collaboration with other websites and search facilities.

Mobile telephones ('M-marketing')
- To stimulate product interest, maybe through V mobiles links, text alerts and so on.
- As a sales alternative to the Internet. Novel : fits 'sense of fun'.
- Could be used to arrange a follow up by passing details on to associates.
- To deal with range of customer enquiries. (Need sophisticated IT)

B1(f) **Ethical issues**
Ethical stance of an individual business is determined by organisational culture and philosophy.

- What we know about V: entrepreneurial (takes risks?), different, quality products, affordable prices and fun. These factors will be relevant as will legislative frameworks.
- Issue of using associates: are they being fairly treated? (Requirement to buy basic stock, continue to sell products, is remuneration appropriate?)
- Issues of using parties for selling: (Other examples: Tupperware, Virgin Vie, Ann Summers.) Is the public being tricked/pressured into using their home in this way? What is in it for them (gifts, discounts, fees, etc.).

- Issue of selling approach: are associates obliged to adopt impolite or 'pushy' sales techniques, which is unfair on the customer.
- Issue of targeting customers through Internet and mobiles: may be overly intrusive or abuse of databases/relationship (with possible implications for data protection legislation).

B2(a) Level capacity strategy: difficult for a firm wishing to adopt a JIT philosophy. About level capacity:

- Level capacity involves building inventory levels to deal with increases in demand beyond 'normal'.
- This suggests a building of buffer stocks of (for instance) cars to deal with excess demand.
- The notion of buffer stocks is wholly inconsistent with a firm wishing to adopt a quality-driven just-in-time (JIT) philosophy.

About JIT
- JIT is considered key to many organisational quality programmes.
- JIT production methods involve each component on a production line being produced only when it is needed and not before.
- An outcome of JIT is an elimination of large stocks of materials and parts, not a building of them (as level capacity strategies imply).

Key points
- Customer satisfaction may be improved short term by adopting a level capacity strategy (making immediate delivery possible). However, these 'buffer' stocks are inconsistent with the JIT quality approach.
- Level capacity increases stockholding costs and may not be the most cost-effective means of capacity management.
- Organisational requirement: more working capital to build stocks.
- A more lasting means of achieving customer satisfaction might be the full adoption of a quality philosophy instead.

B2(b) The impact of demand strategies on an organisation's marketing practice. About Demand strategies:

- Demand strategies attempt to influence demand to 'smooth' variations so that the organisation is better able to cope.
- presents a type of manipulation and influence over demand so that it is 'made' to 'fit' supply capability.

About marketing
The marketing function will want to ensure that the marketing mix (Product/service, Price, Promotion and Place) is appropriate for the individual organisation and may:

- vary price to encourage/slow down demand
- intensify promotion in 'slack' periods
- restrict sales outlets (place) when there is excess demand.

Marketing practice can in ways such as these support demand strategies.

Key points
- The marketing tactics above represent short-term practices and may not benefit the firm long term. It might, for instance, lead to reduced satisfaction when customers are frustrated by the restrictions of place. They may indeed decide to switch to a competitor's product.
- The use of demand strategies in conjunction with marketing practice suggests that the organisation is not marketing orientated. The main focus is not the customer; it is rather internal production considerations. This philosophy will ultimately hurt quality, which has the customer as central.
- In terms of organisational implications profitability may be affected as a result of financing sales promotions and price reductions.

B2(c) Relationship between chase strategies and the flexible organisation.

About Chase strategies:
- Chase strategies involve constantly adjusting activity levels to shadow fluctuations in demand. This demonstrates market responsiveness and closeness to the customer demands.

About flexible organisations

There is something of an organisational trend emerging that has 'non-traditional' organisational structures and a flexible workforce. These measures allow organisations to display maximum flexibility and responsiveness to customer demands.

By using a flexible organisation approach to accommodate 'peaks and troughs', chase strategies will be possible, specifically:

- Organisational structures: may achieve operational flexibility by becoming less rigid in terms of hierarchy.
- Skills flexibility might be achieved by cross training employees to perform different operations. Integration of tasks can occur both horizontally (undertaking a broader range of tasks at the same level as their original task) and vertically (undertaking tasks previously carried out by employees at other levels).
- Atkinson's worker categories involve core and periphery staff (temporary/part-time) to act as a buffer against changes in demand. Numerical flexibility might be achieved by an increased use of temporary, part-time, short-term contract working and outsourcing work at peak times. Such flexibility might be achieved by using both contractors and agency staff.

Key points
- The two concepts complement one another.
- Such an approach would more easily achieve customer satisfaction.
- It would be consistent with a quality ethos, as flexible manufacturing is at the heart of a quality approach.
- Organisational implications include: structures, HR policies and practice, rewards, recruitment and training. Organisationally there should also be a commitment to continuous improvement, including the use of quality circles.

B2(d) Capacity management: the ways that service organisations differ from manufacturing organisations.
Differences for a service organisation:

- The consumer is a participant in the service process (unlike the purchaser of a manufactured good).
- The characteristics of the workforce determine the effectiveness of the service to a greater degree, as the consumer–worker interaction is central.
- Services are perishable.
- Services are intangible, so communication is more difficult when explaining the benefits of a purchase. This makes marketing more complex.
- Output measurement is less easy to evidence (Outputs for Not-for-Profit (NFP) organisations are often multiple).
- NFP funding may be government determined and may be insufficient to finance to meet all customer demands immediately, which implies a need for a rationing of service.
- For NFP organisations, consumers may be a different grouping from those paying for the service to be provided. This is confusing when concentrating on customers, as there are multiple customers to satisfy each with different, sometimes contradictory demands.

Key points
- The level capacity strategy assumes that units of production are durable and can be stored (as is the case with cars). This may not be possible for perishable goods and services more generally (It is impossible to 'stockpile' consultancy advice).
- There may be a lack of customer satisfaction, if (using a medical treatment example) waiting lists appear.
- Quality issues are more overtly of a human kind as the workforce determine the quality of the service.
- Organisational implications include appropriate HR policies to ensure that employees deal with customers appropriately and impact positively on customer satisfaction levels. Good systems to support delivery of the services are also important.

B2(e) This can be understood in the context of Michael Porter's value chain model, as follows:

- Inbound logistics: one of five primary activities directly concerned with the creation or delivery of a product.
- Support activities: help improve the efficiency and effectiveness of primary activities and include technology development (and therefore software applications).

The issue becomes the *types* of software applications that would help with inbound logistics, including receiving, storing and distributing materials, including material handling, stock control, transport and so on. These applications may be developed in-house or purchased as off the shelf.

Types of applications include:

- Software that assists inventory management inventory (whether method used is continuous, periodic inventory or ABC, etc.).
- Warehousing including storage and reordering (Under a just-in-time system the matching of the receipt of material closely with usage is key to reducing stock-holding levels and costs. Larger organisations would certainly need IT support. Software is capable of producing reports to ensure that quantities held in stock are within the predetermined budgets).
- Software capable of assisting the management of transport including work scheduling.
- Benchmarking database of inbound activities. This allows a convenient and systematic comparison to be made of practice and/or process with suitable comparator organisations and other sections.
- Internet-enabled purchasing software from suppliers possibly using an e-catalogue.
- Software to assist purchasing possibly databases of suppliers where issues of quality and price can be monitored.

One specific example of software:

- Manufacturing Resource Planning (MRP) (e.g. MRP II), a system that assists capacity management through a matching supply and demand. Organisational implications: Reduced stock holding & stock turnover, and improved facilities usage. Customer satisfaction: Fewer delays through materials shortage, certainty over delivery times.

B2(f) Selling cars and wanting to improve demand: the types of computerised assistance that could be used.

Cars are consumer goods and sales and promotion strategies are important to both car manufacturers and dealers. Sales and promotion strategies (along with the others Ps including price) will help 'determine' demand.

Computerised technology might be used in a number of ways in order to communicate with existing, past and potential customers the benefits of the products (car models) and so stimulate demand. Examples include:

Database of potential customers may be good for targeting particular customers and their likely requirements. It enables messages to be personalised. This allows for direct letter mailing of promotional literature. It is also easier to improve customer relationships and hence buyer loyalties by customer follow-up contact after sales are made. In terms of customer satisfaction it might be viewed either positively or negatively as 'junk mail'.

Advertising using the Internet to a less targeted audience. A non-personal presentation using email technology and site 'pop-ups'. In terms of customer satisfaction it might be viewed negatively as 'SPAM' mail and a nuisance, alternatively it might reinforce a positive message.

Engaging in e-Business. A dealer could potentially supplement or replace an existing showroom site by developing electronically based systems and technologies of doing business. Savings made on premises costs could be passed on to customers so enhancing their satisfaction.

Technology-supported market research could help provide in-depth analysis of a single market so enabling informed decisions to be made aimed at improving demand. Technology-supported market research might form a sub-system feeding a more comprehensive marketing database and Management Information System (MIS). MIS might include comparative competitor approaches to stimulating demand.

Vehicle dashboards displays. Cars could be fitted with microchips that indicate when a vehicle is in need of a service (e.g. after 20,000 miles). Alternative examples include a display of dealer contact details when a vehicle is in need of replacement (e.g. after 3 years) and so on.

B3(a) Options to overcome the software not fitting the existing business process exactly. Change will be required as a result of the mismatch between the software and the existing business process. There appear to be two distinct options:

Option 1, Change the software or
Option 2, Change the business process.

The choice should be made taking account of all relevant costs and benefits and might be made using suitable evaluation criteria such as suitability, acceptability and feasibility (or similar).

The applications software is designed to perform specific financial functions of the business. It is essentially an 'off the shelf rather than a bespoke solution but could conceivably be adapted. Such an adaptation could be financially costly. There is also a need to identify the necessary expertise to carry out this software development and the company may need to employ outside source for the purpose.

Changing the business process represents yet another change initiative that staff may respond to negatively. As competitors and peers are using the software already it is reasonable to assume that it will encapsulate industry best practice. These organisations apparently operate in that way that is consistent with the software. This implies that S&C may operate in an inconsistent and possibly inefficient fashion.

B3(b) A phased approach: more suitable than a 'big bang' approach.
The more direct 'big bang' approach generally represents the highest risk, as at a predetermined point in time the old system ceases to operate completely. Using this approach there is no opportunity to validate the new system's output with the old, so management must have complete confidence in the new system. As the software in question appears to be something of an industry standard there is likely to be some general confidence in it. However, there appears to be something of a mismatch between the system and corresponding processes, which could prove a difficulty.

The phased approach involves gradual implementation possibly involving one subsystem at a time. This might involve implementing the system by first converting the customer accounts subsystem, then the reporting sub-system, and so on. This offers distinct advantages in this particular case:

- Staff are likely to be suffering 'change fatigue' from previous initiatives and can only endure so much upheaval while continuing to function effectively.
- The continued support of the partners as project sponsors is important and they are likely to see 'deliverables' sooner with a phased roll-out.

- The phased approach is less risky given that the project manager could be unavailable to oversee the change.
- The project management risk (heightened by the absence of the project manager) will be reduced as issues found in small-scale use of the new system can be remedied in time for wider software roll-out.

B3(c) The ways in which particular individuals and groups within S & C are important for implementation to succeed.

- *Partners*. Support from the top is crucial. They must visibly support the implementation.
- *Users*. Successful user acceptance and must buy-in is also key as they are the main recipients of the change. Meaningful communication is necessary, also participation to get commitment through joint analysis of issues to engender feelings of 'ownership'.
- *The users' managers*. These managers will be called upon to help ensure that disruptions are kept to a minimum during and immediately after changeover. Communication and involvement again is necessary (albeit to a different degree to users).
- *Project manager*. Effective project management is crucial which ensures that S & C's corporate performance does not fail. The project manager has been absent with illness and matters cannot be allowed to 'drift'. If the illness is long term, a replacement project manager needs to be appointed swiftly.
- *HR Department*. If system success depends on people behaving in certain ways (e.g. sharing information across departments, taking greater responsibility, etc.) reward systems may need to be adjusted possibly including new incentives, metrics and evaluation criteria. Effective training programmes will also be needed. Formal policies and structures may also need adjustment.
- *Project steering group*. Need to address the real sources of resistance to change and means of overcoming them. Proposals are also needed in order to successfully align financial systems and business processes (It is important that some members of the group are available in the weeks after going live to answer questions and give support to users).

B3(d) Users involvement in testing the system during the implementation phase.

As mentioned earlier, user acceptance is vital. It is also important to test the system during the implementation phase. It is a good idea to combine these two requirements.

Users might be usefully involved in a number of ways and could be used to:

- Act as guinea pigs for any system developments through testing in association with the new procedures and processes.
- Contribute to quality circles and discussion forums.
- Assess the effectiveness of training programmes, and so on and provide feedback.
- Provide mutual mentoring/assistance 'buddying' to other new users of the system.
- Collect data on the costs and benefits of the overall business change, not just the software application.
- Be involved and act as advocates of change to colleagues.

B3(e) The training topics to targeted groups within S&C.

The nature and content of training will inevitably need to be tailored to the needs of the relevant groups, for example:

- *Partners*. General overview of the system and its benefits possibly through executive training seminars.
- *Users*. Instilling detailed user knowledge on how to operate the new system. Specific detailed applications training (including procedures, commands and data-entry requirements, etc.).
- *Users' managers*. Giving an understanding of the elements of the system for which they are responsible, including particular business issues and security and control features related to a particular system. Possibly general training in basic computer literacy and user skills.

The sort of training provision might include:

- Seminars and workshops and so on
- User manuals, 'help lines' and dedicated support teams.
- Online computer-based support.
- On-the-job training while staff are actively using the new system.
- Quality circles and discussion forums for users to address problem areas.
- Short demonstrations and the use of DVD/ Video media support.
- Updates as users become familiar with the system and require further knowledge and skills development or consolidation of existing knowledge and skills.

This can be provided:

- in-house
- outsourced to specialists or
- some combination.

B3(f) Aims of a post-implementation review.

Post-implementation review should be carried out as soon as the system is fully operational, in order to assess the effectiveness of the system, adjustments that may be required and lessons that can be learnt for the future. This should take place possibly between 1 month and no longer than 1 year after changeover is completed. The findings and recommendations from the post-implementation review should be formally reported on.

The specific aims of the review will include:

- Whether the system satisfies user needs.
- How the actual costs and benefit of the system compare with what was anticipated.
- Making recommendations for improvement (if necessary).
- Determining the quality of systems of change and project management.
- Making recommendations that will help shape future management of implementation and change initiatives where necessary.

B4(a) Corporate governance concerns:

- the ownership and control of profit making organisations and
- the relationship between owners and managers.

A number of reports have been produced to address the risk and problems resulting from poor corporate governance. In the UK the most significant reports include the Cadbury, Hempel and Greenbury reports. The recommendations are merged into a Combined Code which comprises the purpose and principles of good corporate governance for listed companies.

B4(b)
- It is problematic for one person to hold both the role of Chairman and Managing Director since this can result in too much concentration of power being in the hands of one person, and the greater dangers of the misuse or abuse of power. As illustrated in the scenario, it is difficult for other directors to challenge M's decisions. M, through his dominance and associated behaviours, combining chairperson and chief executive roles contravenes much of the recent thinking on corporate governance. This advocates that the separation of the two roles is essential for good control.
- It is evident from the scenario that Board meetings are ineffective, they are held on an irregular and infrequent basis with M wielding his power over other directors. It would seem that he has forced through decisions that are in his own personal interest, and could be detrimental to the company. One of the core principles of the Combined Code is that listed companies should be led by effective Boards, which meet regularly and membership should be a balance of executive and non executive directors so that no individuals or small groups can dominate decision making. It would be appropriate for non executive directors to be appointed to the Board of OK1 to provide independent judgements on decisions.
- It seems that there is a lack of adequate control, accountability and audit in the company. The Board is responsible for presenting a balanced and understandable assessment of the company's financial position. It is responsible for maintaining a sound system for internal controls to safeguard the company's assets and shareholders' investment. OK1 should establish through an audit committee formal and transparent arrangements for considering how to apply the principles of financial reporting and internal control. Non executive directors should satisfy themselves on the integrity of financial information and that controls are robust.
- M has determined his own remuneration package, which he is keen to keep covered up. Good corporate governance practice states that no director should be involved in determining his/her own remuneration. Non-executive directors should be responsible for determining a policy on the remuneration of executive directors and specific remuneration packages for each director, a proportion of which should be linked to corporate and individual performance. It is good practice to include a report on the remuneration policy for directors in the annual accounts.

The above points would help support the Finance Director who has been placed in an awkward situation regarding the questionable accounting practices and M's remuneration.

B4(c) Social responsibility is the concept that gives rise to how an organisation should conduct itself within society and the need to deal with the impact of business decisions on different stakeholder groups. However, the debates about the extent to which organisations should consider issues under the heading 'social responsibility' when they are formulating and implementing business strategies continue to provoke conflict and tension between different stakeholders. Organisations need to weigh up the costs of socially responsible business decisions against the benefits.

Acting in a socially responsible manner concerns the extent to which the organisation should move beyond the minimum obligation provided through regulation and corporate governance. This will vary from firm to firm but can include issues related to a range of factors such as:

- human rights (e.g. job security and good conditions of work for the employees, non discrimination in employment);
- providing products that are fit for the stated purpose; marketing practices, and impact of product/service on customers (e.g. health and exclusion);
- non-production of socially undesirable products;
- environmental impact of products from creation to disposal, (e.g. issues relating to environmental pollution and production of non-degradable products).

B4(d) M's plans to close the existing factories and move operations to L country will have significant HR implications. In L country there are low labour costs and little employment legislation. It is not clear how many jobs will be lost or how many new jobs will be created. The HR Director is aware of as need to develop human resource plans in the light of M's plans.

The main stages in developing HR plans and programmes following M's announcement might be as follows:

Forecast supply of labour
- Analysis of existing human resources (number, skill mix, location, age profile, etc.)
- Projection of likely changes over the period (through natural wastage and turnover of workers if not replaced, etc.).

Identify labour demand implied by M's announcement
- Staffing levels required in factories opened in L country based on level of expertise of the local workforce, levels of automation in new factories, etc.
- Staff mix required implied by operating in another country
- Staffing requirements to operate factories that are to remain open.

Articulate both forecasts in HR plan

Develop programmes with target dates to reconcile supply and demand
- Key parties to be consulted with
- Addressing recruitment, selection, training and development, transfers (if any), redeployment (if any)
- Redundancies required from current operations.

(Note: This explanation is based on Mullins (2005). It is not the only way of understanding the stages. Other thinkers may express a need for internal and external data collection and analysis using models such as PESTLE, etc. Valid alternative approaches to that suggested by Mullins will also receive credit.)

NOTE: IT IS IMPORTANT TO CONTAIN YOUR RESPONSES TO THE GIVEN PAGE LIMIT

C Style Revision Questions 6

> *Note*: in the exam the value of sub questions in section C will total 30 per question. Examples given here represent partial questions..

C1 The country Mythland contains several areas of high unemployment including one where Cardinal Beers was until recently produced. Cardinal was an old, family-owned brewery that supplied licenced outlets including local restaurants with their beer. Cardinal represented one of the last local brewers of any size despite retaining many working practices that were evolved at least a century ago. Situated on a (now) underused dockside site, the company had over the years invested little in plant and machinery and someone jokingly once suggested that much of the brewing equipment should rightfully be in a museum! Despite having an enthusiastic, long-serving, highly skilled workforce and a national reputation for the beer 'Cardinal winter warmer' (thanks to winning several national awards), the company was forced to cease trading last month. The workforce, many of whom have only ever worked for Cardinal Beers, are now facing up to the difficulty of finding alter-native work.

In a press statement the owners said that the brewery's closure was sad for the town, the local workforce and traditionally brewed ale in general. The owners blamed the situation on inefficient and expensive brewing methods, fierce competition from large rival brewers and limited geographical sales. They also mentioned a dependence on seasonal sales that made cash flow difficult (35% over Christmas and the New year period). They concluded that they would like the Cardinal tradition to continue and sell the company as a going concern, however unlikely this was. It is speculated that property developers may be interested in the site as the dockland area is showing signs of regeneration as a leisure and tourism attraction (thanks to the efforts of government). However, two of Cardinal's managers would like to save the business and are drawing up a business plan for a management buyout. They have three main initiatives that they feel could in combination save the enterprise:

- Use the site as a basis for a living museum of traditionally brewed ale (with the dated brewing equipment and methods of working as an attraction).
- Produce bottled beer for sales in supermarkets.
- Employ a more flexible but suitably experienced workforce.

One of the managers (your former boss) has asked for your help in advising him how to draft a detailed human resource plan to inform the business plan.

Requirements

(a) Describe the main issues and stages involved in developing a human resource (HR) plan for the Cardinal buy-out idea. **(10 marks)**

(b) Explain how the buy-out team can achieve workforce flexibility. **(5 marks)**

(c) Explain the concept of market segmentation and how it might apply to the to initiatives to save Cardinal Beers. **(10 marks)**

(Total = 25 marks)

C2 4QX is a large exclusive hotel set in an area of outstanding natural beauty. The hotel is a little remote due to the relatively poor transport network. It is located ten miles away from the region's main centre Old Town (the castle ruins of which attract a few tourists during holiday periods). The hotel has attained a high national star rating and specialises in offering executive conference facilities. Unsurprisingly therefore, it caters mainly for corporate guests.

It is a requirement of the hotel rating system that 4QX has, amongst other things, sports and leisure facilities to an approved standard. In order to attain this standard it has, within the last two years, installed a sports and fitness centre ('the centre'), employing fully qualified staff to give instruction and assistance. (Facilities include a small indoor heated swimming pool, an extensively equipped gymnasium, a spa bath and a steam room.) Due to legislation, children under the age of 16 staying in the hotel cannot use the pool without adult supervision or the gymnasium without the supervision of a suitably qualified member of staff. The centre is costly to maintain and underused.

The hotel's manager is currently drawing up a business plan for the hotel and is reviewing all areas of operation. In discussions with sport and fitness centre staff, a proposal has emerged to offer the facility to carefully selected non-guests at certain times of the day in order to bring in some revenue. This could be in the form of annual membership fees (the manager's preferred idea) or a 'pay-as-you-go' charge. The discussions with staff confirm a number of facts:

- The local economy is extremely healthy. The local population is relatively affluent with high levels of disposable income.
- Professional groups are used to paying annual membership fees for the local theatre, a nearby golf club (the manager is also a member and has contacts there), and substantial fees for their children's activities (e.g. dance academies and junior football teams and so on).
- Old Town has a public swimming pool that is dated but almost of Olympic standards. It is used mainly by school children in the day and by a swimming club in the evenings. Taking advantage of government tax incentives to help keep the population fit and healthy, a privately operated, female only, health and beauty facility has recently opened in Old Town. Beyond these facilities, little else in the way of sports and fitness provision exists in the region.

The manager explains that:

- the hotel is unlikely to upgrade the centre's facilities any further in the short term, despite the fact that new, more sophisticated fitness equipment is coming onto the market all the time
- any promotional budget to attract members would be limited
- an estimate of additional revenue potential is needed to complete the business plan.

Requirements

(a) Conduct a PEST analysis that is relevant to the centre. **(5 marks)**

(b) Explain how the centre should undertake market segmentation and describe the most likely segmentation variables that will be identified by such a process.

(10 marks)

(c) Explain how the centre's income potential can be estimated. **(10 marks)**

(Total = 25 marks)

C3 National Secure is a large insurance company. The company is structured into four Divisions and supported by a small headquarters that includes the personnel function (recently renamed the Human Resourcing (HR) Division). The post of Head of HR is vacant following the retirement of the long-serving post-holder, and the HR strategy is in urgent need of review and revision.

National Secure has recently announced a new corporate initiative of continuous improvement through the empowerment of its workforce. The Chief Executive explained: 'We value our people as our most prized asset. We will encourage them to think, challenge and innovate. Only through empowering them in this way can we achieve continuous improvement. Staff will no longer be expected just to obey orders; from now on they will make and implement decisions to bring about continuous improvement. We want to develop clear performance objectives and be more customer focused.'

Your line manager is one of the four Divisional directors and will soon form part of a panel that will interview candidates for the vacant role of HR director. She is particularly keen to ensure that the successful candidate would be able to shape the HR Division to the needs of the organisation. She is aware of your CIMA studies and has asked for your help in preparing for the interview.

Requirements

Produce outline notes for your Divisional director which discuss the main points you would expect candidates to highlight in response to the following two areas she intends to explore with candidates at the interview, specifically:

(a) The likely role that the HR function will perform in the light of the changing nature of the organisation. **(10 marks)**

(b) The aspects of a revised HR strategy that will show significant change given the nature of recent organisational developments. **(10 marks)**

(c) Explain the concept of empowerment. **(5 marks)**

(Total = 25 marks)

C4 D is an international logging company, which cuts down timber and supplies sawmills where the timber is seasoned and then cut to appropriate sizes for use in a range of industries. D will work with any timber, ranging from softwoods used in construction or paper manufacture to exotic hardwoods used in expensive furniture. Its usual approach is to secure the rights from a landowner, or in some cases a national government, to cut timber. This can often involve the payment of large initial cash deposits to these suppliers, money which D usually borrows. A logging team then cuts down the trees as quickly as possible and hauls the timber to a convenient river where it is floated to a sawmill. Moving on rapidly to the next site, the loggers usually leave considerable surface damage behind them.

Since an increasing proportion of the company's work has been in the tropical rainforest, it has recently come under pressure from environmental groups that have protested that it is not socially responsible to act in this way. Whilst the softwood forests can be regenerated in a couple of decades by replanting, hardwoods in tropical forests take far longer to mature.

The Chief Executive of the company has argued that he is not concerned about these protests since, as far as he is concerned, the company always acts ethically, as it has the agreement of the national government in any country in which the company operates.

A recent development in the timber industry has been the harvesting of timber from the bottom of reservoirs which have been created by flooding valleys. Although the capital equipment required for this approach is significantly more expensive than that used in conventional logging, the operating costs are lower. Waterlogged trees in reservoirs have balloons attached, are cut, float to the surface and are towed to a sawmill. The underwater process is quieter and less disruptive to wildlife and the environment.

It has been estimated that there are over half a billion trees, or 20 years' supply, submerged in reservoirs across the world, but it can take considerable research and expense to find them.

As long as the timber has remained submerged deeply enough, it is of the same quality as timber harvested from the land. There is currently only one company conducting underwater logging, although a number of other companies are also considering this development.

Some of the Board of Directors feel that D should pursue this underwater approach and abandon land-based logging. The Chief Executive and one other director feel that the underwater approach carries too high a risk.

Requirements

(a) Briefly explain the differences between business ethics and corporate social responsibility (CSR). **(5 marks)**

(b) Discuss the CSR issues relating to D's business and how the company might improve its CSR position. **(8 marks)**

(c) With reference to D, evaluate the two approaches to logging and recommend which you think is most appropriate for D. **(12 marks)**

(Total = 25 marks)

C5 CTC, a telecommunications company, has recently been privatised by the government of C after legislation was passed which removed the state monopoly and opened up the communications market to competition from both national and overseas companies – a process known as deregulation.

Prior to the deregulation, CTC was the sole, protected, supplier of telecommunications and was required to provide 'the best telecommunications service the nation can afford'. At that time the government dictated the performance levels required for CTC, and the level of resources it would be able to bring to bear to meet its objectives.

The shares were floated on the C Stock Exchange with 80% being made available to the population of C and up to 20% being made available to foreign nationals.

The government of C retained a 'golden share' to prevent the acquisition of CTC by any foreign company. However, the privatisation meant that many of the traditional ways in which the industry had operated would need to change under the new regulations. Apart from the money received from the flotation, the government privatised CTC in recognition of both the changing global environment for telecommunications companies, and the overseas expansion opportunities that might exist for a privatised company. The government recognises that foreign companies will enter the home market but feels that this increased competition is likely to make CTC more effective in the global market.

You have recently been appointed as the management accountant for CTC and have a background in the commercial sector. The Board of Directors is unchanged from CTC's pre-flotation days.

Requirements
(a) Explain to the Board of Directors why the objectives of CTC will need to change as a result of the privatisation of CTC and the deregulation of the market.

(Total = 10 marks)

C6 CQ4 is a leading European industrial gas production company. CQ4's directors are each responsible for a geographical region comprised of several small strategic business units (SBUs). SBU managers report in monthly review meetings in great detail to their directors. CQ4 is showing signs of declining profitability and a new chief executive has been appointed and wishes to address the situation. She has complete freedom to identify organisational problems, solutions and strategies.

She announces two new initiatives 'to address the lost years when managers were prevented from delivering truly excellent CQ4 performance':

- Revision of the existing performance appraisal system. Bonuses paid on sales will be replaced by performance-related pay for achievement of individual 'performance target contracts'. Individual SBU managers will sign contracts to deliver these targets. Performance will now be reviewed at yearly rather than monthly meetings with directors. The remuneration package will be adjusted appropriately with the current emphasis on increasing turnover shifting to profitability and innovation. At their annual conference she tells SBU managers that they hold the key to improved company performance. She has a vision of CQ4 achieving longer-term strategic goals of increased profitability, risk taking and innovation. Under the slogan 'support not report' directors will in future support and provide assistance to their managers to a greater degree, and the frequency and detail of reporting by managers will be reduced.
- A structural review to focus resources and efforts of SBUs on improving net profit. Part of the restructuring will involve SBUs no longer providing their own 'enabling' services such as finance, information technology and health and safety. These 'distractions from doing the real job' will in future be organised centrally. SBUs will, however, receive far greater responsibility, autonomy and influence over their own profitability.

She tells managers that she is stripping away the things that stop them doing their job properly. In return they must manage their SBU in the way they see most appropriate. They will be better rewarded and 'star achievers' will be fast tracked to senior positions. SBU managers are informed that already the HR department has been tasked with redesigning the remuneration and reward package.

Informal discussions amongst managers afterwards confirm that the new chief executive's message has been well received. Comments such as 'work might be more enjoyable without central interference' and 'for the first time I can do my job properly' were overheard.

Requirements

(a) Explain the thinking behind the two initiatives announced by the new chief executive using Herzberg's motivation-hygiene (dual factor) theory as a framework.

(9 marks)

(b) Discuss the factors that should be taken into account by HR department when redesigning the remuneration and reward package for SBU managers.

(9 marks)

(c) Explain the relevance of what Schein and others have called the 'rational economic man theory' in the context of CQ4. **(7 marks)**

(Total = 25 marks)

C7 XYZ Bank has over 2 million customers and nearly 700,000 credit card holders. The bank employs 4,000 staff in 22 locations throughout the country and each week handles over 5 million transactions. New services are developed by project teams before being offered to customers.

Last year a new chief executive set an agenda some years ago to focus on the features, benefits and drawbacks of contemporary approaches to the management of quality. Since this time XYZ has been involved in implementing a TQM programme and a Quality Assurance section and Customer Complaints section have been established at the corporate headquarters.

Requirements

(a) Explain the critical elements of XYZ's TQM approach to Quality improvement, Customer care and Quality Assurance. **(8 marks)**

(b) Outline a plan so that a new branch needing to introduce TQM could communicate the quality approach to its staff and help overcome resistance to the initiative. **(8 marks)**

(c) Explain with examples the types of costs associated with operation of a quality programme within XYZ. **(9 marks)**

(Total = 25 marks)

C8 ARi9 is an information systems solutions company employing 250 staff. When their staff are not at clients' premises they work from a corporate headquarters (HQ) in the country's capital city. The premises (which are owned by the company) are spacious and modern but have extremely limited car parking.

A senior staff meeting takes place every month. Last month's meeting contained a number of significant issues. (Unfortunately the start of this meeting was delayed because of a public transport strike which led to gridlocked roads during rush hour. Those travelling by car found public parking spaces scarce, and parking charges high.) When the meeting eventually got underway a report by the Director of Human Resourcing identified a number of difficulties:

- ARi9 are loosing talented staff that take career breaks or maternity leave and never return.

- Competition amongst firms in the industry for talented individuals who live within a reasonable commuting distance is intense.
- Recruitment is becoming more difficult as local property prices are very expensive making relocation unattractive.
- ARi9 employs much fewer people with disabilities than the Government's suggested quota.
- Clients are making demands on staff outside normal working hours resulting in staff dissatisfaction and increasing claims for overtime payment.
- Staff productivity is declining in part due to interruptions to work caused by the office environment (which is 'open plan' and has crowded workstations where conversations can be easily overheard).

At the same meeting a review of the company's cost structure by the Finance Director underlined the high cost of office space, which was contributing to reduced profitability. (Someone joked that ARi9 is in the technology not the property business!)

In the debate that followed the option of relocating the HQ to somewhere outside the capital was suggested. The Chief Executive tasked both Directors to collaborate and produce some "radical solutions" for the future.

At this month's meeting their joint report outlined a number of ideas:

- ARi9 should sell its HQ and relocate to much smaller accommodation outside the capital. When they are not at clients, staff would be expected to work mainly from home. On the occasions when they were required to be at the HQ the new building should contain a flexible area where staff can 'hot desk'. There should also be some meeting rooms that could be booked in advance if needed.
- In future staff would be expected to work from their homes staying in touch with colleagues and customers through email, webcams and teleconferencing (so-called 'teleworking' or 'telecommuting').
- New equipment purchased for staff would be financed from anticipated improved productivity gains.

The report concluded with the claims that the proposals were 'win/win/win'. The company would produce significant HR and financial gains, society would benefit environmentally through reduced travel, and the workforce would be given greater autonomy to structure their own working arrangements.

Requirements

(a) Evaluate the claims made by the report's authors that the proposals would produce significant gains **for the company.** **(10 marks)**
(b) Discuss the potential benefits and potential difficulties of the proposals **for the workforce** **(10 marks)**

(Total = 20 marks)

Solutions to C Style Revision Questions 6

> *Important note*: The solutions suggested here (and elsewhere in earlier sections) use specific models, frameworks and theories in order to address the question in hand. The identification of alternative valid approaches by candidates will in the examination also receive appropriate credit.

C1(a) Considerations/Issues:
Human resource planning involves developing a plan for the acquisition, utilisation, improvement and retention of an organisation's human resources. Such a plan needs to be integrated into the broader process of business planning if it is to be useful. In this case the Cardinal's managers business plan for a management buyout.

The HR plan will need to take account and support the three main initiatives identified as part of the buy-out:

- Heritage 'real ale' tours using the dated brewing equipment and methods of working as an attraction.
- Bottling beer for sales in supermarkets.
- Employing a more flexible but suitably experienced workforce.

The plan will need to reflect:

- how HR flexibility will be achieved
- retraining in new skills
- budgets, targets and standards
- reward systems
- responsibilities for implementation and control (including the appraisal process)
- reporting procedures that will enable achievements to be monitored against the plan.

Consideration will need to be taken of what Cardinal represents: tradition, national reputation and 'real ale' production.

The plan itself will need to meet certain key criteria: it will need to be realistic, accurate, suitable, consistent and so on.

Stages:

The HR planning process normally consisting of four main phases:

1. Conducting an audit of the existing human resources in the light of any corporate or business changes.
2. Forecasting future demand for labour.
3. Assessing the external labour market and forecasting supply.
4. Establishing a plan reconciling demand and supply.

Applying this thinking to the scenario:

- *Audit of the existing human resources.* Clearly there have been big changes and technically no existing human resources exist! However, as the shut down only happened last month and as the workforce has specialist skills that are likely to be unused in an area of high unemployment, most will be available for reemployment. HR records can be accessed to determine key pieces of information. The selection process will be important to ensure that Cardinal obtains people with the right skills and/or the potential to develop such skills.
- *Forecasting future demand for labour.* Based on past experience a good estimate of minimum and maximum numbers required will be possible. In addition to numbers the skill requirements of people is also important. Again based on past experience projections can be made. As there appear to be no proposals for new technology/automation/reequipping skills, numbers can be confidently predicted. However, a number of important factors need to be taken into account when forecasting demand:

  - the introduction of anew products: bottled beer which will have new skill implications
  - the development of brewery tours which will have new skill implications the seasonal nature of sales
  - financial limits on manpower costs as part of the business plan (i.e. What can be afforded).

- *Assess the external labour market and forecasting supply.* Supply is likely to be plentiful, due to unemployment and unique skills. It is possible to use personnel (HR) records as the database for analysis of the past Cardinal workforce. From these records it is possible to derive a wide range of information about the numbers, current skill, age, training undertaken, performance levels and so on. This information can provide knowledge of the supply of labour available locally.
- *Establish a plan reconciling demand and supply.* Having made an estimate of the labour required to staff the organisation and considered the supply of labour available, the next step is to put together action plans for the recruitment, and where necessary retraining in new skills of the workforce so that the demand and supply of labour can be reconciled. Considerations of motivation are normally relevant as part of this stage. As the workforce was previously highly motivated, the opportunity to be part of a relaunch of Cardinal that offers them employment means that this is less of a consideration.

It must be acknowledged that in reality the process is rarely as linear and sequential as these phases suggest and many aspects progress together.

C1(b) Work at present is very seasonal (the winter months being heaviest) and although brewery tours and bottled beers may help smooth fluctuations in work, more flexibility in the workforce is demanded for the new company to survive. Change in practices is clearly requited and the new Cardinal organisation may take on a different form to the old one.

To provide for flexibility other firms including have adopted various approaches:

New forms of employment terms (e.g. fixed-term contracts, part-time contracts or systems of 'annual hours') to smooth the use of staff over critical periods such as seasonal shortages. The annual hours approach could work well at Cardinal brewery.

Outsourcing certain functions to outside contractors rather than addressing these directly. For Cardinal this might mean all administrative, payroll and marketing functions for instance.

Handy's 'shamrock' organisation with an employed core of professional workers, a contractual fringe providing specialist and non-essential services and flexible part time and temporary workers might be one model for Cardinal (this is consistent with Atkinson's (1984), ideas for core employees and periphery workers on temporary or part-time staff to buffer against changes in demand).

C1(c) 'Market segmentation' is a technique based on the recognition that every market consists of potential buyers with different needs, and different buying behaviour. These different customer characteristics may be subgrouped (or segmented) and a different marketing mix applied by an organisation to each target market segment.

Market segmentation may therefore involve the subdividing of a market into distinct subgroups of customers, where any subgroup can be selected as a target market to be met with a distinct marketing mix.

The important point of market segmentation is that although the total market consists of widely different groups of consumers, each group consists of people with common needs and preferences, who perhaps react to market stimuli in much the same way. Recognition of segmentation will enable a company to adopt a more refined approach to selling to a given group of potential customers.

Segmentation:

- accounts for the fact that the same product cannot satisfy everyone completely
- allows differentiation to take place
- can improve a company's competitive position
- offers an opportunity for an organisation to select the most appropriate target group.

Two of Cardinal's managers would like to save the business and are drawing up a business plan for a management buy-out. Apart from employing a more flexible but suitably experienced workforce, they identify two initiatives that they feel could in combination save the enterprise:

1 Using the site as a basis for a living museum of traditionally brewed ale (with the dated brewing equipment and methods of working as an attraction).
2 Producing bottled beer for sales in supermarkets.

Through market segmentation the managers might determine whether or not the target segment is significant enough to save the enterprise. Segmentation might produce profiles as follows:

Segmentation variable	Living museum	Bottled beer
Benefit sought	Those who like trips out	Those who drink at home
Occasion and usage	Holiday periods, one off outing	Weekly consumption, repeat purchases
Perception, beliefs	Like a day out with a difference	Prefer real ale
Lifestyle	Families, couples used to trips out	Prefer beer to wine with a meal at home
Gender	Whole family	Mainly male
Socio-economic	Employed (it is a luxury)	Employed (it is a luxury)
Geographic	Near enough to travel	Local: depends which supermarkets stock it

C2(a) **Significant influences**

Political/Legal
- There are some important health and safety requirements in place. Specifically, children under the age of 16 cannot use swimming pools unless supervised by an adult. In addition, children cannot use gymnasiums without the supervision of a suitably qualified person. This legislation translates as a restriction on 4QX. However, management is already well aware of the laws and would probably segment its market accordingly (see requirement (b)).
- Government tax incentives exist to encourage providers so that the population becomes or stays fit and healthy. This is positive from 4QX's point of view. Such incentives should be investigated and reflected in the business plan.

Economic
- The economic factors appear favourable. The local economy is extremely healthy and the local population is relatively affluent with high levels of disposable income. This being the case, there should not be a difficulty in affording the centre's fees so long as the fee level is not set unduly high.

Socio-cultural
- In terms of attitudes to leisure and fees, professional groups within the population are used to paying annual membership fees for the theatre and for golf. In addition, a market exists for charging substantial fees for their children's activities. This is obviously a positive trend, making fee paying assumptions reasonable when developing a business plan.
- The centre is a little remote due to the relatively poor transport network in the region, so it is not known whether people would be prepared to travel to it or not. (The fact that people are relatively affluent might suggest that they can afford their own transport, hence this might not be a difficulty.)

Technological
- New, increasingly sophisticated fitness equipment is coming onto the market all the time, so although the hotel installed the most modern sports and fitness centre

two years ago, it may already be out of date. The fact that the manager has ruled out further expenditure may be a difficulty if the ladies health and fitness centre boasts superior facilities or if another competitor emerges with more state of the art equipment.

C2(b) The practical issues associated with segmentation suggest that a narrowing down of *potential* segments should take place in order to establish a viable, *practical* focus on potential customers.

Marketing wisdom suggests that since the purpose of segmentation is to identify target markets, segments must be:

- *Measurable*. Meaning that abstract segmentation by 'personality' for example might be elusive and difficult to measure. A segment identified as 'those with a belief in healthy living' might present difficulties in measurement.
- *Accessible*. The segment must be 'reached' by the centre through (for instance) promotion without any undue difficulty.
- *Substantial*. The likely revenue streams from the segment must outweigh the effort in reaching the segment or segments.

Use available expertise
The challenge for the centre is to identify the significant bases for segmentation and then access these segments through marketing efforts. This is far from an objective process and in practice is inevitably a matter of judgement. This process should be carried out using the thoughts and ideas of all the sports and fitness centre staff. The apparently positive discussions so far are a good sign. The group might begin considering the issue of segmentation by simply identifying potential segments. A second stage could then follow with the elimination of those that appear impractical or undesirable.

Identifying the potential services that could be offered
In this case the centre's distinctive offering is its gymnasium, which is described as both extensive and fully equipped. This will have an appeal to those who are interested in fitness primarily. 'Serious' swimmers by comparison would not be interested in the centre's small pool. The pool itself does not appear to be an obvious attraction in itself. (The serious swimmer is already catered for at the public baths, which are nearing Olympic standard.) The centre's single Spa bath and steam room are also limited in themselves but (along with the pool) usefully augment the basic product of the fitness centre.

Taking account of potential alternative providers
It may be a good idea to identify potential competitors and to speculate as to the groups they are currently targeting and those they may target in the future. In this way, an unexploited segment of market might usefully be identified and targeted by the centre. In this particular case, the local providers of fitness and leisure, the public swimming pool and the health and beauty facility already target specific segments (serious swimmers, children and females respectively). It would not be desirable to offer exactly the same services to the same segment.

Segmentation variables

Market segments might relate to geographical area, age, gender, income, occupation, social class, lifestyle and so. The centre might identify the following key variables:

- *Geographical area*: The target is the regional market as it is unlikely that few, if any, potential customers would travel a distance to use the centre's facilities. The region is remote and has relatively poor transport links, suggesting that potential customers in the region should have their own transport. An alternative segment might be the tourists visiting the area. Business from tourists would lead to irregular trading patterns (none outside the holiday season) and require potentially more intense advertising effort than that directed at regional customers.
- *Age*: Prohibitive legislation excludes those under the age of 16 as a viable segment as additional supervision costs would be required. Encouraging the use of the centre by children would in any case be inconsistent with the image the hotel wants to project (namely exclusivity and with an appeal to business executives). In addition, local children currently have access to the public swimming pool in Old Town.
- *Gender*: The choices to be made in terms of gender are to focus marketing on males, females or both. It is known that a privately operated, female only, health and beauty facility exists locally. By implication, it could be speculated that nothing, other than the public baths, exists for men. The most fruitful potential segment would therefore be men.
- *Income*: The aim of the centre is to generate income rather than to fulfil a social function within the local community. Those with an ability to pay either membership fees or highly priced one off fees represent a natural target. The fact that those accessing the hotel would need their own transport reinforces this requirement. In terms of *social class* and *lifestyle*, affluent, professional groups are used to fee-paying membership and would represent a likely good fit with the existing clientele of the hotel.

In short, the market segment that the centre should focus on is local men in professional or well-paid employment. There would be a need to limit membership in order to guard against overcrowding and also maintain the idea of 'exclusivity'.

C2(c) *Background*

If the sports and leisure facility were treated as a profit centre, it would show a large loss. Hotel management cannot disinvest in it however, as they wish to maintain their current hotel star rating. Any additional revenue that the facility can generate would therefore be welcomed and offset overall hotel costs. The manager wants to estimate this revenue potential for business planning purposes.

Traditional approaches

The estimation of revenue potential will not, in this instance, follow some of the 'traditional' approaches. (There is no sales force to seek opinions from or estimates based on past sales analysis.) The sports and leisure centre's staff do, however, have some insights which could be useful, and they should be involved in the process suggested below.

A marketing approach
Taking on a marketing perspective will provide one approach to estimating the revenue potential. This approach suggests that revenue will be determined by a combination of factors, mainly the effectiveness and level of commitment to promotion (financial and other-wise), and the price of the service. (Both promotion and price represent variables within the overall marketing mix.)

In terms of promotion and pricing:

- The manager has made clear that any promotional budget would be limited (but no figure is quoted). This means that any promotional effort would need to be both carefully determined and as cost effective as possible.
- An annual membership fee is the manager's preferred choice and this is consistent with the charging structure of other facilities in the region. The fee should reflect the exclusive image of the hotel. As the facilities offered are limited, a maximum number of potential members should be considered and agreed upon as appropriate.

The potential revenue under such an approach will be a product of the calculation.

Annual fee x Potential members
The potential will only be achieved however, if promotional effectiveness is maximised, so the sensitivity of the calculation should be considered. Once an estimate is arrived at, using this thinking, some expert opinion might be sought to validate or critically appraise any assumptions made.

Fee level
The annual fee might be set by reference to:

- Fees charged by hotels in other regions for a comparable membership
- Membership fees for other clubs and facilities.

The attractiveness of the membership to the centre for a range of fee rates arising from this analysis might be tested through a limited market survey. (The design of a standard questionnaire format could be used to canvass the views of a sample of those who form the market segment.)

Number of members
Potential member numbers will have a ceiling of a 'safe' upper limit based upon a need for exclusivity and an avoidance of overcrowding. Beyond this optimistic and pessimistic membership take up might be calculated.

Potential collaboration
The local golf club represent an excellent potential source of expert opinion on the suitability of fee rates. Collaboration with the club in promotional activities is also a possibility (provided that the golf club does not see the centre as a rival for membership fees).

It is likely that a segmentation process has taken place at the golf club and that both and the centre are targeting a similar segment. This being the case, collaboration between the centre and the golf club has potential for the following:

- Promoting the centre at the golf club (which could be reciprocated by promoting the club at the centre). This would prove a low cost promotional tactic.
- Offering dual membership of both the club and the centre for an appropriate (mutually agreed) fee.
- Accessing the golf club membership register in order to conduct a market survey and/or target promotional efforts. (Assuming that passing on this data does not infringe legislative requirements or ethical considerations over data protection.)

The impact of competition

Finally, it should be recognised that future actions by competitors might adversely affect income projections. (For example, if the market is price sensitive the competition may cut prices, alternatively, they may increase their promotional effort, or augment their service, and so on.) In addition, new providers entering the market might impact on income levels adversely. This being the case, income projections should be undertaken for both 'best case' and 'worst case' conditions.

If competitor action is significant, the centre might choose to concentrate on another market segment. Alternatively, it might adjust its marketing mix by:

- Investing more heavily in promotional activity
- Adjusting the membership fee (price) or capacity figures
- Making a case to hotel management to enhance the leisure facilities still further (product). (It is however, noted that the manager has indicated that this is unlikely.)

Under such conditions, income projections may need to be adjusted.

C3(a) Likely role HR will perform in the light of the changing nature of the organisation.

- *Company background.* The company appears to be 'traditionally' structured with four divisions and a small HQ staff. The signals for change include a re-branding of personnel to Human Resources. The retirement of the long-serving head of this function is also of significance. This implies that a traditional well-established way of operating in the past is not required in the future. The fact the HR strategy is in 'urgent need' of review and revision underlines this point.
- *An HR rather than Personnel role.* Personnel Management is seen as focusing on day-to-day 'people-related' issues. In the past, NS's small specialist personnel support function would undoubtedly have attempted to ensure consistency and fairness of treatment throughout the organisation. Personnel Management is seen as ensuring compliance with organisational procedures as well as reacting and responding to external environmental changes (including employment legislation and labour market conditions). The changes taking place at NS mean that the function will have different objectives more easily identified as human resource management (HRM).
- *A strategic role.* The new function would be expected to view employees in a different, more strategic way. A reasonable revised focus would be upon the long-term development of human resources in such a way as to deliver the strategic aspirations of the company (i.e. to achieve continuous improvement). The specialist HR Division should provide support to Divisional Directors and other managers in order to meet detailed organisational objectives.

The new HR function would be expected to have key inputs into the strategic deliberations that are apparently underway including the setting of clear objectives. The HR Division will now be expected to shape and deliver strategies.

- *A training needs role.* NS's new corporate initiative of continuous improvement through empowerment is of major significance for the HR Division. Under the initiative people are seen as crucial, exercising skills of thinking, challenging, innovating and implementing. The function will need to ensure that the workforce have these skills.

Empowerment involves passing power downwards for staff 'closer to the action' to be responsible for making decisions and initiating actions. This involves a high degree of trust in the workforce and less directive, authoritarian control from management. This new management style means that Departmental Directors and managers will need to be encouraged by the function to make this change.

- *A role in cultural shaping.* NS's initiative of an empowered workforce normally involves a major organisational cultural change. There is no evidence from the scenario as to how this is to be brought about other than an apparent rethink of the role of specialist personnel function. The HR function will be crucial in affecting the necessary cultural change and the new Head might be expected to perform a change agent's role.
- *A role in championing corporate initiatives.* In an empowered organisation, people are active in solving problems, looking for better ways of working, and co-operating freely with others in and across teams. Continuous improvement is a collective approach towards improving performance throughout the organisation. Clearly the HR function will need to champion and support these developments.

C3(b) Aspects of HR strategy showing significant change given the nature of recent developments.

Given the changing nature of the organisation and the initiatives being progressed, attention should be given to the following aspects of the HR strategy:

- *Structure and job roles.* The overall structure should be configured in order that individuals are developed to their full potential and encouraged to do 'things right' (what needs to be done in organisational terms), not merely 'the right things' (what job descriptions require of them). The strategy will need to articulate the structure, control and functioning of the organisation. Layers of management that add no value or that damage empowerment should be eliminated as part of a systematic review.
- *Job content.* Job content will also need to be reviewed and then be articulated in overall terms in the strategy. This review could conveniently follow on from the structural review identified earlier and might feature broader spans of managerial control. This should in turn encourage managers to delegate and trust subordinates to exercise their increased autonomy and power effectively.
- *Education and training.* Education and Training in empowerment and continuous improvement will be vital components of the strategy. This might be achieved by facilitating workshops and ongoing support mechanisms such as mentors, buddying systems and/or counsellors. Changes to role requires training at all levels,

particularly senior management, where individuals will need to be persuaded to relinquish power. For 'front line' staff, mechanisms for training and building self-confidence are vital. This will undoubtedly involve enhancing existing skills and the identification of new skill requirements.

It is good practice to undertake a training needs analysis of the workforce and shape the strategy accordingly. Specific likely skills will include problem-solving, data-gathering techniques, teambuilding, listening and customer care. Teams of people will need to be built that co-operate and support one another in continuously improving customer service and improving efficiency.

Senior managers may need training in facilitation and leadership skills. It is vital that senior managers (whose role should include setting the 'right' examples) provide consistent messages and behaviour.

The strategy will need to articulate how this is delivered (whether in-house by trainers, externally, or by the use of existing managers). Systems for monitoring the effectiveness of these 'interventions' will also need to be articulated in the strategy.

- *Reward systems.* These systems represent the ways in which staff are recognised and rewarded for their endeavours. A revised strategy must ensure that such systems are consistent with, and encourage, the identified concepts of empowerment and continuous improvement. The HR function in conjunction with senior managers will need to agree behaviour patterns required in the future and ways of measuring outcomes. Those who actively support and embrace the twin concepts identified (of empowerment and continuous improvement) should be rewarded appropriately. Typical organisational rewards usually include pay, promotion and other rewards. Other rewards need not have financial implications and might, for instance, include still greater empowerment. It is a good idea to communicate these points widely and reward publicly, making role models and heroes of those who achieve. In this way positive performance standards might be signaled.

This thinking should be embodied in the HR strategy.

- *Target setting and appraisals.* A mechanism for review and target setting will need to be considered in the strategy. Although this might already exist, major revisions to these targets will be needed in the light of organisational initiatives. New personal plans/targets/key performance indicators (KPIs) will need to be created for every manager and then cascaded down through subordinates and work groups so that the whole organisation's performance is assessed having regards to the twin initiatives. Reviews of performance after a few months by using small groups should highlight progress, problems and areas for adjustment. Once overall review mechanisms are established, annual appraisal and monthly target setting might reasonably be employed. Upward and 360 degree appraisal schemes might be considered in order to strengthen reflective practice.
- *Review mechanisms.* Revised review mechanisms should concentrate on monitoring progress on the initiatives and taking corrective action where necessary. This should be at the expense of previous forms of control, direction and reporting in order to drive decision-making down to the lowest level.
- *Communication systems.* Channels of official communication should be articulated in the strategy. The existing strategy may already do this but the focus may

need to be reorientated in the light of new corporate initiatives. A new emphasis should be placed upon encouraging open communication, sharing of information and honesty.

C3(c) Empowerment is a management technique whereby power and authority is delegated downwards within an organisation. The effect is that subordinates are trusted to work towards their managers' goals. This is obviously an enlightened and wholly sensible strategy to pursue so long as there is mutual trust, sufficient training and a supportive culture.

The fact that National Secure has recently announced a new corporate initiative based on empowerment underlines their commitment to it. There is clear evidence that the Chief Executive trusts the workforce and provides sufficient encouragement, specifically:

- People are apparently valued and regarded as National Secure's most prized asset.
- Staff are encouraged for them to think, challenge and innovate.
- Clear individual performance objectives are to be determined.
- Staff are no longer expected just to obey orders instead they will make and implement decisions.

The fact that the Chief Executive sees this as bringing about continuous improvement is of relevance. He/She states quite clearly: 'Only through empowering them in this way can we achieve continuous improvement.' The process is meant to enable National Secure to become more customer focussed.

C4(a) Although the two terms, business ethics (BE) and corporate social responsibility (CSR) are often used interchangeably it is wrong to do so.

- BE can be defined as 'behaviour judged to be good, just, right, and honourable, based on principles or guides from a specific ethical theory'.
- CSR is defined much more broadly as 'The continuing commitment for business to behave ethically and to contribute to economic development while improving the quality of life of the workforce and their families as well as of the local community and society at large'.

Therefore BE is only a component part of CSR. An alternative definition of CSR states that society can:

- require business to discharge its economic and legal duties
- expect business to fulfil its ethical duties
- desire business to meet its philanthropic responsibilities.

It has been argued that philanthropy is not the best approach for CSR unless it is guided by principles which will develop the local population economically, and educationally.

C4(b) In the context of D's logging business the chief executive argues that the company 'always acts ethically since it has the agreement of the national government…' This presupposes that the government itself is acting in the best interests of society. This is not always the case and much of the focus of both the OECD and WTO is on the unethical behaviour of governments as well as businesses. With a logging business, which has the potential to create considerable environmental damage in remote areas of a country, the possibility of unethical behaviour is high.

From a CSR perspective, D needs to think carefully about its business practices if it is to continue with land based logging. The ecological damage must be minimised and, once logging has finished, as much as practicable should be done to restore the habitat to its previous condition. In the event that the areas in which it operates have a population, D should be looking for ways to minimise the damage to the livelihoods and wellbeing of those people that live there. This could be done by providing education facilities, offering training for those who previously lived off the forest. If possible, it should consider replanting the area which has been harvested with appropriate trees to provide an element of sustainability.

Taking a more global perspective, D should work with the environmental groups that have criticised them. The company should be seeking to conduct its logging in sustainable forests and take advice to ensure that it minimises its environmental impact.

Having said this, it must not be forgotten that D is a commercial organisation and must continue to make the best, sustainable, profit for its shareholders.

C4(c) Existing business

If D continues to conduct its business by logging on dry land it will be working in a familiar way and will not have to learn new processes. The company has an established business which, presumably, is profitable. The established routines with which it operates will enable it to continue to make a profit for the foreseeable future.

As long as the cash flow continues, there may be no increased difficulty in borrowing the large cash deposits that are necessary to secure the use of the land. It is unlikely that its established bankers will not continue to bear the same level of risk to which they are currently exposed.

However, D is harvesting a diminishing resource and it must become increasingly difficult to find land-based timber that can be harvested. This must be particularly true of hardwood forests which take a long time to mature. Whilst softwood can be replaced and matures in a few decades, hardwood takes far longer to reach a harvestable size.

There is increasing pressure from the environmental lobby to halt the cutting of timber from other than sustainable forests, which will limit the supply of 'acceptable' timber. As sources of timber become less available, the environmental groups are likely to become more forceful in their protests. Increasingly, lobby groups are better able to coordinate their protests because of the increasing ease of communication brought about by the Internet.

The current practice of cutting timber with little regard for the environment and the ecological impact is, increasingly, unsustainable. The views and needs of the local population must be taken into account and, even if national governments are supportive, a more responsible approach to society must be taken by the company.

CSR is an increasingly important consideration for companies. The current logging methods are not the most socially responsible approach to the harvesting of timber, particularly hardwoods. The pressure that companies such as D are under at the moment can only increase.

Underwater business

The prospect of gathering timber from the bottom of reservoirs is certainly a more environmentally friendly approach than that currently used by D.

- There is less environmental disturbance and the timber harvested does not represent a habitat or food resource to local flora and fauna.
- Those companies that have a good reputation in terms of CSR often find it easier to borrow, as many organisations are ranked in terms of their CSR policies and actions. Increasingly, banks are using CSR rankings as part of their risk assessments.
- There is a plentiful supply of timber of all kinds, according to the estimates. Although this timber will need to be found, there should be no shortage of maps and local knowledge concerning the valleys that have been flooded to make the reservoirs.
- As sources of land-based timber become scarcer, this business is likely to be more sustainable and, if D becomes expert in this form of harvesting, the company may develop a significant competitive advantage.
- In terms of corporate reputation, D is likely to gain internationally from taking this more socially responsible approach. This will have an impact on its ability to borrow, attract better staff and improve its negotiating position with governments for access to the submerged timber.

However, the underwater process is not without its difficulties.

- There is a need for a large capital investment for the submersible equipment and this will have to be met in addition to any capital sums for access to the timber.
- There are changes in the required operations – new skills will need to be learnt and possibly new staff hired with those skills.
- Even though the estimates of available timber are high, surveys will be needed to determine where the submerged forests are and this may prove difficult initially until skills and reputation are built in this area of expertise.

Recommendation

On balance, the company should move to harvesting submerged trees from reservoirs because of the availability of sustainable supplies and the CSR implications.

C5(a) Prior to the deregulation, the principal stakeholder was the government of C and it had set a requirement relating to the quality of service within a budget. The emphasis would have been on economy, efficiency and effectiveness. Any objectives set would, therefore, have been based on level of service and/or cost efficiency.

The Board of Directors will also need to be aware of the corporate governance issues that it will now face. The stock market of C will almost certainly have a code of practice which must be followed for listed companies.

Now that CTC is owned by shareholders it will be necessary for it to meet objectives addressing the values of those shareholders whilst still complying with the regulations imposed by the government. Since the telecommunications industry in C has become deregulated it is possible that foreign companies could enter the market and offer a rival service. With this in mind CTC will need to consider the customers as an important stakeholder group whose values must also be addressed. Failure to do this might lead to a significant loss of market share.

Although the relationship with CTC is now 'at arms length' it is likely that the government will want CTC to capitalise on the opportunities offered by overseas expansion and to generate significant tax revenue for the good of C. The shareholders are more likely to want CTC to demonstrate significant, profitable, growth and a reward in terms of both dividend and share price increases. This may lead to a conflict of stakeholder objectives that must be managed by the directors.

The customers will still want to receive a level of service at, in their perception, a cost effective price. This will also lead to a conflict with the interests of shareholders, who will necessarily seek a growth in profitability. Increasing prices may be one of the ways to achieve higher profits.

Now that CTC has become privatised it will be subject to the full range of regulation that commercial organisations have to deal with in addition to any industry specific regulation that the government has created in the light of the privatisation. This may mean that CTC is required to provide some unprofitable services, or be prohibited from providing some profitable ones.

The objectives that CTC sets from now on must address the areas of profitability and reward for the shareholders, customer satisfaction, the competitive position of CTC with respect to any new entrants to the market, overseas expansion and compliance with the new regulatory regime.

C6(a) The initiatives identified using Herzberg's motivation-hygiene (dual factor) theory as a framework.

The first initiative involves a revision of the system that measures managerial accountability (now on net profit rather than increasing turnover). The second involves a restructure and reallocation of duties giving SBUs greater control over their own performance.

This thinking can be explained within the context of Frederick Herzberg's motivation-hygiene, or dual factor, theory. Herzberg's contention was that the opposite of job satisfaction is the absence of job satisfaction and not job dissatisfaction. By extension, the opposite of job dissatisfaction is an absence of dissatisfaction. Herzberg's research indicated that satisfaction and dissatisfaction are influenced and created by different variables. His theory has been very influential across a wide range of jobs, organisations and countries.

His initial study in the 1950s of 203 Pittsburgh accountants and engineers focussed on when they felt either exceptionally good or exceptionally bad about their job. This ultimately led to a two-factor theory of motivation:

- Motivators (or satisfiers) are factors that if present within a job encourage individuals to greater effort and performance through higher levels of job satisfaction (but not dissatisfaction). These factors relate to what people are allowed to do and the quality of human experience at work. These are the variables that motivate people. Examples include job role, organisational recognition, personal growth and a sense of achievement, advancement and responsibility. These factors are said to relate to job content.
- Hygiene factors (or dissatisfiers) are factors including status, pay, interpersonal relations, supervision, organisational policy and administration, job security and working conditions. These factors relate to job context.

In this case both motivators and hygiene factors have been addressed as follows:

Motivators:

- Achievement of individual 'performance contracts'.
- Recognition by the chief executive of the vital role played by SBU managers.
- Promises of advancement by fast tracking to senior positions.
- Greater responsibility to get on with the real job.
- Greater autonomy and influence over the SBU managers' own 'bottom-line' performance.

Hygiene factors:

- New remuneration package reflecting bonuses for increased profitability.
- Organisational policy and administration adjusted with SBU managers in mind.
- Potential to improve working conditions as managers are given greater freedom to run their SBU in the way they see most appropriate.

Both of the initiatives therefore go to the heart of motivation and performance. Measurements of performance within someone's control against corporate objectives such as with CQ4 can in themselves be powerful means of positively influencing individuals. There is also a well-researched connection between reward and performance. The way in which the remuneration package is adjusted therefore is crucial in this respect.

C6(b) Factors that should be taken into account by HR department when redesigning the remuneration and reward package for SBU managers:

- *Control of total payroll costs.* CQ4 needs to decide how much overall it can afford in payroll costs. Once the costs associated with other groups are calculated, the overall base salary costs and bonus payments for managers can be determined.
- *Appropriateness of overall package.* The remuneration strategy needs to appropriately balance base and performance-related pay. The base pay element should recognise factors such as size of SBU, relative contribution to the company as a whole, and specific skills and competences demanded of the individual manager and so on. The reward package will need to address not only internal targets but also market place levels of reward for similar work in order that there are not problems associated with retention of staff. As CQ4 is a European operation it is likely that local pay rates will vary enormously between countries in which SBUs are situated.
- *Money available for performance-related pay.* Performance-related pay represents an attempt to establish closer links between results and rewards. The success of the chief executive's new initiatives is dependent on people, primarily managers, behaving in certain ways. Rewards should be directed towards those who adopt the behaviours required. The incentive of performance-related pay should be seen as no less generous than the previous bonus scheme, and sufficient to make managers innovate, take risk and improve bottom-line performance. HR professionals need to know the total amount available to finance the new scheme. Based on this, decisions can be made as to how the scheme can be implemented (whether as a per cent of basic pay, a per cent of net profit, or incremental flat rate payments, etc.).

- *Rewards encouraging risk taking and innovation.* The new chief executive's vision of risk taking and innovation when translated into reward systems can be problematic. Whilst precise quantitative measures are readily available to measure net profit, the other factors suggest difficulties in identification and measurement. Judgements on, for instance, the number and quality of initiatives taken may lead to feelings of unfairness. In addition there needs to be a shared understanding of the relative weighting given to profitability, risk taking and innovation. Appropriate metrics and evaluation criteria need to be agreed upon and put in place.
- *Impact of adjusted HR policies on other groups.* SBU managers are the main focus of remuneration and reward systems. This can present some difficulties, as it is probable that others (e.g. directors, SBU workforce, etc.) will also be involved in achieving the level of SBU performance. If the manager is perceived to be receiving unfair reward and recognition, this might have a negative impact on these other groups and may lead to workplace disharmony and endanger improved performance. The positive impact of work groups on individual motivation has long been recognised and was famously illustrated by the Hawthorne Studies. The new reward system should not therefore be seen as a cause of undermining teamwork within SBUs. It is likely that HR policies will also need to be reviewed for all other groups to prevent this happening.
- *Accounting for non-controllable factors that influence managerial performance.* An underlying philosophy of performance-related pay should be to provide a fair and consistent basis for rewarding managerial performance. However, other organisational factors, such as the availability of technology, raw materials and financial resources will also have an important effect on SBU performance. Consideration needs to be given as to how to account for these factors.
- *Translating longer-term objectives into short-term targets and rewards.* Strategic objectives such as those expressed by the chief executive are longer term but managers need shorter-term targets and rewards. Careful development of individual 'performance contracts' will need to take place in order to translate these longer-term objectives into shorter-term personal targets split into agreed milestones.
- *Non-financial incentives.* A belief that money alone can encourage the enhancement of individual management performance is inaccurate. Other forms of incentive can also include promotion and career development opportunities. The reward system should therefore involve adjustment to issues such as succession planning and career progression or promotion using developmental pathways and career ladders and so on. The chief executive has promised as much for 'star performers'. This may necessitate a review of the existing structure above SBU level in order to ensure that such positions exist.
- *Consultation with SBU managers, trade union and other relevant groups.* If the revised scheme is to be accepted by SBU managers as appropriate, there needs to be a wide consultation in order that there is universal 'buy in'.

C6(c) The initiatives to encourage managers to deliver 'truly excellent CQ4 performance' includes an adjustment to the current performance appraisal system. Existing sales bonuses will be replaced by annual performance-related pay for achievement of individual 'performance target contracts' (focussed on SBU profitability and innovation).

Managers will potentially be 'better rewarded' suggesting potential for increased earnings from performance-related pay (although the HR department has yet to redesign the remuneration and reward package). The proposal has apparently been well received by managers.

One theory of motivation often used to explain the adoption of financial incentive schemes like that operated by CQ4 is what Schein and others have called the 'rational economic man theory'. This theory assumes that people are motivated by self-interest and that the opportunity to accumulate significant sums of money. This will stimulate individuals into making extra effort that the organisation can benefit from.

In this case it would be the manager meeting his or her performance target contract with targets undoubtedly including increased innovation and improved SBU 'bottom line' financial performance. The fact that the new system offers greater potential for earning means that under this theory all managers would be motivated to achieve the new demands upon them.

The 'rational economic man theory' is simply to understand and easy to apply. The main limitation of the theory, however, is that it is perhaps too straightforward and only recognises the most obvious dimensions of the complex subject of motivation.

It is inescapable that most people are motivated by factors other than money: but this theory takes no account of this. The more complex psychological theories of Maslow and Herzberg, for instance, indicate that although it can role in motivating people, it is not the only incentive (see part (a)). Maslow emphasises that once basic needs are satisfied, people are motivated by things like opportunities to gain status, recognition, a sense of achievement, a feeling of power and self-actualisation. Money and wealth can, of course, act as a measure and a source of some of these rewards for effort, but the point is that many of these things that satisfy deeply felt psychological and social needs can be attained without money as an incentive.

C7(a) Often quality programmes are undertaken for the wrong reasons. It is important that organisations ensure that both internal and external quality needs are assessed and addressed.

The critical elements of XYZ's TQM approach can be summarised as:

Quality improvement programme
- Identification, elimination and prevention of processing errors, rework and wastage via systematic audit processes.
- Design control of all processes, products and services.
- The development of beneficial partnerships with all external suppliers.
- A shift in culture so that the whole workforce becomes active in the quality process.

Customer care programme
(Focusing on the needs of the external customer and internal customer relationships)

- Market research to understand customer needs and current customer perceptions of products and service quality.

- Staff perception: research to ascertain staff attitude to quality and their interactions with external customers. (Staff interaction with customers will determine the customer perception of the service.)
- A complaints-handling service designed to be highly and speedily responsive to customer issues.
- Effective and regular customer care training for all staff.
- Effective customer communication and reporting procedures to keep customers informed on organisational issues.

Quality assurance programme

This should lay down the standards for performance and implement and manage a quality management system, ensuring compliance to standards (ISO 9000).

- Ensure XYZ is an ISO-registered firm.
- Benchmark against other banks and service providers to monitor performance and to ensure constant awareness of external quality assurance programmes.

C7(b) Plan to communicate quality

Overview

The plan should have a clear objective, timescale and resource implication. It may be that for certain stages there will be the need to employ an external consultant or facilitator who has particular expertise in this area.

Stage 1 Present TQM philosophy to the senior management team to instill TQM at the top level. Provide information and be prepared to answer questions. The presence of the chief executive to personally outline the agenda to focus on the features, benefits and drawbacks of contemporary approaches to the management of quality would provide a great impetus.

Stage 2 Set up quality groups/circles within the branch to tackle specific quality issues.
Provide support, encouragement and incentives for participation.

Stage 3 Run TQM workshops and training sessions for circle co-ordinators to ensure the quality message is received and reinforced.

Stage 4 Establish departmental/group quality standards. Possibly implement reward systems for quality improvements.

Stage 5 Agree quality performance data/standards for the branch to monitor quality achievements. (This process should be led by the Quality Assurance section.)

Comparative data from other branches could be used in a form of internal benchmarking exercise.

Kotter and Schlesinger (1979) identify six main strategies for dealing with resistance to change initiatives, one of which is education and communication. This strategy is particularly useful when the basic problem is a lack of information about the need for, or the nature of, the planned change. This is exactly the case with the establishment of the TQM philosophy within the new branch. The approach can be very time-consuming but is generally welcomed by staff and regarded as an ethical management strategy.

C7(c) The TQM philosophy is equally applicable to both the service and the manufacturing sector. Various types of costs are associated with the operation of a quality programme, and although these may be more visible in a manufacturing organisation (e.g. reworking, costs of scrap, etc.) they still remain for a service organisation such as the XYZ Bank.

Prevention costs. These are the cost of activities undertaken to prevent defects occurring in the design and development phase of a product or service. XYZ presumably offers a range of financial services to its customers. Costs associated with engineering quality into the design of its services might include careful supplier evaluation (e.g. if ABC offers insurance services on behalf of a partner) or operational training for its 4,000 staff staff and in particular project team members who will need additional training. Performance indicators should be identified, agreed upon and established for service quality against which measures might be taken.

Appraisal costs. These are the costs incurred while conducting quality tests and inspections in order to determine whether services conform to quality requirements. These may include quality audits and the operation of a Quality Assurance section. Service testing might be performed by, for instance, recording telephone conversations with customers to ensure that staff makes appropriate responses. Statistics will need to be collected in order to determine whether performance indicators are being achieved or not.

Internal failure costs. These are costs associated with the detection and rectification of items that do not conform to quality requirements, but have not yet been passed to the customer. This might include the rejection of proposals to launch a new product requiring a redesign of that product by the project team. Costs will also be associated with the trialling of new services to a controlled group of customers.

External failure costs. These are costs associated with the detection and rectification of items that do not conform to quality requirements and have been passed to the customer. They might include the operation of the Customer Complaints Section and their associated procedure and 'goodwill' incentives for any of the 2 million customers or 700,000 credit card holders who have legitimate grievances.

C8(a) Evaluate the claims made by the report's authors that the proposals would produce significant gains for the company.

It is claimed that the proposals would produce significant HR and financial gains for ARi9. The weight of evidence suggests that this claim is well founded.

Financial gains
- *Savings on premises costs.* There appears to be huge potential for cost reduction in premises costs. The Finance Director has in the past underlined the high cost of office space; indeed it was joked that ARi9 is in the technology not the property business! Clearly ARi9 can make large savings on premises costs, including associated overheads and labour cost. With the reductions in office occupancy and the proposal for a more flexible workspace more modest office accommodation in a less expensive location can be utilised (either through purchase, rent or lease).
- *Improved staff efficiency.* Increased productivity leading to improved income generated per employee may be possible. Under the proposals staff would avoid non

productive travel time and the interruptions of the general office environment. One current problem is that staff productivity is declining in part due to interruptions of the office environment; a difficulty that the proposal deals with.

- *Reduced employee costs.* Thanks to the communication technology proposed teams can be constituted regardless of geography and time zones with minimal need for extra travel. Additionally employees can be recruited without need for relocation expenses being paid. The staff flexibility offered by the proposal means peaks and troughs in workload can be managed by individuals, possibly reducing the need for overtime payments.

However, some balance should be struck. There are two main reasons why these gains might not be completely realised:

1 The anticipated improved productivity gains may be difficult short term, particularly as staff adjust to their new working arrangements. This will at best mean an adverse cash flow, (when new equipment is purchased), at worst a failure to realise sufficient efficiency gains to finance the outlay.
2 There is a requirement for a high investment in new technology which could lead to costly one off investments in email, webcams and teleconferencing in employee's homes where economies of scale offered by a traditional working environment do not apply. As technological developments occur this technology may become dated and will therefore store up a requirement for expensive system/technology upgrade in the future.

HR gains

- Improved motivation through more independent work arrangements. Potentially at least the proposals could be a source of motivation, as staff would be given much greater autonomy to structure their own working arrangements. Some employees may respond well to the trust and confidence that ARi9 management have put in them. Alternatively others may not, and the lack of structure offered by a physical environment and human interaction may be demotivating.
- Potentially, the proposals can enable people in an area of high unemployment and people with disabilities to have access to work opportunities. This may help the organisation meet the Government's suggested quota for employment of people with disabilities.
- *Retention of skills base.* ARi9 are loosing talented staff that take career breaks or maternity leave and never return. Under the proposals those employees who might otherwise leave can remain in their jobs, continue to work part time and remain up to date with the business and its methods. Those taking maternity leave can continue to undertake assignments arranging work around their other commitments. Once they return to work full time they will require less retraining and reorientation.
- *Organisational flexibility.* Staff can continue to work without disruption to their personal lives, irrespective of external factors such as office moves or transport difficulties. They can still operate in 'virtual' teams that can be easily reconfigured in response to their clients' changing requirements.
- *Improved customer responsiveness.* Clients should be better served and staff more productive thanks to a reduction in travel time and more flexible working hours. If properly managed these factors should suit both the member of staff and the

client. Services can potentially be extended beyond the 'normal' working day without overtime costs or the need for staff to work (and travel) at unsocial hours.
- *Organisational resilience.* Thanks to employees operating from different bases, ARi9 is better placed to survive external disruption whether transport strikes, inclement weather, natural disasters, terrorist action, or other reason. (The delays experienced before last month's senior staff meeting due to strike action, traffic congestion and limited car parking illustrates the point.)

There are two main reasons why HR gains could be diminished to a degree:

1 Not all tasks are best performed in an individual, distributed, environment. Some tasks may benefit from the close interactions of a team working together in place, or from the synergy of 'real' teams. This is particularly true of creative tasks, where apparently unstructured personal interactions are an important part of the creative process. The advantages of team spirit, group motivation, new idea generation and visible leadership 'from the front' is lost under the proposals.
2 Management in a new environment. ARi9 managers may not be culturally ready for the proposal. The individual flexibility offered may mean that managers lack the confidence and ability to 'manage virtually'. Other managers may doubt their subordinates' commitment and may believe that the new arrangements may lead to employee underperformance.

C8(b) Discuss the potential benefits and potential difficulties of the proposals for the workforce

Potential benefits

Under the proposals, there are many potential benefits for the workforce, including:

- Reduced travel time (and consequently individual cost savings). This is the most obvious benefit and is likely to be the most persuasive argument for changing working arrangements as far as ARi9 staff are concerned. Annual commuting costs may represent a significant proportion of an individual's income. The move to home working would therefore produce tangible savings for the individual.
- Reduction in stress and consequent ill health. The opportunity now exists to work in a less stressful pattern with fewer office distractions. The potential pressure experienced through a busy commute to work daily may cause anxiety, stress and ill health and loss of time from work. Travelling into a busy capital city with driving, transportation and parking problems may be highly stressful and the removal of this burden may be seen as positive. Potentially at least employees are now at liberty to move out of a city dwelling or suburban environment and relocate somewhere more peaceful.
- More rewarding working arrangements. The proposal offers improved opportunities to work creatively and in ways that are consistent with an individual's desired work/life balance.
- More stable family life. The elimination of a need to relocate in the country's capital can again lead to a better balance of work and family life. It is conceivable that under the proposals staff may put in more hours of effective work, at the same

time there is potential to spend more time with the family or a partner as well as contributing more fully to home and parenting responsibilities. The additional time freed by these arrangements may conceivably lead to greater participation in a person's local community (e.g. acting as school governor or helping in the running of local clubs and societies), so strengthening rural communities.

- The opportunity to control a work/life balance arising from the individual autonomy over hours worked. The flexible approach to working hours implied by the proposal means that individual preferences for work patterns can be adopted. Traditional commuting patterns and fixed office hours condemn everyone to work roughly the same hours. The more flexible 'teleworking' approach proposed implies a degree of individual control over working times and arrangements. Workers who feel in control are less likely to suffer from stress.
- Employment and promotion opportunities for the disadvantaged. Sections of the population with specific difficulties problems and disabilities have difficulty with travel and working in as traditional manner (e.g. nine-until-five working day in the same location). Currently ARi9 employs much fewer people with disabilities than the Government's suggested quota and the proposals may go some way to addressing this difficulty. Now too single parents who need to be at home for the children at certain times and carers with family responsibilities will now be able to form part of ARi9's workforce.

Potential difficulties

The proposals however may present certain difficulties for the workforce, including:

- Motivational issues. Home working may not be appropriate for some employees. Those who have poor personal motivation and are not 'self-starters' may miss the structure and discipline offered by fixed hours and a managed environment.
- Working distractions. Staff productivity is currently declining in part due to interruptions of the office environment (which is open plan and has crowded workstations where conversations can be easily overheard). Far from improving matters home working may offer more rather than less distractions. The distractions of the home may mean that even the most highly self motivated could be distracted by family members (e.g. demanding children).
- The loss of learning from individual human contact. Those new to work or returning after a career break would miss the support offered by a physical rather than virtual environment. Similarly, opportunities for mentoring the vulnerable or those undertaking personal development may be lost in a virtual environment.
- A loss of social interaction and stimulation. The traditional office setting offers a number of distinct advantages including opportunities for casual interaction and mutual learning, the development of camaraderie, effective team working and friendships. Although technically it may be feasible to replicate this social experience at a distance it is not always achievable.
- An erosion of work and own time which may be harmful to the individual and could potentially lead to 'burnout' or damaged personal relationships.
- Homes may not be suitable for teleworking. The physical space required (e.g. a spare room converted to a home office) or the need to secure office equipment may make home working difficult.

Exam Q & As

At the time of publication there are no exam Q & As available for the 2010 syllabus. However, the latest specimen exam papers are available on the CIMA website.
Actual exam Q & As will be available free of charge to CIMA students on the CIMA website from summer 2010 onwards.

Index

Index

5-S practice, 113
16 Personality Factors, 206
180 degree appraisal, 213
360 degree appraisal, 213

A
ABC system, inventories, 109
Abramoff, Jack, 31
Acceptance tests, 61
Accountability issues, marketing, 28, 140–1
Accountancy, 157
Accreditation, 101
Achievement versus ascription, 22
Acquisitions, 13
Adaptative maintenance *see* Adaptive maintenance
Adaptive/adaptative maintenance, 61
Advertising, 153, 154
  using internet, 280
AGM *see* Annual general meeting (AGM)
American Psychological Society, 207
Annual general meeting (AGM), 28
Appleyard, B., 207, 208
Application controls, 57
Appraisals, 96, 209–13
  target setting, 304
Armstrong, G., 134
Armstrong, M., 192, 223
Ascription versus achievement, 22
Assessment centre, 208–9
Atkinson, J., 231
Audit, 28
Australia, 14

B
B2B marketing *see* Business-to-business (B2B) marketing

B2C marketing *see* Business-to-consumer (B2C) marketing
BAE Systems, 31
Baker, Mallen, 26
'Balanced trade', 5
BCCI, 27
BCG matrix *see* Boston Consulting Group (BCG) matrix
Beaumont, P. B., 206, 209
Benady, D., 149
Berens, C., 50, 51, 164
Berry, L., 97
Bertil, O., 6
Bin systems, inventories, 109
Blackmon, K., 84, 88, 105, 109
'Blogging', 52
Boddy, D., 135
Boomer, G., 64, 66
Boston Consulting Group (BCG) matrix, 171, 172
Bowhill, B., 96, 101
Boydell, T., 213
Brand equity, 174
Branding, 174
Bratton, J., 192
BRIC nations, 14
'Bridging', 31
British and European systems, 100
British East India Company, 4
British Psychological Society, 207
British Standards Institution (BSI), 100
Brockett, J., 226
Brown, S., 84, 88, 105, 109
Bruce, I., 138
BSI *see* British Standards Institution (BSI)
Burgoyne, J., 213

321

Business:
  and markets, 19
  and politics, 30–1
Business ethics versus CSR, 25
Business-to-business (B2B) marketing, 143, 160
Business-to-consumer (B2C) marketing, 143, 160
Buyer behaviour, 144
Buying process, 143–4

C

CAD *see* Computer aided design (CAD)
Cadbury report, 27
CAM *see* Computer aided manufacturing (CAM)
Capacity management, 109–11
Career planning activity, 218–19
Carlsberg, 13
Carnall, C., 52, 53
Carrington, L., 223, 227
Cash cows products, 171
Cattell 16 PF test, 206
Cause marketing, 138
CBA *see* Cost benefit analysis (CBA)
Champy, J., 102
Chance events, role of, 9
Changeover approaches, 59
Charities, marketing for, 138
Chartered Institute of Personnel and Development (2008), 198
Checkpoint controls, 58–9
China, 14, 23, 32
Christopher, M., 116
The CIMA Code of Ethics for Professional Accountants, 201
Clegg, B., 42, 65
Clustering, 9
Coca Cola, 13, 160
Code of Best Practice, 28
Code Principles and Provisions, 28
Cognitive paradigm, 144
Cognitive tests, 206
Cohen, D., 206
Collectivism:
  versus individualism, 20–1, 22
Combined Code, 28
Combined theories, 197
Communitarianism *see* Collectivism
Comparative advantage, 6–7, 8
Competence, 9
Competitive advantage, 7–9

The Competitive Advantage of Nations (1992), 7
Complementary competences, 9
Computer aided design (CAD), 42, 110
Computer aided manufacturing (CAM), 42, 110
'Confucian dynamism', 21
Connected stakeholders, 24
'Constructive dismissal', 220
Consumer behaviour, 142–3
Consumer marketing, 159–60
Content theories of motivation, 195
Continuous inventory, 109
Contrived tests, 61
Conway, N., 197
Coote, P., 108
Core competence, 9
Corporate citizenship, 26
Corporate governance, 27–9
  benefits, 29
  Combined Code, 28
  stakeholders and government, 27
Corporate political activity (CPA)
  business and politics, 30–1
  developed markets, 31–2
  developing markets, 32
  relational approaches, 31
  transactional approaches, 31
Corporate social responsibility (CSR)
  versus business ethics, 25
  general principles, 25–6
  marketing context, 140–2
  international variation, scope for, 26
Corrective maintenance, 61
Corus Steel, 14
COSO, 27
Cost benefit analysis (CBA), 56
Country and political risk, 32–3
Cousins, P., 84, 88, 105, 109
Cousins, P.D., 86
Cox, 9
CPA *see* Corporate political activity (CPA)
Crosby, Philip P., 95–6, 127
Cross-cultural education and training, purposes of, 20
Cross-cultural management, 19
  Hofstede, 20–1
  managing across cultures, 19–20
  models, 21–3
CSR *see* Corporate social responsibility (CSR)
Customs valuations, 6

D

Data:
   analysis, 42
   collection, 42
   concept, 42
   encryption, 58
   evaluation, 42
   integrity, 58
   interpretation, 42
   reporting, 42
Data processing system (DPS), 45, 77
'Data redundancy', 47
Database management system (DBMS), 47
Databases:
   definition, 47
   features, 48
DBMS *see* Database management system (DBMS)
DDP *see* Distributed data processing (DDP)
de Jager, M., 54
Decision support systems (DSS), 45
Decision-making process, 44
Deighton, J. A., 163
Demerit goods, 139
Deming, W. Edward, 95
Denton, A., 56, 60
Department of Commerce-led Advisory Committee on Trade Policy Negotiations, 31
Deployment chart, 103
Deregulation, 30
Derrick, S., 227
Devanna, M. A., 202
Developed and developing economies, 26
Developed markets, 31–2
Developing markets, 32
Differentiated targeting, 149–50
Diffuse versus specific relationship, 22
Digital envelope, 58
Direct changeover approach, 59
Direct mailing, 153
Direct marketing, 154, 162
Direct tax, 15
Directors, 28
Directors' remuneration, 28
Dismissal *see* Employment practices
Distributed data processing (DDP), 47
Distribution channels, 162–3
Dogs products, 171
'dot.com companies', 50
DPS *see* Data processing system (DPS)
DSS *see* Decision support systems (DSS)

E

E-business, 51, 164
E-commerce, 51, 164
E-mail, 43
E-marketing, 164
'Economic conception', 26
Economic nationalism *see* Protectionism
EDI *see* Electronic data interchange (EDI)
EIS *see* Executive information system (EIS)
Electronic data interchange (EDI), 42, 117
Emotional versus neutral relationship, 22
Employees:
   and corporate dimension, 198–9
   guest model of HRM, 199
   improving opportunities for, contributions, 228–30
Employment practices, 220–2
Enterprise resource planning (ERP), 105
Enterprise-wide systems, 47
ERP *see* Enterprise resource planning (ERP)
ES *see* Expert systems (ES)
Ethical behaviour:
   management of human capital, 199–201
'Ethical conception', 26
Europe, 17
European quality foundation model, 99–100
Examination:
   format, 255
   planning, 253–4
   preparation, 253
   tips, 254
Executive information system (EIS), 45, 76
Experiential marketing, 174
Expert systems (ES), 45
Expropriation, 32
External failure costs, 96
External stakeholders, 24
Extranet, 51

F

Fax, 43
FDI *see* Foreign direct investment (FDI)
Femininity versus masculinity, 21
Financial flexibility, 232
Financial Services Industry, 15
Fine, J., 156
Firewall, 51, 58
Fiscal policy, 15–16, 17
Fishbone diagram, 112
Five why process, 112
Fleming, J., 53
Flexible manufacturing systems (FMS), 111

FMS *see* Flexible manufacturing systems (FMS)
Fombrun, C. J., 202
Ford, Henry, 107
Foreign direct investment (FDI), 13, 14
Foster, D., 20
Free trade:
   concept, 4
   critics, 4–5

G
Galloway, L., 84
Gargan, J., 86
Garrity, Jim, 156
Gates, Bill, 12
General controls, 57
Glass, N.M., 94
Global business environment:
   comparative advantage, 6–7
   competitive advantage, 7–9
   corporate governance, 27–9
   corporate political activity, 30–2
   corporate social responsibility, 25–6
   country and political risk, 32–3
   cross-cultural management, 19–23
   free trade, 4–5
   government, role of, 25
   international trade, 4
   market multinationals, emerging, 11–15
   national account balances and monetary policy, 15–19
   offshoring, 10–11
   outsourcing, 9–10
   protectionism, 5–6
   regulation on firm, impact of, 29–30
   society, role of, 24–5
   stakeholders, 24
Globalisation, 11–12
Gold, J., 192
Goldsmith, S., 93
Gould, S., 108
Government, 27
   role of, 8, 25
Gratton, L., 194, 222
Gray, R., 157
Greenfield investment, 13
Gross Domestic Product, 19
Gross National Product, 19
Guerrilla marketing, 156
Guest, D., 197, 198, 199

H
Habitual decision-making, 145
Hammer, M., 102
Hecksher, E., 6
Hecksher–Ohlin theory, 6
Heineken, 13
Hellriegel, D., 41, 42, 59
Herzberg's motivation-hygiene (dual factor) theory, 196
Higgs, 28
High context behaviour, 22
Hilmer, 10
Hilmer, F.G., 10
Hodgetts, 32
Hofstede, Geert, 20–1
Holme, R., 140
Home market, demand conditions in, 8
Houston, F., 136
Human capital, management of, 191
   employees contributions, improving opportunities for, 228–30
   ethical behaviour, 199–201
   HR planning, 232–5
   human resource development, 202
      appraisals, 209–13
      career planning, 218–19
      employment practices, 220–2
      induction, 209, 210
      recruitment, 203–4, 205
      selection, 204–9
      training and development, 213–18
   human resource management (HRM)
      and organisational success, 191
      definition, 192
      employees and corporate dimension, 198–9
      eras in managing people, 193
      motivation and opportunity, 194–7
      psychological contract and retention, 197–8
   line managers and HR practices, 230–2
   motivation and incentives, 222
      reward systems, designing, 223–8
Human resource management (HRM) *see* Human capital, management of
Hydrocarbon tax, 16

I
IBM, 14
Import duties, 16
In-house training, 216
In-tray exercise, 208, 209
Indirect tax, 15, 16
Individualism versus collectivism, 20–1, 22

Induction programme, 209, 210
Industrial Revolution, 83, 193
Information systems (IS)
   with business strategy, 65–6
   changeover approaches, 59
   evaluation, 56–7
   features, 46
   implementation:
      challenges in, 55–63
   and information, 41
      role of, 43–6
   IT, contexts and change, 54–5
   organisational dependence on, 46
      IS trends, in organisations, 47–52
      IT enabled transformation, 52–3
      opportunity for work teams, 53–4
   outsourcing, 64
   privacy and security, 57–9
   systems implementation, managing, 59–63
Information technology (IT), 42, 54–5, 217
   see also Information systems (IS)
Intelligence tests, 206
Interactive marketing, 163
Internal environment, 136, 137
Internal failure costs, 96, 129, 313
Internal marketing, 164–6
Internal stakeholders, 24
International influence, and market multinationals, 13–15
International trade, 4, 16–17
International variation, scope for, 26
Internet, 43, 49, 50, 51
Interviews, 205
   individual /one to one interview, 206
   panel interviews, 206
   sequential interviews, 206
   tandem interviews, 206
Intranet, 51
Inventory management, 108–9
'Invisible hand', 6
IS *see* Information systems (IS)
Ishikawa, Kaoru, 111
ISO 14001, 101
ISO 9000:2000, 100, 101
IT *see* Information technology (IT)

J
Jobs:
   analysis, 203
   characteristics model, 229–30
   description, 203
Johnson, G., 53, 55, 137
Jones, D.T., 107, 108
Juran, Joseph M., 95
Just-in-time (JIT) techniques, 85, 105–6

K
Kaizen, 97, 112
Kaplan, R.S., 96
Kent County Council:
   performance-related pay, 226
Kirkby, J., 174
Kirkpatrick, D. L., 217
KM Systems *see* Knowledge Management Systems (KM Systems)
Knowledge Management Systems (KM Systems), 49
Kolb, D. A., 213
Kotler, P., 134, 137, 139, 148, 151

L
LAN *see* Local area networks (LAN)
Lancaster, G., 139, 143, 170
Lane Keller, K., 151
Leaderless group exercise, 209
Lean management, 107
Lean supply chain, 118
Learned behaviour theory, 145
Learning programmes, 213
Legal environment, 29–30
Levinson, J. L., 156
Levinson, Jay Conrad, 156
Liberalisation, 4–5
Line managers and HR practices, 230–2
Local area networks (LAN), 47, 49
Long, B.G., 86, 87
Low context behaviour, 22
Lynch, D., 113
Lynch, R., 52

M
M-marketing, 163
MacArthur, K., 141
Macro environment, 136, 137
Macro-political risks, 32
Maerki, Hans Ulrich, 14
Management by objectives (MBO), 212
Management development, 213–14, 218
Management information systems (MIS), 45, 76
Manufacturing resource planning (MRP), 104–5
Market:
   forecasting, 146

Market: (*Continued*)
  growth rate, 172
  multinationals, 11–15
    globalisation, 11–12
    and international influence, 13–15
    transition economies, changes in, 13
  positioning issues, 145–7
  research, 145–7
  segmentation, 147–9
Marketing:
  B2B, 160
  B2C, 143
  brand equity, 174
  branding, 174
  business philosophies, 134
  buyer behavior, 144
  buying process, 143–4
  campaign, 155
  charities, 138
  concept, 133–4
  consumer behavior, 142–3
  consumer marketing, 159–60
  contexts, 159
  corporate social responsibility, 140–2
  definition, 134
  direct marketing, 162
  distribution channels, 162–3
  e-business, 164
  e-commerce, 164
  e-marketing, 164
  environment, 136–7
  experiential marketing, 174
  finance, 168
  human resourcing, 168
  interactive marketing, 163
  internal marketing, 164–6
  market research, 145–7
  market segmentation, 147–9
  marketing mix, 150–1
  non-governmental organisations (NGOs), 138
  not-for-profit context, 137
  operations, 168
  people, 158
  physical evidence, 159
  place, 152
  planning process, 166
  positioning, 149–50
  price, 157–8
  pricing strategies, 172–3
  processes, 159
  product development, 169
  product life cycle, 169–70
  product mix, 151–2
  products investment, 170–2
  promotional mix, 152
  promotional tools, 152
  public sector, 138–9
  services marketing, 161–2
  social marketing, 139–40
  strategic marketing, 166–9
  targeting, 149–50
  theories, 144–5
Masculinity versus femininity, 21
Maslow's hierarchy of needs, 195–6
Maurer, R., 112
Maxwell, 25
Maxwell Communications Group, 27
Maylor, H., 84, 88, 105, 109
MBO *see* Management by objectives (MBO)
McDonald, I., 84, 110
McDonald's Corp., 141
Meall, L., 54
Media and recruitment mechanisms, 204, 205
Medical examinations, selection techniques, 204, 209
Mentoring, 217
Merit goods, 139
Micro environment, 136
Micro-political risk, 32
Mintzberg, H., 89
MIS *see* Management information systems (MIS)
MNEs *see* Multinational enterprises (MNEs)
Modular changeover approach, 59
Monetary policy, 17–19
Motivation:
  and human resource management, 194
  and incentives, 222–8
  theories, 195–7
  Volkswagen (VW) Group UK, 222–3
MRP *see* Manufacturing resource planning (MRP)
Mulis, H., 223
Mullins, L. J., 161, 194, 195, 233
Multinational enterprises (MNEs), 13

N

National account balances, 15
  business and markets, impact on, 19
  fiscal policy, 15–16
  international trade, 16–17
  and monetary policy, 17–19
National campaigns, 6
National competitive advantage, 9

National Social Marketing Centre, 140
Nestle, 13
Network design, 58
Neutral versus emotional relationship, 22
Newsweb Corporation, 31
NFP *see* Not-for-profit (NFP) organisations
NGOs *see* Non-governmental organisations (NGOs)
Non-financial rewards, 226
Non-governmental organisations (NGOs), 25, 26, 138
Norton, D.P., 96
Not-for-profit (NFP) organisations, 137, 138, 279
Numerical flexibility, 231

O

OCB *see* Organisational citizenship behaviour (OCB)
Ody, P., 115
OECD, 13, 30
Office automation, computers, 42
　examples, 43
'Offshore outsourcing', 10
Offshoring, 10–11
'On-the-job' training, 60, 79, 214, 215, 283
One-to-one interviews, 153, 206
Open learning, 216
Operating core, 89
Operations:
　capacity management, 109–11
　continuous improvement practices, 111–13
　decisions, 44
　examples, 84
　inventory management, 108–9
　lean management, 107
　lean supply chain, 118
　middle line, 89
　operating core, 89
　organisational competitiveness, 88
　process:
　　design, 101–7
　　maps, 102–4
　procurement, 85–6
　quality:
　　measurement, 96–101
　　management thinking, 93–101
　　programmes planning, 113–15
　service organizations, 91–2
　shifing perspectives, 85
　standardizing, 78
　strategic apex, 89
　strategic issues, 86–8, 88–91
　supplier relationships, 115–18
　supply chain, 91
　　management, 116–18
　support staff, 89
　sustainability, 92–3
　systems used, 104–7
　technostructure, 89
　total quality management, 114–15, 128
　variation, 85
　variety, 85
　visibility, 85
　volume, 85
Optimised production technologies, 105
Organ, L., 228
Organisational citizenship behaviour (OCB), 228
Organisational legitimacy, issues of, 24
Organisational remuneration structures, types of, 224
Organisations, 134, 183, 191, 223
　information systems:
　　dependence, 46–7
　　role, 43–4
　IS trends, 47–52
　marketing-orientated, 135
　product-orientated, 135
　production-orientated, 135
　quality, 93–5
　sales-orientated, 135
Outline process map, 103
Outsourcing, 9–10
　advantages, 10
　drawbacks, 10
　growth, 9–10
Overell, S., 212

P

PAC *see* Political Action Committees (PACs)
Panel interviews, 206
Parallel changeover approach, 59
Parasuraman, A., 97
Pareto rule, 112
Particularism versus universalism, 22
Particularist societies, 23
Paton, R., 135
PDCA, 112
Peck, Polly, 25, 27
Pedler, M., 213
Penetration pricing, 173
People, 158
Perfective maintenance, 61

Performance-related pay (PRP), 225–6
Periodic inventory, 109
Perry, B., 234
Person specification, 203
Personal selling, 153
Personality tests, 206
Pesola, M., 41, 58
PEST analysis, 32
PESTEL analysis, 187
Phased changeover approach, 59
Phillips, P., 51
Physical evidence, 159
Physical network, 47
'Piece rates', 224
Pilot changeover approach, 59
Place, 152
Planning process, 166
Political Action Committees (PACs), 30, 31
Political risk:
    analysis, 32–3
    effects, 33
Political 'buffering', 31
Porter, M.E., 90, 91, 152
Porter's Diamond, 7
    demand conditions, 8
    events, 8–9
    factor endowments, 8
    firm structure, 8
    national competitive advantage, 9
    related and supporting industries, 8
    rivalry, 8
    strategy, 8
Positioning, 149–50
Post-implementation review, 56, 57, 60
'Power-distance', 21
Preventative maintenance *see* Perfective maintenance
Prevention costs, 96
Price, 157–8
Pricing strategies, 172–3
Prickett, R., 228
Primary research, 146
Principles of Good Governance, 28
Prithcard, S., 217
Process design, 101–7
Process maps, 102–4
    deployment chart, 103
    outline process map, 103
Process theories, 196–7
Processes, 159
Proctor, T., 139
Product development, 169
Product life cycle, 169–70
Product mix, 151–2
Product packaging, 153
Products investment, 170–2
Profit-related pay schemes, 224
Profit sharing, example of, 224
Promotional mix, 152
Promotional tools, 152
Protectionism, 5–6
PRP *see* Performance-related pay (PRP)
Psychological contract:
    and retention, 197–8
Psychometric testing, 207–8
Public sector, 138–9
    marketing, 138
Publicity and public relations, 153

Q
QA *see* Quality assurance (QA)
QC *see* Quality circles (QC)
Quality:
    approaches, 97–101
    costs, types, 96
    definitions, 93
    management thinking, 93–101
    measurement methods, 96–7
    programmes, planning, 113–14
Quality assurance (QA), 99
Quality circles (QC), 111
Question mark, 171
Queuing theory, 111
Quinn, J.B., 10
Quota systems, 5

R
Radio advertisements, 205
RATER, 97
Real growth, 19
Realistic tests, 61
Reck, R.F., 86, 87
Recruitment process, 203–4, 205
Redundancy, 221–2
Reference checks, selection techniques, 204, 209
Regulation, impact of, 30
Regulation on firm, impact of, 29–30
    legal environment, 29–30
    regulation, impact of, 30
Relative market share, 172
Report-writing exercise, 209
Residual competencies, 10
Reward systems, design of, 223–8
Ricardo, D., 6

Ricardo, David, 6
Risk, sources of, 32–3
Robbins Gentry, C., 106
Ronen, 23
Roos, D., 107, 108
Rossellini, Isabella, 148–9
Royal Mail, UK, 224
Rudzki, R.A., 86
Rugman, 32

S

Saban Capital Group, 31
Sales promotion, 153
Samson, D., 93
Scase, R., 52
Schein, E. H., 197
Scholes, K., 53, 55, 137
SDLC *see* Systems development life cycle (SDLC)
SEC *see* Securities and Exchange Commission (SEC)
Secondary research, 146
Securities and Exchange Commission (SEC), 27
Selection process, 202, 204
    assessment centre, 208–9
    interviews, 205–6
    medical examination, 209
    reference checks, 209
    tests, types of, 206–7
Self-appraisal, 212
Self-directed work teams, 229
Senior, B., 53
Sequential interviews, 206
Sequential time versus synchronic time, 22
Service level agreement (SLA), 10
Service organizations, 91–2
    operations, 91–2
Services marketing, 161–2
Servqual, 97
'Seven Dimensions of Culture Model', 22
Seven-Point Plan, for shift process operator, 204
'Shamrock' organisations, 231, 297
Shangri-La Entertainment, 31
Shareholders, relations with, 28
Shenkar, 23
Simms, J., 159, 160
Six Sigma, 113
Skim pricing, 173
Skyrme, D.J., 54
SLA *see* Service level agreement (SLA)

Slocum, J. W., Jr., 41, 42, 59
Smith, A., 6, 16, 17, 28
Social marketing, 139–40
Social responsibility, 25
Society, role of, 24–5
Soros, George, 12
Specific versus diffuse relationship, 22
Stakeholders, 24, 27
    power, issues of, 24
Star products, 171
Strategic competences, 9
Strategic decisions, 44
Strategic marketing, 166–9
Subsidies, for local manufacturers, 6
Supervisor/appraisee, 212
Supplier relationships, 115–18
Supply chain, 91
    management, 116–18
Sustainability, 92–3
    operations, 92–3
Synchronic time versus sequential time, 22
Systems:
    implementation, 59–63
Systems development life cycle (SDLC), 56

T

Tactical decisions, 44
Tandem interviews, 206
Targeting, 149–50
Task/functional flexibility, 231
Tata Group, 14
Taxes on consumption *see* Indirect tax
Taylor, F.W., 84, 192, 193
Teams:
    dispersed and virtual, 53–4
Technical barriers, 6
Teleconferencing, 43
Teleworking, 53
Theories, of motivation, 195–7
Theory of comparative advantage, 7
Threshold competence, 9
Tichy, N. M., 202
Tobacco tax, 16
Total productive maintenance (TPM), 97
Total quality, 127
Total quality management (TQM), 97, 229
    definition, 128
    implementation, 114–15
    prerequisites, 98
'Total reward packages', 227
Toyota, 13
TPM *see* Total productive maintenance (TPM)

TPS *see* Transaction processing system
TQM *see* Total quality management (TQM)
Training/development:
   human resource, 213–18
Transaction processing system (TPS), 45
'Transition' economies, 13
Treadway Commission, 27
Trompenaars, 21, 23
Turnbull, 28
Turner, Hamden, 21, 22
Turner, Hampden, 23

U
UK, 12, 27, 135, 164, 214, 217, 220, 221, 284
'Uncertainty avoidance', 21
Undifferentiated positioning, 149
Universalism versus particularism, 22
Universalist societies, 23
US President's Energy Task Force, 31
USA, 17, 20, 21, 32, 138

V
Value added tax, 16
Vestel Group, 13
Video conferencing, 43

Viral marketing, 154
Virtual network, 47
Volkswagen, 13, 222–3
Volume tests, 61

W
WAN *see* Wide area networks (WANs)
Watts, P., 140
The Wealth of Nations, 16
Web 2.0, 51
Whirlpool, 13
Whittington, R., 53, 55, 137
Wide area networks (WANs), 47
Withey, F., 139, 143, 170
Womack, J.P., 107, 108
World Bank, 11
World Business Council for Sustainable
   Development, 26
World Trade Organisation (WTO), 17, 30
WTO *see* World Trade Organisation (WTO)

Z
Zaltman, G., 139
Zeithaml, V.A., 97